A

Philip E. Lilienthal (signature)

■   ■   ■

B O O K

The Philip E. Lilienthal imprint
honors special books
in commemoration of a man whose work
at University of California Press from 1954 to 1979
was marked by dedication to young authors
and to high standards in the field of Asian Studies.
Friends, family, authors, and foundations have together
endowed the Lilienthal Fund, which enables UC Press
to publish under this imprint selected books
in a way that reflects the taste and judgment
of a great and beloved editor.

The publisher gratefully acknowledges the generous support
of the following:

The Philip E. Lilienthal Asian Studies Endowment Fund
of the University of California Press Foundation, which was
established by a major gift from Sally Lilienthal

The Asian Studies Endowment Fund of the University of
California Press Foundation

Beyond the Metropolis

STUDIES OF THE WEATHERHEAD EAST ASIAN
INSTITUTE, COLUMBIA UNIVERSITY

*The Studies of the Weatherhead East Asian Institute of Columbia
University were inaugurated in 1962 to bring to a wider public
the results of significant new research on modern and
contemporary East Asia.*

Beyond the Metropolis

SECOND CITIES AND MODERN LIFE
IN INTERWAR JAPAN

Louise Young

UNIVERSITY OF CALIFORNIA PRESS

BERKELEY LOS ANGELES LONDON

University of California Press, one of the most distinguished university
presses in the United States, enriches lives around the world by advancing
scholarship in the humanities, social sciences, and natural sciences. Its
activities are supported by the UC Press Foundation and by philanthropic
contributions from individuals and institutions. For more information, visit
www.ucpress.edu.

University of California Press
Berkeley and Los Angeles, California

University of California Press, Ltd.
London, England

Library of Congress Cataloging-in-Publication Data

Young, Louise, 1960-
    Beyond the metropolis: second cities and modern life in
interwar Japan / Louise Young.
        p.   cm. — (Studies of the Weatherhead East Asian
Institute, Columbia University)
    Includes bibliographical references and index.
    ISBN 978-0-520-27520-1 (cloth : alk. paper)
    1. Urbanization—Japan—History—20th century.   2. Japan—
Social conditions—1912–1945.   3. Japan—Civilization—20th century.
    4. Japan—History—1912–1945.   I. Title.
    HT384.J3Y68 2013
    307.760952—dc23

                                              2012040341

Manufactured in the United States of America

22 21 20 19 18 17 16 15 14 13
10 9 8 7 6 5 4 3 2 1

In keeping with a commitment to support environmentally responsible and
sustainable printing practices, UC Press has printed this book on Rolland
Enviro100, a 100% post-consumer fiber paper that is FSC certified, deinked,
processed chlorine-free, and manufactured with renewable biogas energy. It is
acid-free and EcoLogo certified.

In memory of
Rebecca Conrad Young

CONTENTS

ILLUSTRATIONS

MAPS

TABLE

ACKNOWLEDGMENTS

Among the great pleasures of doing research in Japan are the friends one accumulates along the way. This study took me to four cities and introduced me to wonderful communities of local historians and archivists in each. By remarkable good fortune, I embarked on my research around the centennial of the incorporation of most of Japan's second cities in the 1889 administrative reforms that established the "city, town, village" system. This meant that many municipal governments were engaged in production of centennial histories. With the characteristic generosity that greets foreign researchers, local archivists opened their collections to me and shared materials they had gathered for their own works-in-progress. They also offered their wisdom, insights, and local knowledge. Without their gracious collaboration, I could never have done this study; I acknowledge this debt with heartfelt gratitude.

In Sapporo, Aiuchi Masako and Aiuchi Toshikazu opened their home to me and introduced me to their extensive network of local historians. Yamada Hirotaka made numerous key introductions to local study groups. The Sapporo Municipal History Office extended a warm welcome and generously allowed me access to the materials their history group had assembled to write the superb *New History of Sapporo*. I benefited from the assistance of Endō Tatsuhiko at the Hokkaido Prefectural Archives, and at the Sapporo Municipal History Office, from Enomoto Yōsuke, Hayashi Mikitada, Ishida Takehiko, and Konno Yukari. Special thanks are due Nishida Hideko and Takagi Hiroshi, who both spent hours of their time with me. In Niigata, Furumaya Tadao and Yoshii Ken'ichi were both generous and helpful, as was Minami Ken'ichi. Itō Sukeyuki at the Niigata City Archives provided good company and good advice in equal measure. In Okayama, Sakamoto Jūji gave me excellent research tips and a stack of his wonderful books on the local social movement; Arima Nobutsune, Ōta Ken'ichi, and Kandachi Harushige were all great resources. In Kanazawa Motoyasu Hiroshi at the Ishikawa Prefectural Museum of History provided a treasure trove of materials from the museum archives and a memorable architectural tour of the hidden history of modern Kanazawa. Chiku Kakugyō and Hashimoto Tetsuya also generously shared their knowledge of local history; and Kamura Kōsaku offered guidance at the Ishikawa Prefectural Library. My apologies to anyone I inadvertently omitted from this list because of a failure of memory or record keeping. I am extraordinarily grateful for the opportunity to have met the wonderful communities of local historians in what I have come to think of as "my four cities" and for their generous assistance in my research.

This book was begun while I worked at New York University and completed after I moved to the University of Wisconsin-Madison. Both institutions provided generous financial support: at NYU through a Freeman Foundation grant and the Research Challenge Fund; at the UW through the Graduate School, the Vilas Foundation, and the Institute for Research in Humanities. Colleagues at both schools have shaped my thinking about cities and urban culture. At NYU I benefited in particular from conversations with Ada Ferrer, Manu Goswami, Harry Harootunian, Walter Johnson, Rebecca Karl, Yanni Kotsonis, and Joanna Waley-Cohen. At the UW-Madison, David Lehene, Richard Miller, Emiko Ohnuki-Tierney, Jim Raymo, Steve Ridgely, Ben Singer, Steve Stern, and Sarah Thal read portions of the work in progress and provided excellent feedback.

Financial support for research in Japan came from the Social Science Research Council, the National Endowment for Humanities, and the Fulbright Foundation, where Itō Jinko and Iwata Mizuho offered both timely assistance and good humor. I offer my thanks to Hasebe Hiroshi and the staff at Seikei University Center for Asia and Pacific Studies for providing accommodation and an institutional affiliation during one of my research visits, and to Barbara Satō for arranging the whole visit. I also benefited from a semester in residence at the Kyoto University Institute for Research in Humanities, which Yamamuro Shin'ichi helped set up, and where he and Kagotani Naoto, Mizuno Naoki, Takagi Hiroshi, and Yamamoto Yūzo provided a congenial intellectual community.

Other friends and colleagues whose critical support is gratefully acknowledged include Kim Brandt, Geoffrey Chambers, John Dower, Eguchi Keiichi, Jim Fujii, Laura Hein, Igarashi Takeshi, Mark Jones, Naitō

Sachiko, Naitō Tsuneiji, Nishimura Shigeo, Nishimura Takako, Okabe Makio, Okamoto Kōichi, John Ratté, Lou Ratté, Jordan Sand, Barbara Satō, and Satō Kazuki.

Melissa Dale, Ken Kawashima, Kimiko Osawa, Rebecca Shearier, and Ayako Yoshimura provided research assistance at different stages of the project. I wish to also thank the wonderful editorial staff at University of California Press, including Niels Hooper and Kim Hogeland, as well as Daniel Rivero at the Weatherhead Institute.

Nan Enstad, Carol Gluck, Andrew Gordon, Crawford Young, and an anonymous reader from UC Press read the entire manuscript at the penultimate stage. Their comments were invaluable in helping me tighten and refine the central argument.

A special debt is owed my mother, Rebecca Young, whose irrepressible enthusiasm for all things urban and whose keen appreciation for the aesthetics of interwar culture provided inspiration for this project. My work on *Beyond the Metropolis* coincided with her ten-year battle with cancer; her grace and courage sustained me, always. I dedicate this book to her memory with love and admiration.

PART ONE

———

Contexts

Introduction

URBANISM AND JAPANESE MODERN

THE AGE OF THE CITY

In Japan, the interwar period (1918–37) constituted a time of intensive reflection on what it meant to be "modern." At a moment of rapid urbanization, as expanding city populations remade the social and physical landscapes of their communities, the Japanese began to link modernity with the urban experience. Popular referents for the neologism *modan*—jazz music, bobbed hair, cafés, automobiles, and multistory buildings—all conveyed the sense that what characterized the "modern" was the novel phenomenology of city life. In an outpouring of commentary, urbanites invented new categories to describe the changes they were experiencing in their everyday life. This new consciousness of the modern tried to make sense of the ways that the economic growth of the teens and twenties dramatically altered urban modes of production and consumption. To chroniclers of the new age, transformation of their built environment into a futurescape of paved roads and electric streetlamps, the rise of "social problems" like labor strikes and unsightly slums, and a mass consumer culture linked to the baseball field and the movie palace, all stood out as defining modernity. The city, in short, assumed the face of "modern Japan."

How were ideas about modernity produced and circulated? What were their material and ideological effects? To answer these questions, this book looks at both the subjective consciousness and the social structures of "the modern." Though humanities fields differ in their understanding of this term, historians tend to conceive of modernity as a tale of two revolutions: the political, social, cultural, and economic transformations that attended the advent of the nation-state, and the emergence of industrial capitalism.

The time line of these twin revolutions varied widely throughout the world, as did their particular form; for Japan, the forced opening of the country to the global market in 1853 and the overturning of the feudal regime in the Meiji Restoration of 1868 inaugurated a series of administrative reforms and social changes that ushered in modern times. In the initial phase of this process, industrial capitalism took root through a host of state policies designed to create a national economy capable of securing Japan's independence from the threat of western imperialism. At this moment the nation occupied center stage in Japanese economic thinking, reflected in the popular endorsement of state policies to promote a "rich country, strong military" (*fukoku kyōhei*) and to "encourage production, promote industry" (*shokusan kōgyo*). Throughout the 1870s and 1880s state financial and technical assistance helped to direct private investments into textiles, shipping, and railroads—industries identified as critical to national economic security. The cumulative impact of these policies was to weave together economy and nation: capitalist development served national concerns.

The preeminent symbols of "civilization" to emerge from these years were the emperor and the railroad.[1] Associating the "new Japan" with constitutional monarchy and a national rail grid, such images created an iconography of nationalism for the modern age. But by the early decades of the twentieth century the logics that grounded the identification of modernity as a national project began to change. Ushering in a period of accelerated economic and social change, the economic boom of World War One broadened and deepened Japan's industrial revolution. In the new wave of public and private investments triggered by the war boom, the focus of development expanded into regions and localities. Investments in communications infrastructure added a regional network to the national rail grid built up in the 1880s and 1890s. Factories making consumer products for a domestic market multiplied; a thriving service sector began to anchor urban and regional economies. Prefectural and municipal governments encouraged regional economic development through industrial expositions, the promotion of the tourist industry, local branding, and a variety of other strategies. The cumulative impact of these initiatives amounted to a second phase in the industrial revolution, as provincial development became one of capitalism's new frontiers.

All this brought a new level of engagement with urban centers, which were at once the staging ground and the agents of much of this activity. Rapid expansion of factory production created regional labor markets, and these drew migrants from the surrounding countryside to work the new shop floors. Factory growth generated unprecedented wealth for a new breed of managers and entrepreneurs, whose leadership in civic organizations and political life enlarged the scope of municipal ambition. Municipalities invested in electricity, roads, telephone lines, and other city services to accommodate their burgeoning populations. They extended communication networks to encompass an expanding zone of suburban development. In all these ways the age of the city signaled both a new importance for the urban economy and a new scope of operations for municipal government.

It also became a vehicle for the rising power of a new middle class of professionals and intellectuals within urban society and politics. Growth of white collar employment in factories and local government, the proliferation of public and private networks of city services, and the expansion of urban commerce and culture industries all swelled the ranks of the new middle class, which grew from an estimated 4 percent of the population in 1915 to 12 percent in 1925. Since these figures reflected national averages, one can assume the percentage was higher in cities.[2] Though numerically the middle class constituted a small fraction of urban society, it nevertheless exerted enormous influence over municipal politics and administration, key cultural institutions such as the press and higher education, and business organizations. Commentary on the Taishō democracy movement by scholars such as the famous Tokyo University political scientist Yoshino Sakuzō and the eminent Kyoto University sociologist Yoneda Shōtarō vested great expectations in the leadership of the new middle class. Standing at the vanguard of a host of progressive political and social movements, intellectuals and technocrats would lead Japan into a bright and better future.[3] As these observers noted, the new middle class cast an oversize shadow on the cities of interwar Japan.

At the same time, city growth altered existing social arrangements and generated new ways both of dividing people and, conversely, of bringing them together. Modern institutional structures such as the higher educational system and the publishing industry privileged cities and urban dwellers over the countryside economically and culturally; within cities they helped constitute hierarchies of class. They also produced an ideology of urban-centrism—the idea that modern cities possessed a kind of manifest destiny to expand their territory, power, and resources. Urban-centrism celebrated urban growth and measured the value of cities in terms of their size. It portrayed urban expansion as the diffusion of progress and modernity to the countryside and justified the resulting disparities in the distribution of power and resources. This process did not displace the nation but rather upstaged it, for now urban centers seemed to present the most pressing problems, the most dramatic changes, the most alluring possibilities. The Japanese discovered the city.

They were not alone in this discovery. Indeed, the early twentieth century was a global moment for urban growth, as an international fixation with cities in mass culture, philosophy, literature, and the arts attested. From Baltimore to Moscow, from Paris to Buenos Aires, from Tianjin to Dakar—cities became the staging ground for wide-ranging social, cultural, economic, and political transformations. As in Japan, the rise of social problems, the formation of a consumer marketplace, the proliferation of streetcars and streetcar suburbs, and the cascade of investments in urban development reinvented the city as both sociospatial form and set of ideas. Throughout the world, discourses on social change associated the city with modernity and the future.

This book centers its story on the age of the city in the interwar period, a global moment when the material and ideological structures that constitute "the city" took their characteristic modern shape. As elsewhere in the world, the foundation for much of this was laid in the late nineteenth century, when the spread of industrial capitalism and the nationalization of the masses transformed urban space. For Japan, the political lineaments of the modern city were created in the administrative reforms of 1889 that established the "city, town, village" (*shichōson*) system. The design of a national school system and railway grid provided institutional anchors for cities and connected them with one another. War booms accompanying the Sino-Japanese (1894–95) and Russo-Japanese (1904–5) Wars spurred the spread of urban-based factory production and modern industry, as well as new forms of wealth and poverty. The war booms also stimulated the growth of the publishing and newspaper industry, core elements in the cultural fabric of the modern city. In all these ways the rise of the modern urban form rested on the foundations of the Meiji city. Nevertheless, as the following pages will show, the World War One boom ushered in a new age of the city, accelerating urban expansion to an entirely different level of intensity.

THE VIEW FROM THE PROVINCES

Historians have overwhelmingly told this story from the vantage point of Tokyo, newly designated, in 1868, as the national capital of the empire of Japan. Standard narratives assume that from 1868 on, government and civic leaders in Tokyo invented modern institutions and dispatched them to the provinces. They suggest, moreover, that the diffusion of Tokyo models created a dynamic of imitation that placed localities in a condition of perpetual catch-up with the capital. This is particularly true of interwar urban history, which portrays Tokyo as the center and most active site of the modernist social and cultural movement.[4] In many ways the historiographic tendency toward Tokyo-centrism speaks to a deeper conviction about the homogenizing effects of modernization that shoehorns a wide world of experience into a single mold. However, a closer look at provincial cities challenges such beliefs. In fact, as scholars of regional studies have pointed out, cities outside the metropolis generated distinctive cultures of modernism that often referenced Tokyo models but also influenced new cultural and social forms in the metropolis.[5] And contrary to assertions of homogenization, the history of different localities reveals enormous variation in modern urban forms. By centering the story on Japan's provincial cities, this study breaks apart the assumption that the metropolis can serve as the defining lens for a history of Japanese modernity.

In the history of Japanese urbanism in the teens, twenties, and thirties, much of the action took place outside Tokyo. Beyond the metropolis was the world of the provincial city—*chihō toshi*. Since it included all cities outside the "big six" major metropolitan centers (Tokyo, Osaka, Yokohama, Kobe, Kyoto, and Nagoya), the category of "local city" encompassed cities of a wide range of shapes and sizes.[6] While the World War One boom fed the growth of the big six, equally striking was its impact on the small and medium city. In the regional turn of interwar Japan, local cities rose to prominence as centers of burgeoning regional economies. If the late nineteenth century was the age of the metropolis, the interwar years belonged to the city more generally.

This study focuses on second-tier cities, tracking the discourse on the modern in the four provincial cities of Sapporo, Kanazawa, Okayama, and Niigata.[7] As prefectural capitals, these cities constituted the economic, political, and cultural centers of their respective regions. They were seats of municipal and prefectural government, centers of regional industry, and major transportation hubs. They held a concentration of institutions of higher learning and provided a platform for regional publishing. All four, like the metropolitan giants, grew at an enormous rate in the teens and twenties. Yet with populations in 1920 ranging from 50,000 to 150,000, they not only represented a scale of city different from that of the metropolis of Tokyo (with a population in 1920 of 3.3 million) but also maintained peripheral relationships with the capital of the Japanese empire.

Despite such commonalities, these four cities occupied vastly different positions in relation to the social structures and historical processes of the nation-state and the capitalist economy. Sapporo was a Hokkaido "frontier town" that sprang up on land the Japanese appropriated from the indigenous Ainu population in the late nineteenth century. Seats of provincial commerce and government since the Tokugawa period (1603–1868), Kanazawa and Okayama developed modern urban institutions atop the infrastructures of the castle town. In the waning days of feudal power, the coastal city of Niigata was designated one of five open ports where foreign traders were permitted commercial access. As the port grew, Niigata became a point of entry for European imports into the region and, later, a critical entrepôt for trade with the rest of Asia. The increasing orientation of Japan's economy toward the Pacific coast shaped the fates of cities, leaving Niigata (facing Asia and removed from the economic centers of Tokyo and Osaka) on the wrong side of the geography of power and placing Okayama (on the Pacific side, near Osaka) directly in the path of economic progress. The diverse histories of these provincial cities reflected, on the one hand, uneven application of the centralizing and standardizing tendencies of the nation-state and, on the other, the social and economic disparities generated by capitalist modernization.

The story of urbanization varies considerably when viewed through the lens of particular cities. In the case of Sapporo, the World War One boom led not to the emergence of heavy and chemical industries but rather to the expansion of the service and consumer sectors of the economy. This meant that white-collar employment saw significant job growth, which had profound implications for local representations of class and gender. A large middle class emerged, constructing its identity not so much against an organized working class as against a marginalized underclass of street sweepers, garbage collectors, and foragers. In addition, the nature of economic growth in Sapporo made women more prominent agents of the modern economy. They were visible as consumers, but also as the clerks, ticket takers, and hostesses who represented the public face of service capitalism. This leant a decidedly local cast to the Sapporo image of the "modern woman," or *moga*. Moreover, the towering presence of Hokkaido Imperial University, with its premier agricultural research facilities and wide range of high cultural activities, provided a strong intellectual coloration for the Sapporo middle class.

In Okayama, located along the Pacific corridor close to Kobe and Osaka, the war boom expanded factory production in what was, by 1914, an already industrial city. Economic growth intensified tensions between a large and growing working class and a powerful and increasingly organized business community. Such tensions expressed themselves in citizen's rallies and other forms of popular protest that became familiar elements of local politics well before the war. Even so, when skyrocketing food prices and rice shortages touched off rioting throughout the country in 1918, the scope and violence of local protests shocked the city. Conditions that caused barely a ripple in Sapporo provided a flashpoint for Okayama's politically organized working class. As May Day demonstrations, labor strikes, antiprostitution rallies, and other forms of mass protest followed closely on the heels of the rice riots, Okayama became known as a hotbed of political and social activism and a center of the Taishō democracy movement.

A coastal city and former seat of feudal government, Kanazawa resembled Okayama in many respects. Both cities were proud of their castle town heritage and their traditions of scholarship and artisan crafts. Yet Kanazawa, situated along what had become Japan's "back side," experienced difficulty attracting capital for new industrial ventures. Instead, the city focused on reconstituting its traditional industries—lacquerware, gold inlay, and embroidered fabric. Local entrepreneurs turned remoteness into a selling point, investing in hot springs resorts in the nearby mountains and advertising the city's virtues as a tourist spot. Marketing itself as a city of crafts for the modern age and promoting its old world charm, local boosters turned "tradition" into a Kanazawa trademark.

While Niigata shared with Kanazawa the misfortune of location on Japan's back coast, the long-standing centrality of the port to the urban economy provided an adaptable resource for local development. This legacy helped Niigata secure the distinction of becoming one of the five open ports granted trading privileges in 1858. Although the benefits of this coup did not live up to expectations, fortune smiled on Niigata again when the Meiji government anointed the city as the seat of prefectural government in the new administrative order. As Niigata's experience reveals, however, political privilege does not necessarily trump geographic disadvantage. The city often lost out in the competition for resources and investment in the early years of state-led development. Even so, the town fathers pinned their hopes on the potential of the port, investing heavily in a variety of improvements in the teens and twenties that expanded capacity and improved the city's connection with the national rail grid. Niigata's importance as a transit point increased dramatically during the World War One boom, but the city hit pay dirt in the 1930s, when the invasion of China and the creation of the yen block in Japanese-occupied Asia turned the back coast into a gateway to the new Asian empire.

Diverse local conditions meant that policies of national development and the World War One boom affected individual cities in very different ways. As the stories of these four cities illustrate, there was no such thing as a typical small town in modern Japan. Indeed, the myth of the typical small town is itself a product of this moment in urban history, when Tokyo-centrism and the mystique of the hometown became core elements of social ideology. In choosing these particular cities as case studies, I make no claim that they represent some larger sample of regional or other urban types. Although all four are second-tier cities and prefectural capitals, not only their commonalities but also their idiosyncrasies stand out—the serendipitous and conjunctural forces that shaped their particular historical trajectories. As their diverse stories tell us, there is no single master narrative of twentieth-century modernization; nor is there a standard account for the metropolis and an alternative time line for every other place. Just as the Kanazawa story yields important insights into the particularities of the Tokyo case, a case study of Iowa City can force a rethinking of the place of New York in American history. Instead of conceiving of provincial cities or even Japan itself as an example of some kind of alternative modernity, I suggest in this book ways that the so-called standard-bearers of the modern are themselves outliers and exceptions.

The divergences in the local experience of national development and global capitalism were expressed in the character of libraries and archives, among other places. Embarking on the research for this book, I quickly discovered that historical records are strikingly uneven, and that what one city archive possesses in abundance is nowhere to be found in another. Niigata offered a surplus of guides to local businesses but few arts magazines. Sapporo presented a gold mine of literati journals but little on the local-history movement. Kanazawa lovingly preserved manuscripts penned by local writers, but documents on local politics were harder to come by. As I eventually realized, such gaps provided clues in themselves, helping me to focus on significant variations in the four stories of urban modernization.

In the tracks of the provincial city, I draw on such materials as yearbooks, chamber of commerce records, company histories, social surveys and reports, tourist guides and travel diaries, local magazines and newspapers, city plans, and memoir literature. These sources document the World War One boom and the transformation of urban life in Sapporo as well as the 1918 rice riots and images of an insurrectionary lumpen proletariat in Okayama. They tell the story of Niigata's department stores, Okayama's sports teams, and Kanazawa's community of artists and writers. All these regional cultures of modernity referenced and borrowed from Tokyo models and were inevitably shaped by the prodigious cultural power of the metropolis. But they were also part of a much larger network of cultural production that branched out in all directions, connecting Kanazawa to its own peripheries, Niigata to the Asian continent, Sapporo to its neighboring cities, and Okayama to the Kansai urban complex of Kyoto, Kobe, and Osaka. By engaging urban culture beyond the metropolis, this study shows that Japanese modernity was not simply made in Tokyo and exported to the provinces. Rather it was coconstituted through the dynamic interaction of provincial cities with the capital, as well as through the circulation and exchange of people and ideas throughout the country.

THE CITY AS SUBJECT

This book approaches the modern city from two conceptual vantage points. First, I envision the city as a constellation of institutions—government bureaucracies, factories, schools, department stores, and radio stations among them—that create the material contours of the city. They define its territorial boundaries and structure its social life. They provide the foundation for the economy, channel political action, and mediate the relationship between the local residents and the social world outside the city limits. I also look at the city as a set of ideas—a social imaginary, to borrow Cornelius Castoriadis's phrase.[8] For me this means the intellectual field upon which people projected their beliefs about the city. The imaginary domain of the city housed residents' expectations for urban life and their sense of belonging to an urban community—what they thought it meant to be "urban." By using the term *social imaginary*, I want to convey the open-ended, creative element in the urbanist social thought of these years—its utopian and dystopian moods, the succession of thought experiments that recast urban worlds.

These two dimensions of the city—as a matrix of ideas and as a socioinstitutional network—came together through the actions of the individuals who inhabited the city. The key questions that emerge here concern the human actors who occupy the center of my story: How did urban residents respond to the nationalizing and globalizing forces reshaping their world? How did their actions help construct a community of shared interests, beliefs, and ideals—to produce, in other words, a modern urban subject? In their provocative book on social theory, Nicholas Dirks, Geoff Eley, and Sherry Ortner point out that the organization of space and time structures everyday life and individual consciousness. In this sense the space-time of the modern city is built on the relationship between material structures, ideology, and action: "The organization of space (in homes, in villages, in cities) and time (the rhythms of work, leisure, holidays) embody the assumptions of gender, age, and social hierarchy upon which a particular way of life is built. As the actor grows up, lives everyday life within these spatial and temporal forms, s/he comes to embody those assumptions, literally and figuratively. The affect is one of near total naturalization of the social order, the forging of homologies between personal identification and social classification."[9]

As my study shows, new urban social orders were also a site of contest; emergent systems of social classification were riven with contradictions. Grounded in the space-time of urban life, Japanese social imaginaries provided a space for floating experimental visions of radical transformation, but also for constructing the matrix of urban ideology. In the latter case, a set of myths emerged during this period of intellectual ferment. Ideas such as urban-growthism and Tokyo-centrism naturalized particular sociopolitical arrangements even as they concealed the uneven allocation of the benefits of urbanization.

Methodologically, this approach situates my work at the interstices of social and cultural history. I examine the ways that the subjective dimensions of culture—thought, ideology, and consciousness—condition and are conditioned by the material processes of social life. I look at how cultural production is embedded within political and social economies, is linked to social geography and geopolitics, and determines issues of governmentality and social control. Such a conceptual vantage point lets us bring into focus the ways that culture and economy inflect each other and helps us see how both are shot through with politics. It helps illuminate, in other words, the lived interdisciplinarity of social life.

The book opens with a chapter organized around the question of historical moment: Why did the discovery of the city occur in the interwar period? Chapter 1 examines the ways World War One triggered a widespread rethinking of the meaning of the city as a social and economic space. From here the narrative is divided into two parts, focusing analysis on the spatial and temporal structures that give form to the modern city. The first of these narratives (chapters 2 and 3) looks at the spatial relationships that turned local cities into peripheries of the new national capital, Tokyo, at the very time these cities became centers of regional networks of towns, villages, and rural hinterlands. Here I examine the economic force fields generated by the railway revolution and the new cultural geographies created by institutions of higher education and the publishing industry. As circuits of intellectual circulation and exchange were superimposed on the railway map, they infused geography with new forms of social power. These chapters tell the story of how geo-power gave rise to urban-centrism, tracing the creation of a modern urban-rural system and a national hierarchy of cities with Tokyo at its apex.

The next part (chapters 4 and 5) shifts from space to time, examining the multiple temporalities of the modern city. As municipalities cast about for a means to absorb the flood of in-migration in the teens and twenties, they mobilized the idea of a shared past and a common future to build a sense of community. Here I focus on the invention of urban biography through the local-history movement and on how the idea that "cities = future" spread through regional development movements. Just as provincial cities were constituted as both centers and peripheries, they were also perceived as chronotopes of both the past and the future. As we shall see, commentary on urban change figured provincial cities as a world apart from the metropolis, situating them in a space where the past was still present. At the same time, the pervasive and categorical distinctions between city and country imagined all cities, big and small, as sharing the temporality of modernity—as inhabiting a space where time ticked faster and change happened first. These chapters explore the reinvention of the idea of "the city," tracing the emergence of the belief that urban centers were a natural community that crystallized the past, present, and future of the modern subject.

These sections fit into the book's larger argument that interwar social and cultural movements reshaped the meaning of the city as well as its core structures. Whether through literary movements, regional history-writing, or industrial exhibitions, urban elites in provincial cities articulated a vision of modernity that sanctioned new power relationships, new economic disparities, and new social hierarchies, making them appear natural and inexorable. As this vision of the modern acquired a hegemonic status, it obscured the diverse and disparate experiences of modern life and masked the fact that human choice, not transcendent fate, created the winners and losers in the process of urban modernization. Both the material foundation of the modern city established in the interwar years and the epistemology that sustained it have proven remarkably enduring. They helped shape the faith in municipal governance and social planning that fueled expansion of the national defense state in wartime and the technocratic state in the postwar period. They survive in the commonsense points of reference by which we understand urban worlds even today.

ONE

World War One and the City Idea

In the new wave of investments triggered by World War One, the focus of Japan's economic expectations shifted from the nation to the city, where the capitalist revolution's deepening impact was most dramatically felt. Sudden and rapid urban growth stretched the capabilities of city services and strained the seams of the built environment. The war boom propelled new groups to positions of social prominence, swelling the ranks of the new middle and working classes. Though prosperity proved evanescent, the possibility of gaining fabulous wealth in a short period of time was etched in popular memory as a feature of the urban economy, one dimension of the economic and social volatility of modern economic growth. The war years marked the eruption of a new level of crowd violence, on the factory floor and especially in the street, as rice riots broke out in cities throughout the country. Thus, World War One inscribed the image of the city with a new economic and social identity: one associated with an explosive pace of change, with instability, and with the specter of intensified social violence.

Such visions of the city stood in contrast to older urban imaginaries. The feudal concept of the castle town, burnished over three centuries of political stability under Tokugawa rule, envisioned the city as a monument to the enduring power of the military elite. Tokugawa policies concentrated the ruling caste of samurai in the cities, where they constituted as much as 40 percent of the population. The remaining urban population of artisans and merchants supplied the needs and wants of the samurai.[1] Organized as instruments of samurai rule, cities became seats of higher learning and administration, which Tokugawa law defined as the exclusive province of the samurai. With the overthrow of the Tokugawa regime, samurai dominance of the city ended and the myth of samurai permanence was shattered. In the urban reconstructions of the 1870s and 1880s a new vision emerged of the city as instrument of progress and modernity. Exemplified in the remaking of central Tokyo and the famous Ginza brick town, and in the new government buildings that shot up throughout the country, the urban reconstructions of the early Meiji period telegraphed a message to foreigners and Japanese alike about the city as symbol of Japan's capacity for civilization and enlightenment. And though this urban imaginary embraced a sense of managed progress and controlled change, it little prepared people for the tumultuous transformations of the First World War.[2]

Examining the different ways in which World War One catalyzed urban change, this chapter takes up the following questions: Why did a discourse on the modern emerge with such peculiar force in the wake of World War One? What touched off the extended reflection on the newness of everyday life? To understand the intensity and volume of this intellectual production, the pages that follow canvass the impact of the war years on the urban economy, the built environment of the city, and urban society to show why these issues began to register so dramatically in the consciousness of urban residents.

THE ECONOMIC BOOM

Though of minimal significance for Japan militarily, World War One was the third of a series of wars that stimulated the formation of a modern industrial economy. Beginning with the Sino-Japanese War of 1894–95, and followed by the Russo-Japanese War of 1904–5, war booms shaped the contours of Japanese capitalism. Nascent factory production turned out armaments and ships to meet military demand and textiles bound for the East Asian markets that were captured in Japan's first colonial wars. When war broke out in Europe in 1914 the resulting disruptions in the global economy provided an opening for Japanese trade expansion, ushering in the third war boom in the space of twenty years. Although the initial impact of the war was to depress economic activity because of the rupture to international trade, by 1916 the opportunities opened up by the European war had touched off what amounted to a new phase in Japan's industrial revolution. The withdrawal of European textile and light industrial producers from colonial markets in Asia created a void into which Japanese manufacturers rapidly expanded. War cut them off from

European sources of chemicals, machinery, and other heavy industrial products, stimulating the development of domestic production. European demand for armaments and other military goods further encouraged the growth of heavy industry. Japanese shippers were called on to handle this increased trade and Japanese yards to build the ships. All this generated a degree of economic expansion that surpassed the earlier war booms. Moreover, unlike during those earlier wars, military activity was limited to a bloodless occupation of German holdings in China and the Pacific, which meant that World War One was not associated with the deprivation and sacrifice that had attended the earlier periods of rapid growth. Far from it, this war boom brought with it a sense of sudden wealth, widespread prosperity, and conspicuous consumption.

The war boom profoundly affected urban economies. While the late nineteenth-century wave of industrialization occurred mainly in and around the metropolises of Tokyo and Osaka and their affiliated ports of Yokohama and Kobe, the World War One boom left its mark on cities of all sizes. In terms of raw statistics, Tokyo and Osaka may have grown bigger and more quickly than the second-tier cities like the four in this book, but the impact of explosive economic growth on those smaller cites was just as intense. Fifty new companies were established in the city of Okayama between 1916 and 1920, and 99 in Sapporo between 1912 and 1920.[3] Investments in Kanazawa's economy spurred leaps in production, pushing the value of manufacturing from 18 million yen in 1916 up to 50 million yen in 1920.[4] Between 1912 and 1921, the value of heavy industrial production in Niigata rose by a factor of 11, from 2.5 million yen to 27.2 million yen.[5] The speed of this expansion not only anchored the urban economy to manufacturing but also associated the modern city with dynamism and rapid economic growth. The surge in urban investment reflected a new confidence in the future of the city.

Economic growth signaled a rise in the movement of goods in and out of the city. Though it expanded everywhere, trade grew most sharply in a port city like Niigata, where goods handled by the harbor rose from 13 million yen in 1912 to 30 million yen in 1921, more than doubling in ten years. Over the same period freight passing through the city's two principal train stations quadrupled, increasing from 10.5 million yen to 46.2 million yen.[6] The growth in their economies integrated cities such as Niigata more closely into national and international markets and marked urban space more distinctly as a node within the modern trade nexus. That, in turn, implied the new power of urban economies to influence partners in trade and, with it, new vulnerabilities to the vicissitudes of the market. The growth of trade also raised the economic profile of cities, identifying them with their key exports and stamping them with the character of their productive base. Kanazawa thus became known as a city of crafts, producing *hanabusae* silk cloth, gold leaf, and lacquerware. With its oil refineries, Niigata was seen as a center for heavy industry. Okayama was a textile producer, and the beer that took the Sapporo trademark became the symbol of the city's ties to agriculture and the importance of its food processing industries.

The nature of economic activity changed as well during the teens, stamping the urban economy with the imprimatur of modern factory production. One measure of this was the sharp growth in numbers of urban factories. In Okayama 11 new factories employing more than ten workers were established between 1912 and 1920; Sapporo had 52 factories in 1912 and 121 in 1920. Kanazawa's statistical yearbook recorded 190 factories with 6,141 employees in 1916 and 287 factories in 1919 with 8,556 employees.[7] As an Okayama factory survey of 1921 showed, not only did World War One trigger a numerical rise in factories, it also impelled transformation of existing factory production, both in terms of scale (number of workers) and the shift to steam- and gas-powered mechanization. Even the growth of small factories (employing fewer than ten laborers) signaled a shift in the meaning of production, for the war boom generated a movement from household manufacture and the putting-out system to factory-based manufacture of goods such as furniture, lacquerware, tatami mats, umbrellas, and *geta* (traditional Japanese wooden clogs). For example, the number of factory workers producing lacquerware in Niigata rose from 129 in 1916 to 402 in 1918, a threefold increase. Within the space of a few years production of *geta* shifted from households concentrated in the neighborhood of Getamachi to factories. Such moves to the factory both altered the relationship of workers to production and changed the socio-economic character of neighborhoods like Getamachi.[8]

To the political and economic elites who were privy to this knowledge, such statistics demonstrated the capacity of the urban economy to generate ever greater wealth, one more measure of the potential benefits of modern industry. The broader urban citizenry took much the same message from the evidence all around them of new ways to make and spend money. The transformations taking place before their eyes demonstrated to urban residents that cities were now characterized by rapid, even explosive, growth. Cities had become sites of industrial modernity, symbolized by the conversion to factory production and by factory mechanization. As a tendency to identify cities with their principal products revealed, this new urban imaginary foregrounded economic function: Japanese began to equate cities with their economic base. Wartime developments harnessed Japanese cities ever tighter to the engine of industrial expansion; their fate now hung on the future of the Japanese economy. In all these respects, the latest war boom altered the meaning of the city as an economic entity, and the possibilities for urban growth seemed boundless.

Yet there was a dark side to the new urban dynamics. Even as statistics captured for the record unprecedented economic growth, these numbers did not always translate into improved livelihood for city residents. Perhaps even more than the expansion of urban economic activity, the movements in prices and wages during World War One demonstrated the new volatility of the urban economy, for it could both raise and lower urban living standards. While wage increases were widely welcomed by working-class urbanites, the price increases that soon followed were not. And though price increases improved profit margins of industrialists and merchants, they regarded wage hikes with alarm. Thus while inflation translated into a generalized sense of economic anxiety, the specific impact on prices and wages split workers and capitalists and served as one factor in the mounting tensions between new social groups.

Although wage and price inflation had been a conspicuous feature of the earlier war booms, nothing prepared Japanese people for the increases of the late teens. Wages began to rise in 1915 and 1916 and then suddenly accelerated their upward trajectory until they peaked in 1920. The movement of commodity prices told a similar story. In 1918 newspapers everywhere reported the "violent rise" (*bōtō*) in prices, and they were filled with articles documenting the alarming increase in the cost of living. Okayama's *San'yō shinpō* reported a chamber of commerce survey of various shops in the city that compared basic food prices between 1914 and 1919; in an easy-to-read chart, the paper gave readers concrete numerical evidence on which to hang their feelings of alarm and outrage. Special-grade rice had more than doubled in price, table salt and cooking oil had tripled, and the fourteen other consumer staples included in the chart registered equivalent leaps in price. As *bōtō* became a catchphrase of the late teens, it underscored the dangers of rapid growth and the volatility inherent in the modern economy. Like prices of the late teens, the expanding urban economy could quickly spin out of control.[9]

While the explosive growth of World War One altered the economic meaning of the city, the physical transformation of urban sites over this same period changed the significance of the city in other ways. The rapid expansion of production, the rapid influx of population, and the rapid increase in the circulation of goods and people all placed pressing new demands on urban infrastructure, setting off a frenzy of construction that identified the city as a site of speed and ephemerality.

Electric power, introduced in the late 1880s, became exponentially more widespread in the teens, illuminating the streets, electrifying middle- and upper-class households, and transforming factory production. In Sapporo, for example, there were 255 streetlights in 1911; by 1920 the number had risen to 7,835. Over the same period households that were supplied with electricity increased from 2,695 to 21,075, and factory consumption leapt from four thousand to over 4 million kilowatt hours.[10] While in previous decades, the gaslight and the spindle served as symbols of civilization and enlightenment, they were being replaced by a modernity of the neon sign and electrical appliance.

Like many cities, Kanazawa laid a streetcar line in the teens. Before it opened to great fanfare in early 1919, the streetcar necessitated an extensive reshaping of the city along the path of the rail line, the razing of scores of stores and residences, and the destruction of neighborhoods in order to widen the road to accommodate the streetcars. A vibrant new commercial and entertainment strip sprang up on the foundation of old neighborhoods along the tracks, creating what would become the heart of "modern Kanazawa."[11]

In Niigata, the municipal government had carried out wharf construction and port improvements continuously since 1907, dredging the Shinano River, improving the banks, building a breakwater, and erecting a lighthouse. When Niigata annexed Nuttari, its sister city on the opposite bank of the Shinano River, the two communities commenced construction on an elaborate new wharf to expand Niigata's port facilities. At the same time, the city began an ambitious landfill project on the east side of the river, creating tracts of worker housing next to the industrial zone that was taking shape along the riverbank. The dredging, the riparian works, and the landfill dramatically reshaped the river and altered its course. In the space of a few years the river—which had been the economic and social center of these two port cities for generations—was utterly transformed.[12]

In Okayama, where a river also ran through the heart of the city, municipal government began to reconstruct the main Kyōbashi Bridge in 1915. After two years of work the old wooden structure was replaced with a reinforced concrete construction. Like the lighting of Sapporo's streetlamps, the inaugural run of Kanazawa's streetcar, or the ceremony marking the completion of Niigata's wharf, the opening of Okayama's new bridge was a moment of great civic pride. A photograph of the ceremony published March 25, 1917, shows the bridge thronged with people as they surged up from the embankments to step onto the bridge the *San'yō shinpō* proudly hailed as the "first reinforced concrete bridge in the prefecture."[13]

In these ways, the pressures of the war years spurred municipalities to expand the range of urban amenities and develop basic infrastructure to accommodate the demands of a surging population and burgeoning local industry. As new electrical and telephone services became available, as cities created systems of mass transportation, as they widened and paved their roads, and as they improved sewer systems and expanded the supply of running water, the built environment of the city seemed to become a perpetual motion machine, the streetscape a site of ceaseless change. In the process, the modern city was identified with both the sheer, dizzying pace of change and the endless quest for technological improvement. Modernity signified the replacement of gas with electricity, of wood with concrete, of single stories with double, and double with triple. It meant roads became ever wider and rivers ever straighter. Destined for endless remaking, the modern city could never be finished.

Such notions of the city anticipated the epistemological shift in urban thought that took place in the wake of the great Tokyo earthquake of 1923. In a matter of hours the quake and the fires that followed destroyed vast sections of the Japanese capital. As a new, modern Tokyo arose atop the rubble of the old city, the earthquake became etched in popular memory as a watershed moment: the birth of a Japanese modern. The dramatic reconstitution of Tokyo's built environment seemed to evacuate the capital of its past. But before the operatic scale of the earthquake turned all eyes toward Tokyo, the more modest dramas of the wartime construction booms brought urban residents throughout the country face to face with new meanings of the city. Though it was only after the earthquake that theorists of the modern such as Kon Wajirō and Gonda Yasunosuke began to connect the emergence of the new physical space of Tokyo with the possibility of creating a new urban culture called *modanizumu* (modernism), the groundwork for these ruminations was laid in the multifarious construction booms that took place in Japan's smaller cities during the war years.[14]

Even as the construction boom coupled the concept of continuous change with the image of the modern city, the demonstrable failure of municipal infrastructural improvements to keep pace with explosive growth made it clear to municipal authorities, if not to urban residents, that there was no easy solution to the crisis of infrastructure. Like perpetual change, the ongoing crisis of infrastructure appeared to all to be a piece of the modern urban condition. In Okayama, just before the war broke out, the municipal authorities undertook a large improvement in the urban waterworks. Anticipating a population influx with the establishment of a local army division in the city, they planned to expand the water supply to accommodate the new residents. But the sudden urban growth spurred by the war boom threw this careful planning out the window. The rapid expansion of city industry caused water use to rise an unprecedented 27 percent per year. Even as the project was nearing completion, it became clear that increasing demand would strain the capacity of the new waterworks. The staggering pace of growth took city planners completely by surprise.[15]

In a similar vein, efforts of local authorities to improve and expand networks of roads in order to facilitate the flow of goods and people through the city met with a new and unexpected challenge: traffic. For Japan, World War One marked the advent of the automobile, which quickly became a major contributor to traffic congestion and bedlam in the streets. Initially fleets of cars were operated by transportation companies, which employed them to deliver goods to locations not served by the train. Taxi and bus companies soon followed, and the numbers of automobiles on the city streets increased. As a 1920 article in Okayama's *San'yō shinpō* observed, "Although automobiles were a rarity three or four years ago, recently there has been a surprising and dramatic rise in the numbers of cars on the road." By contemporary standards, local car ownership was quite modest. Okayama prefecture's first car was purchased in 1912, and only 130 automobiles were registered by 1920; these operated almost exclusively in the capital and a few other cities.[16] Statistics for Ishikawa prefecture and its capital city of Kanazawa were similar: the first car was bought in 1913 and only 130 were registered prefecture-wide by 1921, a year when eight different companies operated fleets of automobiles in the capital.

The problem was not so much the numbers of cars but the hazard a fast-moving, large-bodied vehicle constituted for the narrow and winding road networks that were the inheritance of Japan's feudal cities. What with bicycles, jinrickshas, horse- and ox-drawn carts, and streetcars all sharing the roads with automobiles, "traffic" was beginning to register among the growing host of urban social problems. Although Kanazawa had leveled large sections of the downtown to create the new arterial road system that led through the city center, traffic surveys conducted barely a few years after road construction was completed revealed a new crisis at hand. A survey in April 1921 measuring the amount of traffic that traversed a level crossing near Kanazawa station showed that in a single day, on average, 5,976 pedestrians, 234 bicycles, 703 wagons, 49 carriages, and 5 automobiles made the crossing. This meant that trains were forced to wait at the crossing for a total of four and a half hours a day. As a local newspaper reported, the results of its own survey several years later showed that the deplorable degree of traffic congestion forced Kanazawa residents to move about "like rats trapped in a bag," and the situation cried out for government intervention.[17]

All this suggested that urban growth had accelerated out of control. City boosters who earlier had observed with great satisfaction the leaps in productivity and the mushrooming of new factories now began to sound an ominous note. Their beloved city was rampantly expanding in unpredictable ways, creating an endless series of crises, a daily onslaught of demands for new services that the existing apparatus of municipal government seemed ill equipped to meet. Indeed, the stresses of the wartime construction boom, much like the "violent rise" in prices that overtook the latter years of industrial expansion, convinced urban elites of the need for a stronger hand at the helm. As Japan's cities headed into the third decade of the twentieth century, the experience of the war boom demonstrated both the fantastic possibilities for economic growth and the need to bring some measure of control over its direction. The war boom convinced people that growth was good, but not violent, chaotic growth; this conviction helped fortify public support for a dramatic expansion in the municipal state. In these ways the experience of World War One laid the foundation for the era of city planning and municipal social engineering and stimulated a rethinking of the city idea.

THE GO-GO ECONOMY AND THE *NARIKIN*

The economic volatility and dramatic physical transformation of these years were mirrored in the domain of urban society. More than anything else, the figure of the *narikin*, or nouveau riche, came to symbolize the social effects of the war boom. Taken from a Japanese chess move that aggrandized a pawn into a more powerful piece, the term was applied after the Russo-Japanese War to a handful of speculators like Suzuki Kyūgorō, who got rich quick playing the stock market. After his sudden acquisition of wealth catapulted Suzuki into a position of social prominence, he remained in the public spotlight by frittering away his earnings in a life of ostentatious dissipation. Men like Suzuki became symbols of rogue capitalism, speculators who operated on the boundaries of legitimacy and whose relentless pursuit of profits caused panics and otherwise endangered the economy.

The *narikin* were enhanced by the aura of the stock market, and their reputation was inseparable from popular images of this new capitalist institution. Established in the late nineteenth century, the securities market became an important avenue of business finance; however, the primacy of government-controlled banks, and of the house banks of the big-business organizations known as *zaibatsu*, meant that it would always remain a less reputable and less secure means of industrial finance.[18] Moreover, while government policies that promoted private industry smiled upon upright businessmen such as the founders of factories, stock traders were regarded with some suspicion—the dark twin of the good capitalist who strove to grow the economy in the name of building Japan's wealth and power. As the economic boom of World War One expanded entrepreneurial opportunities, the number of parvenu capitalists multiplied and the *narikin* dominated the ranks of businessmen in all fields of activity. No longer considered economic adventurers and associated with the shady economic underworld of the stock market, the *narikin* entered the mainstream of economic activity and became the symbol of the go-go economy and urban prosperity.[19]

Yamamoto Isaburō of Okayama was a case in point. A local shipping magnate who made his fortune during the war, Yamamoto became a celebrity both for his eccentric and flamboyant habits and for his public munificence. In attracting notoriety, Yamamoto represented a complicated symbol of the modern economy. His meteoric rise into the plutocratic ether was made possible by speculative investments during the war boom, but it also followed a lifetime's diligent pursuit of self-improvement, in which he had followed the sanctioned road to upward mobility via hard work, education, and duty to company. Born into modest circumstances, Yamamoto spent his childhood laboring in a tofu store to augment the family income. Although poverty precluded him from regular attendance at elementary school, he subsequently found the wherewithal to matriculate at middle school, to gain admittance to the elite Dōshisha University in Kyoto, and from there, to move on to and graduate from Sapporo Agricultural College. He used his university contacts to good effect, involving himself in land development and agribusiness in Hokkaido, then using his connection with former teacher Nitobe Inazo to secure a post in a Tokyo trading company. After Yamamoto strove to establish himself within the ranks of senior management, a lucky break left him in a position to take over the firm when the president suddenly died in the early 1910s. The timing could not have been better: on the eve of the First World War, Yamamoto found himself well placed to take aggressive advantage of opportunities in the East Asian trade; by the late teens he had ridden the war boom to amass a reputed fortune of 40 million yen. Thus, through good fortune and hard work, the humble tofu boy had bootstrapped his way to a position of wealth and social influence. Self-made men like Yamamoto united the good capitalist and his more dangerous twin in the new figure of the *narikin*, who was redefining the face of the urban economy.

Yamamoto's rags-to-riches story modified the existing narrative of the *narikin* in other ways as well. Like other wartime parvenus, Yamamoto achieved notoriety both for his good deeds and his outrageous behavior. His most prominent act as public benefactor was a donation of eighteen thousand yen for a public library, built in 1917 and boasting sixty-three thousand volumes. Yamamoto housed his new library in modern architectural splendor, presenting Okayama city with one of its first two-story buildings constructed with reinforced concrete. He demonstrated his public munificence in other ways as well, financing a local newspaper and establishing the Yamamoto Agricultural School in Kume County, where he was born. Probably more than his good deeds, however, Yamamoto's ostentatious lifestyle made him the stuff of urban legend. He earned the sobriquet "tiger magnate" (*tora daijin*) after he led two hundred men on a much photographed tiger hunt in Korea. He enhanced his reputation for extravagant amusement when he staged a sensational contest between Tokyo and Kyoto geisha. Reserving an entire train traveling from Tokyo to Kyoto for a party of friends and a company of Tokyo geisha, he followed these onboard festivities with a lavish party in Kyoto, where the local geisha had their turn to entertain. During the war boom such stories of the eccentricities of overnight millionaires—their excessive generosity and their excessive extravagance—turned the *narikin* into local legends. Standing out from the ranks of the ordinary businessman—the bland and timorous salaryman—the *narikin* exuded brazen self-confidence and hypermasculinity. Symbols of an age of excess, the *narikin* were larger than life, social abnormalities that defined the new social extremes that the modern economy could produce.[20]

Though stories about shipping magnates such as Yamamoto fed the stereotype of the *narikin*, the term also applied to other beneficiaries of the new urban prosperity. In a city like Kobe, where the local economy was anchored to shipbuilding, the demand for ships brought a wave of prosperity that lifted the fortunes of many local residents. As one observer noted in 1918: "In Kobe the capitalists, the ship owners, and the laborers have all become *narikin*. To put it another way, Kobe itself has become a *narikin*."[21] Others commented on the extraordinary wage hikes commanded by skilled labor, especially those working in munitions factories. Workers were said to "disport themselves like *narikin*, hiring prostitutes, some of them even commuting back and forth to work from the red light district. Workers are welcomed in the cafés and restaurants like the god of wealth."[22] In Sapporo, the surging demand for agricultural exports brought prosperity not only to shipping interests but also to farm supply firms and local transport companies and to food processing, marketing, and warehousing operations. Locally, the lexicon of the nouveau riche expanded beyond mere "shipping magnates" (*funa narikin*) to include the "starch millionaires" (*denpun narikin*), who owned potato-processing companies, as well as the "giant radish" (*daikon*), "pumpkin" (*kabocha*), and "pig" (*buta*) *narikin* who were bringing new custom to Sapporo's shopping districts as they accompanied their families to town to spend their newfound wealth.[23] As such commentary revealed, the *narikin* had come to embody the social possibilities raised by the modern economy, as well as to symbolize rapid growth and urban prosperity.

Ultimately the figure of the *narikin* proved a disquieting image, for the fortunes of the *narikin*, like the urban economy itself, fell as dramatically and rapidly as they had risen. If the narrative of the *narikin* that took form in the war boom began with social obscurity, it ended in financial calamity. Yamamoto Isaburō was no exception: he lost his entire fortune in the catastrophic postwar depression that set in after 1920, when European traders returned to reclaim their markets and demand for Japanese shipping dried up. The cascade of bankruptcies among the *narikin* demonstrated that, while growth in the modern economy generated unprecedented prosperity, it also brought unprecedented insecurity, a lesson reinforced by the swelling ranks of the unemployed that became a symbol of the postwar bust. But even as their fortunes fell, the fate of the *narikin* advertised the mixed blessings of the modern economy, for along with memories of the volatility and risk, the uncertainty and insecurity, *narikin* left behind permanent monuments to their fame and munificence. The libraries and the schools, no less than the tales of wild parties and tiger hunts, spoke to the social possibilities of urban capitalism, nurturing hopes for a return to prosperity and stoking dreams of instant wealth and conspicuous consumption.

THE SPECTER OF THE URBAN CROWD

Even more than the oversized figure of the *narikin*, the rise of worker radical-ism and urban protest in the late teens signaled the dangers inherent in the new urban economy. World War One marked the onset of a new level of urban violence, as the eruption of popular rage in the rice riots of the summer of 1918 underscored the instability of urban society. And just as the acceler-ated urbanization of these years generated new meanings of the city in terms of physical space and economic function, the rice riots heightened fears that modern urban society was violently unpredictable and constituted a serious threat to political order.

Volatile rice prices provided the trigger for the riots that engulfed the country in the hot summer of 1918. An unfortunate conjunction of circum-stances propelled the cost of rice in a dangerous upward spiral. The sudden growth of the urban population had led to a rise in demand for rice as a staple of the daily diet and as an ingredient in the manufacture of sake and other rice-based products. At the same time, migration to the cities produced a labor shortage in the countryside, causing a fall in the supply of rice. The situ-ation was exacerbated by rumors of an imminent military expedition to Siberia, which was then officially announced on August 2. Anticipating a redirection of a large segment of the rice supply to feed the troops, the news spurred grain speculators into action. It also encouraged widespread stock-piling, competition between regional markets for a dwindling supply, and rice prices that varied wildly from place to place—all driving the vicious cycle of inflation ever faster. As rice prices rose, the economy continued to boom, and some were clearly enjoying the benefits of prosperity. But while *narikin* engaged in orgies of conspicuous consumption, others found themselves unable to afford even a family meal. In some areas no rice was to be had for any price. Rumors abounded that merchants were hoarding supplies or ship-ping rice out of the district in search of greater profits. In desperation and rage, urban crowds blamed rice merchants for their greed and the government for its failure to rectify the situation.

The rice riots began in July as a "housewives revolt" (*nyobō ikki*) in a small Toyama fishing village, when fisherwomen refused to allow local rice to be loaded on ships for transport to urban markets in the Kansai region. Protests spread quickly along the Toyama coast and into urban centers throughout Japan. By mid-August the entire country was engulfed with rioting, which affected 38 cities, 153 towns, and 177 villages and involved an estimated six hundred thousand to a million participants.[24] Though the riots were touched off in a village, when transferred to an urban setting they took on a more frightening aspect, becoming associated with a dangerous new form of crowd violence. Michael Lewis points out that the urban riots went beyond the rural protests in their sweeping indictment of the political status quo, representing a "massive rejection of the new Japan by great numbers of its citizens."[25] The distinction made between the rural and urban riots was reflected in the words used to describe them. While the media spoke of village *ikki*, employing language derived from the feudal lexicon of peasant uprisings, they referred to urban riots as *sōjō*—a term drawn from the Meiji criminal code, which categorized *sōjō* as a crime of sedition.[26]

The riots drew on a history of urban militancy that had gathered strength since the Russo-Japanese War of 1904–5, and which had schooled the urban crowd in political tactics empowering the disenfranchised. Since the shocking Hibiya Riots of 1905, where unruly crowds overran Hibiya Park to protest the terms of the peace treaty with Russia, urban rioting had become an increasingly familiar feature of urban politics. Over the years, urban residents learned to use *shimin taikai*—"citizens rallies"—as a means of protesting streetcar-rate hikes, new taxes, and other offensive aspects of municipal policy. If the authorities refused to give way, the crowd frequently demonstrated its displeasure through violence, attacking symbols of the political order such as police boxes and government offices. At the same time, the formation of labor unions created another vehicle for collective action that provided a source of social power for the disenfranchised. The labor shortage of the war boom gave workers a new advantage over their employers, an edge that labor activists were quick to seize in their quest to improve working conditions. The war spurred union organizing and emboldened labor activists to use strikes and other forms of militancy to press their demands.[27]

Though both these forms of crowd militancy had created a new source of social power to express political demands, nothing prepared political elites for the extent and force of the rice riots. The nationwide riots pushed the government to extreme measures, forcing it to impose a media blackout and to dispatch troops to 144 locations to put down the disturbances. The aftermath was equally dramatic: for failing to prevent the riots, the Terauchi Masatake cabinet fell in disgrace, signaling the ability of the disenfranchised crowd to determine the fate of the prime minister. The crowd forced a host of new policies concerning rice prices and rice supply, as well as new measures to address poverty and provide social services for the urban poor. Most of all, the riots burned into popular memory the image of a chain of cities engulfed in rioting: the specter of urban revolution.

The media were a key factor in the outbreak and spread of the rioting. Indeed, their role in the rice riots served as an important demonstration of the social power of the press among an increasingly literate, newspaper-reading public. Coverage in the press of the daily rises in rice prices helped inflame public anger in the first place; sensational reports of riots in one locale inspired crowds elsewhere to act. Moreover, the press served as a kind of advertisement for local rallies and other crowd actions, as in Niigata, where the *Niigata shinbun* published the contents of leaflets that called on local residents to gather and discuss the situation.[28] Extensive coverage of an August 12 rally in Kanazawa that erupted into a riot merely brought greater numbers out the following night, when the crowd regrouped at the same public park to renew its demands.[29] Recognizing the inflammatory role of the media, in mid-August the Home Ministry began to censor reports of the riots.

Coverage in the press helped shape public perceptions of the angry crowds and constructed narratives of their actions. Even in cities like Sapporo, where despite the circulation of advertisements for a "citizen's rally to discuss the problem of rice" neither rallies nor riots occurred, articles on rioting elsewhere impressed local residents with the power of the urban crowd.[30] The story told in the newspapers concluded, significantly, with the suppression of the riots and the arrest of the perpetrators, but not before treating the public to hair-raising accounts of crowds of thousands surging down the streets, overwhelming the local police forces, and venting their rage on the political and economic elite they blamed for their troubles by throwing rocks, lighting fires, and smashing houses.

Newspaper accounts of the Kanazawa riots detailed crowds of several thousand gathering on the evenings of August 12 and 13, the first night on the grounds of a local temple, the second at the city's major park. As the paper told the story, on the first evening of rioting, after the crowds had gathered at the temple grounds, they broke into four groups and spread out over the city, stopping in front of residences of rice merchants, wealthy landlords, and political authorities. At each stop they issued a summons to the master of the house to come out and negotiate with the crowd; they demanded provision of cheap rice to the residents of the city. If their call was answered and demands were met, the crowd moved on. But if the gate remained tightly shut, they vented their rage by breaking down the door and smashing up the entry hall.[31]

The local press in Niigata and Okayama told similar stories of escalating violence. In mid-August the *Niigata shinbun* reported that crowds that had gathered in Hakusan Park for Obon festival dancing were roused to action by a series of impromptu speakers denouncing local merchants for their refusal to lower prices. A pack of angry people surged out of the park and headed for the home of Kagitomi Sansaku, where sentiments toward the powerful rice dealer were expressed with a hail of rocks.[32] Likewise, the *San'yō shinpō* reported the outbreak of violence at the Okayama rice exchange, where two brokers were assaulted by an irate mob. Though city authorities tried to avert rioting by dispensing reduced-price rice, an angry crowd gathered at the storefront of a leading rice merchant and, judging the company efforts wanting, broke into the warehouse and distributed rice to those waiting in the street. From there they headed for the residences of the company president and other local merchants, smashing houses of businessmen rumored to have profited from the rice inflation. Though the police were present for most of this, they were overwhelmed by the sheer numbers of the rioters and could only stand by ineffectually. In Okayama, crowd violence was quelled only with the arrival of the local army regiment.[33]

Such tales of urban rioting conveyed in lurid detail modern society's frightening capacity for violence. In the way the press framed their stories, they drove home several points about the significance of the rice riots. The first concerned the appropriation of city space by the crowd. Gatherings at parks, temple grounds, and other public spaces inscribed these as sites of popular political revolt, memorializing and monumentalizing the social power of the crowd and creating an alternative to the town hall as the symbol of grassroots democracy. Second, newspapers told the story of the righteous anger of the crowd that arose from its frustration with the inability of local political authorities to resolve a crisis situation. Though the crowd's methods may have been extreme and alarming, the press tended to portray the cause of the rioters as just. The third message conveyed by the newspaper coverage of the rioting concerned the rioters' political significance. Unable to get results through established political channels, the crowd took matters into its own hands, entering into direct negotiations with local businessmen to seek relief from starvation. In this way the crowd created its own form of political action and its own rules of political ethics. This signaled the growing power of the disenfranchised to express their will through extraparliamentary means and rendered the town hall momentarily irrelevant. Finally, the photographs of battered houses and smashed up warehouses telegraphed to urban elites the message that they ignored the demands of the lower classes at their own peril. If not met with a good-faith effort, the crowd was capable of exacting a high price on the wealthiest and most powerful members of the community. The local police force offered no guarantee of safety.

The denouement to the drama of the rice riots came in the fall of 1918, when the newspapers reported the results of police investigations and the outcome of the trials of those arrested. Here the central focus of the press was the social background of the rioters, highlighting the principal role played by the urban working poor. Although historians such as Michael Lewis have stressed the socially heterogeneous composition of the crowd, journalists at the time judged participants to be "poor" (*saimin*) or "the lower classes" (*kasō shakai*).[34] Later reports reinforced such impressions. In Kanazawa, five of the seven arrested were foil workers—a category of craftsmen who pounded gold and silver foil for inlay in religious accouterments, lacquerware, and other traditional craft products. Since Kanazawa was a center of the foil industry, foil workers comprised a large percentage of local craftspeople that, together with day laborers, small tradesmen, and workers in small factories, were among the poorest paid of urban workers and most vulnerable to rice price inflation. The other two arrested were a secondhand goods merchant and a day laborer.[35]

In Okayama, where a much higher number of arrests reflected the greater scale and violence of local protests, 177 were eventually prosecuted in connection with the riots. Of these, 53 were unskilled "coolie" and day laborers, 35 were craftsmen, and 36 were small tradesmen. Striking in their absence from the list were workers from Okayama's abundant textile factories, reinforcing the impression that the rioters came not from the better-paid aristocracy of large-factory labor but from the underclass of working poor. Moreover, with headlines like "Peremptory Demands of Poor *Burakumin* Terrorize Rice Merchants" (August 20) and "Armed with Bamboo Spears, *Burakumin* Riot Attacks the Wealthy" (August 22), *San'yō shinpō* reports underscored the dominant presence of the former outcasts known as *burakumin* among the protesters, further strengthening the image of a crowd composed of marginal peoples—the poorest of the poor, the most socially debased, and the most economically disadvantaged.[36] These marginal elements of urban society suffered the most from the volatility of the modern urban economy, and their sense of disaffection could be dangerously transformed into violent rage. Images of new forms of urban wealth and poverty that circulated during the war boom suggested that if *narikin* were the beneficiaries of economic growth, these were its victims. Occupying the extremities of the new social unevenness produced by urban capitalism, the violent gestures of the crowd, no less than the conspicuous consumption of the *narikin*, dramatized the new social face of the city.

The economic boom of World War One left its mark on Japanese cities of all sizes and identified urban space as one of capitalism's new frontiers. Urban growth transformed both material realities of urban life and the way people thought about urban economy and society. The city emerged as a powerful symbol of the modern economy, illustrating the hopes and fears of what industrial growth might promise for the future. The ongoing construction boom appeared to bear out the modernist dictum of creative destruction and destructive creation. In the dizzying pace of change, urban development followed the emerging imperative to clear out the old and make way for the new. Amid the social upheaval triggered by the disruptions of the war years, the twin symbols of the *narikin* and the urban crowd seemed to distill the social possibilities offered by urban growth. Unprecedented wealth and unprecedented poverty, the potential for a paradise of riches as well as for insurrection and revolution—the possibilities made visible by the war years inspired a host of utopian and distopian meditations on modernity in the years that followed. If the war years taught people that change could come quickly, without warning, and with awesome force, they also raised the potential of harnessing and directing this power to control the future.

In these ways the tumultuous experience of World War One contributed to the emergence of a new social imaginary that refigured the city as a social, economic, and cultural space. As we shall see, the war prompted an extended historical moment of intensive reflection on the significance of recent change and gave rise to a new social consciousness of the modern. This social imaginary situated cities at the center of modern life and at the vanguard of national progress, leaving behind the social world of the countryside. Uneven development gave rise to new economic and cultural geographies that concentrated wealth and power in cities and subordinated the provinces to the metropolis. Cities became sites of a distinctive temporality, where time sped along and the minutes ticked by faster. Contemplating the dynamism of the interwar years, urban elites determined that cities represented the point where the forces driving modernization seemed to converge in both space and time.

These changes cumulatively defined an identity for the city that was grounded in the conceptual fusing of modernity with the urban form. Although the identification of the city with modernity appears to be common sense today, the conviction that "city = modern" is in fact a historical product. To retrace the genesis of this belief, in the pages that follow I ask the question: How did the city become the center of modern economic and social life? One answer can be found by examining the forces that made Tokyo into a "world city" and center of the Japanese empire while simultaneously producing new lines of division between "city" and "country." The first part of this book, to which we now turn, tracks the development of the cultural and economic geographies that defined the social space of "modernity" through the creation of a new system of centers and peripheries.

PART TWO

Geo-Power and Urban-Centrism

TWO

The Ideology of the Metropolis

One of the most striking effects of Japan's modernization project of the late nineteenth century was the rising prominence and increasing centrality of Tokyo within the new national space. By the 1920s, Meiji government policies of national developmentalism pursued since the 1870s had built Tokyo up and transformed it into the control room for nationwide political parties, the seat of national government and apex of administrative hierarchies, the clearinghouse for the financial industry, the heart of the national transportation grid, a locus of industry and a major concentration of population, and the main portal to the outside world. These policies increased Tokyo's centrality in cultural ways as well, as it became a center of higher education, the high arts, the publishing industry, and the mass media.

In a material sense, these economic, political, and cultural institutions and networks concentrated power and resources in the capital, producing and reproducing its centrality. But just as significant, people came to think of Tokyo as the first among cities: they believed it to be the largest, the best, the foremost, the fastest, the most advanced. And because nothing succeeds like success, this faith in Tokyo as number one augmented the capital's capacity to attract still more economic, cultural, and political resources. In other words, belief in Tokyo as the center had a power-effect, which reinforced and reproduced its centrality. It is this combination of material and ideological forces that I highlight by the term *Tokyo-centrism.*

Intellectuals, the literati in particular, stood at the heart of this process. Literary production in the early twentieth century was concerned, overwhelmingly, with everyday life. Because their depictions of life in the metropolis, in the provincial town, and in the rural village critically shaped urban and rural imaginaries, writers occupied a central role in the production of Tokyo-centrism. Moreover, faith in Tokyo's centrality was most fervently felt in high cultural circles. For writers, artists, and musicians, the metropolitan stage represented a singular pinnacle of achievement. Their fixation with Tokyo emerged from the intimate relationship between the literati and institutions of the press and the schools. Built up in the late nineteenth century as instruments of national integration, newspapers and the educational system created networks that connected urban communities, and they provided a conduit that channeled talent and ambition to the capital. In the process, they became important vehicles for the production and dissemination of Tokyo-centrism. More than any other, these two modernizing institutions gave definition to the literati as a social formation and cultural force. They offered a meeting ground and a stage, shaping the ethos of the literati and propelling them to social prominence and influence. Like the institutions that fostered them, the literati became instruments of Tokyo-centrism.

Though Tokyo's centrality owed something to the Tokugawa legacy of Edo-centrism, Tokyo's rise was determined as much by what happened after the overthrow of the feudal regime in 1868 as before. Soon after the establishment of the new state, fierce competition broke out between two centers of the old regime for designation as the new national capital. Osaka, the economic hub of rice and money exchange, emerged as one contender, and Edo, the seat of shogunal political power, as the other. Edo, renamed Tokyo, or "Eastern capital," won out, but even its new designation called attention to the contingent nature of capitals in Japan, where the physical seat of power had shifted frequently over the centuries.[1] Old Edo bequeathed to new Tokyo its academies of samurai erudition, its shogunal palace and aristocratic estates, its vibrant popular culture, and its demographic dominance over other urban centers. Nevertheless, as Henry Smith points out, in the early years of the transition from Edo to Tokyo the new city became a shell of its former self, losing population as the feudal lords and their samurai retainers abandoned the city for their homelands, taking with them much of the wealth that had sustained the city as a center of consumption and cultural production since the 1600s.[2] Two decades into the new era, Tokyo recovered the million population mark and regained its centralizing momentum through the establishment of a national railway grid, a constitutional government, and other policies of the Meiji developmental state. Though we have tended to assume the inevitability of Tokyo's rise, this history highlights the human contrivance that lay behind Tokyo-centrism.

The same forces that made Tokyo central—that concentrated power and prestige in the capital—provincialized other urban centers, turning them into "local cities" (*chihō toshi*) in relation to Tokyo by marginalizing their cultural and economic production and limiting their political clout. New educational institutions and the publishing market channeled ambitious and talented intellectuals to the capital; the ongoing brain drain held profound implications for local communities. The belief that Japan's modernist cultural movements originated in Tokyo blinded people to the dynamism and creativity of local cultural movements and their influence on the center. And yet, provincial cities did support thriving communities of artists and writers. Cities such as Kanazawa cultivated towering figures in modern Japanese thought such as writer Izumi Kyōka, Buddhologist Suzuki Daisetsu, and philosopher Nishida Kitarō. As the distinctive regional voices of Sapporo's proletarian literature, Niigata's orchestras, and Okayama's new poetry reveal, innovation and originality was possible in the world beyond the metropolis.

This chapter examines the creation of a new cultural geography that privileged Tokyo and marginalized its outside world—a geography that defined Japan in terms of Tokyo and its Others. In the circulation of people and ideas set in motion by the modernizing project of the Meiji state, Japan's cities redefined themselves in relation to other urban centers. Just as Tokyo's metropolitan identity was constructed against a rural imaginary—the *chihō*, or provinces—Tokyo provided the Other against which local cities forged their own self-conceptions.

EDUCATION AND CULTURAL GEOGRAPHY

The architecture of the national education system was created through a series of late-nineteenth-century laws that shunted children into different streams based on gender and status. The Meiji oligarchy initially intended educational reform to become a vehicle for the introduction of western knowledge into Japan, as well as a vehicle for the creation of a national citizenry capable of service to the state and of work in new economic enterprises. The new leadership also saw education as an instrument of social reform, part of the broader effort to phase out feudal status distinctions between samurai and commoners. To this end they created a compulsory elementary school system available to children of all backgrounds, which by 1907 meant eight years of schooling, tuition free. Entry into secondary school was based on competitive entry examinations, grounding higher education on the principle of meritocracy. These reforms ended the samurai monopoly on learning and made upward mobility theoretically possible through the school system, an ideal captured in the Meiji slogan of "rising in the world" (*risshin shusse*).[3]

In practice, however, the elaborate educational tracking system quickly became a vehicle for the reproduction of existing social hierarchies. The first moment of separation, between primary and secondary education, fixed the boundary between an emerging working class on one hand, and middle and upper classes on the other. Because high tuition effectively barred the poor from most secondary schools, the lower tier of primary schools was terminal for children of tenant farmers or of the urban lower class. For children of means, secondary education proceeded along multiple pathways, dividing into a university-bound middle-and-higher-school track, and alternative tracks for normal schools, girls' higher schools, and commercial, foreign language, and trade schools. Students on the exclusive university track moved from a five-year middle school to a three-year higher school, between which stood a brutal weeding process. School statistics reveal that in 1890 there were spaces for 11,620 students at 55 middle schools spread throughout the country, but only 4,356 spots at the nation's 7 select higher schools. By 1920 the numbers of state middle schools expanded to 368 (177,201 students) and higher schools to 15 (8,839 students), an asymmetry that significantly sharpened the odds against passing higher-school examinations. These statistics translated into a higher-school admission rate of roughly 1 percent of the male population between sixteen and nineteen. The good news for that successful 1 percent was that higher-school graduation virtually guaranteed entry into a university.[4]

While numerous private schools emerged to meet the growing demand for education, state schools commanded considerably more prestige and maintained the ranking system that placed Japan's cities in a hierarchy of educational stature. The first public higher schools were named according to their place in this hierarchy; the nation's top school in Tokyo, for example, was designated Ichikō, literally "First High." Tokyo was also the site of the nation's top (and until 1897 only) public university, Tokyo Imperial University. The cities of Kyoto, distinguished by its long association with the imperial court, and Sendai, seat of one of the most powerful feudal domains and a center of learning during the Tokugawa period, tied for second place in this ranking when the new government located the next higher schools Nikō

(Second High) in Sendai and Sankō (Third High) in Kyoto in the 1880s. Establishment of a second imperial university in Kyoto in 1897, and a third in Sendai (Tōhoku University) in 1907 reinforced their positions at the head of the academic hierarchy.[5]

This educational ranking system privileged Kanazawa and Okayama, where the Fourth and Sixth Higher Schools were located, respectively.[6] Sapporo also achieved cultural prominence as an educational center when the Meiji government in 1876 created Sapporo Agricultural College, making it a center for research in agricultural modernization. Its status was greatly elevated when it became the agricultural campus of Tōhoku Imperial University (main campus in Sendai) in 1907, and was made into Hokkaido Imperial University in 1918 (with the addition of faculties of science, engineering, and medicine). In anointing certain cities as centers of modern knowledge, state educational policy created a cultural geography that concentrated human and material resources for knowledge production, in the process helping to constitute a system of centers and peripheries.

Moreover, the tiers in the state's educational tracking system were distributed according to a particular spatial logic that distinguished villages (with elementary schools only) from cities (with a range of secondary school choices), and both of these from the metropolis (where universities were concentrated). This geographic dispersal of educational institutions linked social mobility to geographic mobility, and it laid the channels through which such demographic movements would flow. Thus, in the late Meiji a pattern established itself where the second and third (noninheriting) sons of rural landlords moved from their villages to the cities to be schooled with children of the urban elite, members of old merchant and artisan families as well as former samurai. For these families, education represented one way to transform feudal wealth into human capital and secure the family's fortunes at a time of rapid economic transition. Elite urban in-migration implied upward mobility, social advance secured through access to new knowledge. The rural poor, in contrast, lacked the property requisite to finance secondary education for their children. For them, the labor market, rather than the school system, created the channels of geo-social mobility. In their case, movement to the cities was less upward mobility than outward mobility, since geographic movement, for the most part, changed the social form of their labor but not their position in the social hierarchy. Like the labor market, modern educational institutions became a vessel for the transmutation of feudal social categories into modern social categories, for dissolving status positions and reshaping them into class formations. Moreover, complementing the effects of urban rankings of public schools, the geographically dispersed tiers of school tracks constituted a new cultural geography that was hierarchical and created a system of centers and peripheries.

Beyond the class distinctions it helped to generate, the educational system created cultural disparities between communities. As they were situated on the educational grid, localities assumed places in a new cultural hierarchy that privileged the learning and knowledge production of the metropolitan center. The nexus of knowledge and power concentrated in secondary education was one reason why localities were willing to commit scarce budgetary resources to establish a network of postelementary schools. As communities recognized, schools provided a cultural resource that could become an engine of local development. Secondary schools were magnets for intellectuals who injected into their adopted homes new forms of knowledge that helped cities modernize; they contributed their expertise to city planning, architectural innovation, public health initiatives, and the creation of local libraries, museums, and exhibitions. This could spell the difference between standing at the forefront of urban innovation and growth or being left behind in the competition for private investment and further government financing.

In the case of Niigata, the prefectural government worked hard to build up educational institutions within its jurisdiction. A middle school was built in Niigata city in 1892, followed by schools in Nagaoka, Shibata, Sado, and Takada. By 1910 the prefecture boasted twelve middle schools, with an enrollment of 5,500 students. Of the 500 graduates that year, 85 had submitted applications to higher school. And though 152 Niigata students were currently attending higher schools, all of these were outside the prefecture.[7] Establishing a higher school was considerably more difficult than building a middle school, however. Both required approval of the Ministry of Education, but higher schools had the distinction of being fully funded by the national treasury. Localities could sweeten the pot for the national government by financing the school building or donating an existing facility. Indeed, Kanazawa and Okayama, early victors in the interurban competition for a higher school, were selected in part because they could draw on their legacy as castle towns to provide this type of assistance. In Kanazawa's case, a generous donation from the former daimyo family, plus the large pool of literate young men ready to matriculate at a higher school, tipped the scales in the city's favor.[8]

Though political leaders in Niigata had been active since the late 1880s with a campaign to raise money for local facilities and efforts to lobby the central government, they lost out to places such as Okayama in the early round of competitions. Further campaigns in 1905 and 1911 likewise met with failure, but another drive was undertaken in 1916. Facing fierce competition from other prefectures, Niigata began a new fund-raising campaign and sent an entourage of local dignitaries to Tokyo to appeal for support. This time the efforts bore fruit: flush with cash generated by tax receipts from the war boom, the state approved the establishment of higher schools in Niigata and three other cities.[9] Departing from previous practice, higher schools of the new generation were designated with the names of the cities in which they were based: Niigata Higher, Yamagata Higher, and so on. Though the round of higher-school expansion during World War One brought great prestige to the communities that gained the new institutions, status distinctions persisted between the first generation of "number" schools and the expanded cadre of "name schools," a distinction exacerbated by the overproduction of middle- and higher-school graduates and so-called employment difficulties (*shūshokunan*) of the 1920s.

Undoubtedly a boon to local development, the enormous investment in secondary schools also fixed the position of localities in the educational grid. A city's status as a center of learning ensured cultural dominance in its respective region and, at the same time, cemented its position of cultural subordination to Tokyo. In other words, the educational system created multiple centers and arranged them hierarchically. The metropolis, with its concentration of universities, was one center, but local cities such as Okayama, with its concentration of secondary schools, constituted another, secondary center. Okayama's ability to develop educational resources drew on its rich inheritance as a center of learning during the Tokugawa period; in the late nineteenth century the city moved quickly to build on this legacy. Okayama's first public middle school opened in 1874; a second was built in 1921. The city's two middle schools, together with the private middle school that had opened in 1894, enrolled about 2,600 students. By 1886 Okayama boasted two women's colleges, and additional schools were established in 1900, 1908, and 1925. In terms of commercial and technical schools, the city offered a range of options by 1926: a four-year public technical school, a four-year public commercial school, a private professional women's college, a women's arts school, and city-run industrial arts and commercial schools. In addition, Okayama was home to a prestigious medical school and a normal school.[10]

This impressive array of schools established Okayama's reputation as a center of higher learning for the region, attracting a flow of students from the surrounding counties as well as neighboring prefectures of the Chūgoku and Shikoku districts. Moreover, because employment at Okayama's secondary schools typically required a university degree, the school network generated an in-migration from university centers in Tokyo and, to a lesser extent, Kyoto. In their capacity as teachers, metropolitan intellectuals made enormous impacts on local cultural movements, often acting as conduits for the introduction of Tokyo trends into the provinces, where they encountered thriving local cultures and became part of a cultural melting pot. Whether it was in-migration of Tokyo intellectuals or the influx of students from surrounding towns and villages, the new educational system provided a channel for the circulation of people and local knowledge. It created extended social networks and provided the context for productive engagements and mutual influences, a synergy between artists and writers from different local communities who came together in places like Okayama.

At the same time, their subordinate position on the grid turned cities such as Okayama into way stations on the path to the metropolis, both for students continuing on to university and for the scholars who used employment in Okayama as a stepping-stone to a more prestigious post at a metropolitan university. Modern educational institutions operated to reinforce Tokyo-centrism in other ways as well. Indeed, the status hierarchy between faculty and students became a powerful mechanism for the production of the ideology of the metropolis. Facing their provincial students, Tokyo intellectuals represented the source of knowledge; in the act of teaching and learning, and the relationship of mentor to student, the lived experience of higher education in the provinces naturalized the idea that modern knowledge issued forth from a single source in Tokyo. Performing, metaphorically, the interplay between Tokyo and the provinces, the teacher-student relationship helped to breed condescension for provincial culture, on the one hand, and deference toward the center on the other.

INTELLECTUAL CIRCUITS

Biographies of Japanese intellectuals who lived during these years reveal the power this tracking system had in structuring individual lives. It influenced career choices and shaped decisions about where to live and when to move. The stories of Shida Sokin (1876–1946), a minor figure in the modernist poetry movement, and Mitani Takamasa (1889–1944), an eminent legal philosopher and Christian leader, offer telling examples of the operations of the new cultural geography. As they traveled along career paths prescribed for upward mobility, Shida and Mitani made the trip between provincial city and metropolitan capital multiple times, crisscrossing the country in pursuit of cultural acclaim. Through their peregrinations along the tracks of higher education, intellectuals such as Shida and Mitani laid down circuits of knowledge production and exchange. They also established personal and institutional networks that knit the new cultural geography into a social web. Not only did these intellectual circuits serve as vectors for the diffusion of metropolitan trends to the provinces, but they also did the reverse. They created an intellectual feeder system that channeled the innovations of provincial cultural production into the metropolis.

After studying literature at Tokyo University, Shida Sokin came to teach at Okayama's Sixth High, where he remained for almost twenty years. As a beloved professor of Japanese literature, he mentored many accomplished poets, including one of Okayama's most famous sons, Uchida Hyakken.[11] During his time at Tokyo University, Shida had come under the influence of Masaoka Shiki, the great naturalist poet and founder of the modern haiku movement. Through disciples like Shida Sokin, the new haiku movement established strong provincial links and spread throughout Japan. Indeed, Shida's energetic promotion of haiku poetry clubs made them a cornerstone of Okayama's literary scene.[12] In spite of his established position as a leading figure in Okayama intellectual circles, Shida quit in 1925, after a long and successful career at Okayama's public higher school, to take a post at a private higher school in Tokyo—Seikei Higher School, forerunner of the prominent private college in Kichijōji. Since public schools were more prestigious than private schools in the prewar context, the only reason this made any sense as a career move was because it took Shida back to Tokyo. Critical as it was to the socialization and acculturation of Japan's intellectual establishment, the intellectual life of the provincial higher school simply could not compete with the cultural attractions of Tokyo.

Much like Shida, the scholar Mitani Takamasa exerted great influence on local intellectual and religious movements in Okayama and served as a cultural bridge to the metropolis. While a student at Tokyo Imperial University, Mitani joined Uchimura Kanzō's "nonchurch" movement (*mukyōkai*). When he came to teach at Sixth High, he brought this school of religious practice to Okayama. Though he became famous only after he returned to Tokyo to teach at First High, during his time in Okayama he introduced

Sixth High students to the latest legal debates in Tokyo and Europe and to what later became his hallmark blend of ethics, law, and philosophy.[13] The prominent place Tokyo intellectuals such as Shida and Mitani occupy in local histories testifies to their importance both as leaders of local cultural movements and as conduits for the import of metropolitan intellectual trends into the provinces.

As the stories of Shida and Mitani illustrate, the educational tracking system created a strong material basis to Tokyo-centrism through the circulation of knowledge and human capital. Yet these powerful channels of social circulation and their impact on the way people thought of the relationship between Tokyo and the provinces masked a more complex reality about the movement of ideas and the intellectual formation of scholars. While Tokyo was undoubtedly the single greatest source of academic pedigree, the "Tokyo intellectuals" who staffed Japan's provincial schools had in fact been provincial transplants to the capital. In this sense Tokyo represented only a single phase of an intellectual biography that circulated scholars through various locales; these diverse cultural experiences cumulatively constituted their intellectual formation.

The biographies of professors at Okayama's Sixth High show the common Tokyo polishing but also the typical path of education and employment that rotated cultural elites back and forth between the provinces and the capital. Both Shida and Mitani grew up outside the capital, Shida in Toyama and Mitani in Kanagawa. The professor of Chinese literature at Sixth High, Mitsuda Shinzō, was raised in Fukushima; the English teachers Sasaki Kuni and Sangū Makoto came from Shizuoka and Yamagata. Sekiyama Toshio and Fujimori Narikichi, both of whom taught German literature, grew up in Toyama and Kanagawa, respectively. Japanese history professor Matsumoto Hikojirō and philosophy professor Takahashi Satomi were from Aomori and Yamagata in the Northeast.[14] In other words, virtually none of the academics hired from Tokyo were actually raised in the capital. This suggested a more complex, heterogeneous intellectual formation than their Tokyo branding implied. Though their scholarship and artistic production were associated with the Tokyo pedigree, this was the capstone of a long period of education and socialization, all of which took place outside the metropolis.

This included the critical period of higher school, which for those born outside the metropolis almost invariably took place in a provincial city. As Donald Roden notes in his engaging study of Japanese higher schools in the late nineteenth and early twentieth centuries, these schools were the equivalent of present-day undergraduate institutions. Indeed, after World War Two many converted into four-year colleges. Prestigious and exclusive, they prepared a select group of students for the imperial university. Passing through the gates of the higher school signaled entry into the intellectual elite. The Japanese government designed the higher school to provide—like the French lycée, the German gymnasium, and the British public school on which it was modeled—"the highest level of general education for young men" and "dedicated [them] to the perfection of national morality."[15] As the instrument of molding the higher-school gentleman, these schools developed a set of distinctive customs that included collective life in self-governing dormitories, hazing rituals, school sports, and school magazines. Such practices became the hallmark of the higher school experience and defined the culture of the student elite. They made the higher school a context for intense sociality and socialization, the formation of a school ethos, and the establishment of old school ties between classmates. The cloistered life, the merging of private and scholastic experience, and expectations of mutual assistance based on hierarchical junior-senior relationships meant that higher-school bonds were particularly strong and enduring. Not only did they demarcate social pathways that took the student elite far beyond their school years, but the hothouse atmosphere of the higher schools also incubated the most powerful intellectual tendencies of the time.[16]

Many scholars whose educational trajectory took them from higher school in a provincial city to university in the capital found themselves retracing these same steps in pursuit of career advances. In both senses, then, cities such as Okayama became way stations for aspirants to national acclaim. The life course of writer Sasaki Kuni (1883–1964), who made a brief sojourn in Okayama, was typical in this regard. Born and raised in Shizuoka, Sasaki moved to Tokyo to study literature at Meiji Gakuin. He left Tokyo for his first job, a teaching post at Okayama's Sixth High, where he taught English literature. But he found a way to return to Tokyo, landing a position at the prestigious private Keiō University. It was during his time at Keiō that he achieved renown for his translations of Mark Twain's humorous fiction. The move to the capital was thus a prerequisite for Sasaki's recognition as a member of the elite fraternity of writers known as the *bundan*.

The life of doctor and poet Inoue Michiyasu traced out a similar peregrination. Inoue was raised in Hyōgo prefecture and went to Tokyo to study medicine at Tokyo Imperial University. He took a job at Okayama Medical College but returned to Tokyo, where he opened a private practice and achieved some fame as a poet. In the meantime, his time spent in Tokyo nurturing university connections eventually paid off with an appointment as advisor to the imperial family. Others also used their time in Okayama as a stepping-stone to greater things. Both Gumma-born Aragi Torasaburō, who taught at the Medical School, and Fukuoka-born Matsui Moto'oki, professor of chemistry at Sixth High, went on to become presidents of Kyoto University.[17]

For all these men, career advancement dictated a departure from Okayama. Ambitious students likewise saw provincial cities as way stations on the road to the university. Though Kyoto, too, was a university town—and by 1918, imperial universities in Sendai, Fukuoka, and Sapporo were other options—most set their sights on Tokyo, where the most prestigious and greatest number of universities were concentrated. The allure of the metropolis deprived provincial cities of local talent, creaming off the men and women who would go on to achieve fame and fortune in the capital. Okayama's most renowned intellectuals and artists trod this path, leaving the prefectural capital after higher school and never moving back.

The roster of Okayama-born members of the Tokyo literati included a founding figure in western philosophical studies, Ōnishi Hajime (1864–1900), as well as the writers Emi Suiin (1865–1934), Uchida Hyakken (1889–1971), and Tsubota Jōji (1890–1982). Emi initially went to Tokyo to pursue a military career but took up literature after meeting writers associated with the Ken'yūsha school (Friends of the Inkstone). He became a prominent member of this group, making a name as a pioneer of detective fiction and popular literature. Hyakken was the son of an Okayama sake brewer. He attended the city's most prestigious middle and higher schools, where his encounter with Shida Sokin converted him to the literary life. After moving on to Tokyo Imperial University for German literature studies, where he worked with Natsume Sōseki, Hyakken became a professor at Hosei University in 1916, gaining a name for his surrealist fiction and humorous essays. The path trod by Tsubota Jōji, a prominent figure in the children's literature movement, followed a similar course. Born to a manager of a weaving factory, Tsubota was educated locally, continuing on to Tokyo's Waseda University, from which he graduated in 1915. During his time at Waseda he joined with Ogawa Mimei and others to study folk and fairy stories; later he became a main contributor to the emblematic children's magazine of the 1920s, *Akai Tori* (Red Bird). Others, like the poets Kinoshita Rigen and Arimoto Hōsui, followed similar paths from Okayama to Tokyo.[18]

What stands out in these biographies is that fame and recognition was achieved in every case only after writers had made the journey to the capital. That entrée into the Tokyo literati defined literary success was not simply the conceit of metropolitan intellectuals but was reinforced by attitudes in the localities. Okayama, like other provincial cities, tended to celebrate its native sons and daughters once the metropolis embraced them: with Tokyo's stamp of approval, local talent became a source of local pride. This tendency became even more pronounced after World War Two, with the creation of shrines to locally born artists who had made their careers in Tokyo. The Yumeiji Takiji Museum (Okayama) and the Tsubota Jōji (Okayama) and Izumi Kyōka (Kanazawa) literary prizes all venerated men who abandoned their hometowns to make their fortunes in the capital.[19] But the self-marginalizing impulse to echo the commendations of Tokyo emerged well before the end of the Second World War, evident in the travel promotions and city guides that constituted a growing literature of local boosterism in the twenties and thirties.

In the magazine *Touring Kanazawa* (*Kankō Kanazawa*), for example, an article titled "Kanazawa and the Literati" did not showcase the local arts and culture of a city that had prided itself on being the center of Hokuriku regional culture for centuries. Instead the essay focused on the famous writer Akutagawa Ryūnosuke, who made a couple of visits to the city in the mid-twenties.[20] The *Hokkaido Yearbook* of 1930 singled out the tenor Okuda Ryōzō to honor in its description of local arts and music. An entry titled "Hokkaido Natives Impart a Distinctive Flavor to the Musical World in the Center" boasted that "local art, born amid Hokkaido's magnificent natural beauty, is gradually moving into the metropolis. . . . Hokkaido's participation in the national music scene is a milestone of our progress: this inspires all Hokkaido natives and raises expectations for the future." In a capsule summary of Okuda's biography, the *Yearbook* traced the itinerary typical of the successful artist: early training in Sapporo, migration to Tokyo for formal music study, and the critical career launch made possible on the metropolitan stage, where Okuda "made a sensation." Okuda returned several times to perform in Hokkaido, dusting his old hometown with a touch of metropolitan glitter.[21]

Entries on literature and the arts in later editions of the *Hokkaido Yearbook* institutionalized the practice of monumentalizing the talent of intellectuals who had risen to capital fame. The 1940 edition even noted distinguished writers such as Takebayashi Musōan, a Sapporo native who moved to Tokyo at the age of four, as well as Shimaki Kensaku and Morita Tama, part of a generation of Taishō writers who left Sapporo in their teens and never looked back. Sasaki Chiyuki, who moved to Tokyo at five, and Kubo Sakae who left for Tokyo after middle school, also made the grade. These artists and writers maintained family connections with Sapporo; they wrote about it in their novels and returned for occasional visits. Nonetheless, Tokyo became their adoptive home, and they were identified with their artistic success in the capital.[22] Yet it was these Tokyo transplants whom provincial guidebooks chose to celebrate in their features on local literary stars, rather than the native talent that elected to stay put. Even though Sapporo possessed a vibrant literary, artistic, and musical scene, little of this found expression in places like the *Hokkaido Yearbook*. And while the proliferating local guidebooks of the twenties and thirties championed the autonomy and distinctiveness of local culture, by reserving special acclaim for artists with Tokyo pedigrees, provincial boosters were complicit in a process of self-marginalization that helped install the ideology of the metropolis.

ASCENDING TO TOKYO

The brain drain to Tokyo, channeled through the educational tracking system laid down in the Meiji reforms, became much more than a mere exodus to the capital. When local artists such as Uchida Hyakken made the move to Tokyo, they underwent a kind of mutual appropriation. Part of this process involved their adoption of Tokyo: locally born writers and artists who made it in the capital shed their roots and took on the aura and identity of the metropolis. The mark of their success, induction into the elite fraternity known as the *bundan*, signified their embrace of a metropolitan identity. At the same time, Tokyo adopted them, appropriating their cultural production as its own. Their novels, paintings, and scientific discoveries all became illustrations, not of the cultural fecundity of the provinces, but of the prodigious cultural power of the metropolis—yet another example of Tokyo as the font of modern knowledge and the pinnacle of modern culture. These mutual appropriations erased the provincial origins of metropolitan culture.

The term used to describe the journey from provincial city to metropolis was *jōkyō*—"ascending to Tokyo." The term captured the elevated status of the capital and the ways people saw this trip as being much more than a movement through physical space. Viewed from outside the metropolis, the journey to Tokyo brought cultural elites into a dazzling realm of celebrity intellectuals, famous places, and citadels of higher learning. Nothing symbolized this rarified world of cultural privilege better than the literary establishment known as the *bundan*. Tokyo was identified, similarly, with establishment circles in the arts (*gadan*), music (*gakudan*), and press (*rondan*), but because of the predilection of writers to use their own life experiences as material for their modernist novels, the angst-ridden, solipsistic world of the literary man became a prominent symbol of the highbrow culture of the capital. As Edward Fowler explains in an illuminating discussion of the *bundan*, this group included "writers, critics, and publishers associated with what is commonly called *junbungaku*, or 'pure' literature."[23] Though their output represented a tiny fraction of literary production in the early twentieth century, these metropolitan intellectuals were recognized both as trendsetters in literary modernism and as exemplars of a national literary tradition.[24]

They were defined by three key characteristics that knit them into a socially alienated, self-referential group and accounted for the surprising uniformity of their values and attitudes. First and foremost, shared education at schools such as Tokyo Imperial University, Waseda University, or the aristocratic peers school, Gakushūin, conditioned the social formation of the *bundan*. As aspirants to literary acclaim converged on these elite institutions, they concentrated themselves in literature departments and became disciples of the famous writers who taught there. During their school days they forged the relationships that would become crucial to their artistic production and to their publication opportunities. School connections developed into literary cliques that endured and generated the outpouring of university publications like *Mita bungaku* (Keiō University), *Waseda bungaku* (Waseda University), and *Teikoku bungaku* (Tokyo Imperial University) and, more important, the myriad coterie magazines that dotted the literary landscape. Institutionally anchored to elite schools, both types of magazines provided the primary forum for literary production in the late Meiji and Taishō periods.

The association with the coterie magazine (*dōjin zasshi*), like educational affiliation, powerfully determined the character of the *bundan*. The *dōjin zasshi* featured fiction, poetry, art, and criticism in varying proportions and were brought out to provide a forum for the literary experiments of a young clique of writers. Since their target audience was other members of their group and, with luck, the greater Tokyo literati, circulations were often limited. Finances depended on the resources of contributors and tended to be precarious, which meant that most were short-lived, lasting no more than a few issues. Probably the most famous of the coterie magazines, *Shirakaba* (White Birch), departed from this pattern because its aristocratic contributors were able to fund an exceptionally long run of the magazine. Yet as ephemeral as more typical coterie magazines were, they offered publishing opportunities to untested writers and exposure to a literary community that was intensely engaged in mutual reading and mutual criticism. And since positive reception signaled induction into the *bundan*, coterie magazines provided a critical stepping-stone to career success. Because contributors, publishers, and readership were essentially identical, coterie magazines became a vehicle for producing the practices of mutual criticism and validation, as well as the inward gaze and collective narcissism that shaped the culture of the *bundan*.[25]

Common physical location in the capital was the third defining characteristic of the literary establishment. As Fowler points out, Tokyo was the home or adopted home of virtually all "pure literature" writers. The identification of the *bundan* with Tokyo was sustained by a number of factors. As we have seen, the educational ladder concentrated resources of higher learning and highbrow culture in Tokyo and funneled aspiring writers to the capital. Likewise, Tokyo was home to the major publishing firms as well as newspaper companies like the Tokyo Asahi Shinbun, which employed establishment writers and published their novels in serial form. But synonymy with Tokyo also emerged from the centrality of personal connections within the literary establishment. The constitutive cultural practices of the *bundan* were based on mutual acquaintance and the intense intersociality of the local community of writers. This was true of not just the coterie journal but also the "I novels" and modes of literary critique that dominated literary form in the teens and twenties.

As many literary historians have pointed out, the Japanese inflection of naturalism was based on an unflinchingly honest and unsentimental depiction of everyday life through the thoughts and emotions of the artist.[26] When applied by Tokyo writers, the celebrated literary technique of "sketching from life" yielded intimate, if thinly disguised, portraits of the artist, his friends, and their lives in the metropolis.[27] As naturalism gave rise to the "I novel" form, fiction became part gossip and part confession, focusing in particular detail on romantic entanglements and sexual peccadilloes. These conditions of production also affected the practice of literary criticism, in which commentary on the merits of technique and form jostled for place with speculation about the identity of specific characters and reactions to the personal revelations contained in the text. Moreover, because of the exclusive nature of the *bundan*, much of what passed for literary criticism devolved into a kind of shoptalk whose meaning was readily apparent only to an insider. In other words, the self-referential nature of the *bundan* and its literary production reinforced its identification with the Tokyo locale. Tokyo's position as a national capital elevated this intensely localized and inward-looking social formation—the Tokyo literati—to the apex of high cultural production. The privilege of cultural geography turned a local literature into a national canon and helped foster the misrecognition of the metropolis as the font of the modernist imagination.[28]

What did it mean for the Tokyo literati that most were born and raised outside the capital city? As literary historians have pointed out, such prominent naturalists as Kunikida Doppo, Tayama Katei, and Tokuda Shūsei were all provincial transplants, and the humanist "White Birch" school *(Shirakabaha)* was drawn from the ranks of the provincial aristocracy.[29] With their enthusiasms for Tolstoy's vision of a pastoral life and their romantic exultations of nature, these writers contributed to what Carol Gluck called the "rediscovery of the countryside" in the early twentieth century.[30] The predilection for writing from life experience meant that a city like Kanazawa, which sent a parade of intellectual luminaries to the capital, served as the stage for many classic works of modern Japanese literature. The list of Kanazawa writers included Izumi Kyōka, disciple of Ozaki Kōyō and founding member of the *bundan*, who wrote lyrical melodramas with a touch of the gothic; Tokuda Shūsei, a naturalist whose fiction evocatively captured the lives of the urban lower-middle class; Murō Saisei, the influential naturalist poet; and Nakano Shigeharu, the celebrated poet of the proletarian literary movement.[31]

Though these artists became identified (by themselves and by others) as belonging to Tokyo, their provincial origins left conspicuous traces in their literary production. Thus it is possible to track a shift in subjectivity—their embrace of a metropolitan identity—through their writings. In a literature that was often autobiographical or loosely based on life experience, the Tokyo literati located themselves as men of the metropolis, but also in relation to an earlier, provincial identity. This came through with particular clarity in the way the *bundan* wrote about their old hometowns. As a focal point of their literary production, the "hometown" (*kokyō*) became the lens through which the *bundan* and their readers visualized the local city. Viewing it from the perspective of Tokyo and situating it in a particular relationship with the capital, they provided in fictional and poetic space a powerful symbolic rendering of places like Kanazawa that became integral to the ideology of the metropolis.

One example of this was the frequent emplotment of Kanazawa within the "ascension to Tokyo" (*jōkyō*) narrative. Izumi Kyōka set much of his fiction in Kanazawa, where he grew up the son of an engraver in the 1870s and 1880s, before moving to Tokyo at the age of seventeen to make his fortune as a writer. Kyōka's writings drew extensively on his experiential knowledge of plebian Kanazawa, the realm of the artisan, the merchant, and the geisha that, in his youth, was still heavily flavored with the old-world traditions of the castle town.[32] Like those of many writers, his plots reproduced his own migration to Tokyo and mapped Kanazawa onto a hierarchical cultural geography that situated the metropolis at the center. His first critical success, *Noble Blood, Heroic Blood*, portrayed a doomed love between a Kanazawa geisha and a student, who "ascends to Tokyo" to study law. This journey was made possible by the sacrifice of the geisha, trapped back in Kanazawa, who sends money to support his studies in Tokyo. Sustaining the flow of money proves an almost impossible task, and the geisha is finally driven to theft and murder in order to help the student realize his ambition. Fatefully, she is caught and tried, as it turns out, by her law student, now a distinguished prosecutor. Hewing to the principles of law he learned at the university, the prosecutor feels he must sentence her to death. But to acknowledge her sacrifice and the bond they shared, he commits suicide after her sentence is carried out.

Both the student and the geisha were stock characters in the fiction of late Meiji and Taishō Japan and were used, as in Kyōka's story, to symbolize Japan's future and its past. The student looked forward to his future and to Japan's future; he had access to modern knowledge and was destined for wealth, status, and power. The geisha was shut out of this new world, trapped in a system of entertainment and sex work that harkened back to an earlier era. As in this story, the social encounter between the geisha and the student narrativized the clash between the old and new worlds, a clash that proved fateful for the geisha who was invariably left desolate or dying.[33] The association of the geisha with Kanazawa and the student with Tokyo linked topos to temporality, turning province and metropolis into chronotopes and leaving Kanazawa behind the juggernaut of progress and out of a modernity concentrated in Tokyo.[34] Moreover, just as the student needs the geisha's support, at any cost, to succeed in his studies, the story implies that Kanazawa must be sacrificed to sustain knowledge production in Tokyo. In painting Kanazawa as provender for Tokyo, a way station to the metropolis, a place that existed only to function within the logic of *jōkyō*, such fictional spaces emplotted provincial cities as part of a cultural system trained toward the capital. They shored up the ideology of the metropolis.

Nakano Shigeharu, too, staged his writing in Kanazawa and deployed the *jōkyō* narrative. In one of his forays into fiction, Nakano structured the plot of *Changing Song* (*Uta no wakare*) around his own biography. At least in terms of geo-social mobility, this conformed to type: born to a landholding family in Fukui prefecture, Nakano attended a village elementary school, continued on to middle school in a nearby town, went to Kanazawa to attend Fourth High, and from there moved to Tokyo University. The first two parts of *Changing Song* were set in Kanazawa during his higher-school years. They depict student life in a provincial town as a rite of passage on the path to literary renown in the capital: early romantic attachments, the rivalries and comradeship of classmates—a story of youthful dreams and character formation.[35]

As such stories make vividly clear, an integral part of the memory of youth in a provincial town was the sense of proximity to nature. The force of nature that infused Kanazawa mesmerized Nakano's protagonist in *Changing Song*, Kataguchi Yasukichi. "The town of Kanazawa was for Kataguchi Yasukichi a place of mystery. It had two rivers, the Saigawa and Asanokawa, which ran almost parallel. There were hills beyond the outer banks of the rivers and between the two rivers rose another hill. To Yasukichi it seemed as if the entire city was languidly dozing, draped across these two rivers and these three hills."[36] Nakano was not alone in his penchant for lyrical natural description; the Tokyo literati laced their works set in Kanazawa with sketches of its hilly surrounds and its rivers, as well as with evocations of the snowbound winter landscape, as in Tokuda Shūsei's fictionalized autobiography, *The Snow in My Old Hometown* (*Furusato no yuki*).[37] By minimizing the built environment of the city and focusing on natural landscape, such scenic descriptions framed the provincial town as an extension of the countryside. While the big city never slept, Tokyo writers portrayed the localities held frozen in place by the overwhelming force of nature; Nakano stressed the somnambulant effect this imparted to a provincial city like Kanazawa.

Likewise Murō Saisei (1889–1962) infused his work with natural imagery and scenic descriptions of the country town. Though Saisei is better known for his poetry, he also produced a good selection of fiction, largely set in

Kanazawa. His novel *Sexual Awakening* (*Sei ni mezameru koro*) based on the loves of a boyhood friend, offers one example. Against the backdrop of higher-school life, this was a coming-of-age story that recounted the youthful moment when the protagonist discovered both sexual love and his desire for literature. Much as he did in his poetry, Saisei used natural imagery to convey the protagonist's state of mind, here to capture the pure, fresh quality of youth and the physicality of a boy on the cusp of manhood.[38] In the following passage, Saisei relays the thoughts of the protagonist as he sets out from his lodging house to walk around the town with no particular object in mind.

> I set out aimlessly.
> The border of mountains glittered intensely in the sun, reflecting on the deep drifts of icy snow that piled up like heaps of shavings after hail had fallen two or three times. The ripe heads of grass on the riverbank now trembled against the bleak landscape, unable to stand against the harsh wind of late fall that scoured them to sharp points. Anyone who grew up in the North Country knows the feeling of being suffocated by the stifling monotony of the landscape just before winter comes, when it seems to creep into your very soul and makes you dull and numb with cold.[39]

The striking predilection for landscape rather than cityscape in Saisei's descriptions of Kanazawa conveyed the impression that life in this countrified city was lived closer to nature. Denuded of its built environment, Kanazawa became a place where the moods, the passions, the sensations of the seasons could be felt in all their intensity; its people, defined by the force of nature, were not truly urban. The effect of such literary devices was to subsume cities such as Kanazawa into a vast rural countryside that constituted Tokyo's Other, dissolving the differences between urban and rural into a monolithic *chihō* of the metropolitan imagination.

Moreover, scenic descriptions such as this invariably depicted a Kanazawa of an earlier moment, a time when the writer, now established in Tokyo, was a youth. In the literary spaces of the Tokyo literati, the provincial city became a memoryscape—the mountains Tokuda Shūsei used to climb, the cafés Nakano Shigeharu used to visit, the riverbanks along which Murō Saisei used to tramp. These descriptions provided a snapshot of youth that cast the hometown in the warm afterglow of nostalgia.[40] Critics of Saisei often note the elegiac quality of his writing, the sense of longing for a lost childhood. Certainly this was the effect of his first novel, the autobiographical *Childhood*

(*Yōnen jidai*) published in 1919.[41] Melancholy longing for a childhood far away in space and time also suffused his poetry, as in *The Time of Cicadas*.

> Somewhere or other
> *Sheee*—the cicadas are singing.
> Is it already the season for cicadas?
> A boy runs over the hot summer sand
> Hoping to catch some cicadas—
> Where has he gone today?
>
> In the sadness of summer
> How short its life is!
> Far beyond the streets of the capital
> Beyond the sky and the roofs
> *Sheee*—the cicadas are singing.[42]

The poem captures the sentiments of a man, now living in the metropolis, as he recalls a childhood moment in a country town. Hearing the sound of the cicada he is brought back to his boyhood, when the summer saw him running across the sand.

This kind of literature-as-recollection represented the provincial city through the ideologically saturated metaphor of "hometown." As such, it offers a classic example of the way the hometown metaphor operated to produce the center-periphery effect. From their perches in Tokyo, the *bundan* situated the provincial town at a physical and temporal remove from the metropolis. Paired as Tokyo's Other, the provincial city was lodged within a nest of binaries: the adult contrasted with the boy, the present with the past, civilization with nature. In this way "the literature of a lost home," as critic Kobayashi Hideo characterized it in his 1933 essay, stereotyped the provincial city as childish and unsophisticated, a world of an earlier age and a simpler time. Indeed, such literature narrated the transformation of a Murō Saisei or Nakano Shigeharu from provincial intellectuals to Tokyo literati, tracing this shift in subjectivity. Their embrace of Tokyo required the distancing and marginalizing of the local city. As they assumed their new identity, they minimized the power and vitality of provincial culture and what it had meant to their own intellectual formation.

If they were complicit in its production, the Tokyo literati were also powerfully affected by the ideology of the metropolis, which acted to reproduce the conditions of its own production as a kind of self-fulfilling prophecy. At an institutional level, it aggravated the concentration of resources in the capital; on a personal level it shaped career and life decisions. Sometimes Tokyo-centrism could exercise a fateful and tragic power, as in the case of Shimada Seijirō. Another famous literary figure from Kanazawa and the author of the best-selling novel *The Earth* (*Chijō*, 1919), Shimada was arguably Japan's first literary celebrity. He emerged at a critical moment in the publishing industry, on the eve of the conversion to mass production. A printing of ten thousand copies of the second installment of Shimada's four-volume book sold out in two days, an unprecedented feat in publishing history that opened the doors to the mass marketing of high literature.[43] This triumph owed its success to clever manipulation of the ideologically charged symbols of "the hometown" and "the capital." Shimada's success was wrapped up in a compelling personal narrative—heavily promoted by his literary backers—about a literary novice, plucked from the obscurity of a country town, who become an overnight publishing phenomenon.

The publishing giant Satō Giryū (1878–1951) engineered Shimada's extraordinary burst onto the literary stage. Founder of the influential magazines *Shinchō* and *Bunshō kurabu*, and president of the publishing house Shinchōsha, Satō played the role of kingmaker in the world of pure literature and wielded enormous power in directing literary fashion in Tokyo. In the teens Satō pioneered the library format in Japanese publishing, inaugurating a string of special series on foreign literature, philosophy in translation, and modern Japanese literature. With this hugely successful initiative, he made the publishing firm of Shinchōsha synonymous with highbrow literary production and the gold standard of western translations. Moreover, by making the works of the *bundan* widely available to a national audience, Shinchōsha presaged the era of the *zenshū* (collected works), the *enbon* (one-yen book), and other strategies to market high culture to the masses in the 1920s. In 1917 Satō established a series called "New Writers" that quickly became a passport to *bundan* status.[44] As he began to exhaust the ranks of young Tokyo writers in his search for fresh talent, Satō hit upon the scheme of publishing a complete unknown. To fulfill this role, Satō plucked promising young writers out of nowhere—or at least a place that could stand in for nowhere in the eyes of the Tokyo literati. He enlisted the help of friends to scour the pages of provincial magazines and newspapers for likely candidates. In the pages of a Kyoto newspaper, one of them "discovered" Shimada.

The publication of the first installment of *The Earth* in the prestigious Shinchōsha series transported Shimada into the spotlight of the literary world in the capital. The book was a fictionalized account of Shimada's life, depicting the story of a young man from an impoverished background who emerged from adversity to embrace the mission of social justice and the ambition of becoming a political leader. The book was animated by humanist sympathies for the poor and their suffering and utopian visions of a new, just society. In 1919, this message resonated with the surging optimism of the Taishō democracy movement and the spirit of reform that galvanized the universities and the higher schools, accounting, in part, for its astonishing critical success. At the same time. Satō had been working assiduously to guarantee a positive response to his literary discovery. Shinchōsha promoted the book heavily in the company's magazine advertisements and through Satō's network of contacts in Tokyo. These efforts bore fruit when *The Earth* met with universal acclaim among the *bundan*. Critic Ikuta Chōkō wrote a glowing review in the *Yomiuri;* socialist Sakai Toshihiko commended it with equal force in the *Jiji shinpō;* writers Hasegawa Nyozekan and Tokutomi Sōhō showered it with praise. Rave reviews continued as subsequent installments of *The Earth* were published. A flood of solicitations poured in and Shimada embarked on a frenzy of literary productivity. He was deluged with fan mail. All doors were suddenly opened to him within the hallowed, exclusive world of the Tokyo *bundan*. Not only was he anointed to this privileged fraternity; he became a literary star.[45]

But for Shimada, this was a poisoned chalice. At the vulnerable age of twenty-one, he was suddenly elevated to fame and the full glare of public attention. A young man of reportedly fragile ego, he felt shamed by his family background and his reliance on an uncle's charity for secondary-school fees. His father died young, leaving his mother to fend for herself by working in Kanazawa's red light district. Shimada had difficulty socializing with fellow students of more secure social status and developed an arrogant manner as a defense against his sense of inadequacy. When thrust into the metropolitan spotlight, he began to entertain delusions of grandeur. One day he walked into Satō's office and announced to the flabbergasted president of Shinchōsha that the reason *The Earth* was selling so well was because of a plot by the Seiyūkai political party. As Shimada explained it, he and the party leader, Hara Takashi, were the two best-known people in Japan at the time, and the Seiyūkai feared that Shimada's fame would eclipse Hara. To forestall this they were buying up all the copies of *The Earth* themselves.[46] Shimada published an essay in a Kanazawa literary magazine titled "To the Young Men in My Old Hometown," announcing that he had become a literary messiah.

To the young men born in the snow and storms of the North Country
I grant my blessing to the future that opens up before you.
My courage, struggle, and accomplishment
Opens a path for all the young men that come after me.
Like Moses I stand at the head of all the masses.[47]

Though his stardom had opened up romantic possibilities, even bringing fan letters inviting marriage, Shimada's strange behavior began to drive women away and led to a succession of broken engagements.

Repelled by rumors of Shimada's increasingly bizarre behavior, the *bundan* closed ranks against him. Solicitations for his work dried up; his money ran out; he began to spiral downward. After an incident at a lodging house, he was arrested for disturbing the peace. The police gave Shimada a psychological evaluation and diagnosed him with schizophrenia. He was locked up in a mental institution where he remained for ten years, until his death in 1930. During this decade of incarceration, his condition reportedly improved enough that he began to write again, but none of his erstwhile friends from the *bundan* tried to help free him. At one point a Kanazawa newspaper, the *Hokkoku shinbun*, ran a campaign to push for Shimada's release, but nothing came of it. Even as he languished in the mental ward, episodes from his final days of liberty found their way into print in a story of his broken engagement and emotional deterioration written by Tokuda Shūsei, fellow writer from Kanazawa and sometime friend.[48] Shimada the man might be dead to the world, but Tokyo literati continued to pick over the remains of his literary legend.

Who killed Shimada Seijirō? Is his merely the story of an unsophisticated country boy blinded by the glare of the big city? Certainly the stresses of literary stardom did not create Shimada's insecurities; his mental breakdown was brought on in part by his own psychological frailty. But Shimada also fell victim to the cruelty and capriciousness of the metropolitan cultural marketplace. The competitive pressures of the publishing industry left little room to consider the effects of instant stardom on his emotional stability. Once he had lost his cache as a literary commodity, the Tokyo *bundan* simply disposed of Shimada and moved on. Satō Giryū exploited the vulnerable Shimada in a publishing stunt to enact a mythic tale of the Tokyo literati's "discovery" of a rustic genius and his "rescue" from provincial obscurity. As this story played out, *The Earth* became elevated from an unknown work of fiction to great literature and Shimada from a provincial writer to a literary star through the mediation and largess of the Tokyo *bundan*. Shimada's (or rather Satō's) spectacular success was due in no small measure to the intoxicating appeal of this *jōkyō* fantasy. Reaffirming the basic tenets of Tokyo-centrism—the idea that Tokyo could fashion literary greatness from the rough clay of Shimada's rusticity, that only a metropolitan mind was capable of judging value in a provincial writer—the Shimada story offered comforting validation of the cultural privileges accruing to the Tokyo literati. At a time when so-called pure literature was expanding into a mass market, and when Tokyo's dominance of that market concentrated enormous power in the hands of a few men in the capital, the Shimada story also vindicated Tokyo's dominance of the cultural marketplace. Whatever this meant for the real Shimada was irrelevant to the success of the myth that was widely embraced by Japanese intellectuals, whether they enjoyed the privileges of Tokyo-centrism or simply lusted after them.

THE REGIONAL PRESS AND LOCAL DIFFERENCE

In provincial cities the formation of intellectual communities, the pursuit of scientific and historical research, the growth of new musical traditions and literary movements, and other forms of knowledge production all took place within a cultural geography that privileged the center in both material and ideological terms. The local literati were acutely conscious that they were positioned in a cultural hinterland; they willingly deferred to the presumed superiority of ideas brought in from the capital. Yet while they acknowledged secondary status through their eager absorption of the latest fashion from Tokyo, they also poured energy into a rich variety of local cultural movements. These aimed not simply to ape metropolitan culture but also to build on local traditions to create distinct and original modernist forms.

As in Tokyo, the print media and institutions of higher education were key agents of modernist cultural movements in the provinces. While the schools and the publishing industry served as instruments of Tokyo-centrism—promoting the power and centrality of the metropolis— they also helped to generate dynamic regional cultures, local innovation, and local autonomy. In this sense, the material and ideological impact of the movements channeled through their networks was felt differently in the localities than in the capital. Although cities such as Kanazawa were subject to the self-marginalizing impulses of the ideology of the metropolis, cultural geography and spatial separation also opened up the possibility for a critical perspective on Tokyo-centrism.

The regional press stood at the heart of this process, providing a central exchange for the networks of local literati and their cultural movements. Like higher schools, newspapers served as a conduit for the import of new ideas and practices from abroad and occupied a central place in the processes of cultural transformation in the late nineteenth and early twentieth centuries.[49] From its foundation as a political press in the 1860s and 1870s, the newspaper was an instrument of national integration and centralization. But also like the school system, it became an anchor of local culture and an institutional meeting ground for the provincial literati. In this sense the press effected cultural change at two levels, both local and national.

Although the early twentieth century saw standardization of cultural forms like the newspaper through the integration of local into global and national markets, this did not spell the end of cultural diversity. Nor did it produce a simple bifurcation of metropolitan and second-city variants on the newspaper form. Rather, local conditions in Japan's cities, large and small, led to different configurations of the local news market and generated a variety of newspapers with distinctive local flavors. It is important to keep this heterogeneity in mind when exploring the nature of regional cultures. Since the newspaper, together with schools, libraries, and museums, provided the main institutional base for regional cultural movements in this period, local difference determined the particular characters of the provincial *bundan* as social and cultural formations.

For good reasons, most accounts of the newspaper in Japan focus on the two major markets of Tokyo and Osaka. With the model of the English-language press in Yokohama and a long history as a center of book publishing in the Tokugawa period, Tokyo quickly emerged as the center of the modern newspaper industry in the 1870s. Blessed with the same advantages—proximity to Kobe's treaty port press and the Tokugawa legacy as a book market—Osaka became a competing center in the 1880s. Discussing a measure of metropolitan dominance of the newspaper trade, Eleanor Westney notes that, in 1884, 54.5 percent of Japan's daily newspapers were published in Tokyo, while Osaka accounted for 21 percent of newspaper production the same year. The lion's share of this production was locally consumed. Together, the two cities represented 6 percent of the national population.[50]

Less well known is the story of the regional press. Even though they lacked the overwhelming advantages of the two metropolitan news markets, provincial cities provided the base for an energetic local press, which emerged virtually simultaneously with that of the center. Like Tokyo and Osaka newspapers, the provincial press in its early years was enormously diverse, borrowing from western press models as well as indigenous sources of publishing culture such as the *kawaraban*, or woodblock broadsheet. Not until the pressures of competition intensified in the 1890s with a major expansion drive by the metropolitan papers did the rich varieties of newspaper form begin to converge toward a national standard.[51] The history of the newspaper in Kanazawa exemplified both the influence of metropolitan publishers on the Kanazawa news market and the power of local conditions to generate the singular features of the provincial press. One newspaper history lists at least thirteen different local papers established during the Meiji period. Many of these were short lived; even papers with a longer shelf life went through multiple reorganizations, often reinventing themselves four or five times over the course of a few years. The crooked path taken by Ishikawa prefecture's first newspaper, the *Kaika shinbun* (*Enlightenment News*), was typical of the shifts and starts of the early Meiji press.[52]

The *Enlightenment News* was established in 1871, one year before Tokyo's first three dailies entered circulation. Founded by a Tokugawa book publisher, *Kaika shinbun* embraced the mission of the new government's Charter Oath, engaging to "enrich our grasp of new knowledge and leave behind the taint of the past ... to strengthen our capacity to use new information and expunge persisting resistance" to change.[53] From its first incarnation as a champion of cultural reform, *Kaika shinbun* went through a series of transformations over the 1870s and 80s. When its editors became too partisan in the government debate over the invasion of Korea in 1873, the paper was forced to close. It quickly reemerged as the *Ishikawa shinbun*, transmogrified into a kind of official gazette that devoted itself to publicizing prefectural government policy and directives. Later the paper was bought up by a local politician who turned it into an organ of the Ishikawa Kaishintō, the local wing of the Progressive Party. In his hands the *Ishikawa shinbun* became a highly effective political tool, facilitating his ascent to leadership of the prefectural assembly. Though it maintained its party affiliation, the paper subsequently passed through the hands of a series of owners and editors, was acquired by another prefectural assembly leader, and changed its name twice before it was reorganized in 1893 as the *Hokkoku shinbun*—which it remained through the end of World War Two.[54]

The mercurial shifts in the early life course of the newspaper company that finally settled down as the *Hokkoku shinbun* were typical of the instability, diversity, and flexibility of the early newspaper form in Japan. As was the case for this Kanazawa paper, innovation and experimentation sought a formula for institutional longevity within a particular setting. Certainly, Tokyo represented an important resource in these early years of the provincial press. As company histories recount, early founders of local newspapers drew inspiration from reading copies of Tokyo papers such as the *Yomiuri shinbun* while on trips to the capital; they recruited staff from Tokyo to help set up the machinery of publication.[55] By the early twentieth century, most provincial papers were allied with one of the two leading Meiji period news services, Teitsū (Teikoku Tsūshinsha) or Dentsū (Nihon Denpō Tsūshinsha), which provided access to metropolitan news and a network of connections to the press world in the capital.[56] Nevertheless, in this critical early phase, local newspapers reinvented themselves to address the vicissitudes of their immediate environment and not simply to replicate metropolitan models of cultural modernization. As in the case of *Hokkoku shinbun*'s affiliation with the Progressive Party and the emergence of a different paper to espouse the cause of the rival Liberal Party, much of this was driven by local politics.[57] Indeed, a large fraction of the early provincial newspapers rose from the froth of political activism that attended the establishment of prefectural assemblies in 1878 and the national assembly in 1890.

Thus the early history of the provincial press was very much a local story intimately connected with the dynamics of local politics. The point when the encounter with metropolitan models became decisive was around the turn of the century, with the first big push by Osaka and Tokyo papers to expand into provincial markets. Driven by the saturation of the metropolitan markets and the increasingly fierce competition among big city newspapers, and made technologically possible by the extension of communications infrastructure like the railroad and postal system, the metropolitan press moved aggressively to promote their news products across the country. The war fevers touched off by the Sino-Japanese and Russo-Japanese wars of 1894–95 and 1904–5 provided a fortuitous opening for their marketing campaigns. In the wake of the Sino-Japanese War, the results of these efforts were still quite modest. In 1899, for example, the largest circulation of the *Ōsaka mainichi shinbun* outside its home base was 330 in the city of Ōgaki, Gifu Prefecture, and elsewhere much less. After the Russo-Japanese War, however, the provincial press felt the impact of this expansion more keenly. As the metropolitan dailies intensified their competition and brought out regional editions, local papers began to fail in Saitama, Ibaragi, Chiba, and Kanagawa, the prefectures that surrounded Tokyo. By 1907, only 31.5 percent of the circulation of the *Osaka asahi shinbun* fell within city limits. Another 36.3 percent went to nearby prefectures, and the remainder to more distant locales.[58]

Provincial newspapers mounted a vigorous response to what they called "papers from the center" (*chūōshi*) and, except in the immediate environs of Osaka and Tokyo, were generally able to survive the test. In Kanazawa, for example, the local press sought to match the technological advantages of the metropolitan dailies by upgrading their own production. The *Hokkoku* introduced its first high-speed Marinoni rotary printing press in 1912 and bought a second in 1916. In 1915, when the metropolitan press began to publish morning and evening versions of their regional editions, possession of a high-speed press allowed the *Hokkoku* to quickly follow suit, adopting this hallmark feature of the big city press. In 1921, the *Hokkoku* established new departments and expanded its staff, hiring an editor away from the *Osaka mainichi*. Competition with the metropolitan dailies spurred the consolidation of the provincial newspapers, which put their own rivalries to bed in order to fend off the more serious threat from the center. By the 1920s, the field had shaken down to two main regional papers, the *Hokkoku shinbun* and the *Hokuriku mainichi*. Like the *Hokkoku*, the *Hokuriku* brought in famous figures such as Nagai Ryutarō, a local son who had made a name in national politics, to enhance its public profile. It also raided the metropolitan papers for talented staff and added new features and divisions to match the formats of the big dailies.[59]

This process encouraged the standardization of the newspaper form, which stabilized around certain technologies, format, and marketing strategies. At the same time, the ability of the provincial press to withstand the challenge of the big dailies from Osaka and Tokyo spoke to the strength of local connections to newspaper readers. In the early decades of the Meiji the provincial press had laid strong, deep roots in the community, becoming a fixture in the local cultural matrix and social system. Residents responded to the availability of papers from the center by continuing to support their local press. Those who did buy the metropolitan news tended to do so as a supplement rather than a replacement for their local paper, as we can see from circulation figures for provincial cities in the *Japan Newspaper Yearbook*.[60]

As papers adopted the most effective marketing and technological features of their rivals in order to survive, competition with the center meant that a certain amount of the heterogeneity characteristic of the early newspaper industry was eliminated. Yet this did not lead to a uniform provincial market, by any means. Indeed, a brief overview of the local newspaper market in the prefectures of Niigata, Hokkaido (Sapporo), Ishikawa (Kanazawa), and Okayama conveys the variety of reactions to the challenges imposed by successive waves of metropolitan expansion.

Niigata managed to emerge from the fracas with a large number of vibrant local papers supported by different local communities. As an observer noted in 1911, after the first wave of metropolitan expansion, "Things that Echigo [a premodern designation for the region] possesses in abundance include rice, oil, schools, unfinished railroads, snow, and newspapers."[61] Though Niigata prefecture experienced the same shakedown of the newspaper industry that affected other regions, more than two decades later the *Japan Newspaper Yearbook* still noted the unusually high number of regional papers. Partly this rested on a relatively large prefectural population (almost 2 million), but it also related to strong press traditions in the prefecture's three leading cities, Niigata (population 139,000), Nagaoka (population 63,000), and Takada (population 31,000). The dispersed nature and large number of papers meant that even the prefecture's largest presses, the *Niigata shinbun* and the *Niigata mainichi*, did not circulate much beyond the prefectural capital in which they were based. Comparative circulation figures for the more remote Sado Island, positioned just off the coast from Niigata city, illustrated the limited reach of the provincial press. In addition to supporting a Sado paper, residents subscribed to six outside papers, the *Tokyo asahi* (Sado circulation 2,200), the *Tokyo nichi nichi* (2,000), the *Yomiuri* (1,300), the *Hōchi shinbun* (700), the *Niigata mainichi* (500), and the *Niigata shinbun* (circulation 300). Thus the four Tokyo papers overwhelmed the nearby Niigata press.[62]

In Ishikawa, a much less populous prefecture (768,416 residents), cultural institutions, including the press, were concentrated in a single center, in the city of Kanazawa (population 190,000). This strong base meant that the two main local papers, the *Hokkoku shinbun* and the *Hokuriku mainichi* maintained a healthy circulation outside Kanazawa itself, even though their rivals from Osaka and Nagoya held the advantage in the region.[63]

The situation was different again in the northern region of Hokkaido. With more than 3 million in population spread across a broad territorial expanse, Hokkaido supported thirty-eight daily papers. Their ability to survive was enhanced by limitations in the transportation network, which forced the metropolitan press to rely on local papers for distribution. Because of such obstacles, not until 1936 did the region's leading paper, the Sapporo-based *Hokkai taimusu*, begin to feel competitive pressure from Tokyo papers such as the *Asahi*, the *Nichi nichi*, or the *Yomiuri*. Size and poor transportation meant that newspaper production was dispersed across seven cities, including Sapporo (population 205,900), Otaru (155,400), Hakodate (211,700), Asahikawa (92,600), and Muroran (68,900). Two papers occupied the dominant position, however, the *Hokkai taimusu* and *Otaru shinbun*. Both stood out among the provincial press for their ability to command markets beyond their respective urban bases, boasting high circulations not only throughout Hokkaido, but also to the south, on the main island of Honshū, and to the north, in the colony of Karafuto. The *Hokkai taimusu* achieved this position by employing the same "regional edition" strategy used to great effect by the Tokyo papers: the press operated eleven local editions and managed sister papers in Hakodate and Asahikawa. Statistics for the port town of Hakodate illustrate the success of this strategy in competing both with other local papers and with Tokyo rivals. The principal local paper, the *Hakodate shinbun*, with a circulation of 18,000, dominated the market, but the *Hakodate taimusu* (owned by *Hokkai taimusu*) came in a close second with 10,000. Next came another Hakodate paper, the *Hakodate nichi nichi*, with a circulation between eight and nine thousand, followed by four metropolitan papers, the *Tokyo asahi* (3,000), the *Tokyo nichi nichi* (2,500), the *Yomiuri* (2,000), and the *Hōchi* (1,000).[64]

The newspaper market in Okayama offered yet another variation in the story of the local press. Proximity to Osaka insured a strong infiltration of Osaka newspapers, but the size of the prefecture (population 1,332,647) gave the provincial press some resources to fight back. Likewise the concentration of the news industry in the capital city of Okayama (population 170,000) facilitated an effective strategy of resistance. Competitive pressure from Osaka in the first decades of the twentieth century intensified local rivalries and forced a series of amalgamations. After the dust settled, the two papers left standing were the *San'yō shinpō* and the *Chūgoku minpō*, both political organs that expanded aggressively as a result of the Sino-Japanese and Russo-Japanese war fevers.[65]

Initially, it was competition between the two local papers, rather than the threat from the center, that stimulated a wave of innovation and improvement. In the race for readership that heated up after the Russo-Japanese War, both papers upgraded production with the purchase of high-speed rotary presses and the introduction of advertising and promotional campaigns. In the teens the *Chūgoku minpō* appealed to readers by sponsoring a series of exhibitions, one on western art and another on education. The *San'yō shinpō* in turn funded a tennis competition and a sumo match, with the results prominently featured in the paper. The *Chūgoku minpō* answered this with a track and field competition. These efforts helped both papers to maintain healthy circulations of 15,000 in the late 1920s.[66]

In expanding their operations into the field of public entertainment and in sponsoring various events, the Okayama papers joined with broader trends in the news industry that sought to enlarge readership through new marketing strategies. By the end of the Meiji period, newspaper readers throughout the country were accustomed to seeing newspapers sponsor fund-raising drives for victims of disaster or distress, contests and lotteries and concerts, exhibits, lectures, and sporting events.[67] The ingenuity of the Okayama press in inventing new forums for reader involvement captured the attention of the Osaka news media, where they became known as a source of new marketing ideas picked up by the big Osaka dailies. The Okayama story thus offers an example of provincial innovation and metropolitan imitation, showing how the process of cultural diffusion could move in both directions.

By the early 1930s, however, pressure from Osaka rivals had grown too great; the two local papers merged in 1936 under the new banner *Gōdō shinbun*. This left Okayama with one major regional newspaper, albeit of greatly strengthened capacity. The *Gōdō shinbun* overwhelmingly dominated the prefectural market and soon made inroads in surrounding regions as well, circulating in Hiroshima prefecture, the island of Shikoku, Hyōgo prefecture, and parts of the San'in region. In terms of circulation within the prefecture, in 1938 *Gōdō* held its own against the Osaka papers. Its circulation of 80,000 dwarfed the *Osaka asahi* at 35,000, the *Osaka mainichi* at 25,000, and a few odd sales by Tokyo papers.[68]

Although histories of the newspaper industry have focused almost exclusively on the large metropolitan papers, the story of the provincial press offers insights that complicate the standard account of the relationship of the press to cultural change. The Tokyo and Osaka case studies have told the story of modernization in terms of centralization, standardization, and cultural diffusion of the metropolitan model; they have stressed the insuperable advantages of scale and capital investment. Yet the metropolitan press is only one piece of the story. As in the proverb of the blind men examining the elephant, there are hazards to making generalizations based on partial data. Even these four accounts reveal enormous variation in the development of a modern newspaper industry. Expanding connections between local, national, and international media markets over the course of the early twentieth century meant increasing competition for local papers, which led to standardization of the newspaper form through common innovations in technology, marketing, management, and organization. At the same time, local newspapers were embedded within distinctive political-economies and social-cultural contexts, which created their own particular set of constraints and possibilities.

The story of variations in the provincial press is important because the newspaper provided a critical institutional foundation for local cultural movements in the early twentieth century. Since Japanese newspapers published both news and literature, people bought papers to read the so-called hard coverage of political affairs as well as the "soft" columns of poetry and serialized novels. Although the intimate connection between the newspaper and the arts was deeply rooted in the broader history of Japanese publishing, the competitive challenges encountered by the local press fortified this connection. Economic self-interest and the quest for survival in the face of competition with metropolitan papers required local papers to carve out and protect a relatively autonomous sphere of local culture, for this was the one place where the papers from the center could not compete. Provincial newspapers provided access to an audience for locally produced knowledge and culture, a market for cultural production that sustained a large cadre of intellectual workers and artists in provincial cities. Thus the regional press became a critical space for the incubation of the local literati. Its organizational structures and social networks lent the provincial *bundan* social cohesion and provided a forum for the creation of a distinctive esprit de corps.

THE PROVINCIAL LITERATI

Newspapers occupied a central position in the culture-space of the provincial city. They brought writers together and offered a place to make connections and contacts. They encouraged the arts through literary pages, poetry columns, and various competitions and awards. They gave financial support, publication opportunities, and prestige to aspiring writers. In all these ways, newspaper companies were critical to the formation of intellectual community in provincial cities. Moreover, local newspapers were a focal point of cultural innovation in their communities. The press stimulated the transformation of literature and influenced modern literary form through the standards they set in poetry competitions, the privileging of certain literary schools, and the common feature of the serialized novel. And like institutions of higher education, newspapers served as conduits for the import of new ideas and practices from abroad: both occupied a central place in the processes of cultural transformation in the late nineteenth and early twentieth centuries.

Through their literary pages, local newspapers and magazines served as forums to bring together local with metropolitan literary trends. As part of their marketing strategy, local newspapers published serial novels by writers with both local and national reputations. In the 1880s and 1890s the Kanazawa press commissioned Tokyo writers such as Ishibashi Ningetsu to publish in their papers and brought back Izumi Kyōka and other local heroes. A list of serial novels published between 1900 and 1923 in the *Hokkai taimusu* featured writers Izumi Kyōka, Tokuda Shūsei, Ōguri Fūyō, and others from the Tokyo-based Ken'yūsha clique, as well as works by staff writers and submissions by other local authors.[69] Though local residents invariably submitted the poetry published in the provincial press, Tokyo intellectuals were frequently employed to edit the poetry column, write critical reviews of the poems that were published, or act as judges for poetry competitions. The Sapporo poetry magazine *Northern Star* appointed Naitō Saiseki and three other establishment poets from Tokyo to judge their competitions. The main regional newspaper, the *Hokkai taimusu*, likewise brought judges from Tokyo to select poems.[70] In this way local papers actively promoted the circulation of ideas between Tokyo and the provinces. The literary networks they helped to forge transcended the parochialism of the Tokyo *bundan*.

The literary initiatives of local newspapers also fostered the dynamic fusion of old and new cultural forms. In Niigata, one of the prefecture's earliest and most successful newspapers helped reinvent the social practice of poetry writing. Established in 1877, the *Niigata shinbun* achieved a certain national prominence as a forum for political opinion by publishing a string of articles by influential party leaders such as Ozaki Yukio, who was invited to visit and write a piece for the paper.[71] The *Niigata shinbun* also introduced a column to feature local poetry with critical commentary, using the poetry column to draw readership from the wealthy rentier class in a region known as the Kingdom of the Landlord. Throughout the nineteenth century and well into the twentieth, a handful of wealthy landowning families dominated the local political economy. This group composed a highly literate and cultured elite, which provided the core membership for the amateur poetry circles that flourished in the late Tokugawa period as a form of male sociality and connoisseurship. Much like groups of wealthy merchants and samurai in the castle towns of Okayama and Kanazawa, Niigata poetry circles would meet to write together and judge each other's work; for these men, poetry signified a mark of status and an expression of erudition. Such poetry circles brought out the first coterie magazines in the Niigata region. Through its poetry columns, *Niigata shinbun* mobilized this cultural practice to draw an important social constituency into newspaper reading.[72] In the process, the social and performative mode of writing associated with the traditional poetry circle was grafted onto the individualized, text-based mode of writing for the modern print media, creating a hybrid form that incorporated elements of the old and the new.

Like the press, institutions of higher education provided a forum for the local arts, nurturing talent and encouraging the spread of different art forms. Here, too, poetry circles and other literati practices of the late Tokugawa migrated into the higher schools, where they were adapted to become an integral component of the ethos of the new student elite. New poetry movements offered particular appeal in provincial higher schools, where they became a center of student social life and an instrument of male bonding. Accounts of literary youth at places such as Fourth Higher in Kanazawa capture the intoxicating discovery of poetry that many young men experienced during their time at school. For Kubokawa Tsurujirō, one of the talented coterie of young men that included Nakano Shigeharu, Moriyama Kei, and others, the encounter with poetry altered the course of his life. His story was typical of the ways in which participation in local arts shaped a sense of self for a generation of student elite.

Kubokawa was born in 1903 in a small village in Shizuoka, the son of a country doctor. Raised in a strict, old-fashioned household, the young Kubokawa was schooled in the Confucian classics and kept away from what his family regarded as the corrupting influence of boy's popular magazines and newspapers. When Kubokawa was in his teens, tragedy struck the household, leaving both parents and an aunt and uncle dead. He was sent off to study at Fourth Higher by his adoptive family, with the understanding he would train to become a doctor. But during his years in Kanazawa, he sought solace for his grief in poetry and fell under the spell of literature. He joined the school's *tanka* association (*tanka* is a classical Japanese verse form of thirty-one syllables), became friends with other literary youth, and spent all his time talking, thinking, writing, reading, and performing poetry. Eventually he made his mind up to abandon a medical career. Apologizing to his adoptive family, he quit school and headed off to Tokyo to pursue a literary calling.[73] Like many students who became caught up in the literary movements at their schools, Kubokawa's life was changed as a result of his encounter with the all-encompassing experience of poetry. Before it changed his future, poetry took over his life. Poetry engaged higher-school students so intensely because of the way it was practiced: it was not simply a text on paper but a rich and multifaceted cultural form and a lived experience. Through their introduction to new cultural forms such as this in higher school, elite youth like Kubokawa experienced a change in subjectivity: they now thought of themselves as part of that elite fraternity the *bundan*.

The poetry-writing practices fostered by higher schools found expression in an expansion of coterie magazines in provincial cities. Much as in the case of the metropolis, local magazines were striking both for their quantity and their ephemerality. And like *dōjin zasshi* in the capital, such journals were central to the coherence and identity of the local literati. They created a community of readers, writers, and critics and encouraged the self-referential character of the local *bundan*. The coterie magazines focused intellectual attention on the local literary scene and themselves defined local trends in high culture. Also like the coterie magazines in Tokyo, provincial literary journals fostered practices of mutual criticism that blurred the roles of writer and critic, an ambiguity characteristic of Japanese literary practice in this period. Because the higher-school experience and provincial magazines engaged literary youth at a critical juncture in their lives, it was here, in the local city, that these youth were groomed to think of their reading and writing as broadly integrated intellectual practices, and that they came to see literature as a way of life.

In contrast to the *bundan* in Tokyo, who formed a closed and exclusive society that reveled in its alienation from the broader urban social world, the local *bundan* were better integrated into their communities. In part this reflected their diminished status relative to Tokyo—local intellectuals lacked many of the cultural and social resources used by metropolitan intellectuals to place themselves in a world above the clouds. In the context of their own communities, however, they enjoyed great status, and here the smaller scale of the city gave them a certain advantage. As big fish in small ponds, local intellectuals found it easier to command the attention of their communities against the competing attractions of the modern cityscape, since provincial cities possessed a tiny fraction of Tokyo's myriad department stores, restaurants, movie palaces, entertainment districts, newspapers, and publishing houses.

Intellectuals' leadership in local cultural movements made a powerful impact on the cultural and social life in their communities. New poetry movements promoted through the elite schools and the local press offered one point of contact. Though the old-boy web of connections smoothed the way to publishing opportunities for cultural elites, the frequent poetry contests held by newspapers and magazines encouraged aspiring writers of all backgrounds to send their selections in. Young men such as Shimada Seijirō sent scores of their poems around to juried competitions published in their own local papers as well as other regional and national papers.[74] In Kanazawa, poetry banquets sponsored by student organizations were advertised on the street, and these organizations actively sought to involve poets from the broader community. Such activities identified the cultural production of the *bundan* with an intellectual community that transcended the exclusive world of the higher school. Unlike Tokyo—where isolation defined the *bundan*—Kanazawa literati were identified with their urban community.

Indeed, the event Kubokawa Tsurujirō remembers capturing his interest as a freshman at Fourth Higher was not even hosted by a student group. Shortly after he arrived in Kanazawa, he noticed an advertisement posted on a wall announcing a haiku party at the Kenrokuen Public Gardens. During this unforgettable event, participants wrote poem after poem, inspired by the convivial atmosphere of food, drink, and cherry blossoms. In a particularly elegant touch, the poets were requested to affix their favorite creation to the branch of a blooming tree, and the reveling crowds were invited to take away those they judged superior. In its focus on process rather than product, and in defining aesthetic value in terms of both creative writing and critical judgment, the practice of poetry writing as social event harked back to the poetry circles of the late Tokugawa. As in the previous era, the practice of writing served to create an intellectual community. Where the Taishō-era banquet departed from precedent was its expansion of the social range of participants; the exclusive social world of the literati poetry circle now embraced the Kanazawa public.[75] In the different forums it provided for poetry writing, the literary scene in Kanazawa offered the simultaneous experience of old and new cultural forms. Literary youth and other amateur poets could shift from the social and performative mode of the banquet to print culture, where publication monumentalized the literary product and where newspapers and magazines provided a medium of anonymous communication between a solitary writer and a solitary reader. The oversized importance of the higher school or the local newspaper in the provincial city magnified the importance of literati within the urban cultural scene. These new forms of cultural practice were at once more public and more part of "our city" in a place like Kanazawa.

The democratization of literary practices symbolized by the haiku banquet revealed one of the most dramatic shifts in the cultural landscape in the early twentieth century. Public schools and the press encouraged this social opening, as did institutions such as public libraries. Despite limited public support, a network of libraries sprang up in the teens and twenties in most areas of the country. In Niigata prefecture, for example, there were 199 libraries by 1924, 123 of which were privately funded. The three main cities, Takada, Nagaoka, and Niigata, all had public libraries; the largest of these was based in the capital city of Niigata. Established in 1915, by 1925 the Niigata Prefectural Library housed a collection of more than 50,000 volumes, 2,503 of which were in western languages. The library was open 326 days a year, and in 1924 the library recorded 370,153 visitors, an average of more than a thousand patrons a day.[76] People went to the library to read books and magazines they could not afford and especially to read newspapers. For literary youth of modest backgrounds, libraries offered crucial access to the world of literature and ideas. Shimaki Kensaku, a leading figure in the agrarian literature movement, who grew up in a poor Sapporo household, wrote that his love of literature and ambition to become a writer were acquired by visiting the local library.[77]

Local businesses also provided a venue for the social diffusion of elite cultural movements. One of the most striking examples of this was the spread of new forms of musical performance and appreciation from schools out into the streets, where they became part of the broader cultural life of the city. In Niigata, western music was initially introduced through choral groups in the mission schools. A teacher at Niigata Women's High School, Takada Sen, became an advocate for music education, promoting school bands and choral groups in the both secondary and elementary schools. From these foundations, interest in new musical forms and imported musical instruments spread through the community as school bands and orchestras offered public performances at local festivals, public events, and field days (undōkai). Local businesses began playing music in front of their shops to entice customers in; movie theaters and playhouses hired bands to provide musical accompaniment for their entertainments. The Niigata city government started to sponsor concerts in the 1920s, bringing famous musicians from Tokyo and overseas to perform for city residents. School bands, orchestras, and glee clubs multiplied as urban residents increasingly embraced music as a hobby. By 1927 Niigata's local music scene supported four musical instrument stores that sold mandolins, violins, and organs.[78]

The stories of the musical groups in Niigata and the poetry movement in Kanazawa were typical of modernist culture in provincial cities, where the interactions of old with new cultural forms, and the entry of new social groups into literary and artistic movements, together shaped the local cultural scene. Through the growing networks of cultural institutions—newspapers and magazines, the school system, libraries, and bookshops—provincial cities nurtured thriving local cultures and groomed a provincial *bundan*. These men, and to a lesser extent, women, assumed positions as cultural leaders, the creative voices of their communities. In the process, the meaning of the term *bundan* underwent a subtle shift: rather than an exclusive fraternity living "above the clouds," as the metropolitan image construed the literati, the provincial literati were the artistic voice of the local community.

The formations of a provincial literati and its position within the culture-space of the local city had a doubled effect on the power dynamics of local and metropolitan culture. On the one hand, by bringing in Tokyo literati as poetry judges and feature novelists, regional newspapers set the metropolis up as the arbiter of aesthetic value and standard-bearer for local cultural production. The press reinforced lessons learned in the local schools, where the educational hierarchy of metropolitan teachers and provincial students promoted a sense of cultural deference to the capital. On the other hand, through their literary pages newspapers provided a forum for the articulation of an independent local voice, one that emerged from and spoke to a local audience, one that made appeals to a particular community of artists and that laid claim to a local identity. While the migration of provincial intellectuals to Tokyo had provided the catalyst for the dynamic interaction of diverse cultural traditions in the capital, the provincial tours of Tokyo intellectuals also energized cultural movements in local cities. In the ways they mobilized the cultural authority of metropolitan intellectuals, provincial newspapers and schools reinforced an opposition between this local artistic voice and metropolitan art. But while working under the shadow of Tokyo often led to an inferiority complex, it could also inspire a defiant regionalism.

The encounter between Sapporo poets and missionaries for Masaoka Shiki's Tokyo-based new haiku movement offered one example of this sort of productive engagement. It was a story that began before the local literati had heard much of Shiki or his celebrated poetry magazine, the *Cuckoo*

(*Hototogisu*). The man usually credited as the father of haiku in the region was Ushijima Tōroku, who came to Hokkaido with the early wave of immigration from the south in the late nineteenth century. Tōroku was an employee in the planning office of the railroad bureau, but his real love was poetry. From the early 1900s, he poured his energies into the publication of a string of very successful literary magazines, including *White Snow (Shirayuki), New Leaf (Wakaba),* and *Northern Star (Hokusei),* which featured haiku of the old school that hewed to traditional conventions of seasonality and natural imagery. After the Railroad Bureau transferred him to Sapporo, he hooked into the networks of writers there and became the editor of the poetry column for the newspaper *Otaru shinbun.* He connected with students and faculty at the Sapporo Agricultural College (the precursor to Hokkaido University), joining their poetry circles and publishing in their coterie magazines. In this way Tōroku exercised a powerful influence on the founding moment of the regional poetry movement, operating through a strong base in local institutions such as the press and the schools.[79] The other key figure in Hokkaido poetry circles was Aoki Kakkō, who arrived in Hokkaido in the late 1880s and remained a major force on the literary scene until the 1940s. He joined the staff of the *Hokkai taimusu* newspaper and, through his position, helped secure jobs for other young poets at newspapers in the regional network of the newspaper. Through his poetry columns and connections Kakkō became a kind of literary godfather and, with Tōroku, encouraged the regional poetry movement.[80]

Thus it was that in the teens, when a parade of Masaoka Shiki's disciples from Tokyo appeared in Sapporo, they encountered a thriving local poetry scene centered on the university and the newspaper. Kawahigashi Hekigotō and Takahama Kyoshi, Shiki's two most famous students, both spent time in Sapporo during tours of Hokkaido and northern Japan. Hekigotō's trip was part of an ambitious project to establish local branches of the new haiku movement throughout the country, leading him to crisscross the archipelago between 1907 and 1911, traveling from Okinawa in Japan's southern tip to Hokkaido in the far north. Kyoshi came to the area in part for family reasons, since he enrolled his son at the Otaru Commercial High School. But he, like Hekigotō, actively promoted the extension of the haiku movement to the provinces through regional competitions for poetry columns in the *Cuckoo (Hototogisu)* and the establishment of magazines affiliated with the Tokyo-based publication. Traveling to places like Sapporo, joining poetry banquets, and encouraging the founding of new poetry journals, they helped spread Shiki's gospel of haiku reform. In the wake of their visits, other young poets of the Masaoka Shiki school, like Ogasawara Yōyō, came to Sapporo to join the regional poetry movement. Through the efforts of both Hekigotō and Kyoshi, the national network of *Hototogisu* organizations became the institutional strength of the haiku movement and the site of creative interactions between provincial and metropolitan literati.[81]

The ability of the new haiku movement to take root in local communities rested in part on the affinities of this poetry form for expressions of regionalism. During the Tokugawa period, haiku emerged as a vehicle for depicting famous scenic spots, a spirit of rustication and pilgrimage, and seasonality evoked through natural imagery. Critics of these older writing conventions, like Shiki, charged that arcane rules about seasonal symbols, as well as the dense accumulations of allusions to past poems that governed word choice, had come to stifle creativity. In their stead he advocated the technique of painterly description—"sketching from life"—and viewed poetry as a means to capture spontaneous reaction to everyday life. This opened haiku up to a range of new subject matter, encouraging compositions that dealt with change and "the new." Yet even with these reforms, practice remained wedded to the evocation of place that had defined Tokugawan haiku, and poets maintained a predilection for natural imagery.[82] In both its earlier form and its modern incarnation, haiku possessed a singular capacity to capture the specificity of time and place, to convey the individual rhythms of everyday life in a particular locale. This made it the perfect vehicle for regionalist literary movements that sought to express the distinctiveness of local culture, local society, and the local environment. In Sapporo, the new haiku movement channeled an outpouring of this kind of sentiment, with poems on the awesome natural beauty of Hokkaido, the pioneer spirit of its residents, and the unique way of life in the far north. One of the first expressions of the strength of this local movement was a poetry collection published in 1912, *Hokkai haikushū (A Collection of Hokkaido Haiku)*, which showcased twenty-five hundred works by Hokkaido poets previously published in *Hototogisu* and the *Hokkai taimusu*.[83]

As with haiku, regionalism emerged as a powerful force within other local literary movements in the teens and twenties. In the university town of Sapporo, it was college students who formed the core of the local *bundan* and provided the principal energy behind these movements. They published a stream of literary magazines beginning in the early 1900s. Until *North Country Literature (Hokkoku bundan)* began publication in 1912, few of these lasted more than a year or two. Though founded by university students,

North Country Literature quickly became the key literary journal for aspiring writers in and outside the university. While literary critics had already begun to comment on regionalist tendencies in the arts, and the phrase *Sapporo bundan* had appeared in the press as early as 1906, this journal explicitly embraced regionalism and committed itself to fostering a writerly ethos particular to the Hokkaido region.[84]

Though *North Country Literature* remained the standard-bearer of the local movement, new Sapporo magazines continued to stream forth, with the *Street* (*Rojō*) and *Lily of the Valley* (*Suzuran*) appearing in 1920, and *Hokkaido University Arts* (*Hokudai Bungei*), *Blue Sky* (*Aozora*), *Bystander* (*Robōjin*), the *Plain* (*Heigen*), *Roar* (*Todoroki*), *Glacier* (*Hyōga*), and the *Town* (*Machi*) coming out in 1921. These magazines provided forums for the progressive ideas that transformed Japanese universities after World War One, inspired by the Russian Revolution and Wilsonian internationalism abroad and the upsurge of radical activism in their communities closer to home. While tapping global currents of reform and revolution, students in Sapporo took their own literary movement in self-consciously local directions, seeking to set their narratives of social transformation within the particular conditions presented in Hokkaido. As the mission statement in the inaugural issue of *Glacier* declared, they aimed to constitute a proletarian literature on the unique grounds of "Hokkaido with its hidden strength and immense frame." The *Plain* devoted itself to literary depictions of the brutal conditions of farm life in Hokkaido, embracing the mission of transforming social conditions in the countryside.[85]

In Kanazawa and Okayama, local poetry movements that had been heavily influenced by Tokyo writers Masaoka Shiki and Yosano Tekkan likewise turned to an assertive localism in the early decades of the twentieth century. In 1921 the Kanazawa Poetry Association (Kanazawa Shijinkai) formed as an organ of regionalism, bringing together writers from Fourth Higher, Kanazawa Commercial School, and the newspaper *Hokkoku nippō* in the city, as well as writers from throughout the prefecture. In 1924 a larger organization, the Hokuriku Federation of Poetry groups (Hokuriku Shijinkai Kyōkai) was created to extend the regional network of poets into the neighboring prefectures of Fukui and Toyama. As its mission statement declared, "We are dedicated to innovation in the art of local poetry and to the spread of poetry writing in our region." Both groups published house journals and sponsored a series of poetry festivals and events, including a spring reception for Tokyo poets to showcase the creative products of the regionalist project.

They actively collected local literary works, maintaining an archive of local cultural production and acting as a clearinghouse for local publications.[86]

As in Hokkaido, leaders of these local movements framed their appeals in a celebration of difference. Though this was frequently expressed in positive terms highlighting what was special about the locality—a specific cultural heritage, the distinguishing marks of landscape and climate—just as often it rested on a critique of Tokyo. In this spirit, Irisawa Ryōgetsu, the founder of the acclaimed Okayama poetry magazines *Young Blood* (*Chishio*) and *White Rainbow* (*Hakkō*) called for the creation of a Kansai region *bundan* capable of resisting the power of the center. In a 1907 issue of *White Rainbow*, Ryōgetsu issued an appeal addressed to "Writers in Provincial Magazines," asking them to look to themselves for creative inspiration and denouncing the metropolitan *bundan*.

> At a time of excessive production of irresponsible literary magazines, must we gentlemen of the provinces lose our self-respect? When there is little to hope for from the metropolitan *bundan*, mired in their internal factions, cannot the provinces become the site for a literary revival? . . . It falls to us, with our commitment to justice and truth to seize the day. Let us give full cry to our outrage! . . . Let us take this one small provincial magazine and through it build an authentic provincial *bundan* and exclude those frauds that have haunted us.[87]

The Kanazawa poet Sengoku Kiku echoed Ryōgetsu's defiant localism in his poetry collection *Manifesto on Civilization*. In response to hearing the news, in 1923, that an earthquake had leveled much of the capital, Kiku penned a harshly critical poem about Tokyo-centrism.

One Kind of Vision

When I think longingly of rosy possibilities for the good life
What springs to mind are the wondrous trappings of civilization—
The grand buildings and skyscrapers of the capital,
The beautiful women of Tokyo in their splendid attire,
And the glittering streetlights at night.

Is Tokyo really a marketplace for the good life?
It certainly holds an awesome power to capture the young soul.

And yet,
First of September 1923—
You have offered a powerful reminder
That this is a dream with a price, thrust on it by reality.

This vision of Tokyo masks an ephemeral civilization.

I can no longer even imagine
A balance between material civilization and human happiness.

The great force of nature hidden deep within the ground,
And the earth, which floats like a ship upon this force,
The seeds of a fate buried far below
They grab, powerfully, at my heart
That has shriveled unbearably.

And before I know it
The dream of the metropolis that had taken over my soul
Is despoiled by the shadow of the doubt that now grips me.[88]

Here the marginalizing effects of the *kokyō* metaphor were reversed: the hometown became a haven from the excesses of Tokyo. Instead of portraying a backward provincial culture, Sengoku Kiku's images spotlighted the corruption at the heart of the capital: a false civilization with its meretricious allure. Like Irisawa Ryōgetsu, he acknowledged the pull of the capital, the power it exerted on provincial youth and local talent. But here he exposes this pull as a chimera. As the earthquake shakes through the dry rot of Tokyo's putative civilization, nature exercises an awesome judgment on the narcissism and vanity of the metropolis. Nature, the trope of the provinces, of the hometown, strikes back at the center and destroys it.

None of this exactly countered the ideology of the metropolis, but rather the poem reframed it. Regionalism and the calls for local pride echoed and reinforced the idea of a dichotomy, defining the local in opposition to the center, just as the center defined itself against the localities. But instead of redounding to the glory of the center, the comparison highlighted the authenticity and depth of the local in contrast to the falseness and superficiality of the center. The hometown's affinity for nature meant that provincial culture was genuine and true, in contrast to the fleeting civilization of the capital. In these ways the regionalist cultural movements borrowed the tropes of Tokyo-centrism to reverse its logic, generating a vision of the local that possessed the capacity for creative and distinctive cultural production.

From their perches in provincial cities and in the metropolis, writers and artists wielded enormous power to shape the epistemology of Japan's modernity. Moving through the circuits of exchange laid down by the educational grid and publishing industry, intellectuals traversed a social and cultural geography organized in terms of centers and peripheries. While they were products of this environment, their actions and their artistic production also helped create the inequalities that characterized it. In the visions of modern urban life that spun from the fancies of the *bundan*, the distinction between the capital and the provinces became a defining feature of urban subjectivity. In its figuration of the metaphor of the hometown, highbrow literature elaborated the Japanese inflection of that most classic trope of modernity— city and country.

Though the spatial divisions between centers and peripheries were not conjured out of thin air in the late nineteenth and early twentieth centuries, the defining features of Tokyo-centrism were peculiar to modern times. Here I have focused on the spatializing effects of institutions of the press and education—the one driven by private industry, the other by the state. Both institutions emerged in the late nineteenth century as powerful forces in the local cultures of Kanazawa, Sapporo, Tokyo, and other cities; they channeled the circulation of ideas and artists between urban centers and encouraged complex, crosscutting influences among them. Moreover, both newspapers and higher education served as conduits for the introduction of literary trends from the capital and abroad. In the process, they became crucibles for autonomous local cultures, even as they fostered national integration and the formation of a "Japanese" national style. They also helped to generate a creative encounter between old and new cultural forms, between Tokyo and the provinces, between the competing epistemologies that yielded modernist expression not just in literature but drama and the arts as well.

Though we are most familiar with the material and institutional aspects of Tokyo-centrism, its ideological operations were equally powerful. The ideology of the metropolis legitimated and sanctified a set of unequal power relations and geographic disparities that concentrated resources in the capital. Tokyo-centrism masked the provincial origins of metropolitan knowledge; it obscured the heterogeneity of local culture as well as the creativity, vibrancy, and local self-generation of cultural life in the provinces. Thinking critically about Tokyo-centrism—both its historical-material origins and its ideological operations—can also help to rethink the problem of modernity more broadly, especially for a place like Japan, which became positioned in the late nineteenth and early twentieth centuries within a global matrix of centers and peripheries. This story of Tokyo-centrism points to the inadequacy of the diffusionist model that still tends to dominate our understanding of the process of modern transformation, suggesting instead that we look to coconstitution and mutual determination in the production of the new knowledges, new institutions, and new structures that defined "the modern."

The story here has examined the modern logics of centers and peripheries through an analysis of the cultural geography that defined the relationship between the national capital and provincial cities. Although I have focused on cultural institutions, the expanding networks of communications grids—especially the railway revolution—exerted an equally powerful impact on the social production of space. New cultural geographies that were developed through schools and the publishing industries were overlaid by new economic geographies following the contours of the railroad map. Both operated to produce the modern logics of centers and peripheries. While Tokyo and its provincial cities defined one matrix, the relationship between regional cities and their own hinterlands constituted another part of the dynamic, since every periphery was also a center.

THREE

Colonizing the Country

As Raymond Williams famously observed, the city-country binary constitutes one of the most prominent tropes of modernity. The opposition between the two, as well as their mutual dependency, emerged as a fundamental condition of industrial capitalism. Moreover, this new relationship between city and country was the product of both material and ideological forces—the operation of labor and commodity markets, the geographic distribution of industry and agriculture, and ideologies of progress and development.[1] For Japan, the late nineteenth and the early twentieth centuries constituted a time of transformation in the urban-rural relationship. This process began in the latter part of the Tokugawa period, as rural industrialization and the growth of merchant capital in villages and along the main transportation routes created cracks in a political economy centered on castle towns and their enfeoffed rural estates.[2] Incorporation into a world economy in the late nineteenth century accelerated and redirected the pace of change, vastly expanding the scale of industry and shifting its locus to the large metropolitan centers along Japan's Pacific coast. After the explosive urban growth that followed in the teens and twenties, the proliferation of industrial centers forced a reorientation of rural economies, breaking down the old patterns of self-sufficiency and obstacles to demographic mobility that were characteristic of the Tokugawa socioeconomy and replacing them with a new dependency on the urban market.

Discourses on urban growth and development that circulated through the city planning movement and the domestic tourist industry naturalized the new order of urban hegemony taking form. In city guides, travel magazines, and planning documents, local boosters promoted a vision of urban triumphalism that positioned the city at the vanguard of progress and cast the village variously as an appendage, supply house, or backwater. In the process, the countryside became modernity's Other. This marked a striking contrast with Tokugawa-era neo-Confucianism, which portrayed the countryside in idealized terms as the wellspring of economic value and the home of farmer producers who occupied the apex of virtue in the hierarchy of economic morality. In the new social imaginary, villages were bound to cities in a reciprocal, if unequal, relationship. Meiji developmental reforms underwrote this vision and pitted town against country. The new system of public finance relied overwhelmingly on the land tax, channeling fiscal resources from agriculture to industry, from village to city. The labor force for the infant textile industry drew on the *dekasegi* labor system—short-term, underpaid female workers from villages. As Japan industrialized on the backs of poor, rural women, the Meiji elite embraced urban-centrism, privileging the city as the engine of growth and the font of modernity.

More than anything else, the advent of the railroad transformed the relationship between town and country in the provinces, changing the way urban residents thought about the rural areas that surrounded their cities. Though we usually understand the railroad as an instrument of nation building, from a local vantage point the impact on the production of regional space appears even more striking. Railroads facilitated the movement of tens of thousands of rural migrants into provincial cities year after year. Railroads opened up possibilities for short-term travel, stimulating the development of tourist retreats at nearby hot springs, mountain resorts, and seashores. Railways altered patterns of land use, accelerating conversion from agricultural production to residential and industrial land uses. Offering new opportunities for the circulation of goods and people, railroads helped extend the orbit of local capitalism through the creation of new labor, agricultural, and commercial markets. With the coming of the railway, nothing would be the same again.

This chapter takes up the history of the railway and its production of social and economic space. Complementing the cultural operations of institutions such as the press and higher education, the railway constituted a force field of economic modernization that helped determine the location of centers and peripheries. The processes of transformation set in motion by the railway happened at multiple spatial scales—national, regional, and local—and their impact was felt unevenly. Using provincial cities such as Niigata and Okayama as an optic through which to examine this story brings into sharp focus the vicissitudes of railway-led development. New patterns of circulation and production determined the fortunes of communities: opportunities opened up for those near the iron track and closed down for others. And in this period of rapid expansion, such fortunes could change quickly. The initial victors in the railway sweepstakes sometimes found themselves the losers when the opening of a new station reduced the strategic value of their established junction. As such episodes reveal, the economic geography produced by railroad-led development was highly unstable.

Intense competition for the economic favor bestowed by the railway accelerated the expansion of railroad networks and whipped up a fever for growth. The reordering of urban-rural relationships that resulted was sanctioned by an emergent ideology of urban expansionism. With the annexation of surrounding territory, cities were reborn and the term *Greater* was added to their names; Niigata became "Greater Niigata" (*dai Niigata*). Told from the perspective of an urban-centered subject, accounts of urban growth echoed narratives of colonial expansion: a triumphant march of progress, the juggernaut of urban modernity expanding inexorably outward, the inevitable decline of the countryside. In fact, the surrounding countryside did not disappear but was radically transformed into the hinterlands of regional urban centers. Although the ideology of urban expansionism imagined "city" and "country" as mutually exclusive, self-contained categories, the material process of urban growth gave the lie to such a crude bifurcation. Indeed, the rise of the suburb as an integral element of urban space exposed the tensions between the material and the mythical dimensions of the urban-rural relationship. Neither one nor the other, the suburb emerged as a place where the ecologies of town and country were thoroughly interpenetrated. The following pages explore these different aspects of the impact of the railway: how it shaped local economies, the physical expansion of the city, and what urban Japanese made of these developments.

THE RAILROAD REVOLUTION

The process of railroad building in Japan began in the 1870s; the first line was built with government capital along the coastal corridor between Tokyo and Kyoto that was part of the old Tōkaidō road. Private railway building accelerated in the late eighties and nineties, increasing the existing 138 miles of track in 1881 to 1,696 miles in 1890. Over the next ten years, the size of the system more than doubled, totaling 3,854 miles of track by 1900. When the government nationalized the railway in 1906, its network covered some 5,000 miles of track. Though by this point in time the railway network traversed the four main islands of the Japanese archipelago, best served by far was the central island of Honshu. There, the Pacific coast provided superior rail access. Along the coastal corridor that faced Europe and America, railroads offered tip-to-tip service, from Aomori in the northeast to Shimonoseki in the southwest. Thus, during the first phase of building, Japan's rail system developed to maximize the goals of national development, and the railway emerged as the strategic connection between domestic and international markets.

Extension of the system to the Sea of Japan lagged behind, in part because of the engineering challenge of tunneling and bridging the mountainous terrain in the center of the archipelago. The more important reason, however, was the higher demand for rapid transport to move goods along the corridor that connected the ports of Yokohama and Kobe with the rapidly industrializing regions of the Kantō and Kinai plains. Since the economy was growing fastest along the Europe-facing Pacific coast, cities seeking to build themselves into centers of trade and industry on the Asia-facing side along the Sea of Japan found it more difficult to attract investments in transportation infrastructure. In this way physical geography reinforced economic geography, which privileged Tokyo and Osaka as dynamic centers of trade and industry within a national economy only recently incorporated into a European-centered global market. Still, by 1906, trunk lines had been built that crossed over from the Osaka region to connect with Tsuruga and Toyama, and from the Tokyo region to connect with Naoetsu and Niigata, cities along the coast of the Sea of Japan. Moreover, a northern route ran up the Pacific coast to Sendai, arcing north and west to make stops in Aomori and Akita before looping south to reconnect with Tokyo. At this early juncture, rail service in the outer islands of the archipelago was likewise uneven. In the far north, the recently annexed island of Hokkaido enjoyed a fairly extensive regional network that serviced its coal industry. On the southern island of Kyushu, track ran only across the northern tip to connect with the port of Nagasaki. And across the Inland Sea, the island of Shikoku had virtually no train service (map 1).

A glance at the Meiji railroad system alongside a Tokugawa highway map reveals a striking feature of the national rail network: the new lines were overlaid almost entirely along the existing communications grid. The Pacific coast route between Tokyo and Kyoto followed the old Tōkaidō road, the most important and frequently traveled of the five official highways of the

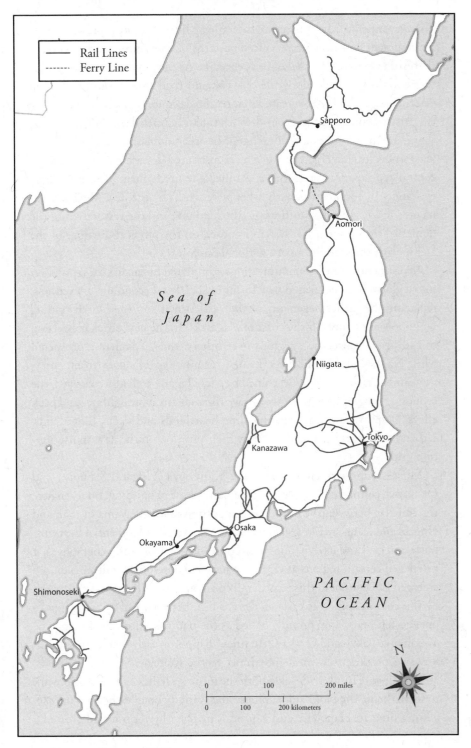

MAP 1. Japanese railway map, 1906

Tokugawa period. In this sense, the railway lines did not represent a new development, but rather reproduced patterns of communications and trade that had existed for decades, if not centuries. At the same time, however, the reorientation of trade along the old Tōkaidō road from an internal to an external market helped to create a new national economic space framed along the existing communications grid. With trade channeled through port cities that marked the boundary of exchange between domestic and foreign markets, a new link emerged between a reconstituted domestic market and the centralized Japanese state that controlled the mechanism of international exchange. In conjunction with other state works by the new Meiji government, such as currency unification, the land tax, and the restoration of the domains, the national rail system imposed on the physical territory of the archipelago the scaffolding of a national economy.[3]

Investments in rail communications stimulated by Japan's incorporation into a global market created new forms of social and economic unevenness, replacing the earlier hegemony of the castle town and the Dutch trading monopoly at Dejima off the coast of Nagasaki. In the new order, conversion to rail privileged certain regions over others; thus, Yokohama prospered while Nagasaki languished. As the new terminology of *omote* (front, entryway) and *ura* (rear, backdoor) coined by Meiji Japanese vividly conveyed, the economic geography of the railway gave rise to main thoroughfares and back alleys, gateways and rear exits, bustling heartlands and sleepy hinterlands. Urban economies became defined by their position on the new transportation grid.

Most second-tier cities were, like Kanazawa, Niigata, Sapporo, and Okayama, connected to rail during the early phase of building. But even here the time lag between the link up of Sapporo in 1880, Okayama in 1891, and Niigata and Kanazawa in 1898 reflected the uneven development of the transportation grid and its dynamic interaction with an economic geography that privileged certain regions as targets of national developmentalism. Sapporo emerged as a winner in this regard: rail construction to the city was proposed by the colonial office as early as 1870; a link between Otaru and Sapporo opened ten years later, proudly hailed as the nation's third railway after the Yokohama-Tokyo and Osaka-Ōtsu lines.[4] Sapporo's early success in the railway sweepstakes drew on its proximity to the strategic Ishikara coalfields, attracting state funds to develop both the mining facilities and a rail network to serve them. The Hokkaido Colliery and Railway bought these up in 1889, adding lines to Hakodate and Muroran in 1892; by 1900 it had created a

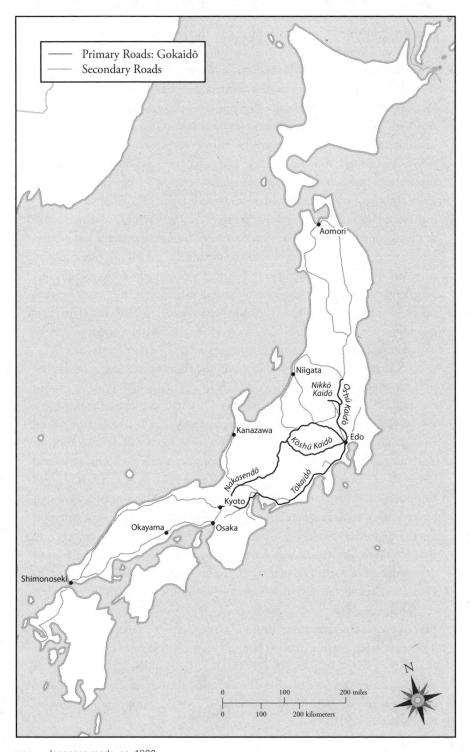

MAP 2. Japanese roads, ca. 1800

regional grid that connected Sapporo to the nearby towns of Asahikawa, Nayoro, and Wakkanai.[5]

Okayama's seven-year advantage over Niigata and Kanazawa exemplified the benefits of its proximity to the industrial heartland of Osaka as well as its location along the economically strategic coastal corridor. Okayama station was built as a hub in the network of the San'yō Railway Company, established in 1886 as a leader in the private railway construction boom of the late 1880s. The San'yō Railway quickly acquired a reputation for progressive innovations, pioneering the use of electric lighting for passenger cars and the adoption of porters and "red caps"; it built Japan's first station hotel and introduced the country's first limited express train.[6] Credited with high standards of construction and service, San'yō grew into one of the largest and most successful of the Meiji railway companies. San'yō took nine years to complete its network, which ran from the city of Himeji (just outside Kobe) via Okayama and Hiroshima to terminate at Shimonoseki on the far western tip of Honshu. In 1898 the Chūgoku-sen, another private company that developed a railway network in the region, connected Okayama city to Tsuyama, the largest city in the northeast part of Okayama prefecture.[7]

In Kanazawa, as in other cities along the coast of the Sea of Japan, the initiative to build railways emerged more slowly and with less vigor. In 1893 the Hokuriku Railway announced the Diet had authorized funds for a twelve-year plan to complete a regional network that would include fifteen tunnels and twenty-three stations.[8] By 1900, this network reached over Toyama and Ishikawa prefectures, connecting Kanazawa to nearby cities and to the Pacific corridor line near Osaka.[9] Rail service to Niigata also lagged behind. As in other Japan Sea coastal cities, this delay became one more sign of economic "backwardness" that gave rise to the stigmatizing designation for the region of *ura Nihon*—the posterior, backside, or rear entrance to Japan.[10] Much like Kanazawa's case, local entrepreneurs pressed hard for rail development, in part to connect with the emerging industrial complexes in Osaka and Tokyo, but also to develop the possibilities of trade with the Asian continent. The Naoetsu Railway opened in 1888, crossing the Usui mountain pass in Nagano prefecture to link the coastal city of Naoetsu with Tokyo. Ten years later, track extended from Naoetsu to Niigata, connecting the city to the capital. By 1912, the Hokuriku Railway pushed its network into the Niigata region, connecting the cities of Kanazawa and Niigata and creating routes for both to the Kansai and Kantō metropolitan regions on the Pacific coast.[11]

Thus, by the time the railroad network was nationalized in 1906, trunk lines connected main provincial cities to the metropolises of Osaka and Tokyo, to ports and mines, and in some cases, to each other. Part of a global boom in railway building, the expanding rail network in Japan served as an instrument for the production of a new, nationalized economic space. The national economy created by the railroad reoriented the topography of the Japanese archipelago according to the logic of a domestic capitalist market enmeshed in a global economy. The signs of the transformation appeared in an economic geography that marginalized *ura Nihon* and granted privileged status to the industrial and export centers on the Pacific coast. The winners and losers in the new regime were easy to identify: along with the Tokyo-Osaka corridor, northern Kyushu and southern Hokkaido became beneficiaries of the restructuring of economic space; regions on the island of Shikoku and along the coast of the Sea of Japan lost out. The advantageous position of Okayama and Sapporo, and the unfortunate situation of Niigata and Kanazawa, set the terms by which these local communities could participate in the project of national developmentalism. Even for Sapporo, blessed with an early rail link because of nearby coal mines, the technological challenges of bridging the waters between Hokkaido and Honshu retarded the city's full integration into the mainland economy.

ENGINES OF UNEVEN DEVELOPMENT

Although the physical scope of railroad building may have been uneven, the railway's penetration of consciousness was widespread. As Carol Gluck observes, "In the popular iconography of the Meiji period two ubiquitous images gradually emerged as symbols of 'civilization': the monarch and the locomotive."[12] This "symbol of civilization" carried with it expectations of progress and faith in an almost magical capacity to bring economic development in its wake. As a newspaper observed in the late 1880s: "Since people have become persuaded . . . that the country's material progress depends, in a great measure, on the extension of railways, there has . . . developed something very like a mania for this species of enterprise, and the appetite having been whetted by issues of public securities, few localities could now be named where projects of railway construction have not been formed. It may be said, in short, that Japan has entered her railway age."[13]

To some degree, historians have unconsciously echoed this triumphalist vision of the railway. According to standard accounts of Japanese capitalism, investments in railways, along with textile production, became the engines of economic development in the critical phase of industrialization in the 1880s. In his classic study of the Meiji railroad, Steven Ericson disputes this notion, arguing instead "for the relative unimportance of railroads to the economy of Meiji Japan." With the notable exceptions of interior landlocked locations such as Nagano or the coalfield railroads, Ericson points out, so-called forward linkages (reduction of transport costs and consequent widening of markets) and backward linkages (demand for industrial products and inputs) were minimal.[14] The histories of Kanazawa, Niigata, and Okayama certainly support Ericson's contention. For small- and medium-size cities, the stimulative effects of railway development awaited the establishment of regional networks in the teens and twenties. In the Meiji period, since new rail lines paralleled previous sea and river routes, they merely replicated existing transportation grids. Hence, the advent of the railway in these regions did not initially stimulate new economic activity; it simply redistributed this activity from a water-centered transportation and commercial complex to one based on rail. With this shift, the loss of business for riparian and coastal transport companies and the communities they supported became the gain for railway transport and warehousing businesses, as well as for the commercial enterprises that flourished in the vicinity of the train stations. Contrary to the myth that the railroad brought material progress to all, it became an engine for uneven development.

Within cities, this process dictated the fate of neighborhoods, whose fortunes rose and fell according to proximity to the train station. More than any other single element of physical infrastructure, rail transport reshaped the spatial organization of the city in early-twentieth-century Japan, transforming the castle town into the modern cityscape. In Okayama, for example, prior to the opening of the railway station in 1898, commercial life centered on patterns established during its Tokugawa life as the administrative seat of the Okayama domain. A survey conducted in 1898, the year the railway station opened, showed that Okayama city dominated the commercial life of the prefecture. It commanded the lead over the nearby towns Tsuyama and Tamashima in terms of numbers of wholesale and retail merchants, as well as in terms of statistics on commercial activity. These numbers reflected the persistence, from feudal times, of Okayama's position as regional center of distribution and consumption. In the Tokugawa era, daimyo authorities used domain monopolies and the guild system to concentrate economic power in castle towns such as Okayama. Castle towns also housed the samurai population, which meant they served as the locus of consumption, drawing rice taxes, goods, and services into the urban economy to support the nonproductive samurai population.

In feudal Okayama, goods were moved in and out of the city by the river, which ran through the center of town to the main commercial districts and circled back behind the castle, forming a natural line of defense. Typical of the spatial organization of the Tokugawa period, Okayama was laid out in a pattern of streets centering on its castle complex. The castle was ringed by a series of concentric protective moats; within the first ring of moats and next to the castle were located the estates of the senior retainers. Since senior retainers served as the daimyo's military leaders, this arrangement was designed to fortify the castle. The main commercial district—Kaminochō and Nishidaiji—lay adjacent to the castle-side estates, just across the first of the encircling moats.

The advent of the railroad shifted commercial life away from the river, inaugurating the spatial reorganization of the city. This process began immediately and happened quickly. In the first year after the railroad opened, 75 percent of Okayama's freight traveled by rail and 25 percent by water. Mercantile neighborhoods near the river, such as Hashimotochō and Funatsukichō, lost their edge as custom shifted to warehousing and transport companies in the vicinity of the train station. It is possible to track the impact of the railway on commercial geography by comparing digests of local businesses published in 1898 and 1920. In terms of the numbers of merchants and of commercial taxes collected, the main neighborhoods of the old commercial center, located near the castle and the river—Nishidaiji, Kaminochō, and Nakanochō—emerge as the top three commercial districts in 1898. One-fifth of Okayama's merchants were concentrated in these three districts; together they paid a total of 2,452 yen in business taxes.

By 1920 the economic center of the city had shifted. A single neighborhood next to the train station, Kamiishichō, took the lead in commercial activity, attracting many of the city's larger firms and generating 2,917 yen in business taxes. A former agricultural village, Kamiishi was annexed to the city in 1898. Within twenty years, the railway transformed the village of Kamiishi into the district of Kamiishichō and the commercial heart of a major provincial city. Though they lost prominence to the neighborhoods near the station, former river-based mercantile districts such as Kaminochō were able to hold their

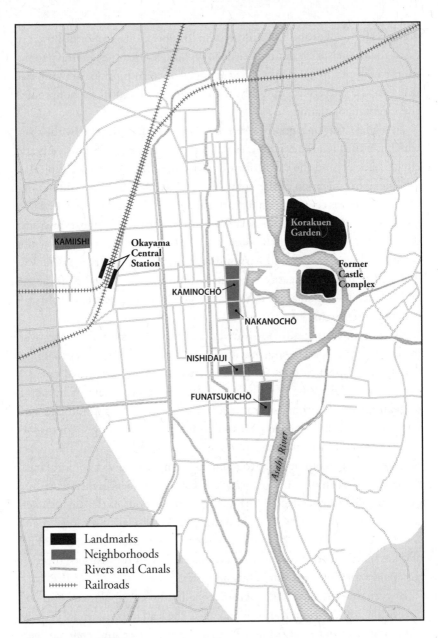

KAMIISHI

Okayama
Central
Station

Korakuen
Garden

Former
Castle
Complex

KAMINOCHŌ

NAKANOCHŌ

NISHIDAIJI

FUNATSUKICHŌ

Asahi River

Landmarks
Neighborhoods
Rivers and Canals
Railroads

MAP 3. Okayama, 1906

own as retail centers selling clothing and dry goods and, later, boasted department stores. In contrast, warehouses and trading operations, and banking and financial services, clustered in the Kamiishichō station district.[15] Much as it did for the national economy, the railroad reoriented local economic space, making peripheries into centers and turning cities inside out.

People at the time perceived the railway both as an engine of development and as a zero-sum game. Thus, along with schools, the location of the railway emerged as an object of intense competition between local communities. This competition dominated local politics in the Meiji period, creating the grounds for the spread of a nationwide party system through the mechanism of pork-barrel politics. Much as in the case of school building, national parties used promises of train routes to extend their influence into local communities, while local elites allied themselves to the political party best situated to deliver on local development aspirations. Adding to the mix was a lively debate between proponents of alternative conceptions of railway building: one advocated the establishment of rail in economically backward regions as an instrument of development, the other prioritized profitability, which dictated that new track had to be sited in areas with an established commercial and manufacturing base.[16] Success or failure in the railway sweepstakes often depended on local boosters' ability to deploy one or the other of these arguments, as well as on the strength of their political network. The politics of railway building frequently pitted neighboring communities against one another, and the bitter feelings engendered in these disputes often lived on to haunt schemes for urban expansionism for decades afterward.

In Niigata, railroad politics intensified in the 1890s, when the Hokuetsu Railway was deciding between alternative routes and station sites for the network that would connect the region with Tokyo. The Naoetsu Railway already ran as far Karuizawa, crossing the Usui Pass to the Pacific side of the Japanese Alps. The Hokuetsu Railway planned to link up with this track at the port city of Naoetsu on the coast of the Sea of Japan. The chosen route ran from Naoetsu along the coast to Kashiwazaki, where it tracked inland to Nagaoka and Niitsu, then headed back toward the coast to terminate at Niigata. On the eve of construction, scheduled to begin in 1896, this much was decided. But for Niigata city leaders the critical question remained: Where would the train terminal be located? Would it be in the city proper or in the neighboring town of Nuttari?

Business leaders in these sister towns on opposite banks of the Shinano River mobilized quickly to press their claims for the station. And both sides lobbied energetically with the Hokuetsu Railway, which was headquartered locally. As seat of prefectural government, Niigata felt it had the higher political claim, but Nuttari pressed its case based on physical geography and ease of construction. Since the Hokuetsu track approached the city on the Nuttari side of the river, a Niigata station would require a new iron bridge across the Shinano River, an expensive proposition. A group of Niigata entrepreneurs sought to counter this disadvantage by raising funds for the bridge. Large shareholders from Niigata pressed the company hard to make the city the site of the terminal. When the company appeared to be leaning toward a Nuttari site, Niigata citizens formed an organization to promote a station in their city, staging public rallies and firing off a series of petitions opposing the Nuttari station. The pressure grew so intense the Hokuetsu Railway Company felt compelled to move its headquarters from Niigata to Tokyo.

Though the politics of railway development mobilized both communities in opposition to one another, it also catalyzed divisions within the cities. In spite of the anti-Nuttari tone that dominated the Niigata station movement, there were those within the local organization who called for a different strategy. One group questioned the wisdom of hostility toward Nuttari and argued that Niigata's long-term economic interests were best served by cooperating with Nuttari to promote local development. When the company indicated its preference for the Nuttari location, they proposed that Niigata accept the loss with good grace and, at the same time, took the opportunity to push for administrative amalgamation between the twin cities and for joint investments in port facilities. Although in the long run this voice of conciliation would win the day, in the heat of the moment it was overwhelmed by the clamor for a short-term victory.

Cost considerations prevailed. The failure to finance the bridge doomed Niigata's hopes for a station on the west bank of the river. As a consolation, the railway company promised to build the station at the river's edge, just across from the (wooden) Bandai Bridge that constituted the main thoroughfare from Nuttari into Niigata. But because of the high price of the land, even this plan was abandoned, and the company chose a site some distance from the bridge, in the Takigashima district of Nuttari. To make matters worse, it was named Nuttari, rather than Niigata, station. Niigata residents were outraged, not the least because they foresaw that the new location, so distant from Niigata's commercial and manufacturing zone, would shift economic activity from Niigata's city center to a new hub around the Nuttari station. Feelings ran so high that when the company confirmed the choice for Nuttari, a group of angry residents impeded construction by blowing up an iron bridge on the Awanogi River. In 1899, in spite of obstruction and opposition, service opened on the Hokuetsu line between Ueno station in Tokyo and the newly constructed Nuttari station on the outskirts of Niigata. In the history of the railway, every station had a tale to tell. While the picture maps proudly trumpeted the expanding rail network as the march of progress, they concealed the trail of tears for those left off the iron track: the routes not taken, the losers in the politics of the railway. In Niigata's case the defeat was, at least, short-lived. Soon after the Nuttari station opened, the Hokuetsu bowed to pressure to build a second station; in 1904, on the east bank of the Shinano River, just steps from the Bandai Bridge, Niigata station opened for service.[17]

Nevertheless, hopes vested in the railway's ability to boost economic growth were destined for disappointment, at least in the near term. Indeed, the Niigata story largely supports Ericson's contention about the minimal economic impact of the railway in Meiji Japan. Though the city was connected to the railway through Nuttari station in 1899, both freight and passenger traffic remained essentially flat until 1904, when the Russo-Japanese War triggered a rise in rail use. Even worse, with the switch from water transport to rail, the port city seemed to have lost the geographic advantage of being located at the convergence of exterior and interior waterways. Before the advent of the railroad, Niigata's economy depended entirely on its port, which drew goods overland via river networks and by sea via coastal shipping routes. Through their strategic position in the water transportation grid, Niigata's merchants controlled all the freight in and out of the region. Now, landlocked cities such as Nagaoka and Sanjō, which formerly imported and exported goods by way of Niigata's port, could bypass Niigata and transport goods directly in and out of their towns. In this way the transportation revolution transformed Niigata from a hub in a water grid to a terminus in a rail network, siphoning business away from its merchants and placing it in the hands of Nagaoka and Sanjō businessmen. Regionally, the railroad produced very little net economic development; rather it shifted economic activity and profits from one site to another.[18]

But later, the situation changed again, as local entrepreneurs sought to turn the terminus back into a hub through the modernization and expansion of Niigata's port facilities. After the railroad killed the port, now its presence revived it. Both the opening of the Jōetsu line in 1931, which shrank travel time to Tokyo from twelve and a half to seven hours, and the acceleration of economic involvement with China after World War One enhanced the strategic importance of Niigata's port. And after the Manchurian Incident of 1931, with the reorientation of the Japanese economy toward Asia and the development of the yen bloc, fortune began to smile on Niigata's geography once again. Japan's economic thrust into China and Korea turned Niigata into a booming transshipment site, stimulating the rapid growth of warehousing, banking, and freight industries.[19] The unevenness of Niigata's experience demonstrated that the railway, like other agents of capitalism, could stimulate both the shrinking and the expansion of the local economy. Depending on the larger market context in which it operated, the railway could just as easily divert economic activity away from Niigata as toward it. After 1931 this larger market context shifted from the economic space of the Niigata region to the imperial core of the yen bloc—Korea, Manchuria, North China. As Niigata's economy grew fat off the profits generated by the port and the carrying trade with Asia, a new economic redistribution was at work, draining the Manchurian, North Chinese, and Korean economies, siphoning off their economic surplus through the ports along the coast of the Sea of Japan into Japan.

As the Niigata story reveals, the economic impact of railway building was complex and uneven. The new railway grid—organized according to the logic of a capitalist market, guided by state development policy, and oriented to a world economy—produced integrated, economic space that was territorialized along the physical sites of the railway lines. The economic stimulation of the railway was allocated unevenly; fortunes of regions, cities, and neighborhoods rose and fell depending on where they were located along the railway grid. But this was not a simple story of winners and losers, of fateful and permanent underdevelopment. As rail lines proliferated, economic space shifted again and again, making winners of losers and losers of winners. Moreover, as local residents embraced the instrumentalities of the railroad for a variety of developmental projects, an animated and frequently pugnacious railroad politics emerged. Economic space became shot through with politics, creating a political economy around the railroad.

REGIONAL TRANSPORTATION GRIDS

In terms of urban economies, the first phase of railway building effected a number of changes. In a large sense, the railroad repositioned cities relative to one another. Coastal cities along the Sea of Japan linked up to Osaka and Tokyo instead of each other; Nagaoka gained importance and Niigata lost importance within regional trade routes. Within cities, new rivalries broke out, pitting former villages against the old commercial centers. But the constitution of the urban-rural system singularly characteristic of Japanese modernity awaited the second phase of the transportation revolution. For the regional transportation grids laid down in the teens and twenties opened up new kinds of relationships between city and country—creating "town and country" as an integrated economic space and an economic system that structured the dynamics of regional markets. The impact of this regional railroad building was both material and ideological: it created a communications and market infrastructure that was connected to a new set of ideas about the importance of urban growth.

At the head of the train of urban expansionism was the ongoing transportation revolution, which entered a new phase with the economic boom of World War One. Two developments inaugurated the second phase of the transportation revolution: the electrification of existing track, improving speed and performance, and the creation of a network of feeder lines branching out from the main railroad grid, granting rail transportation between provincial cities and their surrounding countryside. In the teens and twenties, cities built streetcars that connected downtown districts with industrial and residential developments springing up on the outskirts of the city lines. They laid tracks for light-rail to nearby mountains and beaches. In surrounding villages and towns, new train stations appeared in rapid succession. If Meiji was the "railroad age," Taishō was the era of light-rail. Over the period (1912–1926), on average, 200 miles of track were added every year, reaching 3,100 miles of new track by the end of the era.[20] The massive expansion of regional rail networks transformed the local landscape, creating circuits of exchange between city and country that augmented the political-economic power of provincial cities. A new economic geography emerged, composed of regional centers and their rural hinterlands. Drawn into the orbit of provincial cities through rail systems, nearby towns and villages became secondary, auxiliaries to the urban economy. This relationship characterized the urban-rural system in modern Japan.

Near Kanazawa, for example, a burst of rail building in the teens and twenties added more than 80 miles of new track to the 150 miles that comprised the Hokuriku and Nanao Railways, laid during the first phase of railway building in the late nineteenth century. By 1927, Ishikawa prefecture boasted eight new regional lines. Some of these connected Kanazawa to hot springs resorts and coastal towns, while others ran from the prefectural capital to other major cities in the region. The newly built city tramway operated a municipal route as well as lines to Kanazawa's nearby towns.[21] Much like the national rail system, the local networks created new forms of economic space. In Ishikawa the transport grid brought people and goods in and through Kanazawa, enhancing its position as the center of a system of circulation and exchange.

Within provincial cities, the success of tramways introduced in the teens led to a succession of improvements in service and the expansion of lines. In Sapporo, the horse-drawn streetcar was upgraded to electricity on the occasion of the Hokkaido Exhibit of 1918 commemorating the fiftieth anniversary of the colonization of Hokkaido. Over the course of the following decade, service expanded twelve times, extending the original three and a half miles of track into a network that encompassed more than ten miles of track. These improvements were accompanied by a dramatic rise in usage. Between 1918 and 1927, the number of riders jumped from 1.5 million to nearly 15 million. Given that Sapporo's population increased over the same period from 90,000 to 150,000, these ridership statistics suggest that a very high percentage of the local population used the trams to move about the city on a daily basis. Although a large share of ridership was probably commuting to Sapporo's new suburbs, the tram was clearly central to physical movement through and about the city.[22]

The extension of light-rail over the course of the teens and twenties meant that provincial cities were transformed from single-station towns to multistation towns. In Niigata, a progression of new stations opened up in the teens and twenties, spurring the extension of urban land use along the rail lines, as well as commercial growth in the immediate vicinity of the stations. Both developments accelerated the trend toward land use specialization and the creation of a new social geography that divided the city into industrial, commercial, and residential zones, and which segregated urban residents by class. Niigata's first station, built across the Shinano River in Nuttari, went up in 1898. A second station in downtown Niigata opened in 1904, offering fourteen-hour service to Tokyo. In 1912 both stations were connected to the Kansai rail network, shrinking travel time to Osaka to seventeen hours. In 1913 the long-distance Echigo Railroad opened two new stations on the western fringes of the city; in the late twenties Niigata built a rail spur for freight service to its port facility; and in 1932 the city began operating electric tram service that ran west to the nearby town of Tsubame.[23] A local industrial guide boasted, "With the new rail connections, Niigata will become the central junction on the rail system along *ura Nihon* [Japan's back coast]." By connecting Niigata's port through rail to the Pacific Ocean ports in Tokyo and Yokohama, the new rail constructions would make "Niigata famous as the hub of rail and sea as well as the commercial capital of northern Japan."[24] As the extension of rail into the city showed, Nuttari had won the first round in the railroad sweepstakes, but the commercial promise of its station was quickly eclipsed by developments in Niigata's western side, where the city's expanding industrial belt and residential settlements grew up around the new transportation grid.[25]

Alongside the proliferation of feeder lines, investments in an improved network of roads and the establishment of bus and taxi services pushed the transportation revolution to a new level. If Taishō was the era of light-rail, it also marked the coming of the automobile, which quickly assumed a prominent place in the iconography of urban modernity. The big initiative in road building occurred in the twenties, propelled by the administrative city planning movement. Starting with the "big six" cities designated by the state as first tier (Tokyo, Osaka, Yokohama, Nagoya, Kyoto, Kobe), the Home Ministry identified particular cities as qualifying for city planning regulation. Responding to urban sprawl and the surging demand for new city services, most cities had, by the late teens, entered into a planning process on their own; nevertheless the City Planning Law (*toshi keikaku hō*) provided a uniform set of guidelines for this purpose. The City Planning Law helped establish mechanisms for public finance and a regulatory framework to control urban expansion through zoning, the development of parks and recreational spaces, the relocation of existing urban amenities to new regions, slum clearance, and the like.[26] The municipal bureaucrats involved in the planning were not antigrowth; far from it, they saw urban planning as the means to promote the physical expansion of the city as a necessary component to economic development and social policy. In their view, the state was best situated to establish priorities and to balance conflicting interests.

For cities such as Okayama and Niigata, part of the second wave of twenty-four cities designated under the City Planning Law in 1923, roads were a major focus of public investment and one of the primary instruments deployed to direct the physical expansion of the city. Prior to the adoption of the city plan, Okayama's municipal government built a few roads into new suburban districts, but after 1923 the modernization of the road grid to facilitate movement of freight and passenger traffic through the city and onto the rail corridors was made a municipal government priority. In the vision of city planners, the new road grid became a primary mechanism for the division of the city into residential, commercial, and industrial land use zones. Much of the rationalization of road networks took place in the late twenties and early thirties, a point when Okayama developed a modern taxonomy for its road system, classifying them by width. Under the city plan, thirty boulevards, twelve avenues, and fourteen streets were widened to the prescribed dimensions and rerouted to transform the winding circle of roads centering on the castle into a grid pattern designed to converge on the town center and the railway station.[27]

Prior to the second wave of town plans, there were few cars outside the metropolis, and even in Japan's first tier cities the numbers were unimpressive. Statistics for 1910 reveal seventy cars registered to owners in Tokyo, five in Osaka, and none in Kyoto. The road building of the 1920s that stimulated the physical expansion of second-tier cities also ushered in the era of the automobile. Although the first generation of car owners included foreign dignitaries, aristocrats, and a few company presidents, the automobile did not spread in Japan as a single-family vehicle, but rather through the fleets of passenger transport companies running bus and taxi services. Before improvements, however, road quality posed a major obstacle to any attempt to exploit the potential of the automobile for mass transit, as one car-owning entrepreneur in Okayama discovered.

The first car in Okayama was a Studebaker purchased by Nishio Gentarō for five thousand yen in 1912. His driver commanded a salary of fifty yen, a handsome sum at a time when a rookie patrolman earned nine yen per month. Nishio initially used his car to operate a ten-sen taxi service from Okayama station to Higashiyama, where a Children's Fair was being held. In 1914 he secured a license to run the city's first bus service, making round-trips between Okayama station and Tamashima station in the neighboring city of Kurashiki. But because of opposition from drivers of jinrickshas, the hand-pulled carts that had served as urban taxis since the early Meiji period, he was forced to close operations. Next he tried switching routes, but the roads were too narrow for comfort. The noise of the car continually startled the livestock in its path, and his driver found himself colliding with horse-drawn carts and wagons. Nishio's bus service shut down after a brief, difficult run: the poor roads had defeated him.[28]

The real growth of bus service awaited the road-building projects of the twenties. The Japanese buses of the interwar period were the equivalent of present-day minivans, seating between six and ten passengers. By the late twenties, this form of mass transit had taken root in most provincial cities. According to statistics in the *Japan City Yearbook*, in 1930 there were 17,522 vehicles nationwide, owned by 3,770 companies and individuals. These fleets of cars served routes covering 68,829 miles. For Okayama prefecture, this broke down to eighty-five bus companies operating 330 vehicles over routes that covered 1,643 miles.[29] Bus service developed to complement and extend the rail and tram service, often running between cities and towns. In Okayama, after Nishio's failure, a bus service opened in 1917 between Okayama city and Bizen city. Service was extended and improved in the 1920s, with a new route established between Okayama and Tsuyama city. By 1927, the bus company operated a fleet of six vehicles, making nine round-trips per day; by the mid-1930s, bus service had become so competitive in terms of service and fare that it began to compete with the railroad, prompting the Chūgoku Railway Company to buy the local bus company.

As the following table shows, the automobile had, by the late twenties, cut into the number of other forms of transportation, in particular jinrickshas and horse-drawn carriages. Despite their resistance, carriages were all but eliminated and jinrickshas fell sharply between 1912 and 1928. The other striking statistic to note here is the dramatic rise in bicycle use. The spread of this form of transportation, like that of the automobile, followed the development of a paved road system. Paved roads that connected cities to nearby towns and villages made commuting by bicycle possible not only for work but also for shopping and entertainment. Like the expansion of suburban bus service, the rise in bicycle use expanded the territorial reach of the urban economy. The ubiquity of both automobiles and bicycles in provincial cities such as Okayama was captured in a 1932 photograph of Kyōbashi Bridge, which shows several pedestrians, some fifteen bicycles, and nine cars making the crossing.[30]

The transportation revolution of the teens and twenties made the electric streetcar and the automobile into preeminent symbols of urban modernity, even as they transformed the built environment of the city. Images of sleek, streamlined trains and fleets of automobiles neatly lined up alongside the train station became ubiquitous decorations in city guides of the period. The modernist aesthetic that invariably infused graphic representations of trains and automobiles conveyed a sense of innovation and progress. Such images captured popular belief that the transportation revolution would become an engine for local development and the key to vigorous economic growth in the

Vehicular statistics for Okayama Prefecture

Type of Vehicle	1912	1919	1924	1928
Motorized passenger vehicles	1	42	220	610
Motorized freight vehicles	0	0	4	254
Horse-drawn carriages	44	30	7	2
Jinrickshas	4,787	3,746	2,685	1,490
Bicycles	15,000	54,000	108,000	138,000
Motorcycles	0	46	183	616

SOURCE: Hōgō Iwao, ed., *Me de miru Okayama no Taishō* (Okayama: Nihon Bunkyō Shuppan, 1986), 17.

future. And yet, hidden behind the seductive vision of the train as an engine of progress were the vast numbers of communities left out of its path, for whom railway development signified loss of resources and missed opportunities.

For both winners and losers in the railway sweepstakes, the impact of light-rail and road building was readily apparent in both visible and invisible ways. In a large sense, these developments produced integrated regional economies that territorialized circuits of production and exchange along the physical sites of tracks and roads. The new spatial logic imposed by the transportation grid reoriented local geography and altered forms of production. Its effects, moreover, were distributed unevenly, as placement of roads, train lines, and stations opened up possibilities for some communities and closed them off for others. This dynamic shaped the patterns of land use and the divisions of labor within cities and regions, constituting space around economic function and giving rise to new social geographies. All this transformed the status of cities within their regional economies.

THE "BIG CITY" MOVEMENT

The proliferation of regional transportation grids led in the twenties and thirties to the production of new forms of economic space. Rail and roads, trains and buses, extended the economic reach of the city, expanding the boundaries of local labor, commodity, and retail markets. The impact registered most dramatically on the rural communities located in close proximity to cities; these communities were brought into subordinate relationships to the cities because of transport systems. What had formerly been autonomous, self-sustaining villages now became orbital communities and extensions of the urban economy—part of a larger field of economic specialization that reorganized social and productive space. As cities grew and commerce and industry concentrated in urban centers, nearby communities were absorbed into a widespread reorganization of space. New geographic divisions of labor and specialization of land use turned nearby villages into economic dependents; many were subsequently slated for annexation. Even if they maintained their nominal independence, satellite communities now had their fate determined by decisions made in the city; fortunes rose and fell on the vicissitudes of the urban economy. They became, in effect, urban colonies: targeted for housing tracts to accommodate urban workers, for industrial development zones to accommodate new factory production. Throughout Japan, this dynamic reshaped regional economies into a characteristic pattern, where large provincial cities connected themselves to a ring of satellite communities—the villages and towns that lived in the shadow of the urban economy.

Urban expansionism, with its characteristic geography of orbital villages, represented a phenomenon widely embraced by urban boosters in the interwar period. This was the age of the "*dai*" (greater) movements, when cities added the prefix *greater* to their designations to applaud the territorial aggrandizement of the city. When the language of "Greater Sapporo" and "Greater Niigata" infused the lexicon of urban administration and business plans, cities loomed larger: they were monumentalized.

The impact of these movements registered in the primacy of the urban form and its triumph over the countryside, even as urban expansionism encountered a surge of rural fundamentalism and the rise of agrarianism as a potent political movement. The institutional structures that undergirded the city's domination of the countryside included the growth of municipal governments and their expanded authority through city planning and social policy. Urban power was likewise anchored in the interests of private enterprise—real estate developers, manufacturing firms, the leisure and tourist industry—and their increasingly powerful business organizations. Municipal power brokers deployed all the considerable tools at their disposal to promote urban growth, disseminating an urban-centric view of the countryside under the banner of the "big city" (*dai toshi*) movements that flourished in the teens and twenties. Nevertheless, there were many who viewed urban expansionism with trepidation. Defenders of the countryside pointed to the importance of protecting "Japanese tradition" and the viability of the agricultural economy. They noted that urban expansion had exacerbated problems associated with rural overpopulation and poverty and led to the rise of social tensions in the countryside. But although appeals to communitarian ideals and calls for a return to the simple life may have found favor among segments of the Japanese population, and although agrarianist political parties were bankrolled by some powerful people, agrarianism did not prove a match—either as ideology or as politics—for the material forces driving urban expansion. While urban growth was welcomed in some quarters as the triumph of progress, others denounced it as a modern leviathan. If the proponents of urban growth and their adversaries agreed on anything, it was that the forces pushing cities outward were indeed overwhelming.

The urban expansionism set in motion by the transportation revolution gave cities a voracious appetite for land. Spreading outward into the surrounding countryside, cities colonized nearby farm villages, bringing them into the orbit of the city and reshaping them into part of an urban-suburban complex. This occurred in part through the conversion of agricultural land for urban use as city populations rose—the physical expansion of the city by building houses and factories in the rice paddies. Though new transportation grids accelerated this process, they did not always precede it. Certainly, rail access facilitated the enormous and rapid demographic growth of cities in post-World-War-One Japan, but this represented only one of the factors driving the great rural-urban migrations of these years.

Niigata's experience was a common one and reveals how demographic growth generated intense outward pressure to alleviate the shortage of housing at factory sites. Niigata's population rose from 65,475 in 1912 to 131,675 by 1930, an increase arising partly from the amalgamation of Nuttari village but also from a significant in-migration to the city. Growth of industry and population influx created an acute housing shortage. In 1924, of the 20,850 urban households in Niigata, 5,422 owned their own home.[31] Many of these were longtime Niigata residents who lived in neighborhoods like Furumachi and Honchō, the old city center near the entry ramps to Bandai Bridge. There was only limited rental housing available in these areas, mostly along the backs of commercial property. New rental housing was erected in Gakkōchō and Tanakachō to accommodate the new arrivals, whether they came for white-collar employment or as factory hands. Much of this was shoddy construction for factory workers and day laborers, but even middle-class housing was substandard and subject to collapse. With new oil-processing factories built along the Shinano River, working-class tenements sprang up in Sekiya, at Niigata's ragged urban edge. Amalgamated with Niigata district prior to its incorporation as a city in 1889, the west side neighborhood grew rapidly, even before the Echigo Railway opened Sekiya station in 1913. In 1888 Sekiya's population comprised 88 households (572 individuals); by 1911 it expanded to 306 households, with a total population of 1,573.[32] Niigata was not alone in experiencing this pace of growth. Here, as elsewhere, the development of factories and housing along the urban edge propelled cities to chew up agricultural land along their peripheries. The drive toward suburbanization had begun.

Alongside the birth of the suburbs through land use conversion, urban expansionism brought nearby farming villages under the domination of the city. Turned into agricultural suppliers for the urban economy, such villages simultaneously became dependent for commercial supplies on the urban market, which drew them ever more tightly into the economic orbit of the city. And like suburbanization, economic integration proceeded rapidly in the wake of the railroad. In Niigata's case, for example, commercial life was decentralized and dispersed among the nearby farm villages prior to the advent of rail. Both the city of Niigata and its proximate agricultural villages possessed retail economies; the latter were largely independent of the Niigata market. Nearby villages like Nuttari, Ryōkawa, Matsugasakihama, and Uchinō, which relied on river transport, all ran thriving markets and supported a small number of merchants along their main streets. Markets were held three times a month and typically drew between thirty and fifty stalls that sold foodstuffs, secondhand clothing, sundries, and other goods for daily life. In spite of Niigata's size and more extensive range of goods, nearby residents traveled there infrequently, perhaps once or twice a year.

This situation began to change dramatically around the turn of the century. With the establishment of railway stations in Nuttari and Niigata, both sites became commercial centers for the region. The number and frequency of their markets rose and merchant establishments proliferated. In nearby villages, markets did not disappear, but the mix of goods available for sale changed. Now they sold vegetables and fruits, and Niigata customers became some of their main clientele.[33] Moreover, as villages reoriented their production toward the urban market, they replaced rice with new crops and began to specialize. Villages like Toriyano and Ishiyama focused on vegetables, with particular hamlets concentrating on single crops such as radish or eggplant. Other villages brought out new crops such as tomato and cabbage.[34] In this way, regional transportation grids extended the reach of Niigata's urban economy, turning farmers in nearby villages into producers for and consumers of an expanded, urban-centered market. Whether it was houses or vegetables that took their place, the rice paddies were gone and the countryside would never the look the same.

Urban expansionism and the passion for "bigness" were reflected in the ongoing waves of annexations in the teens, twenties, and thirties—an urban juggernaut with no end in sight. In Sapporo, sections of four of its seven satellite villages were annexed in 1910, adding more than ten thousand people and 3 million tsubo of land to the city population.[35] Another major annexation occurred in 1934. Niigata amalgamated the neighboring village of Nuttari in pieces in 1915 and 1918, adding close to 2 million tsubo to the city and almost doubling the territorial jurisdiction of the city.[36] Extended negotiations with three nearby villages in the 1930s yielded a major amalgamation in 1943, multiplying the city's territory nearly fourfold and increasing the population to 191,000.[37] Kanazawa annexed parts of three nearby villages in 1910 and 1925, and Okayama amalgamated nearby villages in 1899, 1921 and 1931.[38] The consequences of these annexations varied widely for the communities involved; as we shall see there was no single story of "the Japanese suburb." But such variations—the costs as well as the benefits and the unevenness that attended urban expansion—always seemed to get lost in the consuming fever for growth.

Blessed by the central government and proliferating rapidly throughout the country, town plans drawn up in the early twenties leant credence to the idea that territorial expansion of cities was an inexorable force of modernization. And because the city planning movement endorsed rational growth as an instrument for progress, it helped install the idea of a manifest destiny for the city. Designed to place development under administrative control and to bring urban sprawl under a regime of planned and managed growth, city plans included in their purview the nearby villages that had come within the economic orbit of the city. Even villages not administratively annexed to a municipality came under its informal economic jurisdiction. When these villages were brought into the administrative gaze of urban planners, infrastructural improvements and new road systems sealed their fate and signaled eventual amalgamation of the villages into the city.

Though the experience of amalgamation was fraught with political tensions and its economic impact was unevenly felt, accounts of urban expansion that poured forth from chambers of commerce, travel bureaus, railroad companies, municipal offices, and newspapers turned this rocky course into a smooth highway of progress rolling forth from the city. Paeans to development highlighted the importance of new communications infrastructure, celebrating the building boom that added roads, rail beds, bridges, and ports to their communities. To be sure, disaggregating the interests of the communities and individuals affected by the creation of "Greater Niigata" and "Greater Sapporo" reveals a wide range of costs and benefits for those involved. But whatever the overall balance sheet of urban expansion, the people making the largest investment (taxpayers) and the people making the largest profits (private enterprise) were rarely the same.

Boosters for development in Niigata published stacks of books and pamphlets over the course of the teens, twenties, and thirties, all promoting the message that growth was good. To this end, city leaders advocated the expansion of the port, which they regarded as the linchpin of their strategy for economic development. A pamphlet published in 1936, *Prospects for Niigata's Advance*, explained this course of action. Noting the importance of harbor construction that had taken place in the early Meiji period, the bank work along the Shinano River to protect the city from the catastrophic flooding that occurred nearly every winter, as well as the improvement in harbor facilities in 1926, the book proclaimed, "Riparian construction constituted a major turning point for industrial development in the Echigo region and stimulated the growth of Niigata. . . . Now in name and reality Niigata boasts the only river harbor of its kind. With the establishment of educational institutions and a railway grid, and the flourishing of commerce, Niigata has become a metropolis of water, a city of willows, and a harbor of beautiful women . . . and is advancing by leaps and bounds."[39] And with the timely establishment of the puppet state of Manchukuo in Japanese-occupied Manchuria "ushering in the age of the Sea of Japan," Niigata was poised for further improvement, "expanding its harbor facilities and pouring efforts into city planning to become a great city."[40]

What the port did to nurture the rise of "greater Niigata," the railway did for Kanazawa. The new communications grid broke Kanazawa's stultifying isolation and catalyzed the growth of commerce, industry, and population. Deploying the classic enlightenment trope of awakening, the *Kanazawa City Reader* explained:

Looking back, we see that until the mid-Meiji period, our city was in a state of extreme stagnation and decline; half the former samurai estates were empty and overgrown with weeds. But afterward, with the completion of the

Hokuriku Railway and the reemergence of social prosperity, the great efforts of our leaders have brought about the rise of production, especially industrial production, and Kanazawa has awakened. Today our city is proud to occupy the heart of the Hokuriku region. The 1919 street improvements and the beginning of operation of a city tram—and before this, the amalgamation of the two villages Nomura and Yumitori—have made Kanazawa into a great city.[41]

In the views of local boosters, the new communications infrastructure triggered a wave of growth and ushered in a halcyon age of urban prosperity. In Sapporo, too, local boosters celebrated the development of transportation infrastructure. Arguing that "roads are the forerunners of civilization," *A Guide to Greater Sapporo* proudly detailed "expensive and difficult" investments in roads during the first stages of colonization that yielded the proliferating network of roads and rail in the city.[42] For the promoters of "greater Sapporo" roads represented the agent of progress and civilization, much as railways and ports signified engines of local development elsewhere. Roads meant growth, and growth was good, not just because it ushered in progress, but also because it produced "greatness."

For the interwar generation, the principal marker of urban greatness was size. To be great meant to be big; and the bigger the better. Urban size, measured in population, number of factories, and territorial jurisdiction became the new metric of value for cities. Books like *Prospects for Niigata's Advance* were laced with laudatory references to "greater Niigata" and the "great city" that specified these terms through attendant data points. Pointing triumphantly to Niigata's population growth "from 34,375 in 1877 . . . to 65,475 in 1912 . . . to 149,175 in 1935," *Prospects* applauded plans to amalgamate more nearby villages and "boost the population over the 150,000 mark."[43] Likewise the book spoke approvingly of the proliferating bus and train routes connecting Niigata with surrounding towns and villages, and the city plan for further growth with its blueprint for a "grand industrial zone near the harbor, with access to worker housing, water supplies, rail transport, and a large market."[44] Territorial amalgamations, multiplying factories, rising population, proliferating rail lines, an expanding market—these were the touchstones of progress and the sign of a vital, healthy city. Niigata, they promised, was destined for greatness.

Much like city boosters in Niigata, those in Kanazawa endorsed the city plan as the key to bringing about the benefits of growth to ensure "greatness": "For our city of Kanazawa the city plan is the ideal instrument for bringing about rapid development of Greater Kanazawa internally and externally, making us the greatest city in *ura Nihon* [Japan's back coast] in name and reality. In its promise to bring the best minds to build houses, roads ... railways, sewer systems, hospitals, music performance halls, playhouses, zoos, sporting grounds, parks, libraries, religious facilities, schools, and government buildings, this city plan is the best gift we could bequeath to our future generations."[45] Greatness here was defined in terms of rapid development, in boasting the "best" new urban amenities. The city plan would secure Kanazawa's place as a regional leader—the "greatest city in *ura Nihon*." Therefore Kanazawa boosters applauded annexations, as well as industrial, communications, and physical expansion—echoing the growth agenda of the city government.[46]

The growth agenda encapsulated in the first generation of city plans embraced many laudable goals: infrastructural improvement to reduce public health threats such as typhus and tuberculosis, the creation of public amenities such as libraries and parks to improve the lives of urban residents. And yet, these plans also promoted a set of assumptions about the relationship between city growth and urban health. Physical expansion of cities became an indication of urban vitality. By extension, a lack of population rise or territorial growth signaled stagnation and crisis. Likewise, town plans assumed that the only means to address urban social problems such as public health or lack of recreational facilities was through physical expansion. Whether or not there were other means to the same end, the city plan validated the colonization of rural space for the prosperity of the modern city.

The ideology of the "big city" taking hold at this time also expressed itself through urban-centrism. Urban-centrism was signified in many ways: the material advantages accruing to cities through their privileged capacity to attract human and material resources; the idea that cities were modern and that they represented Japan's future; and the tendency to frame arguments from the vantage point of an urban subject. In the literature of the "big city" movements, urban-centrism emerged in the tendency to trumpet a particular city's position as a regional center. In Okayama, local boosters liked to boast about their city's importance to the region. An article titled "Expanding Okayama" exclaimed, "From a variety of perspectives our Okayama is clearly the single greatest city in the Chūgoku region."[47] The "Okayama City Song" stressed the blessings of geography that situated Okayama where it could look down upon the towns and villages around it. Penned during a fad for urban anthems, the "Okayama City Song" was a classic example of its kind, disseminating the mantra of urban expansionism and linking this idea to civic pride and local identity. As the song stressed, the city's rising economic and cultural position mirrored its geographic prominence.

Overflowing with the riches of the Great Kibi Plain,
Looking out onto the Inland Sea,
Sitting astride the Asahi River,
The great metropolis that expands day after day—
Our own greater Okayama city!

To the West and East and South and North
Assemble and are redistributed people and commodities.
Unashamed to be called an industrial and commercial city,
A communications hub on sea, air, and land—
Our own greater Okayama city!

The single cultural capital of the Chūgoku region,
Gathering praise and glory from throughout the land,
Boasting every variety of school,
The heartland of an education prefecture—
Our own greater Okayama city!

The sites of old Bizen, redolent of a great past,
Like the smart colors of the tower of Ujō Castle
Or the striking cranes of Kōrakuen Gardens,
These scenic places that still evoke the spirits of illustrious retainers and wise
rulers—
Ah! Our own greater Okayama city.[48]

What made Okayama great? Natural topography, a unique cultural heritage, natural bounty—but especially, its position as the axis of economic activity and as the cultural capital of the region made Okayama a "great metropolis that expands day after day."

Similar sentiments infused the enthusiastic embrace of "Sapporo-centrism" (Sapporo chūshinshugi) and the celebration of Sapporo's rise in the official city ranking.[49] "Now our city occupies a territory of 7,320,000 tsubo and commands a population of 170,000—ranking us tenth in the country. If the trend in rapid growth continues, we are looking at a population of 500,000 in the near future. To embrace this population we should have a hundred-year great plan, starting with the city center and encompassing the five nearby villages."[50] Great expectations, indeed, for the Sapporo community. In celebrating "bigness" and trumpeting rapid and ongoing growth as the mark of a prosperous city and a matter of local pride, the Guide to Greater Sapporo joined a chorus of urban boosters who constructed a manifest destiny for the city—an ideology of urban expansionism.

In spite of the drumbeat of support for the growth agenda, for the city that "expands day after day," there were those that refused to join the march. In Niigata, amalgamation with Nuttari in the teens was delayed because of squeamishness on both sides of the river generated by the earlier battles over the railway. Later in the thirties, industrialists promoted amalgamation of nearby villages as part of ambitious plans for a sprawling industrial zone stretching out from the city on all sides. Again, opposition from the village populations concerned effectively blocked these plans until wartime demand accelerated local industrialization. When the spread of industry into the villages made incorporation a fait accompli, villagers relinquished their opposition and agreed to merge with the city.[51]

In Okayama, the same economic journal that published the "Okayama City Song" also ran a sharp critique of the "fever" for amalgamation. The author, Okada Chō, was a local businessman who questioned the idea that expansion universally benefited cities on both economic and political grounds. Okada's concern with the issue arose from the concentration of his business interests in downtown Okayama. He wanted neither the rise of a rival business district on the outskirts of the city, nor to have precious taxes diverted to infrastructural investments outside the central city. To this end, he advocated a careful examination of the costs and benefits of amalgamation, adjuring city residents not to be blinded by the dazzle of "greatness."

> Recently, city residents look upon the expansion of the city limits as a matter for celebration. At the same time people from nearby villages are proud to become urbanites. . . . Though urban amalgamations of local towns and villages has become a kind of fad, . . . we should distinguish between amalgamation proposals based on sound financial considerations and those that are simply harebrained, bumptious schemes. . . . We need to encourage the former and soundly reject the latter.
>
> When Yokohama recently expanded its city limits, there was nothing harebrained about it, but next came Nagoya's expansion—a project puffed up by mindless boosterism. The annexations undertaken by Osaka and Kyoto were crude appeals to urban pride, plain and simple. And needless to say, expansionism in places like Hiroshima is only more of the same.[52]

Pointing out the inflated promises of the annexationist agenda, Okada highlighted the ideological dimension to urban expansionism.

Trying to puncture the puffery of "mindless boosterism," Okada countered the case for amalgamation point by point. Since boosters frequently invoked population growth as a benefit of village amalgamation, he noted that even with the additional population, Okayama's national ranking would not change: "we would still be ranked 18, doing nothing to satisfy our vanity and ambition."[53] In answer to claims by advocates of the "garden city movement" that more city land promoted access to green space and a healthier, freer lifestyle, Okada countered that urban beautification could take place within the existing city limits. The annexation of undeveloped farmland would provide nothing new to Okayama residents, he insisted. And while the push for amalgamation of Hirai, Uno, and Fukuhama villages was intended to gain access to the seashore for Okayama, mere annexation on paper would not serve this purpose because the three lacked the basic infrastructure to attract people and to accommodate them when they came. Annexation, in his view, was premature.

He also made a fiscal case against amalgamation:

> If you look at the different elements of urban infrastructure, from education, to construction, to waterworks, most of the new roads, new elementary schools, and new sewer facilities are being built in newly amalgamated areas. What this means is that these areas are sucking up the city budget. The main burden for paying for this new development falls, needless to say, on the business district in the city center. In other words, the main share of the tax burden falls on the residents in the center, who are reaping no benefit from the allocation of their tax yen.[54]

Okada explained that blueprints for third and fourth amalgamations would only exacerbate this process, diverting scarce financial resources into the suburbs and draining the center of funds it required for its own infrastructural needs.

Finally, Okada argued that territorial expansion held a political downside for the city center. With Okayama's first amalgamation, the new suburbs gained eight representatives to the city council; the districts in the second amalgamation received five. The amalgamation currently being contemplated would add another four or five new representatives. What this meant, he stressed, was that about half the city council would represent the suburbs, considerably diluting the voice of the central business district and the urban core of Okayama in local politics.[55]

In the short run, Okada's worst fears were not realized. The amalgamations he opposed were forestalled until after World War Two, when they occurred as part of a new wave of annexations that followed reconstruction and economic recovery. Nevertheless, the fever for urban growthism that picked up steam in the postwar built on the foundations of the big city movement. By the 1930s, the idea that growth was good was already etched in the popular mind as a bromide of modern life. According to the growth creed, cities that did not expand were stagnant, on their way to obscurity and decline. Because size conferred power—economic, political, and cultural—cities needed to grow, and the bigger the better. Growth benefited cities, but boosters stressed the advantages for villages, as well. For the rolling concrete frontier brought social progress, economic development, cultural uplift, and political empowerment to the countryside, the putative fruits of urban life. Bequeathed to future generations, the growth fetish structured the governing approaches to cities in postwar Japan and endorsed the seeming inevitability of urban expansionism.

In the context of interwar Japan, this vision of urban triumphalism exerted extraordinary influence on the politics of city planning. The most serious assault on urban-centrism was mounted by the agrarianist movement in the 1930s, where antiurban feeling found purchase in calls for the resurrection of an agriculture-centered social order and a redistribution of resources back to the villages. But even here agrarianists made little headway in their efforts to stop the urban colonization of the villages. Instead, they were bought off by the promise of free land in Manchuria—the empire providing a spatial fix to the "problem of the villages" triggered by urban expansion of the teens and twenties.

The ideology of urban expansionism composed one thread of a tapestry of meaning that constituted the city idea in interwar Japan. Like the myth of the railway as an engine for development, the fever for growth spread the idea that cities represented the singular path to progress and economic betterment. Not only did the city represent the best entry point to the future, it was the only way to get there. Just as the railway mythology overlooked the losers in railway-led development, the idea of urban expansionism created a conceptual vocabulary that expressed development only in terms of a limited menu of lifestyle improvements, and in which a term like *modern village* was an oxymoron. One place where these modern myths came together with peculiar force was the suburb. Though suburbs came to be imagined as the ultimate symbol of the homogenizing effects of urban modernization and cookie-cutter development, the idea of the suburb that took hold during these years masked a material reality of striking unevenness and variation.

One of the most momentous consequences of urban expansionism in the teens and twenties was the proliferation of suburban communities in the orbits of Japan's cities, great and small. This was the moment when the suburb emerged as a sociospatial form: when suburbs developed particular material characteristics, and when they became integral components of urban economies, polities, and societies. As we have seen, the expanded road, rail, and other transportation networks became engines for uneven development at national and regional levels. Within cities and their orbital communities, these same networks were central agents in the social production of space. Though historians tend to ignore suburbs as marginal and uninteresting facets of the urban story, in fact suburbs underlay the rise of urban-centrism and constituted a central component of the urban-rural system taking shape at this time. And yet the idea of "the suburb" was uneasily located in the epistemology of "town and country" as mutually exclusive categories. Neither one nor the other, the suburb occupied a liminal social and physical space between city and countryside.

Just as the suburb emerged as an integral element of Japanese cities, it also began to capture the artistic imagination. In the depictions by writers such as Tanizaki Jun'ichirō and directors such as Ozu Yasujirō, an image of the suburb took shape: middle class, bucolic, and modern.[56] So-called garden cities (den'en toshi), "culture villages" (bunka machi), and the like conjured up images of rows of single-family homes along tree-lined boulevards. With their cookie-cutter, vaguely western-style appearance, the homes in these imagined suburban communities seemed culturally hollowed out, places without tradition or heritage. Much like broader stereotypes of city and country, such images masked the tremendous diversity in suburban social forms.

Though the particular configuration of the suburban landscape varied from city to city, some sense of the magnitude and scale of the urban transformation of these years can be gained by focusing on the case of Sapporo.[57] As happened in other cities in this period, the suburbs became an integral part of Sapporo's urban system after World War One, necessary to the economic and social functioning of the city. Under the banner of "Greater Sapporo," a spatial revolution organized the city and its suburbs into land use zones defined by function, creating distinct spaces of industrial, residential, and commercial activities. These zones of economic specialization tended to be overlaid with a social character, segregating urban residents by class and limiting social interactions between different income groups. With these transformations in urban and suburban space, the social geography that undergirded the feudal town, and which persisted for most Japanese cities well into the Meiji period, all but disappeared.

One of the exceptional features of Sapporo, of course, was that it had no history as a feudal town. Founded in the early Meiji period as part of a state colonization program, immigrants came to Sapporo—and Hokkaido more broadly—from the main islands under two settlement programs. One, known as the *todenhei*, was a military colonization program to resettle former samurai in the new territory. The state intended the military colonization project to be both a welfare program for the deposed feudal aristocracy and a means to fortify the land against the potential threat from Russia and the native Ainu. The military colonists were given a high degree of state assistance to facilitate their adaptation to an unfamiliar and harsh climate. This assistance included a free grant of land, a house with a stove, initial rice rations, seed subsidies, and agricultural implements. A second emigration program recruited ordinary peasant farmers to settle in Hokkaido under much less generous terms. As F. C. Jones observed, each migrant in this settlement project was "assigned to poor land, given housing which was quite inadequate against the winter cold, and in general treated not much better than a convict."[58] The fate of the latter class of colonists was depicted in the proletarian literary classic *The Absentee Landlord* (*Fusai jinushi*), which condemned the plight of poor farmers lured to a life of social exploitation and physical hardship with false promises of good land and state aid.[59] The villages in the vicinity of Sapporo were largely settled by the *todenhei*, and this heritage figured prominently in attitudes toward the nearby city. It also meant that village residents, like the migrants who composed the population of Sapporo itself, were castle town transplants. Thus, even though Sapporo itself had no history as a feudal town, memories of this earlier spatial experience of the city served as a point of reference for its urban and suburban residents.

Beginning in 1897 and continuing into the following decade, Hokkaido's system of local administration underwent a large-scale reform, bringing it into conformity with the mainland as part of an overarching administrative and political integration.[60] The seventeen immigrant villages situated on the outskirts of Sapporo were amalgamated into seven village jurisdictions; these became the iconic Sapporo suburbs in the 1920s. The metamorphosis from agricultural colony to suburb varied from village to village, producing communities with radically different economic functions and social characters. The localized social and political dramas that accompanied incorporation into the urban market are aspects of urban history usually overshadowed by the more captivating spectacles in the city center. And yet, each suburban village had its own tale to tell. These included stories of urban sprawl and the improvement of urban leisure facilities, showcase developments, and unsightly slums. Amalgamation benefited some communities, while others suffered. There were places changed in utterly unforeseen ways. And in contrast to the emerging stereotype of the interchangeable subdivisions of single-family homes, the interwar suburb came in all shapes and sizes.

Analyzing Sapporo's seven orbital villages in terms of land use and social character, one may discern three general patterns in the process of suburbanization. Individual trajectories depended in large part on where the village lay on the expanding transportation grid. The villages of Kotoni, Teine, and Shiraishi turned into outposts for Sapporo's factories because of access to the main rail line. The villages of Toyohira and Moiwa, linked to the central city by bus and tram, became residential "bed towns." Two others, the village of Sapporo (a separate jurisdiction from the city of Sapporo) and Shinoro, expanded their agricultural production, directing their economies toward supplying the growing urban market. Although Sapporo and Shinoro villages' specialization in food crops emerged in part to compensate for declining agricultural production in the other industrial and residential suburbs, even the most urbanized of these orbital villages retained something of the smell of the farm, setting them apart from the "real" city.

The first of these patterns is a striking feature of Sapporo's factory suburbs: the power of rail to produce economic space. Even before the World War One boom triggered an intensification of industrial production in Sapporo's city center, Kotoni, Teine, and Shiraishi had begun to suburbanize because of their position on the Hakodate main rail line (Hakodate honsen). Connecting the city with the port of Hakodate to the west and the military base city of Asahikawa to the east, the Hakodate line ran from Teine and Kotoni on Sapporo's northwestern edge, cutting through the city center before moving east through Shiraishi. As early as 1880, stations were opened in Karugawa (Teine village), Kotoni (Kotoni village), and Shiraishi (Shiraishi village), leading to residential and commercial development in the vicinity of the rail stations. In Kotoni, for example, the neighborhood around the station became a middle-class residential suburb for white-collar workers in

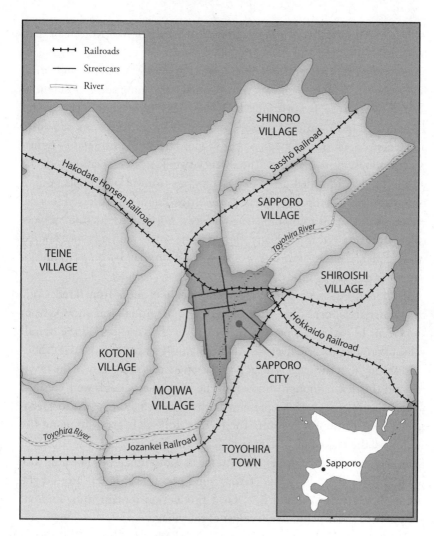

MAP 4. Sapporo and suburbs, ca. 1925

Sapporo's banks, companies, and government offices. Moreover, children of the military colonists (*todenhei*) took advantage of rail access to commute into Sapporo for secondary school. These children and grandchildren of deposed samurai nurtured ambitions for reclaiming status through educational pedigree and government employment. In these early years, it looked as if the Hakodate main-line suburbs would become Sapporo's first middle-class bed towns.

Despite this early beginning, large-scale urbanization in Kotoni awaited Sapporo's economic and demographic expansion of the 1920s, when easy access to city services and freight transport attracted a wave of industrial investment. This investment transformed the embryonic residential community into a factory suburb. When the city located experimental agricultural and industrial stations in Kotoni in 1922, clusters of houses and storefronts soon cropped up nearby. Conversion of farmland to industrial production accelerated. The twenty-two factories operating in the village in 1932 included a cement factory, an ironworks, a paper mill, a pharmaceutical company, and a *shōchū* (rice liquor) distillery. Housing estates sprung up to accommodate employees. Adjacent to the factory, blue-collar workers lived in company dorms, while single-family homes housed white-collar workers some distance away.[61] Kotoni had become a center of Sapporo's expanding industry.

Economic statistics capture this striking metamorphosis from farm colony to industrial suburb. The share of agricultural production shrank from 59 percent in 1925 to 24 percent in 1939. Over the same period the overall value of production rose fivefold. After remaining steady at around six thousand throughout the teens, village population increased steadily in the twenties and thirties. Although almost half the village households were engaged in agriculture in 1940, this represented a dramatic remaking of the socioeconomic constitution of Kotoni. The factory zone that grew up along the stations of the Hakodate line integrated the village into Sapporo's industrializing economy. Although in certain respects Kotoni had become a factory town, within the village the factory zone was concentrated around the station; away from the rail line, farm production remained an internal periphery to the new industrial center of the village.[62]

The village of Teine, situated along the Hakodate rail line to the west of Kotoni, also developed as an industrial satellite. Opened in 1881, Teine's Karugawa station was located strategically between Otaru and Sapporo and offered easy access to the nearby Ishikawa mines. Much as it did in Kotoni, early rail access touched off urban development in the vicinity of the Teine station. The Ishikari road opened in 1888, attended by another burst of local development. The government set up a post office (1899), a police substation (1900), and a firehouse (1901) in Karugawa to serve the growing population. The rail station was expanded and improved in 1900 to accommodate rising demand. Industrial production in Teine began in 1912, with the establishment of an oil distillery (Nihon Sekiyū), supplied from the nearby Ishikari oilfields. The same year, Karugawa was connected with the city center by a horse-drawn tram that carried both passengers and agricultural produce. When the tram was electrified in 1922, it triggered a flurry of residential real estate development. Over the course of the 1920s, a number of agricultural processing plants set up shop nearby, including Maeda Agribusiness, Hokkaido Timber, and Far Eastern Condensed Milk. Thus Teine, much like Kotoni, transformed from farm colony to factory suburb because of the proximity of rail transport. Much as it territorialized markets along the railway grid at a macro level, at a micro level the railway became a force field of the local economy, shaping and reshaping the social and economic character of communities within its domain.

Resources, especially mineral resources, also exerted a powerful influence over the fate of Sapporo's orbital villages. In Teine's case, the discovery of new deposits of gold, silver, and copper in a nearby mine in the early 1930s put Teine on the map as the nation's largest source of copper and gold. Mitsubishi purchased the mine in 1935 and expanded operations rapidly. By 1940, 2,000 miners dug for gold and copper at Teine; a mining town of 6,932 grew up around Mitsubishi's operations. The same mountainous terrain that yielded these mineral riches offered opportunities to develop leisure facilities. Stimulated by rail and road access, hotels and restaurants proliferated around the hot springs of Teine Mountain, attracting visitors to a lively resort that offered skiing in winter and mountain climbing and flower appreciation in summer. Thus, as in Kotoni, the industrialization of the suburb was spatially dispersed, creating a localized economic geography that operated according to its own internal logics.[63]

Statistics tell the story of Teine's transformation, too. The value of economic production doubled between 1925 and 1939. The share of the pie accounted for by agriculture shrank from 32 percent in 1925 to 21 percent in 1939. Although Teine's economic growth did not match the fivefold expansion in next-door Kotoni, this was a substantial increase, reflecting the growth of the oil distilling operations of Nihon Sekiyū and yields from the Mitsubishi mine. In terms of demographic trends, Teine also trailed neighboring Kotoni. Both communities remained stable throughout the teens, and Teine's population did not begin to increase by substantial numbers until the late 1930s, when the expansion of the Mitsubishi mine brought migrants into the area. Behind the story of the population growth in both communities was a shift from their exposure to the vicissitudes of crop production to their exposure to the vagaries of the market economy. In the teens, a series of crop failures limited in-migration to this largely agricultural community; strong demand for industrial goods stimulated population growth in the 1930s.[64]

One point to take from this brief comparison of the histories of Kotoni and Teine: even these tiny suburbs of a colonial city exhibit striking points of variation. Both were Sapporo factory suburbs, and both developed a characteristic mix of agriculture and industry; and yet in its development, Teine, whose economy was grounded in extractive industries such as oil and minerals, departed dramatically from Kotoni, which was characterized by a mix of types of factory production. As these differences suggest, a closer look at orbital communities can yield a more nuanced understanding of the suburb as a sociospatial form and prompt us to rethink its place within the historiography of the modern city.

Shiroishi was the third of Sapporo's industrial satellites, located along the Hakodate main line to the east of the city center. Unlike the other two, Shiroishi remained evenly split between industrial and agricultural sectors and did not develop much suburban housing. Early on, Shiroishi became the site of major investment in a brick and mortar factory, located in the village because of rail access. Production began in 1884, and new investments expanded the facility substantially in 1909. These were the bricks that made Shiroishi famous, at least locally; they built Sapporo's emblematic buildings—the beer factory, Hokkaido Prefectural Hall, the Normal School, and the dormitories of the Twenty-Fifth Regiment. The second industry to develop in Shiroishi was rubber manufacture: boots, gloves, rain ponchos, and other consumer products. In the twenties, rubber factories opened up one after another, eclipsing Shiroishi's famous brick factory. In spite of the proliferation of factories, Shiroishi's agricultural production remained strong, shored up by investments in model livestock farms, which provided sites of innovation in animal husbandry tailored for the local climate.

Though residential development lagged behind that of Kotoni and Teine, the relocation of the Sapporo licensed quarters from the city center to Shiroishi-chō in 1920 provided a major stimulus to commercial development in the area. The new grounds of the red-light district were just inside the city limits on former village land—a slice of Shiroishi that had been annexed to the city in 1910 (Shiroishi-chō). The proliferation of brothels, restaurants, and cafés on both sides of the boundary knit the severed section of the village back into itself. Moreover, the development of new train lines in the vicinity greatly encouraged the growth of commercial establishments catering to the sex trades. With the establishment of the Jōzankei (1918) and Sapporo (1925) lines, three of the four local lines made stops at Shiroishi station. These lines also made station stops at the new Higashi Sapporo station, offering closest access to the new red-light district. The relocated licensed quarters quickly became a magnet for new settlement. Within Shiroishi-chō (on the Sapporo side) population increased tenfold in the space of five years, and this dynamism spilled across the city limits into Shiroishi village as well.[65] Indeed, commercial growth in the vicinity of the red-light district accounted for much of village population growth over the early decades of the century.

The pattern of economic development, and Shiroishi's character as an industrial suburb, departed in significant respects from that of Kotoni or Teine. Shiroishi's industrial base was laid early, with a secure connection to Sapporo's ongoing construction boom. Though its later replacement by rubber manufacture signaled a shift from dependence on the state-financed construction industry to production for a local consumer market, as well as a move from reliance on one large factory to many small manufacturers, these changes did not substantially alter the composition of economic production. The agricultural share of production actually increased from 55 percent in 1925 to 62 percent in 1939, with the share of manufacturing dropping by a like amount. Moreover production values overall rose less dramatically than in neighboring Kotoni and Teine villages. Thus, although the expansion of rubber production and the sex trades certainly changed the economic and social character of the village, the impact of suburbanization on Shiroishi did not echo the experience of either Kotoni or Teine. Commerce shaped Shiroishi's economic development as profoundly as industry did; this also meant that Shiroishi's urban/suburban boundaries were less clearly defined, since the sex and entertainment zone on Shiroishi's west side blended seamlessly into the red-light district in the city proper. Moreover, unlike in Kotoni, industry in Shiroishi never became an engine of local development and economic expansion. Lacking this dynamic, village land converted more slowly from agriculture to industry, and farm production continued to color Shiroishi's suburban identity.[66]

As the stories of Kotoni, Teine, and Shiroishi reveal, the early history of the suburbs was an elemental dimension of urban industrialization. The drive to build factories that swept urban areas called for access to labor and transport. Both were readily available in the city center, but suitable land was less easy to come by. Thus for many Japanese cities, the earliest suburbs were developed as factory zones. Although factory zones may have been typical of the early Japanese suburb, no template of a "typical" factory suburb emerges from this examination of Sapporo's case. Indeed, the abstraction *industrial* conceals a host of differences. Different land use patterns characterized Sapporo's three industrial suburbs, as well as different political economies, economic geographies, and demographic trajectories. The social character of Teine's mining community was worlds away from the community adjacent to the government-sponsored factory zone in Kotoni. Neither possessed anything resembling Shiroishi's lively commercial district. And yet all three were major loci of industrial production: they were Sapporo's factory suburbs.

While Kotoni, Teine, and Shiroishi developed as industrial suburbs, a second form of suburbanization emerged in the villages of Moiwa and Toyohira. These became the precursors of the bed towns that ring Japan's cities today. Much better than the factory suburbs, Moiwa and Toyohira fit the emerging stereotype of suburban garden cities that advertised a tasteful modern life apart from the hustle and bustle of downtown.[67] Though residential settlement took place to some degree in all Sapporo's neighboring villages, nowhere did this happen as rapidly and relentlessly as in the two villages on the city's southern frontier. Several factors accounted for the concentration of residential development in Moiwa and Toyohira, but as in the factory suburbs, new transportation networks exercised an oversized influence. The difference here was access by bus and streetcar. While the industrial suburbs grew up along the northwestern and eastern fringes of the city, where the Hakodate main line connected Sapporo to long-distance destinations, a more localized communications network developed in and beyond Sapporo's south side. With the exception of a tram running to the university, just north of the main train station, streetcar and bus lines overwhelmingly favored the southern reaches of the city. The development of residential suburbs in Moiwa and Toyohira followed the contours of this transportation grid (see map 4).[68]

Moiwa, located at the foot of the Moiwa and Maruyama Mountains on Sapporo's southwestern edge, became prime suburban real estate in the 1920s. Middle- and upper-class housing predominated, linked to leisure complexes that grew up around the two mountains. Moiwa experienced the most dramatic population growth of any of the suburbs in the twenties, adding more than seven thousand people between 1921 and 1930. Here, more than in any of the other suburbs, the role of aggressive real estate developers drove the conversion from farmland to residential subdivisions. By the end of the decade Moiwa's famous "morning market," long a symbol of its high-quality farm produce, was reduced to a tourist attraction.

Moiwa village grew out of the first wave of military colonies settled by former samurai in 1870. They occupied a prime piece of land at the foot of Mount Muruyama, a site of striking natural beauty and historic associations. Town plans for the new settlement at Sapporo oriented the city toward the twin mountains, which had been written up by a famous Tokugawa explorer, Matsuura Takejirō. Matsuura's travel diary included Ainu legends about the mountains and descriptions of their holy places, lending to the new colony of Sapporo a prefabricated patina of archaism. After the land was claimed by the Meiji state, the site of the main Ainu shrine on Maruyama was converted to Sapporo Shrine, which became the centerpiece of a large landscape park leading up to its entrance.

One of the arresting features of the Moiwa story is the powerful role played by village politicians and entrepreneurs. This was one of many examples where the forces behind suburban development were located in the suburbs themselves. Moiwa's conversion from vegetable plots to urban housing tracts began in the late Meiji and proceeded rapidly, as multiple forces converged to drive the development of new housing estates in the village. Rail access was one influence, as was the establishment of local government; the rise of land speculation also added to the pressures for development. In 1910, after the original village center, Yamahana, was annexed to the city, administrative offices were relocated to the Maruyama section of the village. Village authorities and the local landlord association actively pressed for investment in road improvement and the extension of light-rail into the area, efforts that were rewarded with a streetcar station in 1923 and a new road in 1927. In the meantime, rising values meant that it was more lucrative to develop land for housing subdivisions than to keep it in agricultural production. In Asahigaoka, the original home of the first generation of military colonists, farm lands were broken up and sold for housing lots in the midtwenties; the area facing the front gate of Sapporo Shrine, Miya no Mori, soon followed. In striking contrast to the historiographic convention that tends to stress the outward push of a city into its hinterlands, the Moiwa village story highlights the fact that the suburb became the driving force of urban expansionism. Not only did suburbs such as Moiwa become the agents of their own production, but also, as they influenced city planning and transportation policies enacted in the center, the tail began to wag the dog.

In a signal example of the periphery representing the advance guard of the center, the village of Moiwa emerged as one of the preeminent symbols of modern life in Sapporo. Its residential subdivisions were typical of the high-class "culture houses" (*bunka jūtaku*) that became emblematic of urban middle-class life in the twenties and thirties. Moiwa offered to Sapporo's most sophisticated consumers an elegant lifestyle unavailable in the cramped downtown districts of Sapporo. Glossy posters circulated by the developers association depicted a pastoral landscape broken up by a grid of new roads and lined with single-family homes nestled among trees. Streetlights, paved roads, and white picket fences added to the picture, and the streetcar was just steps away. The Moiwa and Maruyama Mountains, with their ski slopes and landscape parks, rose dramatically in the backdrop.[69] Offering a vision of an idyllic suburban life for the expanding ranks of Sapporo's white-collar workers, such advertisements helped make Moiwa synonymous with the latest fashion in house and home.[70]

The importance of housing in Moiwa's economy was reflected in statistics. Of the seven villages, Moiwa ranked fourth in population in 1906; but by 1930 it had pulled ahead of all but Toyohira, and by 1939 it emerged as the most populous of the suburbs. At the same time, it was the least productive, generating under a million yen of goods in 1939. While little industry was built in Moiwa, a small group of agricultural producers protected a small share of village land from the rolling frontier of housing development. The Maruyama morning market, founded in 1897, established Moiwa's reputation early on as a provisioner of high-quality produce for urban dwellers. By reinventing itself, the market managed to survive in the face of rapid urbanization until late in the war. In the 1920s, when residential development accelerated, some local farmers resisted appeals to sell and instead formed a cooperative to operate the Maruyama market. The co-op succeeded in maintaining the high reputation of the market and turned it into a stop on the itinerary of weekend visitors.[71]

Like Moiwa, Toyohira grew into a residential suburb, but with one significant difference: Toyohira's social composition was considerably more diverse. While Moiwa became a bed town for the expanding ranks of Sapporo's salary men and middle-class professionals, Toyohira attracted concentrations of petty merchants and manufacturers, a large slum population, and pockets of upper-middle-class settlement. The largest of Sapporo's suburbs both physically and demographically, Toyohira was incorporated as a town (*chō*) in 1908 when its population topped the ten thousand mark. Although in 1910 the most commercialized section was amalgamated to the city, Toyohira remained the most populous of Sapporo's suburbs, until Moiwa outpaced it in the late 1930s. At 723 square kilometers (1925 boundaries), it was almost twice as large as all the other suburban villages combined.

Three hamlets made up the administrative village of Toyohira: Toyohira, Tsukisappu, and Hiragishi. The first, Toyohira, bounded the city limits to the southeast. As with Sapporo's other suburban villages, transportation development provided the main stimulus to Toyohira's metamorphosis. Because the Muroran road into Sapporo cut through the village, Toyohira became the gateway for nonrail transport into the city. This was the principal route used for supply wagons bringing farm produce from nearby villages and charcoal from farther away. Wide enough for two wagons to pass one another, the road supported a steady stream of traffic into and out of the city. Small-scale commercial and manufacturing establishments sprang up along the transport corridor selling secondhand clothing, sundries, liquor, and food products, as well as supplies, tools, and repair services for wagons.

As befit the gateway to the city, the suburban village of Toyohira—and its eponymous hamlet and river—stood as a symbol of the social diversity of modern urban life. A former vineyard in Nakajima, just across the banks of the Toyohira River from the Nakajima fairgrounds and amusement park, was developed in 1926 as a Moiwa-style upper-class subdivision of 180 units of culture houses. The city fortified and rebuilt the main bridge over the Toyohira River in 1924. Proudly advertised as the "only three-arch bridge north of Tokyo," the spectacular iron bridge was featured on postcards and city guides as a monument to Sapporo's distinctive brand of modernism. Just steps away, along the edges of the river, a ragged urban slum grew up, home to Sapporo's swelling underclass of day laborers, ragpickers, street entertainers, and other working poor. Households sustained by lower-end commercial and manufacturing stalls settled along the main road, a community of petty merchants and manufacturers located socioeconomically only one notch above the slum. Though city guides failed to mention the Toyohira slum, for Sapporo residents the presence of this monument to urban poverty at the city's main entry constituted an equally powerful symbol of urban modernity.[72]

If Toyohira's internal divisions mirrored the social diversity of the city as a whole, the village divided into zones of economic and political specialization that echoed the different facets of the city's personality. Farther down the main road from the hamlet of Toyohira, Tsukisappu emerged as the political-administrative heart of the village as well as a center of commercial and residential development, replicating in miniature the overarching character of Sapporo. The hamlet of Tsukisappu housed the local Twenty-Fifth Regiment; when Toyohira was incorporated as a town in 1908, the town hall was erected along the main street near the regimental headquarters. Both the military and local government presence stimulated commercial growth. A map of the neighborhood in 1921 showed some fifty-odd shops down the main street, including bakeries, candy stores, fish shops, bathhouses, shoe stores, a bicycle shop, and a tofu stand. Unlike the commercial activity in Toyohira hamlet, closer to the city, shopkeepers here catered to local residents rather than to traders passing through into Sapporo.[73] Thus, while Tsukisappu developed a lively commercial sphere, this was an inward-directed service economy, ancillary to the hamlet's primary function as the political-administrative center of the village.

The third of the village hamlets, Hiragishi, occupied the long ribbon of land that followed Toyohira River upstream from Nakajima Park to the mountain resort of Jozankei. Filled with apple and persimmon orchards, Hiragishi benefited from a number of agricultural outreach initiatives. State-funded research and model farms with links to Sapporo Agricultural College helped to develop pesticides and introduce new cultivation methods to minimize crop damage, also bringing infusions of agricultural investment to the area.[74] Much as in Tsukisappu, public investment fueled suburban growth and reshaped Hiragishi's social and economic character.

The rapid shifts in Hiragishi's social environment also illustrated the ways that the character of a suburb could turn on a dime. In addition to being the center of the Toyohira's experimental farms and fruit production, Hiragishi became home to the hot springs resort of Jozankei, located in a mountainous section of the hamlet near the headwaters of the Toyohira River. Like the rest of the hamlet, this part of Hiragishi had remained largely agricultural until a gold and silver mine opened in 1915–1916. Driven by the rising price of precious metals during the war boom, mine owners expanded operations at a frantic pace. By 1918 the mine employed a thousand hands and was the second-largest employer in the region. The miners were housed in a camp town nearby; investments in spa and entertainment facilities soon followed. Initially the mountain resort was developed to cater to miners, but when the mining operations collapsed in the postwar bust the resort reinvented itself, marketing its amenities as a weekend retreat for Sapporo's urban masses. Offering a variety of bathing and entertainment facilities in a site of exceptional scenic beauty, the Jozankei resort soon became known as the "back parlor" of the city. The shifting economic base of Hiragishi—from agricultural production, to mining center, to leisure complex—shaped and reshaped the social character of the hamlet, all within the space of a few years.

In the wake of World War One, ongoing rail improvements accelerated Hiragishi's development as a leisure complex. In 1918, the opening of a dedicated train line running from Shiroishi station out to Jozankei connected the resort to downtown Sapporo by rail and provided the first impetus in the reorganization of Jozankei from a camp town spa to a weekend resort. Electrification in 1929 reduced travel time to an hour, improving access and enhancing the appeal of the resort.[75] In the process, the new, high-speed Jozankei railway became emblematic of the importance of regional transportation networks in developing a diversified commercial economy in this sprawling Sapporo suburb. With station stops in Toyohira and elsewhere, the Jozankei line accelerated commercial development and integration into the greater Sapporo economy. In 1924 a track extension brought streetcar service across the river and added several new stops in Toyohira. Although lobbying by local officials failed to extend the track as far as Tsukisappu, the sting of this disappointment soon disappeared when the Sapporo branch line of the Hokkaido Railway opened a train station in the hamlet the following year, in 1925. The Sapporo line ran from Naebo station on the Hakodate main line and connected with the Jozankei line at Higashi Sapporo. From there it continued east to Nunotan. Complementing rail and streetcar lines, Toyohira developed an extensive network of roads, some branching out from the Muroran Highway and others offering the ability to travel by automobile from Sapporo's main train station to the Jozankei resort. In these ways railroad track, streetcar lines, and roadways crisscrossed the village, providing easy access to the city center and opening up the village interior to commercial and real estate development.[76]

The overall result of transportation-driven development on Toyohira was a mixed economy. Like Moiwa, Toyohira provided a hospitable site for the expansion of leisure and residential facilities. But while the closer in, more compact Moiwa favored extensive growth of housing estates, Toyohira's sprawling geography encouraged a broader mix of land use. In contrast to Moiwa—with the lowest production values of the seven suburbs—Toyohira stood near the head of the pack. A threefold rise in production between 1925 and 1939 (from 1.5 to 5 million yen) was driven by expanded investments in both agriculture and industry. Though both helped sustain the local economy, agriculture (mainly livestock farming) remained dominant, shrinking only slightly, from 72 percent of production in 1925 to 60 percent in 1939, against industry's rise from 6 percent to 22 percent over the same period.[77] As these statistics suggest, transportation provided a critical resource for Toyohira's economic development and shaped the diversity of its land use. Since access to the city by multiple road and rail routes facilitated the movement of goods and people in and out of the town, it was no coincidence that the Sapporo suburb with the best transit network was also the most diverse in terms of land use and economic base.

Alongside the growth of new industrial and residential zones on the outskirts of Sapporo, a third pattern of suburbanization emerged in the villages of Sapporo (a separate jurisdiction from the city of Sapporo) and Shinoro. Here agricultural production continued to dominate the village economy, with a few key changes. As Sapporo pulled the two villages ever tighter into the orbit of the urban economy, their crop mix shifted to cater exclusively to the urban market. The metamorphosis from agricultural colony to suburb transmogrified Shinoro and Sapporo into vegetable gardens for the city. And as other villages reduced agricultural production, Shinoro and Sapporo took up the slack, increasing in both absolute and relative measures. This process was most dramatic in Sapporo Village, where agriculture increased from 62 percent of total production in 1925 to 95 percent in 1939.[78] Thus, the process of suburbanization distilled these communities into a more "pure" version of the agricultural village.

The path by which Sapporo village achieved this position was curious indeed. Beginning in the late nineteenth century, this village experienced intense urbanization in patterns also seen in the city's other suburbs: residential development, factory growth, and commercial development, all encouraged by improvements in rail access. And yet Sapporo village developed into an entirely different suburban form. Before this village's metamorphosis from a center of manufacture, commerce, and housing into a farming suburb, it was one of the most urbanized of the seven suburbs. Precisely because of this, as Sapporo village's early urbanization integrated it furthest and fastest with the urban economy, pressures for annexation increased. A wave of amalgamations in the teens and twenties transformed Sapporo village back into an agricultural community. As a series of amputations lopped off the urbanized sections of the village in succession and grafted them onto the city proper, the remaining parts of the village depended increasingly on agriculture for local production.

The neighborhood of Naebo was the first to go, precisely because of its growing importance to the urban economy. The main rail line ran through Naebo, which fell within an expanding factory zone along the ragged urban edge of northern Sapporo. By the time it was annexed to the city in 1910, Naebo housed two major industrial facilities: Sapporo Beer and the Ministry of Railways ironworks. With the opening of a train station the same year, the neighborhoods on both sides of the city limits continued to attract a stream of new investments: a *geta* (wooden clog) factory opened in 1917; a lumber mill, wooden carton factory, and fertilizer plant in 1918; and an oil refinery in 1919. And because farmers from Sapporo and Shiroishi villages utilized Naebo as their main trading post, commercial development in the area expanded, turning it into a "second city center."[79] At the same time, housing estates proliferated and other urban facilities followed. Among the most prominent, the Tenshi Hospital opened in 1911, and in 1922 the Hokkaido Girls Higher School moved to the district. When the Motomura road was built in the late teens and enlarged in 1925, it created another major road corridor into the central city. Like the Muroran road that ran through Toyohira, Motomura helped eliminate the boundary between the city of Sapporo and Sapporo Village. Residential development of the Shingawazoe neighborhood accelerated; following Naebo's path, this section of Sapporo village was annexed to the city in 1934.[80] The wave of annexations reflected the rapid degree of urbanization in the village, as well as the extent of integration into the downtown socioeconomy. Even more than this, the history of Sapporo village illustrated the strategic position occupied by suburbs within a rapidly shifting urban economic geography. As Naebo's informal designation as "a second city center" suggests, the suburb was never a marginal element in the urban economy, but the potential site of new force fields of capitalist development.

Although the acceleration of urban development in the village of Sapporo seemed to feed on itself—factories begetting more factories, the spread of housing estates generating the proliferation of commerce in the vicinity— again something strange happened in Sapporo village. The remaining parts of the village forestalled urbanization by setting up, in effect, an agricultural line of defense—investing in agricultural development and securing markets for local products. From early on, the village had already established a reputation for quality produce—especially onions, but also eggplant, cabbage, and squash. Beginning in the late 1890s, local producers expanded onion production to take advantage of new markets in the Philippines and Siberia. When

Sapporo village, like the others abutting the Hakodate main line, experienced pressures to convert land use to factories and housing, the ability to develop a lucrative export market for local produce preserved the profitability of agriculture. Instead of stimulating conversion, rail access offered local farmers the means to transport their goods abroad. Government purchases of local produce also helped maintain the profitability of agricultural land use. In 1909 the army set up a provisioning station in the village, contracting for large-scale and reliable purchases of oats. Around the same time, the University of Hokkaido established several experimental farms to improve oat production in the village. Through the rail system, the provisioning station, and the experimental farms, the local and central governments made investments in the village economy that helped Sapporo village become a local success story. The strange career of Sapporo village, from agricultural colony to "second city center" to showcase agricultural suburb, revealed the unevenness and variability in the process of suburbanization. In this sense, the colonization of the countryside by the city yielded many outcomes; not all of these were predictable, nor were they wholly controlled from the center.

Sapporo's last suburb—Shinoro—offered a strikingly different example of an agricultural suburb. In contrast to Sapporo village's image of agricultural profitability, Shinoro presented a grim picture of poverty in a suburban farming village. Of the city's seven suburban villages, Shinoro was the most marginal economically. Unlike Sapporo village, which actively developed its agricultural base and achieved some success with products such as onions and oats, Shinoro lagged behind in both productivity and demographic growth. Much like the strange career of Sapporo village, the twists and turns in Shinoro's fate confounded both the predictions and the efforts at management by the city's central authorities. Colonial planners of the late nineteenth century had confidently predicted Shinoro would become the most successful among Sapporo's agricultural colonies. One of the early *todenhei* settlements of former samurai, Shinoro initially outstripped the other colonial villages. Anticipating further growth, an administrative reorganization in 1899 made Shinoro into a separate jurisdiction. But soon afterward, the colony began to falter and Shinoro, once the largest and most robust of Sapporo's seventeen colonial settlements, became the smallest and most troubled of the seven suburban villages. On the thirtieth anniversary of the colony's founding, Shinoro celebrated negative population growth: by 1919 the original 1889 settlement of 220 households had shrunk to a mere 100 households.[81]

Residents initially grew crops such as barley and legumes while trying to develop strains of rice that were sufficiently hardy for the colder Hokkaido climate. In this the colony achieved some success, and it acquired a name as the "rice bowl" of Sapporo. After the army provisioning station set up shop in nearby Sapporo village, Shinoro also began to grow oats. In spite of these achievements, the village struggled in its efforts to attract new settlers and to maintain adequate farm yields. Part of the problem was chronic flooding by the nearby river, but the village also suffered from poor soil quality. In their attempts to open up new fields for cultivation, residents discovered that much of the village land was covered in peat bog that resisted tilling. Suburban transportation grids built during the teens passed Shinoro by, compounding the challenges facing villagers. When new plans to extend the light-rail network circulated in the 1920s, Shinoro lobbied heavily for a local station stop. In spite of these efforts, the village had to wait until 1934 for its first train station—more than fifty years after the earliest suburban train stations opened in 1880 along the Hakodate main line.[82]

Of Sapporo's seven satellite villages, Shinoro was the least integrated into the greater urban economy and also the poorest—conditions that were mutually constitutive. Road and rail linkups lagged far behind those of Shinoro's neighbors. The difficulty and expense of transportation made farming less profitable; it also discouraged investments in new economic ventures. Like Sapporo village, Shinoro specialized in agriculture, which accounted for virtually all local production throughout the twenties and thirties. The difference was that Sapporo's land use specialization reflected its success in developing specialty crops for a targeted market; Shinoro's focus on agriculture was a mark of its distress. Poor profit margins threw local families into debt, and over time many lost their land. In 1921 the tenancy rate in Shinoro reached 74 percent (compared to the national average of 28 percent), a statistic that revealed the poor standard of living for most village households. The marginal living of Shinoro's farms made the village more vulnerable to the vagaries of weather, and a series of crop failures between 1930 and 1935 devastated the village. In the worst year, 1931, more than half the local population was forced onto public assistance.[83] Largely left out of the blessings of regional developmentalism in the interwar period, Shinoro emerged from under the yoke of poverty only when Japan went to war. As conscription pulled more and more men off the farms and agricultural shortages turned the terms of trade in favor of producers, villages such as Shinoro suddenly found themselves commanding unprecedented sums for farm produce. As the tenancy system became an obstacle to efficient resource mobilization, state procurement bypassed landlords and dealt directly with tenants, placing more of the profits in the hands of direct producers.

Several larger observations can be drawn from the stories of Sapporo's seven suburbs. First, these stories highlight the overwhelming importance of the railroad in suburban development. Railroads and, to a lesser extent, road networks created a socioeconomic force field that stimulated economic development—commercial, residential, industrial. The railway also created micro-economies within Sapporo's suburbs, generating new suburban centers and internal peripheries that organized socioeconomic space within satellite villages. In this, the railroad joined other state developmental forces of the interwar period, in particular the city planning movement, which erected infrastructural systems encompassing a greater urban area. In the process, public policy, state investment, and the private capital that followed reshaped cities and their proximate villages into the urban-rural system that defined regional space for much of the twentieth century.

A second feature of interwar suburban development that this account illustrates is the striking variety in suburban forms. Even if Sapporo's suburbs roughly conform to the three-part taxonomy I lay down here, the villages differ enormously within these categories. "Industrial" suburbs encompassed government production, large and small factories, and mining operations—each of which had a different impact on settlement patterns and social formations. Suburban development of leisure facilities included the red-light district in Shiraishi, Maruyama's baseball field, and the hot springs resorts at Jozankei. These catered to different clientele, and they stimulated different sorts of commercial development in their vicinity. Rich and poor, socially diverse and socially uniform, built-up and largely agricultural—suburbs came in all shapes and sizes.

Nevertheless, the discourse on the city compresses these different shapes and sizes into a single mold, and this is my third observation. In the emerging symbology of the suburb, different images of land use competed for center stage. In descriptions of Kotoni, Teine, and Shiroishi, the factory stands out as the symbol of urban expansionism and capitalist modernization: to observers it proclaimed both the city's intent to colonize the countryside and the power of industry to command and transform rural space. The factory portended the retreat of the countryside, whether one viewed this retreat in elegiac or triumphalist terms. Yet the semiotics of the factory coexisted uneasily with images of the suburb as open, green space, an association reinforced by the tenacity of agricultural production within both industrial and residential suburbs. Indeed, the selling point of middle-class suburban life in Moiwa and Toyohira was its bucolic attractions: the proximity of parks, mountains, and outdoor leisure amenities. That two of Sapporo's seven suburbs—the villages of Sapporo and Shinoro—were active farming communities injected yet another set of images into the social imaginary of the suburb. In the dualistic constructions of city and country that circulated in the interwar period, the suburb occupied a liminal space. Neither urban nor rural, the suburb somehow managed to be both at once. In a suburb, Japanese could pretend they were in the country (even knowing they were not); at the same time they could imagine they were in the city (though not quite). In a world that pitted city against countryside in a battle for survival, and where activists and intellectuals of all political stripes were urging people to take sides, the suburb offered a place to be both rustic and urbane, to find a performative fix to the clash between city and country.

One of the epic tales of the twentieth century is the rise of the modern city as a sociospatial form. This is a story about roads and railways, about trains and automobiles. Modern cities were products of new transportation networks that reshaped economic geographies within cities, among cities, and between cities and their surrounding countryside. They were embedded within the social production of regional space and the emergence of a new kind of urban-rural system that positioned rural villages within a market network centered on cities. In other words, the story of the modern city is about urban expansion, the ongoing colonization of the countryside, and the rise of the suburb as an integral component of the urban form. The historiography of urbanization has tended to tell this story in terms of convergence—the process of urban modernization transforming cities to look more like one another—and to view modernization as a single, common process undergone by all cities as they experience the catalyst of capitalist modernity. And yet, as this chapter has shown, every case was different: there was no such thing as a typical small town or a typical big city. Instead, every place had its own strange career, full of unintended consequences, twists of fate, and reversals of fortune. Since the new force of the market affected regions, cities, and suburbs in different ways, the story of urban modernization is one of infinite variation: this unevenness defined the experience of urban modernity.

Among the most momentous consequences of the transportation revolution and the city story was the formation of a new kind of relationship between town and country—the urban-rural system that was set in place at this time. The strength of this system lay in its grounding in both material and ideological structures. In material terms, cities accrued forms of political, economic, and cultural power that permitted them to dominate rural communities in new ways. The enormous demographic growth of the interwar years triggered an expansion of the built environment of the city. Proliferation of urban rail and other regional transportation networks transformed the relationship between cities and the towns and villages that surrounded them. In this sense, the urban expansion of the interwar decades ushered in a new age of the city. The post-World-War-One shrinking of external markets and the deepening of the industrial revolution focused attention on regional development as a new frontier. Investments in communications infrastructure added a regional network to the national rail grid built up in the 1880s and 1890s. A system that interlinked Tokyo with other major cities and facilitated exchange with the world economy now fostered an internal market, channeling goods and people along both regional and national circuits. The expanded communications grid enhanced the prominence of regional capitals, creating multiple economic force fields that complemented and competed with one another. Engineering Tokyo's rise as a great metropolis in the late nineteenth century, the railroad now became the vehicle for a more generic urban-centrism.

The concatenation of multiple forces—the transportation revolution, the urban planning movement, and the physical, demographic, and economic growth of cities—triggered a rethinking of the meaning of the countryside in interwar Japan. As we have seen, suburban development offered a variety of templates for reimagining modern rural space. The passion for urban "bigness" altered the metrics of land use value, privileging urban demands on the land. In a world where growth was seen as both good and inevitable, the city appeared destined to triumph over a countryside in retreat. The metaphors that dominated visions of the country in the new urban-rural system invoked consumption: the inexorable devouring of the countryside by the urban juggernaut.

Complementing the specter of rural land consumed by urban development, urbanites began to view the countryside as an object of consumption in other ways as well. With the creation of new leisure facilities in the suburbs, the rise of "rustic" hobbies such as skiing and mountain climbing, and the growth of domestic tourism, city residents began to view the nearby countryside as a recreational space. Whether they traveled to seaside resorts or read about them, rural space became identified as the playground for urban residents. Alongside images of rice paddies, ancient villages, and other symbols of old-world Japan were sparkling new theme parks and the latest ski equipment. Like the mountains upstream from Sapporo's Toyohira River, the countryside around Jozankei was reconceived through an urban lens when packaged as a destination for the weekend tourist. Whether viewed as a site for consumption—where urban workers went to play and re-create their ability to face another working day in the city—or as a place that was "anti-," "pre-," or merely "outside" the modern, the rural stood alternatively as a symbol of old-world charm and a symbol of less-appealing backwardness; in both cases the country became the city's Other. Along with an unyielding faith in the efficacy of railway-led development and a passionate commitment to the benefits of urban growth, this urban-centered view of the countryside represented the ideological product of the transportation revolution.

PART THREE

Modern Times and the City Idea

FOUR

The Past in the Present

The urban juggernaut of the early twentieth century created new challenges for cities as they tried to deal with the dramatic changes in everyday life. Former castle towns, battered by Meiji reforms that had undercut the towns' source of feudal privilege, recovered and began to grow at a swift pace.[1] The population churn generated by an increasingly mobile labor force destabilized urban communities, as newcomers to the city constituted an increasing share of the local demographic. The city became a melting pot, dissolving the social memory of the community that rested on the geographic stability of successive generations of residents. In the meantime, the establishment of modern industry undermined the economic foundations of city life and gave rise to new occupational structures and economic geographies. As the communications revolution expanded the territorial jurisdiction of the city, and as the building boom of the teens and twenties remade its built environment, the predictability and familiarity of the cityscape seemed to disappear.

Such changes created a crisis of socialization for municipal governments. Their toolbox of policies for managing social tensions had little effect in the new environment, because existing mechanisms to moderate social behavior and guide individuals to conform to norms of public order could no longer function as they once had. As increasingly clamorous social groups competed for public space and political representation, for access to resources and city services, new questions arose: Whose city was it going to be? How could these antagonistic forces be reconfigured into a workable social unit? One response to these questions emerged in the context of regional culture movements, where visions of local community provided new grounds upon which to build a sense of belonging. As they cast about for material from which to fashion a cohesive identity, municipal leaders stretched the meaning of the city, installing the belief that the rising urban centers of the twentieth century represented natural communities that drew on a shared cultural heritage.

In pursuit of a sense of community, urban elites turned to a search for customs that conveyed what was special about their locality. This involved excavating the past to discover the foundations of the modern city and the roots of its identity. It required educating the local population about their history and traditions. In the process, urbanites reinvented the idea of the city, making the urban community into a vessel of regional culture and a core component of their selfhood. Urban residents imagined their cities as self-enclosed lifeworlds with corporate identities, as organic communities with political centers. They wrote urban biographies that told the stories of these collective subjects, the history of a community's birth and development to the present age. Much the way we think of nations, we tend to think of cities as natural communities vested with primordial sovereignty. But the concept of the city as organic community and sovereign subject actually took shape in the interwar period, a product of regional culture movements in the service of urban development.[2]

Though it constituted a fraction of the urban demographic, the middle class commanded an oversized role this process. Teachers and librarians, city officials and journalists, businessmen and politicians, headed a host of regional movements that remade their urban communities and reinvented the city idea over the course of the 1920s and 1930s. Through chambers of commerce, the city planning movement, and regional arts movements, the middle class monopolized the creation of the modern urban form—which was both envisioned and constructed through the institutions they dominated. Middle-class urbanites invested their hopes and ambitions in the development of their communities in a number of ways. They lobbied the national government for city planning designation and the establishment of new schools. They created baseball teams and sports tournaments. They promoted their products, celebrated their artists, and cheered their sports stars, especially when these symbols of the vibrancy of local culture made the jump to the national and international stage. As urban residents identified themselves with the success of their communities, urban development came to signify not simply constructing infrastructure and factories, but the cultivation of a distinctive brand and local tradition—something that could identify their city and set it apart from the rest. Staking their fortunes to the future of the city, middle-class urbanites poured their energies into the regionalist movements that elevated the importance of the city in modern life.

While regionalist movements were forward-looking, they also mobilized history in the service of urban development. Thus interwar regionalism defined the city as a work in progress representing a moment in time: cities were cultural communities that built on the past to move toward the future. The spread of local history, folklore, and folk-craft movements became powerful instruments in the production of this idea of cities as time-space. Beginning in the teens and accelerating in the twenties and thirties, a local-history boom took place across the country, producing and disseminating story lines that came to define the regional community. A growing local tourist industry picked up on this movement, promoting local history and folklore that turned provincial cities into museums of regional culture. The obsession with collecting and preserving local crafts, local arts, and local myths, and resurrecting local dialects, local foods, and local festivals, reflected a desire to grab hold of a vanishing past, a desire that urban merchants helped map onto the physical space of the city. At the same time, teachers participating in a hometown-education movement embraced local history as an instrument for a new liberal, child-centered learning process. Both the tourist industry—in its attempt to sell the city—and local educators, in their effort to make education more utilitarian and democratic, placed history in the service of regional identity. In the process they deployed temporal strategies to develop a local brand and spirit of community, linking past to present to define the unique character and singular story of their communities.

While historical novels and so-called histories of civilization (*bunmei shi*) had captured popular imagination in the late nineteenth century, here the object of concern shifted from the nation to the region. And if the Meiji obsession with excavating the past in the service of the nation was part of a global phenomenon, the romance of the local in interwar Japan also resonated with a contemporaneous fashion for folklore and folk crafts in other societies. For Japan, the rise of regional movements was overdetermined by the accumulations of the modernizing project of the Meiji period. The capitalist revolution turned to the development of regional markets, stimulating the expansion of domestic consumer industries. The maturation of the central organs of constitutional monarchy led to a new dynamism in local politics and the bureaucratic proliferation of regional governments. Vehicles of nation building and central control, such as the educational system, established themselves as fixtures in their communities. Once they sank local roots, schools could be recaptured for local agendas.

This is not to suggest that nation building—now complete—was replaced by region making. Rather, regionalism emerged as an invented tradition alongside the nation. While the central state continued to nationalize its citizenry through the schools, the army, and other institutions of national developmentalism established in the Meiji period, the prefectural and municipal governments engaged in their own projects of community building and regional development, often making use of the same institutions and deploying similar tactics. Indeed, technologies of nationalism proved easily adaptable to building imagined communities at other sociospatial scales. But although region making did not follow upon nation building in a simple sequential process, the relationship between regionalism and nationalism did change in character over the course of the late nineteenth and early twentieth centuries. In the Meiji period one of the major challenges of the new state was to overcome institutions of local autonomy: to nationalize the feudal domains, systems of taxation, local militias, and so forth, all of which had grown accustomed to regional government over the three centuries of Tokugawa rule. At the same time, the local occupied a prominent place on the agenda of the new Meiji state, through the efforts to establish a uniform set of administrative units at the prefectural (*dōfuken*) and city, town, and village (*shichōson*) levels. By the teens, the situation had changed; the central state commanded sufficient authority over localities that it no longer viewed the region as a threat to the nation. Far from it, the national government looked with favor on the variety of local culture movements of the interwar period, movements that now constructed forms of regional community within a national frame.

This chapter looks at the formation of a modern regional identity in the 1920s and 1930s and how it became associated with the idea of the city as sovereign subject and organic unity. Rapid urbanization in the interwar years meant that many of the constituent elements of Japanese cities were new, including their populations of recent in-migrants, their territorial base of newly annexed land, their built environments, and their forms of governance. Nevertheless, community-building efforts and the regional development movements of the interwar period helped install self-understandings of provincial cities as imagined communities with ancient pedigrees.

Over the course of the teens, twenties, and thirties, a local-history boom took off across the country. In the north, Akita's local historians published more than eighty works in the years before 1945, half of these in the 1930s.[3] On the Japan Sea coast, every county in Ishikawa brought out its own history, as did many villages. The first wave of prefectural histories emerged at this time; some of these, such as the two-volume *General History of Okayama Prefecture* (1930) and *A Seventy-Year History of Okayama Prefecture* (1936), were published by the local press, while others, such as *A History of Hokkaido* (1933), were published by the local radio station.[4] In many cases publishers doubled as editors, convening the committees of scholars, reporters, and government bureaucrats that conducted the research and wrote the text of these studies. This was also the founding moment for city histories, which were likewise collectively authored and locally published, running into multiple volumes produced over years, sometimes even decades. Barely forty years after its founding, Sapporo brought out its first city history, a fat volume that topped a thousand pages. In 1930, Niigata published a two-volume study twice this length, and Kanazawa produced an astonishing fourteen-volume city history between 1916 and 1937.[5]

The studies that emerged from this flurry of activity were strikingly diverse in both subject matter and form. While some took local administrative units—cities, counties, and prefectures—as their subject matter, others focused on local specialty products, like the books on Shizuoka's sericulture industry and its tea production, or the *History of Sapporo Beer*, written in-house by the Japan Beer Company.[6] One after another, localities brought out histories of their schools, newspapers, and hospitals, of their chambers of commerce and railroads, and even of station names, merchants associations, and entertainment districts.[7] In addition to branding cities in terms of prominent institutions, these efforts established the company and institutional history as a standard form of historical research and a key strategy for public relations and organizational promotion.

Biography was another popular category in the new wave of local histories, including biographical dictionaries and document collections. Many of these were paeans to political leaders, heirs to the Tokugawa-era biographic form, where scholars combed the lives of rulers for exemplary virtues that justified and explained their exalted position. Biographies of the early twentieth century, however, went beyond the Confucian homily to ground the qualities of good leadership in the particularities of the local community. With titles like *Shikoku: A History of Local Progress and the Men Who Led It*, the new biographies engaged in a kind of local boosterism that highlighted the accomplishments of local leaders along with the success of the locality itself.[8] Former castle towns published works that showcased the leadership of their great daimyo families, such as the string of biographies on Kanazawa's Maeda men, the clan who ruled the Kaga domain.[9] Often, biographies and biographical sourcebooks were actually produced by scions of the great families, a circumstance that exacerbated the tendency toward hagiography. In Kumamoto, descendants of the Hosokawa daimyo household spent the teens and twenties working on editing and annotating documents from the clan archives. The results were ten volumes of documents, published in 1931 and 1932.[10] While Tokugawa-era biographies strove to abstract universal principles of good governance, the new biographical literature aimed to particularize the qualities of leadership, linking these great men to the heritage of local history and highlighting their legacy for the present.

Like other genres of the new local history, the biographical research produced during these years became foundational, as these works aged into standard reference texts for later generations of historians. A recent account of Kumamoto prefecture spotlighted interwar works such as Sumita Masaji's biographical dictionary, *Higo jinmei jiten*, and Yamazaki Sasatada's biography of nineteenth-century political activist Yokoi Shōnan as classic texts in the field of local history.[11] In this way the interwar movement crystallized the genres that have defined the practice of local history through the present: the company history; the bureaucratic–institutional history; prefectural, town, and village histories; the annotated document collections; and so forth. While local history stabilized as a form in the successive waves of history-writing after World War Two, during the peak of the first local-history boom the enormous variety in subject matter reflected both the vibrancy and the heterogeneity of groups involved in the movement.

The local histories of the interwar years were diverse in matters of content as well. Some followed the Tokugawa precedent of local gazetteers, such as the fourteen-volume *Kanazawa City History*, which divided its narrative into thematic sections on topography (four volumes), administration (two volumes), and education (four volumes), with additional books on industry, religion, and customs (*fūzoku*).[12] Although Kanazawa borrowed an earlier schematic for local history, the relative weight placed on topography and education in the overall narrative, as well as the overwhelming focus on the period of the castle town, reflected a more contemporary and particular set of concerns on the part of Kanazawa's historians. Under the rubric of "topography," compilers described the minute history of settlement as well as the physical expansion of the city, neighborhood by neighborhood, during the city's administration by the Maeda clan. Volumes on education dealt with educational-policy shifts under subsequent daimyo administrations, the growth of Confucian academies and temple schools during the Tokugawa period, and the works of the domain's most prominent scholars. These choices signaled the authors' conviction that the essence of Kanazawa inhered in the physical environment of the city, in its position as a center of higher learning, and in the heritage of its years as a wealthy and powerful castle town. They reflected the generalized concern of the local-history movement to link past and present, even as they conveyed the idea that Kanazawa's local culture comprised the inheritance of a particular past.

Other communities chose to foreground different features of their histories to capture the essence of the local character. The two-volume *Niigata City History*, like the Kanazawa history, devoted sections to customs, politics, and topography but produced a strikingly different narrative. The history of the built environment in Niigata was recounted in a section on the port which occupied the heart of the narrative. In contrast to Kanazawa historians, who anchored local identity to development as a castle town, Niigata scholars highlighted the role of the port in the constitution of local culture. The *Niigata City History* also stood out for its extensive definition of the political, a category that subsumed administration, finance, and transportation. Here the balance of the text concentrated on post- rather than pre-Meiji times.[13] In Kanazawa's history, the discussion of topography branded the city as a visible relic of its feudal past, and sections on education showcased its status as a center of traditional learning and culture. The *Niigata City History*, in contrast, defined the community through the economic activity of the port and the leadership of city government in local development. This signaled the belief that what made Niigata special, what captured its power and essence, was the dynamism of the contemporary economy, the growth of its industries, and its function as a port. In other words, local historians defined the city of Niigata as an economic space, and Kanazawa as the cultural legacy of an earlier lifeworld. Later generations of local historiography would tend to smooth out such variations: today, multivolume local histories tend toward an identical format and conform to a standard periodization. But in this first wave, the striking diversity in story line and emphasis was an expression of the local genesis of these ideas as well as the premium placed on locating the particular character of a community. Caught up in the exuberant regionalism of the interwar period, communities celebrated the individuality of their locales and paid homage to that distinctiveness by harnessing it to a particular past.

There were many forces driving the upsurge in local history in the twenties and thirties. The movement tied in with new initiatives to develop tourism and efforts to promote local products, as local governments struggled to come to grips with the economic fibrillations of the 1920s. It was inspired by writings that celebrated the importance of the local as a storehouse of national culture, such as Nitobe Inazo's local studies (*chihōgaku*) and Yanagita Kunio's folklore (*minzokugaku*).[14] The movement also tapped the same well of sentiment that fed regional literary, poetry, and arts circles in the interwar period. But most important, by far, were local schools. Here a combination of central government initiatives and teacher activism came together to energize a drive for local history.

For the national government, education became the linchpin of efforts to counter the rise of radical thought in the wake of World War One. As part of a hometown-education (*kyōdo kyōiku*) initiative, the Ministry of Education encouraged local school boards to adopt provincial history and geography as part of the primary school curriculum. Their goal was to inculcate a sense of local attachment and loyalty to community. By pumping up local pride, the state hoped to foster commitment to local development and to redirect popular energies away from protest and opposition. If people loved their hometowns, the idea went, they would work harder at their jobs and stop complaining about low wages or adverse working conditions or poor government.[15]

The state's hometown-education policy also aimed to counter the rise of the liberal-education (*jiyū kyōiku*) and other movements that sought in the 1920s to use educational institutions to promote a progressive agenda. The liberal education movement called for reform of the authoritarian pedagogy and rote-learning style that characterized the educational system; its leaders pushed to retool schools to provide utilitarian, child-centered learning that would instill values of autonomy and individuality.[16] This movement commanded a wide following. The journal *Jiyū kyōiku*, one of its principal organs, was based in Chiba prefecture on the outskirts of Tokyo, but a large share of the subscriptions went to places like Akita in the northeast and Tokushima on the island of Shikoku. Through magazines such as *Jiyū kyōiku*, the movement exerted enormous influence on elementary school teachers and normal schools in regions around the country. As part of their efforts to instill the values of liberal education, teachers created school newspapers, worked field trips into the curriculum, and instituted the practice of group travel for school children.[17]

Though the state envisioned hometown education as an alternative to this movement, hoping to co-opt teacher activism and redirect it toward state goals, the results did not always conform to expectations. Teachers already energized by the liberal education movement embraced the possibilities offered by hometown education because they saw it as an extension of—not an alternative to—liberal education. They picked up the themes of local empowerment and enthusiastically redesigned curricula to incorporate local history and geography; they produced new textbooks for local use. Following the principles of liberal education, they looked at the creative potential of producing local history and saw community-centered learning as a cognate to child-centered learning. Studying local topography and the flora and fauna specific to the region provided a method for practical learning and incorporating education into daily life. All this may have nurtured the sense of loyalty to home and country desired by the national government, but it also encouraged values of utilitarianism, autonomy, and self-reliance.

Like liberal education, the hometown-education movement drew an enthusiastic following. Schools established special classrooms (*kyōdoshitsu*) and published textbooks on local history and geography (*kyōdo dokuhon*). Teachers' colleges and elementary schools provided the base for the movement. In Okayama, elementary teachers formed organizations such as the Okayama Culture Study Group and the Central Japan Folklore Studies Association in the late 1920s and undertook a variety of research projects. Teachers in Okayama Normal School took their students on trips around the prefecture to conduct historical surveys that became the basis of works such as *A General History of Okayama Prefecture*, *Monumental Epigraphs in Okayama Prefecture*, and *Okayama City History*, all published in the late 1930s.[18] In Ishikawa, the Ishikawa Danjo Normal School established a local-history archive in 1932, with assembled materials on local habitat, climate, industry, geography, history, and culture. Like Ishikawa Danjo, other normal schools in the region compiled and published materials relating to local history; an organization of Ishikawa normal school teachers founded a local-history journal called *Kyōdo kenkyū kiyō*.[19] Similar activities took place elsewhere throughout the country, generating a groundswell of interest in local history and contributing to the proliferation of new textbooks on local communities.[20]

Outside of schools, libraries provided another institutional base for the local-history movement. In Ishikawa, for example, the Ishikawa Prefecture Library Association was formed in 1929. Based in the central prefectural library in Kanazawa, the organization drew members from libraries throughout the prefecture. They worked with local educators to promote reading through readership surveys, reading tests, and other mechanisms. The Ishikawa libraries took an active role in the local-history movement, publishing a series of document collections between 1931 and 1938 and holding exhibitions on local themes, such as the 1936 Sea of Japan Regional Culture Exhibit.[21] Groups of folklorists and antiquarians joined forces with the movement. In Kanazawa, building on the foundations of efforts by the Maeda family (that of the former daimyo) to preserve and publish collections of historical documents, local intellectuals founded the Kanazawa Culture Association, the Ishikawa Prefecture Geography Society, and the Kanazawa Folklore Association. Like the teachers and the librarians, they engaged in document compilation and annotation, sponsored exhibitions on regional themes, and published books on local history.[22]

The profusion of new local-history texts of the twenties and thirties grew out of this sort of grassroots activism, which also accounted for the texts' variability and uneven distribution. The normal and elementary school teachers who were principally responsible for setting off the local-history boom were products of the new institutional structures laid down in Meiji educational reforms. By the 1920s, the national school system had sunk deep local roots. Schools were more than mere vessels for the dissemination of knowledge for national development and national citizenship: they were sites for the production of local culture and for forging a more narrowly bounded sense of community. The local-history movement was both cause and effect of this process.

At the same time, the local histories of the interwar years drew on institutions of scholarship and education that went even further back in time. One reason that intellectuals seized upon history so enthusiastically as a medium for local expression was the extensive legacy of history writing and an abiding respect for the moral and political uses of historiography in Japanese culture. Beginning in the seventh century, the early Japanese state imported the norms and forms of history writing from China, along with religion, art, writing, and a variety of other cultural practices. The Chinese model continued to dominate Japanese intellectual production well into the nineteenth century, when it began to retreat before internal critiques and the challenge of alternative knowledge systems imported from Europe and America. But in its heyday, neo-Confucianist historicism was a thriving enterprise for samurai intellectuals. Historical analysis occupied the heart of the main philosophic, religious, and political debates of the day; it generated the ideological lifeblood of the Tokugawa political and social order.

Neo-Confucianism held that the universe was systematically and rationally ordered, and that its principles were accessible to human understanding. The principles that guided the universe extended from the metaphysical realm through the physical and social order; they interlinked individual and public domains. A principal object of neo-Confucianist analysis was to prescribe models for good government, ethical social order, and virtuous behavior. In pursuit of this goal, neo-Confucianism privileged historical study, viewing history as the means to illuminate the operations and order of the universe and looking to the past for ethical norms and models of good government. Since a stable political and social order reflected a "mandate of heaven" that rewarded good rulers and punished bad, a careful examination of past administrations could identify both the recipients of "the mandate" and the policies that secured their success. Such an approach yielded the normative historical narratives derisively labeled the "praise and blame" school by critics in the late nineteenth century, who rejected normative history in favor of the objectivity they identified with German scientific historiography.

The other key feature of neo-Confucian historicism was a commitment to *kōshōgaku*—research based on classical texts and documents. The high value placed on old texts as an evidentiary base for historical writing gave rise to a powerful empiricist orientation in neo-Confucian historiography, and it explained the enormous efforts devoted to the discovery, authentification, and compilation of document collections and ancient texts. Thus, leading historians of the Tokugawa period devoted decades of work to a punctilious linguistic analysis of the original meanings of characters and words in classical texts such as the mytho-historical *Kojiki*, the romantic narrative *Tale of Genji*, and the great poetry collection *Manyōshū*. Successive generations of historians working on the Mito domain's *Great History of Japan* took field trips to temples and aristocratic storehouses to search out documents. Not only did this leave a prodigious legacy of document collections and preserved literature for later generations to work with, but it also associated history writing with positivism and empiricism.

Both of these tendencies informed the practice of local history in the Tokugawa period. Following Chinese practice, domains produced local gazetteers and studies of local administrations that conformed with the tenets of neo-Confucian historicism. These studies tracked the fortunes of daimyo clans and wrote the history of the domains in terms of daimyo administration. Provincial gazetteers served as guidebooks to the domain, offering information on such topics as roads and waterways, manufactured and agricultural products, officialdom, literature, and inspirational men of distinction.[23]

Historical consciousness and practice began to shift in the mid-eighteenth century, when internal critiques of excessive reliance on China emerged with a nativist school of historiography and the Mito historians started to question the reliability of the classical texts that had served as the basis of the Tokugawa shogunate's authority and legitimacy. These and other centers of samurai scholarship had already begun to chip away at the verities of neo-Confucian orthodoxy when they confronted a radically different European epistemology in the late nineteenth century. The encounter with the West revolutionized Japanese thinking on a wide range of topics; the introduction of German positivism and the ideas of the British enlightenment signaled the birth of a modern historiography. From the 1870s and 1880s, as part of the "civilization and enlightenment" movement, a fountain of historical writing appeared, including translations and adaptations of western works, historical novels, histories of civilization, and a major project to produce a national history through the new government's Historiographic Institute.[24] Running through this wide-ranging and exuberant movement was a new global perspective on history and an overarching concern with defining Japan within the world community of nations. The consequence of "civilization and enlightenment" thus laid the groundwork of a national history that turned the purpose of history writing away from accounts of daimyo and shogun— their battles, negotiations, and administrations—to the history of a people: their customs, inclinations, and characteristics. This national turn constituted the central thrust of the historical revolution of Meiji.

Though this process is usually understood in terms of a historical break or rupture that divided a feudal from a modern epistemology, it is perhaps more accurate to say that the import of western historical and social thought provided a new set of tools that intensified and accelerated a revolution well under way. Thus, Rankean appeals for "objectivity" were deployed to reinforce the ongoing attack on Confucian modes of narrating history from an ethical perspective; calls for a "scientific method" highlighted problems in the use of mytho-historical texts like the *Kojiki* as sources for actual historical events. In other words, the late Tokugawa critique of received historiographic practice was continued in the Meiji period on European epistemological grounds.

At the same time, late-nineteenth-century Japanese intellectuals found it easy to embrace western ideas because they resonated so well with many of the tenets of their own historiographic practice. Rankean positivism could absorb Confucian empiricism—both privileged the document as the source of historical Truth. Moreover, the Rankean focus on the state as key historical actor dovetailed neatly with the Confucian preoccupation with statecraft. The new world-historical perspective that situated Japan along the time line of civilizational evolution could be grafted fairly easily onto a regional-historical perspective that placed Japan within a Sino-centric culture zone, also structured hierarchically. With Japan now fixed in a larger global setting, the Euro-centric universalism of the enlightenment stepped into the mold cast by the universal principals of the Chinese state system. Advocates of Herbert Spencer's stagist historiography used categories of "civilization" and "barbarism" that were also part of a Confucian worldview, but deployed them to describe a new set of international relationships. Here, as with so much of the epistemological revolution of the late nineteenth century, certain western ideas were embraced precisely because they felt familiar: they made sense in terms of the existing historical consciousness.

The new local histories written in the twenties and thirties bore the imprint of Tokugawa precedent, as well as of the innovations of Meiji historiography. But when the Meiji history boom went local, it also departed from precedent in interesting and important ways. First, unlike national-history writing, which was centered in organs of higher learning such as new universities or the Historiographic Institute, the institutional vehicles of the local-history movement occupied a lower rung on the educational hierarchy— elementary and secondary schools. This meant that the knowledge effects of local history percolated out into a wider social field. Indeed, one could argue that it took the local-history movement to bring the epistemological revolution of the Meiji period out beyond the circumscribed world of the educated elite. Second, when the object of historical inquiry shifted from the nation to the locality, it followed a broader turn that focused on the region in the wake of World War One. The deepening of the national-institutional revolution of the Meiji era occurred through the localization of initiative and momentum in areas such as industrial development, representative government, and public education. As the Meiji reforms sank roots and generated local off-shoots, the national-development thrust of the reforms was supplemented by proliferating regional initiatives. In the process, national leadership, the central government, and the metropolitan intelligentsia lost much of the voice they previously had in Meiji historiography. Finally, unlike the self-conscious cosmopolitanism of national-history writing that looked to the West for intellectual models and points of reference, the local-history movement directed its gaze decidedly inward. Although Meiji reforms created the conditions of possibility for local history, and the hometown educational policy of the 1920s galvanized teachers into action, local control meant that national concerns could be relegated to the periphery—and they were. Moreover, local historians did little to reach out to their counterparts in other cities. Indeed, if there was any point in common in the prodigious intellectual products of the interwar local-history movement, it was their insistent provincialism.

TIME LINES OF LOCAL IDENTITY

The local-history movement produced new forms of knowledge that linked localities with a particular temporality. Through the construction of distinctive narratives of a place—its origins, its turning points, and its defining features—local identity became tied to local time. In the process, the interwar local-history movement invented the quintessentially modern form of local history—the urban biography. As the *Niigata City History* put it, "Just as nations have national histories and families have genealogies, local communities [*kyōdo*] have their own histories."[25] Both the clan and the nation were symbolic reference points for the new urban biographies. Drawing heavily on the models and inspiration of national historiography, the profusion of urban biographies brought out in the twenties and thirties told the story of the city as the birth and rise of an organic community that was rooted in a particular place. And yet, local historians did not make their community into a microcosm of the nation, nor did they draw their accounts simply in reaction or reference to the larger national story. Rather, these histories laid down a set of time lines specific to each community: historical time was heterogeneous, not uniform. Within the narrative frame of the urban biography, the single historical time line of the nation was inhabited by the multiple temporalities of the local.

Like the new national history of the late nineteenth century, local history was concerned with the question of origins. Historians of national history pursued this question in a variety of ways. Archeologists excavated the great shell mounds in search of Japan's preliterate society. The discovered remains of Jōmon and Yayoi societies touched off a debate over whether these were ancestors of modern-day Yamato or Ainu people, a question not settled in favor of the Yamato until the twenties. Philologists looked to ancient texts for the origins of Japanese civilization, while the enlightenment historians tracked the stages of social evolution back to their foundations in hunter-gatherer society.[26] Although national history was concerned with locating the origins of a commonly, if vaguely, understood "Japanese civilization," local scholars encountered more difficulties with the question of beginnings. Should the essence of the city be tracked to the original locus of settlement, the foundations of the built environment, or the ancestors of the local community? Urban biographers laid out multiple starting points for the life story of their cities, whose fractured origins reflected the dilemmas of the interwar generation as they struggled to define a form and method for urban history.

The *Niigata City History* provided at least four accounts of the origins of the city. The preface began by tracing the first recorded mention of city place-names. The district of Kōtō, annexed by Niigata City in 1914, appeared in accounts of Kōtoku's Court (seventh century) as a stronghold for frontier defense. Kambara (another Niigata place-name) was described as a famous harbor in the Engishiki, a tenth-century sacred legal text. An earlier designation for Niigata itself—Tōsai—proved more of a challenge. In the absence of clear documentary evidence, historians speculated that Tōsai/Niigata was established when the daimyo Uesugi Kenshin became lord of Kasugayama Castle in 1549. During the great civil wars of the sixteenth century, the Uesugi clan controlled an enormous estate in Echigo province, whose boundaries were redrawn to create Niigata prefecture in the wake of the Meiji Restoration. The historical time line became easier to trace from the seventeenth century, when records documented Tōsai's relocation in 1615, its rebuilding in 1655, and its dynamic growth by the end of the century.[27]

A second accounting of origins tracked the development of Niigata's characteristic local culture, noting that it evolved out of the peculiarities of topography and climate—"in Echigo the snowy season lasts a long time"—that impeded the development of overland communications and cut the region off from the major centers of population to the south and west. Here the account highlighted Niigata's temporally imprecise point of origin in a snowbound harbor and a people defined by residence in the "snow country." Its position on the northern coast also meant that the ships plying their trade along Japan's coastal ports provided a conduit for cultural exchange. Thus the constraints imposed by geography and climate shaped the development of local character; Niigata's beginnings as a port city whose seasonal opening offered painfully brief opportunities for the trade that sustained the local population stamped the local personality. In the self-stereotype proffered in the *Niigata City History*, the "snow country" encouraged the development of "a determined and hardworking character" in local residents.[28]

A related story focused on the origins of the port itself, seeking the first emergence of a harbor in the vicinity of contemporary Niigata. Here, history began in the early tenth century, when Kambara harbor rose to prominence. Then for many centuries the trail went cold, as the port either died or was lost to the historical record. The history of Niigata port resumed in the Tokugawa period, when the port city grew and thrived once again.[29] Yet another account of the city's origins focused on the roots of human settlement on the physical site of present-day Niigata. Tracking the shifting course of the river, along whose banks the road grid was laid out, historians speculated about when settlement became possible on the current location. Offering an environmental time line that traced Niigata's beginnings to the late sixteenth century, they understood Niigata in physical terms—as the built environment of a riverbank town.[30] In the multiple origin stories contained in the *Niigata History*, the word *Niigata* signified a physical location, the people who founded it, the community that grew up in the vicinity, and the port that constituted its economic foundation. The inability of local historians to settle on a definitive beginning reflected the fact that what defined the essence of a city was not yet fixed.

The *Kanazawa City History* relayed the same fractured tale of urban beginnings. Its authors searched for the roots of Kanazawa's physical location along the ancient Hokuriku highway and tracked the etymology of the name *Kanazawa* in classical texts. They scrutinized topographical records of land use along the Sai and Asano Rivers for the earliest signs of a permanent settlement and looked closely at the founding of a religious community around Honganji, a temple of the Ikkō-shū sect, in the fifteenth century. They examined the birth of the castle town in the 1580s, tracing the rapid urban growth in the seventeenth century under the direction of the Maeda clan—Kanazawa's fortunes rising in tandem with the power and glory of the Kaga domain.[31]

The difficulty in fixing a precise point of origin in these urban histories reflected the ambiguity in identifying the city with a polity, an economy, the land, or a human settlement. As historians groped for a definition of "the city," their first attempts at urban biography bore the trace of their struggles in these multiple points of origin. What exactly was Kanazawa? Was it the location on which the contemporary city was sited? Was it the natural topography, the peculiarities of the local environment that gave the town its character? Or was it the urban polity—Kanazawa the capital city of Ishikawa prefecture—the city-state that traced its roots back to its origins in the castle town? Was Niigata defined by its port economy? Or was it the port culture—the peculiar snowbound place cut off from inland Japan but connected to the sea? The fractured story lines tracked both place and community, both polity and production, through time. In the process, they created a local time line that adhered to late-nineteenth-century concepts of linear, progressive time and that fixed local identity to a particular chronology. But identity also inhered in the place itself—in a territorial locus of origin that proved just as difficult to fix as the city's temporal beginning.

As historians worked through these conceptual challenges, their ideas about local identity tapped intellectual currents circulating through their communities. While the local-history movement took form in the twenties and thirties, local boosters in other venues—in business organizations and local government, in the press, schools, and tourist organizations—staked competing claims on an urban identity constituted through a key commodity, a signature art form, or an iconic topographic feature. The possibilities that local branding offered for the accumulation of political and financial power were just beginning to be understood. The first generation of urban biographies were drafted at this moment of creative opening. At a time when the city idea could be stretched to accommodate new demands for building a sense of belonging to a "greater Kanazawa" or a "greater Niigata," just what the "greater city" meant was still open to debate. As politicians, artists, and businessmen tasked the local brand with a growing list of expectations, urban biographies were called to serve an expanded definition of "the city": not just settlement but also economic base; not just cultural persona but also political character; not just topography but also patois. Through their thought experiments about urban origins, elementary school teachers and municipal librarians helped reinvent the city idea.

The painstaking research published in the multivolume accounts such as the *Niigata* and *Kanazawa* city histories was popularized contemporaneously through a variety of means, including local guidebooks, as well as the exhibits and textbooks generated by the local-history movement. In these abbreviated forms, the ambiguities in points-of-origin were compressed into a highly distilled urban biography. In the process, the impossibility of empirically fixing the origins of the city was resolved through mystification. The *Kanazawa Citizen's Reader*, compiled between 1924 and 1927 as a textbook for use in the Young Men's Training School and the Kanazawa Municipal Institute of Continuing Education, provided an example of this narrative sleight of hand.[32] Like many such texts, the *Kanazawa Citizen's Reader* was assembled by committee, which included the mayor, the headmaster of Fourth Higher School, the secretary of education for Ishikawa Prefecture, and a score of individuals drawn from the chamber of commerce, municipal government, and secondary schools.[33] Its declared purpose was to "democratize knowledge" by depicting the most "up-to-date portrait of the city . . . historically, geographically, and as an urban center."[34] Such textbooks sought to promote civic pride and build a sense of community by educating urban citizens with a common framework of local identity, which drew heavily on the insights of the new local histories.

The *Kanazawa Citizen's Reader* began with an account of the etymological possibilities of the place-name *Kanazawa*, condensing a discussion that ranged over many chapters in the *Kanazawa City History* into eight brief pages. The *Reader* singled out three potential sources of the place-name *Kanazawa*, presenting the problem of origins as a kind of mystery to which several solutions had been proffered. First, *Kanazawa* may have derived from a Heian-period agricultural estate (*shōen*) that occupied the present-day site of Oyama Shrine and Kenrokuen Garden. A second possibility was that the city took its name from Kanazawa Genji, retainer of Inoue Saemon, whose arrival in the locality was recorded in 1185. The third source was the legend of Fuji Goro the hermit, who sold potatoes at the local market. According to the *Kanazawa City Reader's* account of this story, one day as Fuji Goro dug potatoes he discovered gold dust or nuggets, which he washed nearby—in the *kana* (gold) *zawa* (spring) that reputedly gave the city its name. An ancient landmark in Kenrokuen Garden marked the site where Fuji Goro was said to have washed his gold.[35] As the *Reader* emphasized, however, which of the three possibilities represented the true origin remained a mystery. Thus, in repackaging the detailed empirical investigations into etymology from the city history as these three legends of the name's origin, the *Citizen's Reader* conveyed the sense that Kanazawa's origins were lost in the mists of time—ancient, mystical, and primordial.

A more concrete time line centering on political history emerged in the second chapter of the *Citizen's Reader*, "The Maeda Family and Kanazawa."

Here the *Citizen's Reader* noted that the "cradle of local history" could be traced back to a spot in the vicinity of present-day Kenrokuen Garden, where the ancient village of Yamazaki once stood. The *Reader* traced Kanazawa's progress from these humble origins: erection of Honganji Temple on the future grounds of Kanazawa Castle, the fortification of the temple and the coming of the warrior-monks in the late sixteenth century, and urban settlement on the outskirts of the temple complex. From this point on, as the *Citizen's Reader* observed, "the history of Kanazawa city and the history of this fortification became one and the same." What followed was the train of events that marked the rise of the castle town: Oda Nobunaga's campaigns against the monks of Honganji, the razing of the temple, the construction of a castle on its ruins, the territory granted to the Maeda clan, the Maeda's establishment of the castle town and, from this base, their rule of Kaga domain until the fall of the Bakufu in 1868.[36]

In these brief sketches the *Kanazawa Citizen's Reader* wove the multiple historical threads laid out in separate chapters and volumes of the *Kanazawa City History* into a single strand. Opening with speculation about the derivation of "Gold Spring," from there the story turned to the evolution of an agricultural village into a fortified castle town, in a seamless shift from legend to history. Circulated through the conduits of the hometown-education movement, repetition and reproduction elevated these newly fashioned historical vignettes to the status of local gospel. As they became part of a canon of hometown knowledge, such stories of a common heritage constituted a shared field of meaning that bound the local citizenry to one another and set them apart from other communities.

Local histories placed an invented temporality in the service of regional identity in other ways as well. While the search for origins encoded local subjectivity in a common set of roots and a primordial identity, these histories also laid out new chronologies that were specific to the locality. Like the question of origins, the organization of local histories around the concept of linear, progressive time reflected the powerful influence of Meiji historicism. To be sure, the impact of modernist historiography was somewhat uneven, and sections of local histories frequently reproduced earlier practices of stringing together documents and listing exemplary activities of successive administrations. But in their exposition of the development of the port in Niigata, or the evolution of the city plan in Kanazawa, or the opening of Hokkaido, local histories subscribed to a narrative of progress borrowed from the Meiji enlightenment.

The force of national-history writing was also felt in the intrusion of national time into the local chronology. Local histories signified national time by reference to standard historical periods such as Heian, Kamakura, Tokugawa, or Meiji. Specific events were marked by the imperial calendar— for example, Bunji 3 (A.D. 1188) or Eiroku 1 (A.D. 1558). In these ways local histories referenced a single chronology that was structured according to the succession of dynastic rulers at the center, a time line privileging centralized political administration and authority. Clearly situating their narratives within this larger sense of nation-time, local histories made no attempt to reject their subordination to centralized authority or to assert autonomy from the nation. By the same token, these histories operated within multiple temporalities. Nation-time progressed according to the logics of political administration at the center, but local time ran by a different clock. Local histories conveyed the interplay of these two time lines—their simultaneity and their points of intersection, but also their relative autonomy. The strength and prominence of the local chronology in local-historical narratives height-ened consciousness of these multiple temporalities—the complexities of modern time—in the provinces. At the center, Tokyo-time and nation-time were more closely aligned, but in the provinces local history could convey a sense of simultaneity without synchronicity.

For Hokkaido, the story of contact and colonization drove the chronology and its periodization. In *The New History of Hokkaido* (1936), the chapters marked the march of progress toward the Japanization of the island of Ezo in a series of stages. The earliest stage—"prehistory"—began with a portrait of Ainu/Ezo society on the eve of Abe no Hirafu's campaigns against the Ezo between 558 and 560. The first Japanese explorers who followed in the wake of the campaigning brought the seeds of historical change to a static Ezo, ruptur-ing a way of life that had existed, unchanged, for centuries. Chapters on first contact described the cultural and religious influence of Japanese explorers on Ezo society, as well as the opening of a trade relationship. From there the story moved forward to the establishment of the Matsumae domain and its efforts to develop Ezo: missions for reconnaissance and trade, the opening of ports, the rise of a discourse on colonization, and the establishment of the fishing and other important industries. The next stage emerged with the decline in Matsumae's political fortunes and the beginnings of Russian encroachment on Ezo. Matsumae's inability to effectively counter this new threat from the north galvanized the Bakufu into action; the shogunate took control of Matsumae administration, attempting to reestablish Japanese primacy in Ezo and drive the Russians out. Next, negotiations with the United States and the opening of a foreign port in Hakodate signaled the beginning of a new phase of foreign trade, the birth of modern industry, and the general influx of modern culture from Japan and the West. The opening of the port was followed by the inauguration of the "management of Hokkaido" through the ten-year colonization plan of the island, annexed and renamed in the aftermath of the Meiji Restoration. Under the plan, local administration was established to guide development of the island, while the first waves of Japanese settlers moved north to Hokkaido. The final chapters brought the story up to the close of the Taishō period (1926), with details on city building in Sapporo, Hakodate, and elsewhere; the establishment of modern farming techniques on Hokkaido's virgin tracts of land; and the impressive expansion of mining, manufacturing, and commerce.

The most striking aspect of this Hokkaido time line was that the signposts of national history were eclipsed by a local set of milestones. National time lines of the nineteenth-century transition from feudalism to modernity usually included a set list of events: the failed efforts to resolve the feudal crisis in the Tempō Reforms of the 1830s and 1840s, the coming of the American squadron of "black ships" and the opening of Japan in 1853, and the Meiji Restoration of 1868 that overthrew the feudal regime. For the nation, these were epochal moments, each signaling a sea change in economy, culture, and polity, and each a key stage in the formation of the modern nation-state. Yet the history depicted in the *New History of Hokkaido* placed this national chronology in the background, choosing to highlight a different series of events. For Hokkaido, these local milestones of progress marked stages in a teleology of colonization: first contacts, the opening of trade, the beginnings of Japanese settlement, annexation, and so forth. Together they told the story of the evolution of Ezo into Hokkaido.[37]

Like the primordial origins of the city, these time lines of local history became a core component of the narrative form of urban biography. The chronology of colonization became incorporated into Sapporo's life story through textbooks produced for the local school system in the 1920s and 1930s. *Sapporo chiri dokuhon (Sapporo Geography Reader)*, an elementary school reader published in 1927 by the Sapporo Board of Education, distilled the detailed account laid out in the four volumes of *The New History of Hokkaido* into a simplified story that outlined the history of Japanese colonization in two phases. Sapporo's story began in the age of exploration in the late eighteenth century. In the days when Hokkaido was still called "Ezo

Island," Bakufu agent Kondō Chūzō toured the Ishikari Plain and settled on the site of present-day Sapporo as a good location for the capital of Hokkaido. The Japanese took the name of the prefectural capital from the Ainu word *Satoporo*, a term used to describe their fishing grounds along the Toyohira River. Two hardy Japanese pioneers, Shimura Tetsuichi and Yoshida Shigehachi, moved into the vicinity of the Toyohira, making a living off the river and the land. Commemorating the first phase of Sapporo's history, the *Geography Reader* recommended a visit to the historical monument erected near Toyohira Bridge.

The establishment of the Colonization Bureau marked a new stage in the history of the town, making Sapporo into Japan's gateway to Hokkaido. Magistrate Shima Yoshitake began the program of urban construction that transformed Sapporo from wilderness to civilization, clearing the forests of elm and oak, where deer and bear roamed freely, to make way for paved streets and government buildings. This was the period the first settlers laid foot in Hokkaido, inspiring generations to come with their tales of suffering and forbearance: "They bravely endured life in the forest and helped to build the city. . . . Roads were laid, bridges erected; the city grew and thrived."[38] Statues in city parks and along the main thoroughfare of Sapporo's city center commemorated these founding fathers, agents of the Meiji government who devoted themselves to building the city and colonizing Hokkaido.[39] The history texts, the school readers, and the network of commemorative statuary worked together to shape public understandings of Sapporo as a showcase settlement, exemplar of Japan's capacity for colonization. Colonization and the transformation from wilderness to settled, city life became central to the narrative of urban progress, a triumphalist story line of expanding government, services, and urban-based collective life. As the Japanese colonized Ezo, homeland of the Ainu, its urban outposts were colonizing the countryside.

Other cities had different story lines. For Niigata, the logic of the port drove the chronology. New histories of the city were written to commemorate the expansion of the port in the twenties. They told the story of the city in terms of its development as a port town and trade center. Niigata's epochal moments, its dramatic turns, were determined by the rise and fall in the fortunes of the harbor. As the urban anthem "Niigata Port Song" proclaimed, "This village that served as harbor for river boats for many generations became one of the five ports that governed Japan's routes to the sea." Pointing to the moment when Niigata joined Kobe and Yokohama as an open port in the mid-nineteenth century, the song highlighted the role of Niigata's port in ushering in the era of civilization and enlightenment for the country and urban growth for the city.[40] Whereas the Niigata plotline told the story of "humble beginnings; a leap to greatness," Kanazawa's urban biography traced out a history of decline and recovery.

> During the 300 years of the great peace the samurai who lived beneath the castle that commanded 1,000,000 *koku* [of rice revenue]. . . . Under successive administrations they avoided intercourse with other domains and, like the still water at the bottom of a well, grew accustomed to the safety and security of this untroubled time. Lacking the stimulation of the struggle for survival, there was little of the spirit of enterprise and action. . . . People were complacent and self-satisfied with their place at the center of Japan's back coast [*ura Nihon*].[41]

For Niigata the Edo period signified a sleepy time of river transport; for Kanazawa it stood for stagnancy and complacency. Warning its citizens against "remaining intoxicated with the rosy dreams of . . . the ancient metropolis," the *Kanazawa Citizen's Reader* dismissed such dreams as "hollow and empty, the tarnished remains of a past glory." To be able to "grow and expand," required the "total elimination of the evil practices of inactivity and stagnation nurtured over the three hundred years of the Tokugawa and the deeply conservative ideas that permeated the inner core of our townspeople over those years."[42] Only eviscerating the past and embracing its opposite—movement, dynamism, and expansion—could guarantee Kanazawa's future.

Unlike Kanazawa, whose samurai community had been shattered by the social and economic transformations of the early Meiji, Okayama experienced an easier transition to the new capitalist order. Perhaps because of this, the eulogies to urban progress that circulated in Okayama took a different approach to the city's heritage as a castle town, portraying the past as a potential resource for future progress. Thus, the "Okayama City Song" celebrated the city's heritage as a castle town:

> The sites of old Bizen, redolent of a great past,
> Like the smart colors of the tower of Ujō Castle
> Or the striking cranes of Kōrakuen Gardens,
> These scenic places that still evoke the spirits of illustrious retainers and wise rulers.
> Ah! Our own great Okayama city.[43]

The multiple time lines of local identity stamped these cities with their characters, whether the pioneer spirit of Sapporo, the castle town legacies of Kanazawa and Okayama, or Niigata's history as a great trading entrepôt. In the place of the charismatic heroes and epochal events that children learned about through national-history texts, the hometown-education movement introduced a separate set of distinctive protagonists and telling episodes. The flattering urban biographies constructed and circulated through the local-history and hometown-education movements did not displace a national history erected on a wider stage, but they did not make the stories come together, either. Rather, local history asserted the primacy of the local urban frame: the city constituting an organic, indivisible unit with its own story to tell. Urban biographies of Kanazawa were entirely self-referential, conveying the message of a self-made city, a force unto itself. Local storytellers turned the city into an organic community and a sovereign subject.

CULTURE AND COMMUNITY

The idea of community as a cultural formation occupied a central place in the new modes of urban biography that emerged from the local-history movement. Seven of the fourteen volumes of *The Kanazawa City History* were devoted to aspects of cultural history: one on religion, three on scholarship and education, one on crafts, and two on customs. *The Niigata City History* placed public health, social policy, local finance, transportation, the military, and administration under the rubric of "politics"; together with urban expansion and the history of the port, these issues took up the first of two volumes. The second volume was almost entirely devoted to different aspects of local culture, including sections on shrines and temples, education, literary practice (*bungaku*), and customs (*fūzoku*). Measured against local-history writing after World War Two, this degree of attention to "culture" seems disproportionate. During the second and third waves of local history in postwar Japan, politics and the economy eclipsed culture, which subsequent historiographies tended to relegate to a single volume appended to the ends of the series. Thus, when the form of the local history stabilized in the sixties and seventies, "culture" had shifted from a central to a residual category. In the first wave, however, "culture" defined local history.[44]

This foregrounding of culture as a determinant of local history was consistent with the national turn of late-nineteenth-century historiographic practice. The new national histories began to relocate their object, turning from an examination of successive administrations to focus instead on the record of a people and their civilization. The Meiji boom in "histories of civilization" (*bunmei shi*) took up questions of educational reform and the impact of climate on culture. Historical compendia detailed Japanese cultural practices under the category "clothing, food, and shelter" (*ishokujū*). Local histories followed this lead, embracing culture as the central sphere of human activity that connected the community with its past.

Like the quest for origins and the delineation of a particular chronology, the focus on culture offered yet another temporal strategy to constitute local identity—to forge a sense of shared meaning by linking past and present. Such connections between history, culture, and community emerged in the genealogies of local educators, scholars, and artists that figured prominently in the histories of the twenties and thirties. For example, the volume on craft production (*kōgei*) in the *Kanazawa City History* traced the succession of teachers and students who established the distinctive schools of pottery and lacquerware, as well as the schools of Confucian textual exegesis and ethical interpretation that historians now marked as an expression of Kanazawa's local culture.[45] Permeated with the residue of Tokugawa historiographic practice, these genealogies expressed cultural value through the biographies of intellectual leaders whose merit was grounded in Confucian principles. At the same time, local histories enclosed their genealogies within a modern epistemology. By explicitly linking Tokugawa intellectual and artistic traditions to twentieth-century Kanazawa, local historians excavated an instance of what Reinhart Koselleck has called "futures past"—an inherently teleological past that gave rise to the present.[46]

The category of culture that figured so prominently in local-history narratives of the interwar years was also influenced by developments in other venues of intellectual life. In particular, the growth of regional arts movements in the twenties and thirties galvanized interest in local culture. Poetry associations, musical groups, theater organizations, and the like sought to give voice to a regional aesthetic style. The dissemination of their artistic production in local newspapers, magazines, and radio, in theaters and department stores, and through libraries and schools helped shape the idea of a distinctive regional culture. A project pursued by self-consciously modernist colonies of local artists dovetailed neatly with the aspirations of local historians to catalog and preserve their cultural heritage. Local historians surveyed their regions for survivals of a preindustrial past in arts and crafts, in traditional ceremonies and festivals, in folk beliefs and local legends, and in dialect and figures of speech. Their research methods were influenced by metropolitan intellectuals such as Yanagi Sōetsu and Yanagita Kunio, whose prolific writings helped establish folk arts (*mingei*) and folklore (*minzoku-gaku*) as important objects of study. Both men traveled the country in the early decades of the twentieth century, searching for examples of an indigenous folk culture that could define an authentic core of Japanese national character. Joining established networks of intellectuals and antiquarian enthusiasts in provincial cities, both men helped spread a mania for collecting and for the seductive charms of discovery.[47] As they applied these ideas to their search for regional identity, activists in the local-history movement amplified their common concern with the preservation of provincial cultures. Yet unlike Yanagi and Yanagita, who tended to examine local difference through the frame of a national culture, local activists were squarely focused on the region. This created a certain amount of tension in the concept of folk—which became a sign of difference between Japan and the West on the one hand, and of regional distinctions within the nation on the other.

For those interested in regional culture, the social networks of intellectuals involved in the local-history movement provided a point of intersection with local arts groups, collectors of folk art, and folklore associations. The widely respected Niigata folklore association, Koshiji, offered one instance of this sort of overlap. The organization held regular meetings, sponsored surveys and collecting trips, and published a magazine, *Koshiji*, which became renowned as a sterling example of a regional folklore journal. Members of Koshiji included Kanda Kyotarō, a prominent intellectual who was at once a professor of Japanese literature at the local girl's higher school, a priest at a local shrine, the head of the historical archives for Niigata's main local bank (Dai-yon Ginkō), and a respected poet and secretary of the local *waka* (classical Japanese-style poetry) association. Andō Bumpei, vice president of Niigata's Chamber of Commerce and senior editor of the *Niigata History Reader* (*Niigata kyōdo dokuhon*) was also a founding member of Koshiji, as was the head of the Niigata Historical Association, Fujita Fukutarō, and Hasegawa Shō, a professor at Niigata Commercial College whose resume included a stint at the prestigious Tokyo University of Fine Arts. Calling themselves "hobbyists of the local" (*chihō no shumika*), members of Koshiji saw themselves as men of aesthetic discernment and erudition. And yet their use of the word *shumi* signified both "hobby" and "taste," reflecting the somewhat ambiguous position of organizations such as Koshiji between expertise and amateurism.[48]

Members of Koshiji were prominent public intellectuals in their communities. Their commitment to the folklore project was both personal and professional and reflected their concerns with regional culture both old and new. "Hobbyists of the local" aimed not only to preserve vanishing folkways but also to contribute to the production of a vibrant modern culture.

The name of the Niigata folklore association—Koshiji—was a reference to an archaic name for the region that comprised the ancient provinces of Echigo, Etchū, Noto, Kaga, and Echizen, and which covered the modern prefectures of Niigata, Toyama, Ishikawa, and Fukui. But while the temporal scope of Koshiji's research reached back to the origins of human settlement in the region, the geographic scope was more limited than its name implied. The association's work was actually confined to the region encompassed by the modern prefecture of Niigata; its research agenda sought to give cultural definition to a twentieth-century state-territorial structure. Other prefectures and their urban capitals had their own folklore and history clubs that, like Koshiji, made the production of prefectural identity an explicit goal. As *Koshiji*'s editors announced in the magazine's founding issue: "The prefecture has recognized the need to reawaken consciousness of the locality [*kyōdo*] and is creating a museum for that purpose."[49] Koshiji saw research on regional culture as part of this broader project.

What made this task so urgent was the impression—widespread in the 1920s—that "traditional" culture was vanishing. As *Koshiji* pointed out, "If you look at many of the old ceremonies of New Year's, their traditional flavor is thinning. Dialect is gradually becoming assimilated into standardized speech [*chūōka shite*], and the distinctive northern style is disappearing. This is both good and bad, but in any case calls for 100 percent scholarly research to track and preserve the traces of these local customs before they vanish entirely."[50] Such sentiments suffused the literature of the folklore movement, in which the category of "regional culture" held a distinctly old-world flavor. Here, local custom represented a kind of preindustrial, indigenous culture that reposed in the provinces among the "folk" and their traditions.[51]

In pursuit of this vanishing object, Koshiji members poured their energies into research on a wide range of topics. They studied the racial origins of *koshi-bito*—the people who settled the coastal areas of northern Honshu along the Sea of Japan; they explored evidence that tracked these settlers back to Manchuria and Korea.[52] They scoured the area for folktales and legends specific to the Echigo-Sado region. "Legends exist everywhere in the country," wrote one of them, "but stories connected with Echigo and Sado can only be found here in our native place: they have a distinctive flavor."⁵³ They investigated Echigo dialect, explaining, "Although at first glance studies of dialect [*hōgen*] may seem irrelevant, local speech connects to our everyday life in deep and profound ways. Linguistically, dialect flows in our blood; it constitutes our way of life. This is perhaps an extreme way of putting it, but so-called standard Japanese [*hyōjungo*] is actually an admixture of many different elements; originally no one spoke a purely 'standard Japanese.'"⁵⁴

Members of the folklore movement viewed forms of traditional culture such as local dialects and local legends both as vessels of national character and as examples of regional identity, a source of tension in the folklore project that tended to divide metropolitan folklorists from their local counterparts. For Tokyo intellectuals "the folk" embodied the cultural essence of the Japanese nation, and they viewed with alarm the danger posed to indigenous Japanese folkways by an expanding western modernity. But while people situated in the capital operated from a national perspective, local intellectuals tended to view the threat to dialect and other forms of regional culture as coming from Tokyo itself. Whether it was children's stories, popular sayings, local idioms, pottery design, or folk toys, the distinctiveness of the local custom appeared to be under siege by forces of homogenization emanating from the "center."

In the tracks of a folk untainted by contact with modern progress, researchers sought out remote mountain villages and farming hamlets on their collecting expeditions. The less accessible they were, the farther they were from "the center," and so the more authentic they appeared to be. As one Okayama study group explained, "Visiting a village off the beaten paths, somewhere you have never been before, staying the night with a village family, listening to the old stories told by the locals, hearing the strange sounds outside your door at night[,] . . . these things convey the seductive beauty of a past lifeworld. The old stories capture the dream of that older world, an evocative and haunting dream."⁵⁵ Entering a village that was off the railway grid and not yet hooked up with electricity, urban intellectuals felt as if they were stepping back in time, visiting living relics of their own past. Romanticizing the putatively simple lives of "the folk," they found it fun to camp out for a day or two, listening to folktales and poking around storehouses. The experience was especially gratifying if they returned to town with a good haul of material to add to their collections. Such field trips also produced a sense of imagined local community, although with a decidedly urban-centric inflection. Indeed, in collecting and carefully preserving examples of a vanishing regional culture—and carting them off to urban archives—folklorists could take pride in the service they were providing to their communities. But if this was not quite the same as Elgin shipping the Greek marbles off to the British museum, there was nevertheless something imperious about their approach to village culture. Quick to sense a patronizing tone from a metropolitan intellectual, local activists were less conscious of their own condescension toward the villages in the orbit of their cities.

Folklorists compiled catalogues of the things they discovered, and these lists found their way into guidebooks and travel literature. A 1929 travel guide to Okayama included a glossary of famous products (*meibutsu*) that visitors could purchase as souvenirs, complete with explanations of the history of their regional associations. Readers were directed to specialty stores for local crafts and provided with the genealogy of their artistry—such as the *bizenyaki* pottery with its distinctive brown glaze that had been produced by a local colony of potters since the Kamakura period. They were advised to buy sweets such as *Kibi dankō* cakes and *ōte manjū* bean paste, which had been developed as local specialty products during the Tokugawa period.[56]

Another Okayama guidebook appended a dictionary of Okayama proverbs detailing the etymology of forty-one different sayings. As the author explained, "While still in its infancy, research on puns, wordplays, and aphorisms began about fourteen years ago in Okayama. You cannot research such things in libraries and storehouses, but need to seek them out in a village pub [*izakaya*] or backstreet bar." The guidebook included such sayings as "Niino cakes might look good" (*Niino oyakidekata bakari*), explaining that this expression indicated something that looked appealing at first but was a poor buy. The source of the phrase was a shop called Niino, formerly located on the north side of Okayama just in front of Kamiifuku. Niino's roasted rice cakes were enormous and cost only two mon. They seemed like a real bargain until you tasted them—atrocious! Now when something looks good but tastes bad or is, in other words, a deceptive practice, it is known as a Niino cake.[57] The guidebook also offered other examples of what it called "local color." Readers were informed that if they spent time in the area, they might hear the phrase "the mane of Lord Niwase's horse never changes" (*Niwase no tonosama de ouma no ke ga kawaranu*), another saying with specific local references. "When the Lord of Niwase rode in the festival of Gongen, he always rode the same horse. Therefore when you want to poke fun at some bumpkin who always wears the same clothes or brings the same things with him, you say, 'Just like the lord of Niwase.'"[58]

Like the Niino cakes and Niwase lord, names of shops, neighborhoods, festivals, or families marked the other thirty-nine sayings listed in the dictionary of Okayama proverbs. Part of a system of local knowledge, these references to proper names represented words and meanings that circulated within the geographically bounded community of Okayama and which defined its regional culture. Armed with guidebooks such as *A Tale of Okayama Past and Present*, visitors could drink in the "local color" and experience the exotic flavors that set that community off from their own local place. And they could purchase a piece of pottery and collect memories of the quaint proverbs, embodiments of a vanishing past, as souvenirs of their encounter with difference.

The "100 percent scholarship" standard of folklore aficionados was sometimes relaxed when applied to the historical bona fides of the local specialty product, or *meibutsu*. Responding to tourist demands for products with "local color," souvenir shops began selling *meibutsu* that were gilded with old-world flavor, alongside "genuine" traditional products such as *bizenyaki* pottery. For example, Okayama's so-called rice tree pastries (*kome no naru ki*), whose name referenced a famous Edo-period poem, were new "traditional style" products that became popular local specialties in the travel boom of the 1920s. Similarly, "crane egg" sweets were new *meibutsu* whose name alluded to the famous cranes of the historic Kōrakuen Garden.[59] As they promoted local color to attract visitors to their communities, guidebooks added to the folkloric penchant for "the old." Local culture was old-world, traditional culture; it seemed more authentic if it had a patina of local history.

Collectors of folk craft, and activists in the folklore movement, helped shape the concept of local culture and the conviction that it represented the heritage of the local community. Such ideas about the relationship between culture and community found their way into local-history narratives, shaping the time lines of local identity. Culture connected place-based communities through time, creating a sense of isomorphism between territory, history, and community. And yet, while the idea of progressive time was a central element in the new narratives of urban biography, the temporality of local culture did not always follow a linear time line. Categories of "custom" (*fūzoku*) and "yearly events" (*nenjū gyōji*) featured prominently in the local histories' discussions of culture. In their treatment of custom and yearly events, local histories theorized culture as a collective act of creation that persisted through repetition. By joining in the yearly cycle of festivals and rituals, in shared forms of speech and dress, and through regional foodways, local residents created and reaffirmed their community. Embedded in a particular calendar, these cultural practices bound the community together and set it apart by continuously re-creating "local time."

Descriptions of these festivals in local-history texts figured local time—the temporality of custom and culture—as the endless loop of events that cycled through the movements of the calendar. Yet this did not imply that local culture was timeless or stagnant. Indeed, texts such as *Niigata City History* articulated a dynamic vision of local culture that was strikingly at variance with representations of Tokyo intellectuals such as Yanagita Kunio. Yanagita's folklore studies did much to stimulate the study of regional customs and provided a methodology for thinking about the relationship between yearly events and local time and place. Nevertheless, as Harry Harootunian and others have pointed out, Yanagita's concept of "the abiding folk" (*jōmin*) that emerged in his later writings tended to envision local culture as an enduring vessel of an authentic Japan increasingly lost to metropolitan Japanese.[60] In this sense, Yanagita's folklore studies theorized a torpid view of regional culture, linking "the local" to an image of rural people outside of time and history. In their quest for regional identity, local historians understood custom and culture in different terms, imbuing their culture with a temporality and a historicity.

In its detailed descriptions of Niigata's yearly events, the *Niigata City History* conveyed the complex ways that the past persisted in the present. Beginning with the particular festivities associated with the New Year's practice of decorating entryways to the home with *kadomatsu* (pine ornaments) to welcome benevolent spirits, and ending the yearly cycle with Niigata's variation on the ritual of *shūmon ninbetsu aratame*—the collective registration of births at the local temple—the *Niigata City History* detailed some twenty-seven current and past customary events. The list included customs of recent vintage, such as the "opening of the river" (*kawa hiraki*), which was a fireworks display inaugurated in Meiji 21 (1888) over the Bandai Bridge. Promoted by local transport companies, this new festival celebrated the centrality of the river to Niigata's livelihood. The *Niigata City History* enumerated events, such as the "festival of the dead" (*o-bon*), that were celebrated throughout the country on different dates, as well as customs that were particular to the region. Coastal inhabitants of northern Japan celebrated the "docking of the ships" (*kakoi bune*) in the late fall, marking the point in the season when the ships plying the coastal waters docked their boats for the winter in Niigata and a handful of other ports.[61]

Also included were customs no longer practiced, such as the *dōsojin matsuri*—the festival of the Shinto god of the road—celebrated locally on January 15 through the early Meiji period. As the *Niigata City History* explained, children would parade around the town during the *dōsojin* festival, gathering at the stone shrine that marked the *dōsojin's* home. There they set fire to newly cut bamboo and their New Year's decorations as offerings to the god and to supplicate him for his help in protection from theft. Sumptuary reforms of the 1840s proscribed the harvest of bamboo for the ceremony; in 1874, for reasons left unspecified in the text, the festival was banned outright.[62] Although it was included in the *Niigata City History* as one of the local "yearly events," the festival of the Shinto god of the road was no longer actively practiced. It existed as a memory, referenced in text and marked with a physical trace—the stone shrines that reminded the citizenry of what had once been a prominent part of local culture in the Tokugawa period. From the "opening of the river" festival to the "shrine of the god of the road," "local custom" could signify cultural practices that were dead or living, newly invented or long-standing. They occupied an ambiguous status between linear and cyclical time.

The authors of *Niigata City History* highlighted the dynamic character of these cultural practices, clearly setting their concept of "local culture" apart from metropolitan images of an unchanging rural folk. They opened the chapter on "customs and annual events" with an observation: "There are some ancient customs that are completely obsolete today, but whose traces survive, like the festival of the Shinto god of the road or the docking of the ships [*kakoi bune*]. There are also customs whose essence [*fūbō*] survives though the form has changed, like the port festival. Other festivals can reemerge and gain popularity with the changing times."[63] Here, Niigata's historians saw in present practice traces of the past; they also saw the possibility of a renewal of former custom. But at the same time they could envision the disappearance of old practices: obsolete customs that were no longer part of present cultural practice. In other words, they understood culture to be adaptive to new conditions. They identified entirely new customs and events, suggesting that local traditions emerged through a process of cultural creativity and invention. Such a theorization of cultural transformation was nested within their description of the yearly cycle of events that repeated themselves, renewing year after year the contemporary community's connections with its past.[64]

Moreover, Niigata's historians highlighted the heterogeneity of Japanese culture and its localized nature. They pointed out, for example, that types of *kadomatsu* decorations varied considerably even between the Niigata and Nuttari districts of the city. Traditions surrounding the decorations were heavily influenced by Tokugawa-period sumptuary regulations, which were determined by domainal governments. Although Nuttari and Niigata were amalgamated into a single municipal district in the twentieth century, during the Tokugawa period they had fallen under separate jurisdictions: Nuttari was part of Shibata domain, while Niigata lay within Echigo domain. Other festivals, like that of the Shinto god of the road, protector of villages and travelers, were likewise found throughout the country, where they were said to banish evil spirits, demons, and illness. The *dōsojin* was represented by stone markers on the side of the road or at the edges of fields or villages. Though it acknowledged such commonalities, the *Niigata City History* stressed the distinctiveness of the local variation. Niigata celebrated this on January 11, other places on different days in January. The choreography of the parade, the appearance of the doll representing the *dōsojin*, and the order of the ritual, all offered additional opportunities for Niigata's historians to argue for the importance of local variations in cultural practice.[65] The take-home message of the interwar regional heritage movements was that these variations—the local distinctions in custom and culture—defined the community and bound it together through time. Local culture was the lifeblood of an imagined community.

Even though such representations of regional culture stressed its vibrancy and dynamism, they also marked the locality as a space where the past was still present. In this sense the local-history and folklore movements helped associate the provinces with a vanishing lifeworld and authentic traditional culture. In the process, they contributed to the same phenomenon of self-marginalization that provincial artists and writers engaged in. By linking the hometown with old-world rusticity, both groups reinforced stereotypes of a contrast with metropolitan modernity even as they insisted on the vitality of the local. They also took part in the larger project of reifying culture that became central to fascist ideology and wartime nationalism. Wartime propaganda invoked cultural tradition to promote the idea of the family-state and the "national body" (*kokutai*), claiming that ancient ties of blood and spirit bound the Japanese people to their emperor. Local historians, in contrast, placed culture in the service of regional identity, making a shared set of particularized cultural practices the fulcrum of an imagined community of "the city."

Together with the introduction of local history into the elementary school curriculum and its dissemination through social education, youth groups, and the like, the rapidly developing tourist industry provided another powerful vehicle for the broadcast of a temporally inflected urban identity.[66] Throughout the twenties and thirties, railway companies, municipalities, and chambers of commerce undertook a series of campaigns to promote domestic tourism, part of a larger project to stimulate economic development. An outpouring of local travel guides published in cities such as Okayama and Sapporo in the interwar period shaped a new image of the provincial city for both visitors and residents. Here, local boosters packaged their communities as tourist attractions, presenting their cities as a glittering necklace of *meisho*—or famous sites—each of which captured the character and distinctiveness of the city and which together accounted for its magnetic appeal.

By the 1930s, cities such as Okayama offered a wide choice of guides to their communities. The municipal government began publishing *Okayama* in the teens, a 150-page guide to the city printed by the San'yō newspaper company and updated nearly every year. *Okayama* opened with scenic views of the city: a panoramic photograph taken from a nearby mountaintop, an old picture of Okayama Castle, the emblematic Kyōbashi Bridge, and the modernist facade of the central station building. The photographic highlights included the city's main commercial streets and its rivers, as well as its iconic buildings, temples, and shrines. The guidebook provided information on bridges, roads, and waterways—when they were built and improved, their widths and lengths. *Okayama* enumerated the city's banks, companies, and factories; registered average temperatures and rainfall for the previous few years; gave descriptions of local restaurants, inns, and outdoor markets and their times of operation; and listed local newspapers.[67] Visitors could avail themselves of a variety of other materials introducing the city: in addition to *Okayama*, there were travel dairies, magazines, yearbooks, postcards, maps, and timetables of bus and train service. A 1936 guide, *Touring Okayama*, offered an introduction to the city's suburbs and suggestions for side trips to the city's outskirts via the Chūgoku, Uno, and Bizen train lines. It provided readers with itineraries for a two-hour, half-day, and full-day tour of the city, with thumbnail descriptions of each stop along the route.[68] Such tourist materials collectively defined the "tourist attractions" of Okayama and fixed routes to apprehend them—a circuit that, once traveled, captured the essence of the place.

The travel circuit, the tourist attraction, and the guidebook itself constituted core elements of modern tourism as it developed in interwar Japan. All
three were grounded in new notions of urban culture and community as well
as in the conceptual lexicon of the local-history movement. Guidebooks drew
on local-history texts for their source material; they promoted the idea of
urban biography—that cities were organic communities with life histories.
They frequently opened with condensed versions of the historical narratives
developed in multivolume texts such as *Kanazawa City History*.
Recommended routes drew visitors to historical sites, whose importance had
been documented by the painstaking efforts of historical committees. Thus
books such as *Okayama* and *Touring Okayama* included a brief history of the
city and a roster of famous places (*meisho*), ruins, and relics. *Okayama*
devoted extra pages to a history of the castle and a guide to the castle grounds;
Touring Okayama appended a handy map of the city's main historic sites.[69]
Guidebooks conveyed the message that being steeped in history made places
like Okayama attractive as tourist destinations, with "their abundance of
famous old sites [*meisho kyūseki*] that excited historical curiosity."[70] Through
the vehicle of the travel guidebook, cities became open-air historical museums that invited residents and visitors alike to apprehend these communities
as nexuses of past and present.

The key category for mediating the relationship between past and present was the famous site. Here, place became associated with a history that
was particularized and a temporality that was modern. The modern incarnation of this concept emerged in part through the bureaucratic historic
preservation movement, a series of laws aimed at protecting and preserving
national heritage by designating sites of historic importance and scenic
beauty for special status as "national treasures" (*kokuhō*).[71] From the late
nineteenth century, the central government established a succession of
national museums designed to preserve certain categories of material
culture—religious statuary, architectural structures, works of art—as
vessels of national identity.[72] While state designations of *meisho* signified
the heritage of a national culture, guidebooks framed their meaning within
a more localized system of reference. Both reinforced the idea that the *meisho* crystallized a connection between past and present. Like historical
objects displayed in a museum, the *meisho* represented a past far removed
from the modern world—a place that appeared exotic and otherworldly
from the vantage point of the present day. Whether invoked as a signifier
of national or local culture, the famous place was tied to the identity and

genealogy of an imagined community—one that both defined the *meisho* and was defined by it.

By the time the tourist industry of the early twentieth century began promoting the idea, the "famous site" had accrued a variety of literary, religious, and commercial meanings from centuries of use. Past usage made the *meisho* a particularly dense and evocative metaphor when deployed to concentrate the new sense of past. This history went back to the ancient and medieval periods, when poetry anthologies, travel diaries (*kikōbun*), narrative tales (*monogatari*), and the like established *meisho* as a lyrical and literary space. In a series of intertextual images that grew more layered and formalized over time, particular places were associated with the visits and creative imagination of literary travelers of an earlier age. By the late Heian period (794–1185), writers could consult compendiums of so-called pillow words, or *utamakura*—poetic phrases that linked particular sites with natural symbols, with mood, and with aesthetic flavor. Although a *meisho* might mark the site of an ancient battle, a sacred place, or the exile of a fallen hero, what infused these sites with meaning was not their concrete historical referents but rather their literary associations—their location on a transcendent poetryscape. In what Laura Nenzi calls a "lyrical cartography," literary travelers interacted with their predecessors, moving from symbol to symbol as they traveled through physical space. Traversing the stages of the ancient Tōkaidō highway meant retracing the peregrinations of the aristocratic poet Ariwara Narihira (825–880), whose "descent to the East" was narrated in the classic *Tales of Ise* (tenth century). Passing Mount Fuji in later years, any literate traveler would recall Narihira's admiring verse that described "the mountain that knows no season . . . dappled with fallen snow," a poem invoked in the *Tales of Ise* and over and again in subsequent literary and visual depictions. In this chain of lyrical associations, successive writers and artists connected themselves to their predecessors through the perception of Fuji as *meisho*.[73]

Building on this literary heritage, the political and commercial revolutions of the Tokugawa period (1603–1868) transformed the epistemology of the "famous place" and injected new layers of meaning that twentieth-century guidebooks would draw on. Ending the civil wars of the sixteenth century, the Tokugawa dynasty created a system of centralized feudalism that imposed hegemony over regional lords (daimyo), the imperial court, and powerful monasteries. The Tokugawa regime effectively maintained the peace for nearly three centuries, and spatial strategies were central to the success of this effort. The new rulers confiscated and reallocated land among the daimyo on a massive scale, creating a political geography centered on their power base in Edo. They established a network of official highways and regulated movement along them through a system of checkpoints and travel permits; they deployed official cartographers to measure and map spaces of strategic importance.

In the process, they reinvented the concept of *meisho* from the strategic and administrative perspective of the state. State logics created new sites of importance as certain post stations (*shukuba*) acquired special value in the strategic ranking of the officially sanctioned main roads. Established as part of the Tokugawa system of regulating movement within the realm of the state, the post stations provided checkpoints (*sekisho*) where travel permits were inspected and also offered lodging and other forms of accommodation for travelers. Among the five major highways (the Gokaidō), the Tōkaidō route connecting the imperial capital in Kyoto and the center of Tokugawa authority in Edo was clearly the most important. While older lyrical cartographies concentrated *meisho* around Kyoto and the other ancient capitals, now the fifty-three post stations of the Tōkaidō gained special prominence through the actions of the state. Reversing the long-standing centrality of Kyoto, the new rulers inaugurated a shift toward Edo-centrism through a variety of tactics, not least the marking of distances along the Tōkaidō from a starting point at Edo's commercial quarter in Nihonbashi. Over the course of the seventeenth and eighteenth centuries, both the stations of the Tōkaidō and Edo itself would become densely populated with *meisho* as the political revolution continued to generate new frames of reference for the famous place.

The impact of the commercial revolution on the perception of *meisho* was equally dramatic. Places like the Tōkaidō road and Edo that were privileged by the new regime also became focal points of a thriving market economy. Building on the political structures put in place by the Tokugawa, the dramatic growth of commerce from the seventeenth century shaped both a new publishing culture of travel literature and the commercialization of travel itself. Various genres of travel literature emerged in Japan's burgeoning urban print culture: guidebooks, maps, travel diaries, fictional travel accounts, and gazetteers, as well as collections of famous places in woodblock prints and poetry.[74] Indeed, many of the classics of the period fall into the category of travel literature: the woodblock artist Katsushika Hokusai's *Thirty-Six Views of Mount Fuji*, Ikku Jippensha's comic masterpiece *Shank's Mare*, and Matsuo Bashō's celebrated poetry collection, *The Road to the Far North*.

The spread of a commercialized print culture led not only to the development of new genres of travel literature but also to its broader social circulation. Part of the reason for this was that leisured travel—much like literature itself—was no longer the exclusive preserve of the aristocracy. Among the sanctioned reasons for travel was religious pilgrimage, a practice that developed among aristocrats during the latter part of the Heian period and spread to the commoner classes during the Tokugawa era, actively encouraged as a revenue stream by major shrines and temples. As Constantine Vaporis points out, travel became, for commoners, virtually synonymous with pilgrimage. The numbers of people making the thirty-three-temple circuit in western Japan, or traveling the eighty-eight holy sites of Shikoku, grew exponentially over the eighteenth and nineteenth centuries. Every month hundreds of thousands made the trip to Ise Shrine; enormous numbers came to climb the stations of Mount Fuji. To cater to people on the road, commercial hostelries sprang up at post stations and villages along the main transportation routes and at the entry points to castle towns. Entertainment booths, souvenir shops, and food stalls lined the approaches to major shrines and temples. Clusters of theaters and brothels grew up on the outskirts of religious complexes and near roadside rest stations. Increasingly wealthy and literate commoners provided a market for this effervescent culture of pilgrimage. They both consumed and produced the expanding literature on travel. And most of all, they took to the road, joining a broad cross section of Tokugawa society—men and women, old and young, from the great lord traveling with a retinue of thousands of samurai attendants on procession to Edo to the common peasant joining a group of compatriots on a once-in-a-lifetime pilgrimage to Ise.[75]

Both the social expansion of pilgrimage and the commercial expansion of travel generated yet another set of famous places—sites renown as bustling centers of entertainment and consumption. Pilgrimage sites such as Mount Fuji, which figured prominently in Heian-period poetic space, were overlaid with new meanings on a travelscape that foregrounded bodily pleasure and commercial transactions. The peregrinations of pilgrims and their demand for roadside entertainment reinvented the idea of *meisho*, turning it into an intoxicating mix of devotion, decadence, and profit. This definition of the famous place became increasingly common in the guidebooks, travel literature, and maps of the late Tokugawa period. Overlaying and sometimes competing with lyrical, strategic, and religious alternatives, the *meisho* of commercialized travel defined iconic space in an ever more popular mind.

The guidebook form and the *meisho* of the early twentieth century drew on this accumulated heritage. The long history of the famous place was evident in the kinds of sites that merited inclusion: government buildings, scenic views, commercial and entertainment districts, shrines, and temples all appeared on the list. They won recognition for the same reasons particular places became famous in the Tokugawa period—because of their poetic, commercial, sacred, or political importance. Into this mix, the quintessentially modern projects of national and regional developmentalism added something new, as *meisho* became vehicles for the production of imagined communities. For their part, cities vested famous places with meaning as symbols of a shared history and a link between past and present. Municipal governments and the travel industry appointed them, in effect, as main exhibits in the city-as-museum display. By mapping local identity onto physical space, *meisho* created a perception of isomorphism between place, people, and history.[76] In the process, *meisho* and the guidebook form helped constitute a temporally inflected urban identity.

Interwar city guidebooks made a distinction between "new famous sites" (*shin meisho*) and "sites of historic importance" (*meisho kyūseki*). New *meisho* symbolized the modern city and the novelty of its built environment and daily life: they portended the shape of things to come for the urban future. Historic *meisho*, in contrast, represented the city as it used to be, a relic of a vanishing lifeworld. In *Niigata City Guide*, for example, the opening chapter introduced readers to "Niigata, past and present," using the term *konjaku*— "past and present"—a word that appeared regularly in travel literature of the period. Highlighting the city's origins as a sleepy port town, the chapter "Niigata, Past and Present" juxtaposed a distant past with the large, bustling city of the present. At the top of the list of Niigata's *meisho* stood Hakusan Park, a "new famous place" created in 1873 on the site of the old Hakusan Shrine. Descriptions of the shrine highlighted the antinomy of past and present that characterized definitions of the modern city. The old shrine lay buried beneath the new park, an earlier incarnation of Niigata's civic culture that was invoked in contrast with the modern quality of the new famous place. In one corner of Hakusan Park, visitors could locate Senbon Matsuura, the site of a once glorious forest where, today, "only a small part of what once was a wide expanse of old pines" remains. As the *Niigata City Guide* explained, "The countless pines and bracken growing thickly here recall the former glory of the pine forest, where people used to illuminate lanterns in the evening to light the way for boats traveling on the nearby river." Readers were called on to mourn the lost pines and cherish those that remained; they were invited to see the city through the contrasting frames of past and present.[77]

The self-conscious objectification of "old *meisho*" and their association with earlier, especially Tokugawa-era, usage mapped the historic sensibility of the urban biography onto iconic elements of the built environment of the city. A 1936 guidebook, *A Tale of Okayama Past and Present*, opened with a series of famous woodblock print images and poems reprinted from celebrated Tokugawa-era travel guides to the castle town of Okayama. Each image was extensively annotated, citing the source, the artist, the date of production (if known), and where the original was located (most were in the former Ikeda daimyo family archives). The captions also described the image's literary allusions and points of historic interest. Both the inclusion of older travel images in a modern guidebook and the historic annotation of the images highlighted the contrast between old and new *meisho*. Presented through the empiricist gaze of the local-history movement, the "old *meisho*" became more than a mere symbol of Okayama's past; it also invoked a sense of temporal distance between the urban subject of the present and the earlier lifeworld to which the old *meisho* belonged.

One of the prints that prefaced *A Tale of Okayama Past and Present* showed a famous fish market under the caption "Scene of thriving market at Kyōbashi Bridge" *(Kyōbashi fukin no inshin)*. The fish market had vanished and the old wooden bridge was long gone, but Kyōbashi Bridge itself remained an iconic image of the city. Okayama guidebooks and postcard collections invariably included a shot of the bridge. Rebuilt in 1917 using the latest engineering technology, and often thronged with automobiles, the bridge, with its distinctive profile, was a symbol of the new Okayama. Thus, to twentieth-century audiences the "scene of a thriving market at Kyōbashi Bridge" would be both familiar and unfamiliar. The gloss on the print situated the bridge within the temporal coordinates of an earlier era and called attention to the particular fish products that were characteristic of Okayama and illustrative of its distinctive foodways. The market itself may have disappeared, but the new bridge was there and "specialty products" were still available at souvenir stores throughout the city.

A Tale of Okayama Past and Present reproduced other prints from the Ikeda family collection, including an image of the *torii* gate marking the entrance to the famous shrine on the island of Takashima, associated with Emperor Jimmu, legendary founder of the imperial state. As the annotation explained, this beautiful image of the shrine surrounded by ancient pine trees and wreathed in morning mist was part of the Tokugawa-period collection "Looking to Bizen's Past" (Bizen onko). The scenic outlook to the Takashima Island shrine was one of the "Eight scenic views of Bizen"—an older name for the province—and a favored subject of woodblock prints and poetry. While the view from shore of the Takashima Island shrine remained an iconic image of present-day Okayama, the Tokugawa-era print reminded readers of its links to the literary and artistic heritage of the castle town, when the scene became regarded as one of the eight top *meisho* in Okayama domain. Thus, the prints and their annotation highlighted the contrasts between "Okayama, past and present." The documentation marked the prints themselves as material objects of historical interest and situated a familiar sight at a temporal remove.[78]

Like poetic invocations of *meisho* in earlier times, interwar guidebooks listed places renowned for their scenic beauty. Yet in the modern context what leant these sites aesthetic value was not the dense accumulation of symbols that hung about them but rather scenic beauty as an instance of local pride. The *Niigata City Guide* pointed out the distinctive beauty of local geography that drew people to cities such as Niigata and bound them to the place. Guiding visitors to Ariake Inlet, a famous place along the Niigata coast, the *Niigata City Guide* noted the inlet's fame as a site for moon viewing. From here one gained a commanding perspective of "the minute and limitless waves of the Sea of Japan . . . the autumn moon over Sado Island."[79] Though in past eras visitors would have seen the moon as a symbol on a literary landscape, now they were called upon to appreciate this scenic snapshot as an instance of the natural beauty of the Niigata seascape. Instead of a literary history that connected the cultured observer with poets of times now past, the scene invoked a natural history that connected the distinctive features of local topography with the development of Niigata's society, economy, and culture.

Niigata City Guide also invited readers to make a stop at Hiwa Mountain, a scenic coastal overlook that "in spite of its name is not much more than a sand dune. At the top of the rise is a tower, recently rebuilt after the original burned down in Meiji 13 [1880]." In earlier days the tower was used to detect changes in weather and as a lookout for incoming ships; it was now preserved as a scenic outlook. Like the remains of the pine forest in Hakusan Park and the moonscape on Ariake Inlet, Hiwa Mountain was presented as a *meisho* that connected past with present. The site offered a vantage point for appreciating Niigata's distinctive scenic beauty, but it also recalled a vanishing past. The old tower was gone, a new one built in its place. This served as a reminder of the destruction and rebuilding that characterized the modern city. In much the same vein, an Okayama guidebook directed visitors to the scenic Takashima Park, with its views of the inland sea and the iconic outlook onto the Takashima Island shrine. Modern attractions included a sunbathing beach and amenities for a family day out, but the haunting view of the famous shrine with its ancient links to Emperor Jimmu also called attention to Okayama's connections with the archaic. Again, this highlighted the contrast between the old and the new, the modern city and its primordial roots.[80]

In such descriptions, viewers were instructed to visualize a site of scenic beauty as an inscription of a particular history, an instance of urban biography. Even a garden, a scenic lookout, or a beautiful pine tree was the product of a singular historical development, of the collective progress of the community, and of the linearity of modern history. An Okayama guidebook description of the famous Kōrakuen Garden stressed the progressive development of the garden as part of the history of the city. Kōrakuen was initially created for the estate of the Ikeda family—the domainal lords during the Tokugawa period. Gifted to the prefecture in the Meiji period, Kōrakuen opened as a public park and became one of the crown jewels of the city. A section on "the history of gardens" noted the important place occupied by Okayama's jewel in the history of the Japanese garden. Its notable features—the teahouse, islands in the garden pond, and a dry field as a garden element—were all innovations of the garden form from the Edo period. As the guidebook proudly noted, Kōrakuen was the first to use elements like the island in the garden pond.[81] Such descriptions inscribed the *meisho* with a linear history, part of a narrative of progress and development that followed the urban biography to the present day.

As visitors moved through the city along the travel circuit, they embarked on a voyage of discovery, coming to understand the place and its people by learning its history. *Touring Okayama*, a guidebook written in 1929 by Okayama native Utani Takeji, encouraged readers to look beneath the city surface to discover its historical core. He was prompted to write the book after friends visiting from Tokyo had asked him for a tour. Realizing how little he knew about his birthplace, he embarked on the task of writing a guidebook based on scientific research of old texts and diaries and a "field survey." In other words, he looked to local history to learn more about his community and himself.

This journey of discovery began with the founding of the castle town. Utani wrote:

Tracking the history of our Okayama [*waga Okayama*] brings us back to the point when Ukita Naoie built Okayama Castle in the first year of Tensho [1573]. The 350 years that have passed since then have seen wondrous development [*subarashii hatten*], from the administrations of Kobayakawa and Ikeda, who took over the domain, through the reforms of the Meiji Restoration and on to the present day. . . . Even the changes that have happened since I was a child are truly startling. In the area south of the castle . . . what was once a field where we caught dragonflies has grown into a bustling shopping street lined with elegant buildings.[82]

Here progress and development—the time lines of local identity—were materialized in the changing physical appearance of the city. *Touring Okayama* led readers on a stroll through its altered built environment, urging them to see Okayama as it once was, to feel the past that underlay the present.

Although Utani celebrated Okayama's "wondrous development," he also expressed a sense of ambivalence about the impact of modern progress. The central train station was a modern-style reinforced concrete building with the latest amenities, and "the only one of its kind in the East." Despite his obvious pride in the engineering prowess of local builders, something disturbed Utani about this symbol of Okayama's greatness: "as a gateway to the city, the station building might seem almost too grand, out of proportion" to the real, historical city.[83] The implication here was that the modern exterior of the city was somehow artificial or false, masking an authentic urban core. Indeed, Utani read the city in terms of surfaces and depths that corresponded with a temporal division between the old and the new.

From the central station, according to Utani's directions, travelers would turn left and walk three blocks to a major thoroughfare: to the west stood the neighborhood of Banchō, and to the east Iwadachō. Banchō housed the headquarters of the local military brigade, the West Policy building, Seishin Women's College, Kansai Middle School, Chūgoku Railway headquarters, and the Okayama Insurance building, among other important enterprises. These buildings, which served as focal points of city government, higher education, and major business interests, were described in brief, even perfunctory, terms followed by an evocative account of the neighborhood as it had once been. In earlier times, Banchō was the entry to the castle town from the west. The main gate to the city was located here, as were the rooms of domainal officials. In the aftermath of the Restoration, impoverished former samurai had plied their new trades in the neighborhood. When their efforts to recoup their fortunes in craft manufacture largely failed, the neighborhood went to seed, overtaken by downscale brothels and drinking establishments. The district of Nadayachō—now home to the Sekaikan movie theater, the Amagi Radium Bath, the municipal employment center, and the public market—was once a merchant neighborhood that catered to the nearby Ikeda family estate; the area occupied by Okayama Industrial College was once farmland; and so on.[84] In this way Utani's commentary directed viewers to look through the structures of the present and visualize older uses of the land and previous social meanings of Okayama's neighborhoods. And while descriptions of the present focused on its buildings, the historical references spotlighted its people—suggesting that the true spirit of the place, its vital human core, was enclosed within Okayama's past.

Utani's descriptions conveyed the importance of this heritage: the past provided the foundation upon which the modern was built. To the reader walking past the Women's Normal School, *Touring Okayama* had nothing to say about Okayama's current schools, but it pointed out that the Normal School was the site of the old domain academy and reflected at length on the Bizen scholarly tradition.[85] Utani noted the etymology of place-names: Ishiseki-machi was called "stone wall street" because a stone wall had been built up against an interior canal that diverted water from the Asahi River; Rimboku-machi was called "lumber street" because it was formerly a center for lumber merchants; the downtown neighborhood of Kaminochō used to be known as "vegetable street" (Yaoya-machi) to reflect merchant activity along the inner moat.[86] He walked readers past the place where the Ikeda family had lived and pointed out the former locations of their principal retainers. He told them where the shrines and temples used to be and how these arrangements changed over time. Through such descriptions he gave the modern city a quality of pentimento—the earlier image of the cityscape showing through the modern surface. This conveyed a sense of the city as the accumulated experiences of generations that lived on the same spot.

As visitors moved through the city, going from *meisho* to *meisho* along paths directed by guidebooks, they were provided with a series of encounters with the past. In this sense both the *meisho* and the guidebook were part of a web of signification that turned cities into historically redolent spaces. In presenting the city-as-museum, guidebooks mapped the urban biographies produced by the local-history movement onto a travel circuit, crystallizing the city's past on a set of tourist attractions. The built environment of the city, viewed through the experience of the tourist circuit, became a vessel for the particular historical narratives that scripted local identity. By weaving together urban biography, the interiorized subjectivity of local residents, and the external landscapes they inhabited, guidebooks took the effect of the local-history movement one step further: they deepened the identification of history, community, and place.

The lure of regionalism appeared in various incarnations in the interwar period, as organizations of amateur historians and folklorists proliferated in provincial cities. The obsession with collecting and preserving crafts, arts, and myths, and with resurrecting dialects, specialty foods, and festivals, reflected a desire to possess the past—to grab hold before it disappeared entirely. The local tourist industry stoked this desire, marketing specialty foods and local crafts as the indispensable point of access to an authentic cultural experience. Tour guides and travel magazines included glossaries of local idioms, catalogs of proverbs, schedules of events, and lists of famous sites (*meisho*). Claims of historical particularity, ancient pedigree, and the unique affinity of the local city to a vanishing past were mobilized to sell the city and its products. The commercialization of the local-history movement turned heritage into a commodity, reinforcing the idea that urban identity was grounded in a newly discovered past.

In all these ways, the local-history movement deployed temporal strategies to constitute a regional identity. Following innovations developed in the context of the national turn in historiographic practice, local historians created urban biographies for their cities that explained the cities' particular cultures and personalities. Like the national-history writing of the late nineteenth century, the spread of local history in the twenties and thirties established certain conventions of the form. This first wave of modern city histories required a starting point—the origin of the community, the founding moment of settlement. They told stories of the rise and development of the local polity and its claims to territorial jurisdiction. They characterized the distinctive culture and customs of the local community. And most important, they mapped these elements of urban biography onto the physical space of the city. As the writers of each modern city history stitched a particular narrative of development onto their city's topography and its built environment, they imagined their community as a chronotope. In the process, they helped establish the lasting conviction that "the city" embodied a particularized time-space in modern society.

As this chapter has argued, the conceptualization of "the city" as an organic unity and sovereign subject represented one product of the local-history movements of the interwar years. Here the technologies of nationalism—both imagined communities and invented traditions—were applied to the creation of urban identities and the city idea. Much like nations and nationalism, cities and urban-centrism were newly constructed forms and ideologies that masked their modern origins under the veil of primordialism. Although local histories created origin myths that reached back through the mists of time and plotted urban development as the natural growth of an organic community, the expansion of modern Japanese cities was neither spontaneous nor natural. The modern urban form emerged through the 1889 administrative reforms that established Meiji cities as administrative-political units with territorial jurisdictions; the modern city took shape over the succeeding decades with the growth of urban-based industry. Upon this foundation, the local-history movement constructed the form of urban biography and the idea of the city as a cultural community that existed through time. Spread through hometown education and the tourist industry, such ideas became core elements in the ideology of the modern city. Like the presumed isomorphism of the nation that imagined an identity between people, economy, and territory, the city idea brought territory and culture into a single unit. Deploying this idea, guidebooks and hometown-education texts interpellated urban residents, calling them to a sense of membership in their urban communities.

The local-history movements that helped give rise to the modern city idea were part of a broader flowering of regional movements in the teens, twenties, and thirties. In some ways these movements reinforced nationalism; in some ways they operated in tension with the forces of central government. The facility with which regional movements appropriated the narrative form of national history, as well as instruments of socialization such as the school system, revealed the portability of that form and those instruments: the products of national developmentalism could be used in the service of regional identities, and the reverse held true, as well. Just as the production of a national social space contained a nested hierarchy of centers and peripheries with metropolitan Tokyo at its apex, regional identity could be enclosed within a national frame. Against this backdrop, regionalist movements conveyed the message that the citizenry of an Okayama or a Niigata was shaped as much by its membership in a distinctive urban society with an ancient pedigree as it was by the imagined community of the nation. And yet, neither the creation of a complementarity between nation and region, nor the subordination of the region to the nation, was ever "complete." As much as regionalist movements participated in the reification of culture as the fulcrum of identity, and as much as they reinforced the preoccupation with cultural authenticity that ran through nationalist discourse of the 1930s, the "hobbyists of the local" also challenged certain claims being made about "national culture." In other words, while the romanticization of the past is often seen as part of a Japanist elevation of the nation, the local-history movement generated ideas that were often at odds with the wartime program of the state. Municipal schoolteachers transformed the hometown-education movement from a project that sought to harness the community's loyalty to the nation and transform it into an instrument of community activism and empowerment. In contrast to neonativist depictions of local custom as a reservoir of unchanging tradition, local historians portrayed their culture as dynamic and modern. The local-history movement signaled not the "return to Japan" (*Nihon kaiki*) that swept metropolitan literary and philosophic circles in the 1930s, but rather a step away from a nation-centered epistemology.

Although ostensibly focused on the past, regionalist movements were primarily concerned with the future. Participants viewed such movements as a form of urban development; they joined regionalist movements to help ensure a bright future for themselves and their cities. While local-history texts and regional craft organizations identified the provinces with a rapidly vanishing past, provincial cities shared with the metropolis the identification of the city with modern life and the world of tomorrow. Complementing the regional culture movements, chambers of commerce and municipal governments put local development plans in motion that harnessed the city idea to a forward-facing time horizon. At the same time, the rapid transformation of the physical and social environment of these years oriented urbanites toward the future and provoked intense speculation about what that future would bring. Such speculation firmly identified cities with change and "the new," another dimension of the city idea that took shape in the early decades of the twentieth century.

FIVE

The Cult of the New

The social and cultural movements of the interwar years expressed a fascination with "the new"—the new products, new fads, new pastimes, new lifestyles, and new types of men and women that erupted onto the urban landscape, only to be replaced with the new "new." The regional turn reflected in the local-history movement also expressed itself through an upsurge of interest in what the face of the urban future would look like. The tourist industry, town planning, industrial exhibitions, and other forms of local boosterism promoted the locality and its capacity for progress and development. Guidebooks trumpeted the modern face of the city, pointing with pride to the transformation of the built environment and its iconic symbols—new *meisho* such as department stores and station buildings. City fathers celebrated their locales as technotopias filled with engineering wonders—multistoried buildings, elevators, and escalators; and magical instruments like telescopes and radios—holding out a tantalizing vision of an uncertain future controlled by technology.

Such celebratory visions of the destiny of the modern city were reinforced by broader intellectual trends that oriented people toward the future. Systematic attempts to study and chart the course of "fashion" guided department stores in their plans to develop markets for consumer goods.[1] A new mania for government planning expressed itself in the rise of town plans, economic plans, and plans to rehabilitate villages. A boom in popular science and science fiction created what Hiromi Mizuno called the "mobilization of wonder" in the service of nationalism.[2] A new faith in the efficacy of measurement and prediction, statistics, and prognostication took root in the social sciences, management ideology, and government policy.[3] All these developments shaped a habit of thinking forward and fueled the collective imagination about the future.

These discourses on local development and futurism interlinked the city idea with a cult of the new. Bullish views on the future identified urban space with the world of tomorrow. Urban boosters saw cities in terms of their potential, projecting rosy scenarios of economic and social development. Embracing growth, bigness, speed, and acceleration, the cult of the new celebrated an aesthetic of dynamism and vitality. Although the metropolitan establishment promoted the idea that modern institutions were invented in Tokyo and exported to the provinces, the discourse on "the new" in cities outside the capital suggested that progress was etched in local colors. Like the multiple temporalities of local history, individual cities offered particular time lines into the future. Running counter to the image of "hometown" produced in the capital that figured localities as a past lifeworld, provincial cities imagined themselves in terms of chronotopes of a future-space. Futurism took hold of the city idea.

Partly this had to do with the rise of a powerful new urban-based middle class of professionals, technocrats, and managers who helped bring an agenda of urban progress to the forefront of popular consciousness. A confluence of forces helped propel the new middle class to this position. The growth of a service economy created new jobs for white-collar workers and expanded the scope for these workers to redesign urban social life. Proliferation of educational institutions and the culture industry expanded paid employment for scholars and artists and provided them a platform on which to shape the cultural life of their communities. The expansion of municipal government opened opportunities for college graduates to work for local government and participate in an unprecedented experiment in social engineering. Significantly, the city was the staging ground for all of these developments. The growing size and influence of cities within the social space of the nation also augmented the power and influence of the new middle class, who hitched their fate to urban growth. Through their dominance over key institutions of municipal government, the mass media, the entertainment industry, and the service economy, urban expansionism became a vehicle for middle-class hegemony. What was good for the city was good for the middle class. Equating growth with progress, the intellectual workers who occupied these important new positions possessed both the tools and the ambition to aggressively promote urban development.

In the process, the new middle class became agents of "the new." They wanted urban time to tick faster and their cities to grow up and out. They envisioned the infrastructural investments that accelerated communications and brought technological advance. They foresaw the development of the local symphony and arts academies. They imagined radio towers, airports, and entertainment complexes. They formed a chorus of local boosters trumpeting the future, because what was good for their local city strengthened the organizations they worked for and enhanced their social status and cultural capital. These agents of the new formed the core constituency for *machizukuri*, or "city-making," a word that signified community building through urban planning and local development schemes. Though this term did not come into circulation until after World War Two, its conceptual coordinates were laid in the future orientation of the city idea that took root in the twenties and thirties. Here "the city" became a site of intense engagement around future prospects: looking forward with an eye to creating opportunities, channeling resources, directing the course of future development. Hitched to the concept of *machizukuri*, the city became not so much a fixed entity as a process, a project whose realization was always just out of reach. Destined for endless remaking, the modern city was never complete.

While it might seem that urban futurism operated in tension with regional culture movements that envisioned the essence of urban identity in the city's past, *machizukuri* drew on both tactics. Together with instructions in authenticity by travel guidebooks and local-history readers, industrial expositions showcased the growth of local industry that equated the city with its economic base and spotlighted milestones of local progress and future development. A tourist industry created "new *meisho*" as an optic for viewing the future; these "famous places" complimented the "old *meisho*" marking the survival of the past in the present. Urban biographies provided instructive tales of hometown heroes and the grand vision of founding fathers, as well as expectations about the next generation. This pedagogy of local identity claimed city residents as members of an organic community whose roots sank down deep, even as it interpellated them as modern subjects who carried their city's torch into the future. In this sense, urban futurism picked up where the history movement left off, projecting time lines of local identity forward in time.

Although urban biography particularized the identity of "Niigata" or "Kanazawa," projections of the future could also make regional particularities converge on a singular set of images of the modern city. Here stereotypes of local cities as markers of difference operated in tension with a more universal model of urban modernity. While paeans to progress showcased the regional brand and celebrated local color, projections of the cities of tomorrow—with their neon towns and modern girls, their high-rise department stores and wide, paved boulevards—tended to make all moderns look the same. As urban futurism turned the association of the city with the future into an axiom of modern life, the cult of the new became a cult of the same. These competing images of an urban past as (mostly) different and an urban future as (mostly) the same created a tension within the city idea, between universalism and particularism. As people came to understand the city as a time-space—a place with a past, present, and future—they also embraced the doubled identity of the modern urbanite. Kanazawa residents embodied local culture: they spoke the dialect, and they took part in local festivals. They could list the best restaurants, knew where to go for a bird's-eye view of the cityscape, and perhaps could even recite the city song. Familiarity with this system of local knowledge defined what it meant to be "from Kanazawa." But Kanazawa residents also thought of themselves as urban, a self-perception that bound them with city dwellers throughout the country and that set them apart from rural people. Urban residents embodied modern culture. They lived in a place with baseball fields and movie palaces. They worked in offices and factories. They rode trains and dealt with traffic. In this sense city dwellers lived a double life: they embodied a collective past that set them apart from other regional communities and a collective future that bound them together with other urban communities. The new idea of "the city" contained within it the sense that particularized pasts shaped the present; it also contained a belief in an increasingly homogeneous future.

The conviction that all urban modernities converge constituted one of the most powerful legacies of the idea of the city during the interwar period. This narrative of convergence, much like the concept of diffusion, shored up belief in Tokyo's centrality. While circuits of intellectual exchange channeled resources, talent, and ideas to the capital, the formation of a literary canon and the trope of "hometown" concealed this flow to the center beneath a narrative of diffusion outward from the capital. Likewise, the idea that all moderns began to look alike led to a readiness to monumentalize the metropolis as the quintessential modern and effaced regional variations in modern life. While the local-history movement analyzed folk crafts and festivals as a sign of difference, the discourse on urban futurism read the appearance of department stores and the modern girl as a sign that all cities were becoming the same. Even though the localized history of commerce meant that department stores in Niigata varied considerably from those in Sapporo, and even though the particulars of the women's movement, the availability of women's education, and employment opportunities altered local meanings of the phrase *modern girl*, such differences were pushed to the side by the narrative of convergence. Expressed in the enduring tendency to conflate the history of Tokyo with the history of modern Japan, these ideas reinforced the ideology of Tokyo-centrism.

THE FUTURE IN THE PRESENT

In myriad ways, the economic growth of the interwar period etched itself in the remaking of the city. The demography of urban society, the culture of everyday life, the built environment of the city, and the economic foundations of municipal wealth altered in dramatic and visible ways. These changes happened quickly and were accompanied by an explosion of public commentary that called attention to what was viewed as a new age of the city. Writers peppered essays on contemporary society with references to the new: new scenery (*shin fūkei*), new customs (*shin fūzoku*), new sights (*shin meisho*), new buildings (*shin kenchiku*). They invoked a neologism—*modern*—to describe everything from "modern life" (*modan raifu*) to "modern trousers" (*modan zubon*). The ubiquitous references to the new and the modern conveyed a breathless enchantment with what was seen as the novelty and exoticism of urban life. The choice of an English loan word, *modan*, rather than the indigenous term *kindai*, to describe the contemporary city marked the phenomenology of urban change as a western—and American—import. The 1920s neologism *modan* was itself defined in terms of a late-nineteenth-century loan word, *hai karaa*, or "high collar." *Hai karaa* derived from the habit of elite men adopting western-style shirts, and it was generalized to signify "western-style," "metropolitan," and "fashionable."[4] Reformulated in the 1920s as *modan*, the word encompassed a broader range of referents: not just fashion in clothing but the latest in foodways, architectural style, urban topography—even the city itself. The expanding purview of "the modern" figured the city as a chronotope: a topos for ceaseless novelty and a place where the future became present.[5]

In the national press and in mass-circulation magazines like the *Central Review* (*Chūo kōron*), *Reconstruction* (*Kaizō*), and *Modern Japan* (*Modan Nihon*), the locus of *modan* was Tokyo. However, provincial newspapers and magazines focused their descriptions of modern urban life closer to home. In such publications as *Modan Kanazawa*, sketches of modern life spotlighted urban landmarks like Kanazawa's Ishiguro Pharmacy or the fashionable Kōrinbō entertainment district. As in the national media, modern fashion meant bobbed hair and western dress for women, suits and walking sticks for men; it was illustrated with photographs of neon lights, broad, paved boulevards, and multistory buildings. But in *A Guidebook to Greater Sapporo*, modern girls and modern boys paraded not across an urban stage in the capital but along Sapporo's city streets.[6] While metropolitan intellectuals universalized "modernity" from observation of Tokyo's downtown, provincial elites associated modern life with their own entertainment and shopping districts (*sakariba*), like Sapporo's Tanukikōji and Niigata's Furumachi. Such descriptions made the *sakariba* into a metonym for the modern—a chronotope within a chronotope that provided a glimpse into the world of tomorrow.

Though residents of provincial cities engaged this world by walking through their own downtowns, they joined with metropolitan intellectuals in identifying Tokyo's Ginza as the epicenter of Japanese modern life. And while the movie industry, department store advertisements, mass magazines, and popular songs initially spread the iconic image of "Ginza modern," local entrepreneurs, municipal leaders, and literati reinforced the Ginza's symbolic power through the widespread adoption, beginning in the mid-1920s, of the name for cafés, bars, and other nightlife establishments, as well as for local entertainment districts. Thus, Furumachi became "Niigata Ginza," and Tanukikōji "Sapporo Ginza." The expression *Ginbura*—to "hang out in the Ginza"—was picked up and turned into *Furubura*—"hanging out in Furumachi."[7] In what Hattori Keijirō identified as a process of "Ginza-ization," 487 shopping districts around the country had, by 1956, named themselves "Someplace Ginza."[8]

What accounted for the Ginza's symbolic appeal? How did a handful of city blocks east of Edo castle in downtown Tokyo come to stand for Japanese modern? The answer says a great deal about Tokyo's division into rising and declining neighborhoods and where the Ginza fit within a broader cultural landscape. Unlike the inhabitants of provincial cities, where typically there was a single central entertainment district, Tokyo's large population supported several geographically dispersed *sakariba*, including Asakusa, Shinjuku, Ueno, and Shibuya, as well as the Ginza. Writers like Kawabata Yasunari, Tanizaki Jun'ichirō, and Nagai Kafū all wrote evocative portraits of Tokyo's "bustling places" in the twenties and thirties. Filled with a cast of social archetypes— salarymen, modern girls, revolutionaries, delinquent youth, writers, and down-at-the-heel geisha—the novels *The Scarlet Gang of Asakusa* (Kawabata

Yasunari), *Naomi* (Tanizaki Jun'ichirō), and *A Strange Tale East of the River* (Nagai Kafū) were staged in particular metropolitan neighborhoods; they laid out what Seiji Lippit has called a "topography of Japanese modernism."[9] The 1929 hit tune "Tokyo March" distilled such symbolic associations into a memorable series of lines. The theme song from a popular movie and a best-selling recording, "Tokyo March" contained four stanzas, each devoted to a separate "bustling place." The lyrics identified the Ginza with dance halls, jazz, and liquor; the Marunouchi business center with the rush hour; Asakusa with the new subway (the first in Japan and the Orient); and Shinjuku with movies, department stores, and the suburban Odakyu train line.[10] As "Tokyo March" suggested, a number of Tokyo's neighborhoods possessed hallmarks of the modern city. And yet, the Ginza emerged from this crowded field of possibilities to monumentalize "modern Tokyo."

Surely part of the reason was the Ginza's ability to lay claim to both the old and the new, particularly after the Great Kantō Earthquake that destroyed much within the low-lying districts of the city. The earthquake hit Tokyo seconds before noon on September 1, 1923. Fires erupted from over-turned stoves that were lit to prepare the noon meal, and soon flames engulfed the eastern wards of the city. In the two days that the fires raged, most of the "low city" to the east of the Imperial Palace was destroyed. Three-quarters of the city's housing stock was burned to the ground. More than one hundred thousand people were killed, and more than 2 million rendered homeless. Economic activity came to a standstill. In the massive reconstruction that took place afterward, the city's center of gravity shifted west, to the hilly "high city" that emerged from the earthquake relatively unscathed. As wealth fled the old city and Tokyo expanded westward, ambitious plans for rebuilding the eastern wards were scaled back. In the process, reconstruction congealed divisions between a "high city" on the rise and a "low city" on the decline.[11]

Located next to Nihonbashi, the mercantile heart of the old city, the Ginza was geographically part of the "low city" ravaged by the quake. Though neglect turned much of eastern Tokyo into a concentration of slums and down-market entertainment districts, the neighborhoods adjacent to the Imperial Palace were an exception. The Ginza benefited from new invest-ments in building stock, as department-store and other commercial capital poured into the neighborhood. The impact of reconstruction on the neigh-borhood was profound. Before the earthquake the Ginza provided the city's main outlet for the retail of western imported goods; it was also the center of the newspaper industry and home to a handful of highbrow cafes catering to the Tokyo literati. Laid out in the late nineteenth century as the centerpiece of the new national capital, "Ginza Brick Town" showcased the modernization project of the Meiji government. With its haberdasheries for western clothing and rows of publishing houses, the Ginza seemed to embody the national pursuit of "civilization and enlightenment." When the earthquake destroyed much of the low city, the Ginza's capacity for revitalization drew on this foundation.

As Yoshimi Shun'ya points out, the resonance of the formulation "Ginza equals future" rested on two postearthquake developments. The first was the adoption of an aggressive marketing strategy by the large metropolitan department stores. Building magnificent new branches in the Ginza, stores like Mitsukoshi, Matsuya, and Matsuzakaya reached for an expanded clientele among the middle class, marketing domestically produced western-style goods as well as the imports for which the Ginza was famous. Second, the newspaper and publishing industry increased production to serve a national market, transforming itself into mass media.[12] In addition to such investments in a wider market for the culture industries, a third critical change lay in the reinvention of Ginza café culture after the earthquake, as Edward Seidensticker notes. The handful of exclusive cafés that provided a venue for writers' salons expanded rapidly into a diverse and lively nightclub scene that attracted a core clientele among the men who worked in the office buildings of nearby Marunouchi.[13] All three developments built on Meiji-era Ginza. Together, they made the market for "Ginza culture" more national in scope, broader in class terms, and representative of a "Japanese-style" modern. In short, the Ginza was abstracted to symbolize the urban future.

If Tokyo's Ginza represented a chronotope of the future in the present, it also seemed to embody the temporal rupture of modernity. The Ginza captured the moment when the earthquake destroyed the old city, when Edo disappeared and Tokyo rose in its place. The Ginza narrative resonated with the classic modernist formulation of creative destruction and the birth of the modern from the ashes of history articulated by Nietzsche and popularized by countless writers and artists.[14] Indeed, Tanizaki Jun'ichirō actually welcomed news of the earthquake because its destructive force would evacuate the old world and make way for the new. As he later confessed, though he worried about the fate of his family, who were staying in Yokohama at the time of the quake, "at almost the same instant joy welled up inside me at the thought, 'How marvelous! Tokyo will become a decent place now!'"

Orderly thoroughfares, shiny, newly paved streets, a flood of cars, blocks of flats rising floor on floor, level on level, in geometric beauty, and threading through the city elevated lines, subways, streetcars. And the excitement at night of a great city, a city with all the amusements of Paris or New York, a city where the nightlife never ends. Then, and then indeed, the citizens of Tokyo will come to adopt a purely European-American style of life, and the young people, men and women alike, will all wear Western clothes. This is the inevitable trend of the times, and whether one likes it or not this is what will happen.[15]

Like many of his contemporaries, Tanizaki welcomed an urban future that promised to eliminate the old city with its cramped, winding streets, parochial culture, and stultifying predictability. He looked forward to, in its stead, an intoxicating flood of western-style consumer goods and a city rebuilt according to the imposing rationality and geometric certitudes of modernist city planning. On the boundary between the low and high cities, equally part of the old and the new, the Ginza was uniquely positioned to symbolize Tanizaki's vision of a Tokyo risen triumphant from the rubble of destruction.

Laying the ground for the enhancement of the Ginza's symbolic power, the local disaster of the Great Kantō Earthquake became written into the chronologies of modernity throughout Japan. There were many concrete reasons for the widespread recognition of the midtwenties as a turning point in Japanese cities. The damage to Tokyo triggered a extensive exodus from the capital, temporarily shifting the balance of political-economic power toward the rival metropolis Osaka. The conspicuous failure of the more ambitious, utopian plans for Tokyo's reconstruction also shifted the spotlight to the progressive urban planning in Osaka. At the same time, in-migrants to Tokyo from the provinces returned in droves to their hometowns, bringing economic and cultural resources with them. In the process, local experiments in provincial cities took on new importance and appeal. Finally, the origins of the spectacular nationwide bank failures of 1927, which marked the beginning of Japan's Great Depression, lay in the central bank's easy-money policy during reconstruction. In all these ways, the aftershocks of the earthquake reverberated far beyond the city limits, providing the grounds for a commonsense identification of 1923 as both an end and a beginning. Thus, even though the Great Kantō Earthquake was a local disaster, it marked the turning point from old city to new throughout the country.

It is tempting to read the transformation of the Ginza from merely a referent for a particular Tokyo neighborhood into a more general signifier for urban modernity as a privileging of Tokyo as the wellspring of progress, a homage paid to the metropolis as provincial cities sought to follow Tokyo's lead. But was this the entire meaning of "Ginza-ization"? Though it may have signified a desire to "catch up" with Tokyo, the proliferation of "local Ginza" also expressed a sense of identification with the capital. Cities everywhere were changing in similar ways. Residents of Sapporo and Niigata saw in their own downtowns the identical markers of urban progress associated with the Ginza. The point was not that Ginza-Tokyo offered a spectral view of their future, but rather that the "local Ginza" embodied the sign of things to come. The formulation "Ginza = future" transcended the geography of the metropolis.

In city guides, local magazines, advertisements, and the like, Ginza-ization reflected the perception that cities were undergoing epochal shifts: the sense of temporal rupture evoked by the earthquake resonated with the experience of urban life throughout the country. A series of essays on the city of Kanazawa written by Kamoi Yū, the arts editor of the local newspaper, offered a telling example. Initially published in the *Hokkoku shinbun,* the essays were later brought out by the paper in book form under the title *New Scenes of Kanazawa* (*Kanazawa shin fūkei,* 1933). Kamoi introduced his book as an "unconventional" guide, an attempt to present the city in a new way. To this end, he employed the newly created discipline of *kōgengaku,* or "modernology." As Kamoi explained, *kōgengaku* was defined as the modern counterpart to the field of archaeology, or *kōkogaku.* While archeology studied "prehistory," modernology deployed a similar method to look at "posthistory."[16] In other words, archeology investigated human artifacts to theorize the social world before the written record, history traced that record to the present, and modernology took up where history left off, analyzing the material objects of contemporary life to project the social world into the future.

Invented by Tokyo architect Kon Wajirō (1888–1973), modernology is usually identified with the study of the capital. The great classic of the discipline was Kon's *1925 Survey of Customs in Tokyo Ginza in Early Summer,* where he documented, with statistics and graphic illustrations, his observations of the pedestrians at a central Ginza crossing in the summer of 1925. Detailing types of hairstyles, accessories, and footwear, and tabulating percentages of women (and men) wearing various combinations of indigenous and western-style dress (bobbed hair and kimono, bowler hats with men's formal *hakama* skirts), Kon theorized the modern subject through the material culture of their everyday lives. While this famous portrait of the Ginza helped establish a name for Kon and for modernology, he produced studies of other parts of Tokyo that included surveys of urban crowds in Shinjuku, Asakusa, and the slum districts of Honjo and Fukugawa. He also carried out a detailed study of the middle-class suburb of Kōenji, surveying the interior designs and material objects found in Tokyo's new suburban housing developments.[17]

Kon is well known for his idiosyncratic studies of Tokyo after the earthquake and as a chronicler of the new age. Less well known, perhaps, is the spread of modernology to cities outside the metropolis. The discipline never achieved the traction of Yanagita Kunio's folklore studies; but with its infectious enthusiasm for "the new," modernology offered local intellectuals an appealing optic for viewing their own cities. The magazine *Modern Kanazawa* applied Kon's method to a different analysis in "The Modernology of Café and Coffeehouse Names," pointing out that names of contemporary drinking establishments were drawn overwhelmingly from foreign place-names (Paris, London, Brazil, Arabia, Venice), from legendary characters in foreign literature and art (Bacchus, Venus, Carmen), and of course, from Tokyo's Ginza.[18] Adapted to the local cityscape, Kon's modernology focused attention on new customs, new scenes, new things—an anthropology of the new that tried to capture analytically what Tanizaki had called "the inevitable trends of the times." Both Kon and Tanizaki were thinking of Tokyo, but Kanazawa's intellectuals appropriated modernology to illuminate something they understood to be characteristic of urban change everywhere.

Kamoi Yū organized his tour of the "new sights" of Kanazawa by neighborhood. Like Kon Wajirō, Kamoi gave special attention to *sakariba*, those bustling centers of entertainment and commerce that captured the excitement and rousing movement of the modern city, what Kamoi called the "urban march." As in Tokyo, Kamoi's *sakariba* occupied the epicenter of urban change, a chronotope within a chronotope that revealed the shape of things to come. While others highlighted the intensity of visual stimulation in the new city centers—neon signs, display windows, modernist buildings—Kamoi called attention to the encounter with new sounds like the "sound of the train" carrying crowds to the city center and the "clip-clop of wooden clogs [*geta*] along the paved streets." As Kamoi pointed out, when clog hit pavement rather than packed dirt the familiar and evocative sound of traditional footwear was rendered unfamiliar. Like the sound of the train, this was a sensory experience associated with the *sakariba*, a city space that turned the old world into the new.[19]

And as it did for Kon, *sakariba* for Kamoi meant department stores and cafés. As he pointed out, the establishment of a Mitsukoshi branch store in the neighborhood turned Musashigatsuji into a commercial center.[20] Modernology could help illuminate the ways department stores were creating *sakariba* and transforming the character of the city. For Kamoi, department stores captured the quality of perpetual motion that defined the city; they were the place to envision the future in the present. Viewing the new Miyaji Daimaru store through this lens, he wrote: "[It] looks like a square box with windows cut out. Though failing as architecture, as a commercial building it has a certain comfortable, human quality that one grows familiar with as the store expands more and more according to demand. At the moment it is being expanded again; when the new renovation is finished the store will certainly become one of the great sights of Katamachi."[21] As Kamoi's description suggested, department stores possessed an organic connection to city residents through the interface of the local market; they were both cause and effect of the "trends of the times." With their endless projects to rebuild and expand, stores like Miyaji Daimaru resonated symbolically with the modernist axiom that the only constant of the modern age is constant change.

Department stores telegraphed their cultural and economic authority through monumental architecture. Kamoi offered a reading of the visual power of the Mitsukoshi building:

If you look at Mitsukoshi from the front, it stirs the appetite for material consumption; but looking at it from behind, it stokes an aesthetic reaction that greatly transcends material desire.... The pile of concrete you look up at from the back lacks filigree or decoration because it is the rear of the building. Instead, the structure is audaciously finished off as a single unadorned mass that announces its existence with a bracing simplicity. The view from the front is nothing more than an American-style department store, but from the back it has the majestic and dignified appearance of a medieval castle. Just as Oyama castle cast its authority over feudal Kanazawa, Mitsukoshi dominates modern Kanazawa.[22]

In other words, the department store possessed a symbolic power that exceeded its appeal as a palace of consumer desire. Just as the castle provided both material base and symbolic projection of the feudal authority that ruled the castle town, the imposing edifice of the department store telegraphed its command over the modern city through both commercial and symbolic power. Moreover, Kamoi's reading of the iconography of department store architecture gave a new spin to the Japanese appropriations of western modernist design: in the front of the building, crass imitation of "American-style"; in the rear, something raw and simple and honest.

Gazing at the city through the lens of modernology, Kanazawa intellectuals predicted the expansion of Kanazawa's café culture. An article titled "Movies and Cafés, Choice of the Times" in *Modan Kanazawa* explained the rise of the café as the contemporary variation on the timeless human desire for pleasure. In this "age of excess" the urban crowd turned their backs on Kabuki and the teahouse, demanding from their entertainments a more intense form of stimulation.[23] Kamoi likewise pinpointed sensory experience as the core of the café's appeal, identifying the café experience with a uniquely modern and uniquely urban sensibility. As he explained, "The café provided a particular modern sensation available only to urbanites: the ability, in savoring a drink, to feel the latent energy of the city pulsing through your veins."[24] The café, like the department store, constituted a wellspring of the new urban culture.

Kamoi predicted the spread of café culture in Kanazawa from its current base in Kōrinbō to the nearby district of Kakinokibata. As he noted, Kakinokibata was originally developed from land left vacant when clansmen relocated their estates some three hundred years ago. The Maeda lord planted the area with persimmon trees, hence the name Kakinokibata, or "persimmon grove field." "Yet today you can see no sign of a *kaki* tree, and if we study the area through the methodology of modernology we can predict that it will soon develop into a center of up-market drinking establishments. Customers who are unsatisfied by Kōrinbō's ostentatious cafés will want a neighborhood of quiet bars where they can savor their drink. It should be someplace close by to draw in customers from Kōrinbō. The only logical possibility is Kakinokibata." Modernology offered Kamoi a means to pick up where history left off, projecting the linear development of local culture into the future. The numbers of cafés would proliferate as the growing market for modern entertainment divided into elite and "mass" segments. Once again, as this narrative of an expanding café culture in Kanazawa illustrated, the *sakariba* constituted the nucleus of the modern city. In this sense Ginza-ization did not mean the transplanting of the Ginza to Kanazawa, but rather the spread of a universal form of modernity from a local base in Kōrinbō.

Though Kon Wajirō also studied the slums that popped up on the underside of modern Tokyo, the dominant tone of his writing was celebratory. In this sense he joined the chorus of Japanese intellectuals who were bullish on modernity. Likewise, Kamoi's guide to the "new sites of Kanazawa," exuded excitement about the changes in store for the modern city. Being an arts editor of the local paper, Kamoi made his case largely on aesthetic grounds. A description of road construction through the downtown neighborhood of Hikizō conveyed Kamoi's admiration for the modernist order and linearity of the new cityscape.

The boulevard is one of the so-called twelve-ken roads, a wide expanse that appears to run straight out into a vast plain. Looking out onto both sides of this wide boulevard where houses have yet to be built and shops have yet to be established, one sees modern Kanazawa itself standing frozen in place. When you survey the broad Hikizō Boulevard from the direction of Musashigatsuji, the sparse roofline seems to bow down in awe before the mighty power of the roadway.... At the end of the road is the modern edifice of Hikizō Hospital, an imposing symbol of Hikizō.[25]

Rebuilt according the modernist vision of city planners after a catastrophic fire destroyed the neighborhood in 1927, the new Hikizō was defined through the grand boulevard that carved a channel through its center.[26] The geometric simplicity of Kanazawa's "twelve-ken" roads appealed to Kamoi, much as Tanizaki had dreamed of "orderly thoroughfares, shiny, newly paved streets" in a reconstructed Tokyo. The boulevard conveyed a "mighty power" to determine Kanazawa's future.

In adopting the road as metaphor for the modern city, Kamoi envisioned a linear path to the future, with milestones of progress marked by the ongoing erection of new buildings. As he explained the time line, "a modern city was developed first by establishing a road network, then the erection of buildings follows. Hikizō thoroughfare is creating precisely these conditions, this foundation. When business picks up again, Hikizō might well become Kanazawa's high street [daiichi no shigai]. When the roadside trees grow big enough to wrap your arms around, the street will be a lively entertainment district filled with groups of modern boys [mobo] and modern girls [moga]. And today's modern boys will have become modern granddads [mojiji] and modern grannies [mobaba]."[27] As Kamoi deployed it, the road metaphor operated at several levels. Since roads are linear, the metaphor symbolized the modernological projection of Kanazawa's path into the future. The road also represented a blank slate on which the city could be erected, reflecting the conviction that new urban spaces molded new urban subjects. Since modern people were produced by modern infrastructure, the road signified faith in the power of technology to engineer future generations.

The metaphor of the road also invoked the prospect of urban renewal. In the 1920s, roads were the linchpins of city plans. They were central to a narrative of creative destruction in which provincial cities would create their modern selves out of the ashes of the past. Kamoi's urban sketches highlighted this dualism of the traditional and modern; and like Tanizaki, Kamoi welcomed the natural disaster that destroyed the old city: "The large boulevard draws a stark line between feudal and modern Kanazawa. The pedestrian walkway is clearly set apart from the vehicular road. Trees line the side, capturing the appearance of modern Kanazawa. Though it is not the first to be paved in Kanazawa, Hikizō Boulevard represents the first planned road on this scale. In this sense we can say that the great fire that consumed Hikizō also destroyed feudal Kanazawa—and now modern Kanazawa is rising from within its ashes."[28] Echoing the archetypal image of modern Tokyo emerging from the rubble of the great earthquake, Kamoi described Kanazawa's worst natural disaster in modern memory in terms of the possibility of rebirth. Drawing a "stark line" between the old and the new, he embraced the moment of rupture and looked eagerly to the new city taking shape before his eyes.

If the boulevard encapsulated the modernist celebration of straight lines on a horizontal plane, applause for the multistory building reflected a corresponding vertical aesthetic: admiration for the "mighty power" of commanding heights. As Kamoi observed, the tall buildings that dominated the modern cityscape altered ways of seeing. The sightlines of modern perception were defined by the aerial view.

Perceptions of scenic beauty change with the age. The "three famous views" for Japanese of the past will not be the same as they are for modern-day people. If we look at this from the perspective of historical materialism we see that changes in modes of transportation have transformed our appreciation of scenery. In the feudal era, scenery was viewed from the middle of a palanquin, from a boat, or from on horseback. This is the perspective you see in Hiroshige's famous woodblock series, "Fifty-Three Views of the Tōkaidō." But with the advent of steamships and the railway, we move at astonishing speed. This has changed our appreciation of the scenery that we pass through. Take the site in Kiso, for example, famous in the era of the palanquin as a place to break one's journey. Today if you look down at this place from the window of a steam train you can quickly appreciate the transformation— it looks like nothing so much as a clod of dirt rolling by. And then comes the airplane. After the appearance of air travel, the appreciation of scenery characteristic of the era of the steamship and the steam train undergoes yet another epochal transformation. Airplanes and high-rise buildings accelerate changes in perception. To see for yourself the scenic beauty of the new age, it is essential to visit the rooftop gardens of Mitsukoshi, Miyaji Daimaru, and Ishiguro Pharmacy. Unfortunately, Ishiguro's rooftop garden is open only in summer, particularly since it affords the best view. When you look down, you get dizzy—the same feeling you have riding an airplane. As a rehearsal for the airplane age, go to the rooftop garden.[29]

Kamoi saw the multistory building, much like the road or the café, as a feature of the city that produced modern consciousness and modern people. Looking down from above, one could see the entire city at a glance; it created an entirely new frame of reference for the world of daily life.

Access to this totalizing perspective was something that set urban dwellers apart from their rural counterparts. Just as they could "feel the pulse" of modern life in the café, city people could experience the dizzying thrill of commanding heights from their multistory buildings. As Kamoi summed it up, the Kanazawa rooftop gardens had created an "ultramodern" (*uruturaa modan*) way of looking at the world—a uniquely urban gaze that shaped modern consciousness. Country people, unable to "experience the beauty of height," were left "behind the times": they were modernity's Other.[30]

In all these ways the discourse on modern life in the 1920s equated the city with the future. Though from their perches in the metropolis the Tokyo intellectuals understood their city as the epicenter of the modern, the viewpoint from the provincial city identified modernity as a product of the city more generally. The enthusiastic embrace of Ginza-ization represented the conviction that the "city = future"; it was also a ringing endorsement of what that future would bring. The widespread appeal of the narrative of Ginza-ization conveyed the sense that cities were converging on a unitary future, that the modern city would be characterized by a single laundry list of characteristics: wide streets, bustling places, department stores, high-rise buildings. These defined what it meant to be a modern city; they culturally engineered a modern way of seeing and feeling among urban residents and socialized the modern subject. Together, such convictions helped install a metanarrative of modernity where everything that rises must converge, of homogenization and universalism—where the cult of the new became a cult of the same.

And yet, the city-planning and local-development movements of the interwar period also generated thought experiments about the future that operated in tension with this narrative of convergence. Just as the local-history

movement reinforced the sense of a universal national past even while stress-
ing local difference, urban futurism contained competing impulses between
universalism and particularism within the city idea. In the tracks of the multiple time lines of local identity laid down by the local-history movement, the
future could be imagined to unfold according to particularized road maps.
This emerged with special clarity in the exhibition boom of the interwar
years, where the process of local branding for economic development highlighted the heterogeneity of urban progress.

EXHIBITING PROGRESS

During the late teens and the twenties, localities throughout the country
hosted industrial fairs as a tool for promoting economic development. In
what the Kanazawa Chamber of Commerce called the "exhibition boom,"
prefectures and municipalities looked to the industrial fair to counter an
economic slump. As the Sapporo government explained, plans for its 1926
exhibition represented a response to the global depression after the Great
War and the wave of economic problems that spread out from the Kantō
region after the great earthquake of 1923. The exhibition boom also reflected
the rising importance of the domestic market for Japanese commerce and
industry. Japanese exports to Asia had surged during the war and then
shrunk again afterward, as Europeans reestablished themselves in the
Chinese and Indian markets. The increased use of rayon for the production
of stockings in Europe and America cut into Japanese silk exports. The new
challenges facing Japanese products in overseas markets turned attention to
opportunities for expanding sales closer to home. Reflecting this view, the
Sapporo exhibit recognized the limits of "export-led development policies
pursued since the Meiji period under the banner of 'increase production,
encourage industry' [*shokusan kōgyō*]."[31] The conviction that an untapped
domestic market represented the best hope for Sapporo's producers marked
a sea change in the attitudes of Japan's economic elite.

By the time of the interwar boom in industrial fairs, Japanese had developed a long experience with exhibitions. As a study of international and
domestic industrial fairs published in 1937 observed, from their nineteenth-
century origins the exhibition form was designed to pursue four broad goals:
economic development, international relations, commemoration, and colonization.[32] The same study pointed out that exhibitions operated at a number

of functional levels. They were educational, proffering "enlightenment" and introducing new lifestyles. And because they represented a form of investment and offered a return on that investment, they were also a commercial enterprise. Beyond this, they acted as a vehicle for social policy, aiming to steer the country out of recession. Finally, because they provided a venue for cultural exchange and improved relations with foreign countries, fairs were a form of diplomacy.[33] Drawing on decades of experience, Japan's regional exhibitions of the 1920s and 1930s brought together a diverse group of participants and a variety of ambitious agendas. Meticulously planned and logistically complex, these fairs were staged on a grand scale. They were transforming events for the cities that hosted them.

The exhibition boom hit the prefecture of Ishikawa in the mid-1920s. In 1926, twenty-seven different fairs, displays, and product shows were held, most sponsored by trade associations or business organizations. At the same time, local authorities and the Kanazawa business community began to explore the idea of staging a major products fair in the city, culminating in the 1931 Fair to Promote Industry and Tourism.[34] The situation was similar elsewhere. Niigata conducted a six-week fair to commemorate the opening of the port in the summer of 1926. Fifteen years later the city hosted the Great Exhibition on Asian Development and National Defense, linking the expansion of the port to the empire and the war effort. Okayama held an industrial fair in 1928; Sapporo hosted three between 1918 and 1931.

The first of the Sapporo exhibitions was staged in 1918, part of a grand effort to commemorate the fiftieth anniversary of the colonization of Hokkaido. Planning for the exhibition began in 1914 with an initial budget of 330,000 yen, which rose to 459,349 yen by 1918. The city placed thirty-four thousand articles on display at three separate fairgrounds, two within Sapporo and a third in the nearby city of Otaru. During the fifty days of the fair, officials recorded 1,420,000 visitors to the main site at Sapporo's Nakajima Park; 8,000 came on opening day alone. These were impressive attendance figures for the time, and the fair drew numbers comparable to those of fairs in larger cities. The Osaka Fair of 1903 drew 4,350,693 visitors, while a fair in Philadelphia in 1926 drew 6,500,000.[35] Both the city and the prefecture made significant investments in infrastructure to prepare for the exhibition. The horse-drawn city tram was electrified, and twenty new buses were put into circulation to carry people between the central station and the fairgrounds. The city experienced a construction boom as new hotels and shops went up, the display halls were built, and amenities at Nakajima Park were improved. The central rail station, as the gateway to the city, gained three magnificent, Renaissance-style arches, erected in front of Sapporo station to constitute a welcome gate, at a cost of 4,700 yen.[36]

In Kanazawa, the city, prefecture, chamber of commerce, and railway bureau joined in sponsoring the Exhibition on Industry and Tourism in the spring of 1932. Advertised as the first exhibition to focus on tourism, the Kanazawa fair solicited participation from the three special municipal districts of Tokyo, Kyoto, and Osaka, from Japan's forty-three prefectures, and from Hokkaido. Tens of thousands of products were put on display in more than thirty buildings. The city was spruced up for the occasion: stores were refurbished, neon lights installed, new transportation lines created, and extra buses and taxis provided. As statistics collected on the exhibition confirm, such investments paid off handsomely. Attendance topped 1 million. Passengers passing through Kanazawa station during the fair totaled 490,000, a rise of 230,000 over the same period the previous year. Inn and hotel guests rose by 15,000. The streetcar took in 22,000 yen more than previous year. Red-light district receipts went up 10 percent; department store sales were up 35 percent; and souvenir shop receipts increased 30–50 percent. As the business community agreed, the fair was a huge success.[37]

The Sapporo and Kanazawa fairs were part of an interwar exhibition boom that drew upon precedents of the early Meiji period, when the opening of the country, the influx of new products from the West, the stimulation of industry through the "increase production; encourage industry" policy, and the example of international exhibitions generated a wave of domestic fairs starting in the 1870s. Like these earlier fairs, the exhibitions of the twenties and thirties assembled an engaging collection of historical and newfangled curios. They reflected a similar fever for novelty and invention, displaying new products from the West as well as domestic inventions. The Meiji fairs themselves retained a strong flavoring of Edo-period antiquarian exhibits and often included sales of swords and other collectors' items from the estates of down-on-their-luck samurai. By the interwar period, though the fairs maintained their hallmark juxtaposition of old and new, a more coherent historical vision replaced the feel of a curiosity shop.[38] As they developed out of their Meiji predecessors, exhibits became a vehicle for the dissemination of the cult of the new.

Throughout the late nineteenth and early twentieth centuries, exhibitions in Europe and America offered important models for fair design in Japan. After the sensational London Crystal Palace Exhibition of 1851, a succession of world's fairs each competed to outdo the last in its lavish scale and spectacular display. World's fairs provided a venue for introducing new inventions, technologies, and products to an international market. The gramophone, sewing machine, and typewriter riveted world attention at the Philadelphia Fair of 1876; moving walkways and moving pictures captured attention at Paris in 1900; the airplane, automobile, and wireless dazzled visitors to St. Louis in 1904. After first hearing of the London Exhibition of 1862 via newspaper coverage and a write-up in Fukuzawa Yukichi's best seller *Conditions in the West (Seiyō jijō*, 1866), Japanese looked to world's fairs for opportunities to promote sales overseas and for managing their national image abroad. At the invitation of the French consul, Japanese sent exhibits of lacquerware, pottery, screens, and other "traditional" decorative arts to Paris in 1867. From these and subsequent exhibits, Europeans and Americans developed a taste for "Japonism," influencing fashion in visual and decorative arts and in architecture. The potential of exhibition displays for cultural influence was a lesson not lost on Japanese observers.[39]

Like the international exhibitions of the late nineteenth and early twentieth centuries, Japanese industrial fairs became a forum for exhibiting progress as well as for the constitution of a cultural identity that often took "tradition" as its marker. In their juxtapositions of new and old, progress and tradition, and in their adoption of Eurocentric ideas about a hierarchy of civilizations along a time line of development, exhibitions created a powerful vehicle for temporal consciousness. But while the Meiji fairs helped foster a spirit of economic nationalism and international rivalry, the Taishō exhibitions focused spectators on the regional economy, pumping up a buoyant localism and encouraging competition between prefectures and regions. In this sense, exhibitions reinforced the multiple temporalities produced by the local-history movement and helped turn ideas of progress and development into time lines of local identity.

The equation of progress with localism was conveyed through the monumental visuality and spectacle of the exhibitions. Provincial cities used the industrial fairs to market themselves, showcasing urban amenities, modern factories, and new streets and buildings as illustrations of the vitality and progress of their communities. While guidebooks urged visitors to see the city as an extended fairground, visitors' main impressions were drawn from the exhibition space itself. Localities invested enormous sums in expanding city parks and parade grounds for these fairs and in building architectural structures to house the displays. Often divided into main and secondary sites with bus or tram service between the two, the principal fairgrounds were typically laid out like strolling gardens, directing the crowds along a particular circuit. The route channeled visitors through an assortment of some thirty to fifty halls, pavilions, and booths of varying sizes, ranging from large halls housing multiple exhibits to small booths with a single focus. In between, fairgoers encountered fountains, decorative arches, flags, and towers. Along the way they could amuse themselves in a scenic garden, a boating pond, or a "children's country" with rides and playground equipment.

The Kanazawa fair engaged visitors through special events like the "hunt for beauties" (*bijin sagashi*). Photos of celebrated geisha were distributed to the crowd, which fanned out in search of the originals. For two days, fairgoers could also participate in a treasure hunt for certificates hidden throughout the fairgrounds that were exchanged for prizes. On a special "Tokyo Day," the Tokyo pavilion hosted a series of activities, including performances and product demonstrations. The Tokyo sponsors distributed free samples of their goods as well as coupons for use on a trip to the capital. Taiwan Day and Karafuto Day spotlighted the empire, and a "discount day" provided bargain deals for the budget minded.[40] The variety of events decorating exhibition calendars not only enticed visitors to the fair but also associated the city with entertainment and play.

The fairground experience, like the *sakariba*, bombarded visitors with visual stimulation, overwhelming them through the impact of architectural splendor. The 1918 Sapporo exhibition housed its displays in beaux arts, neoclassical style, but most of the exhibitions of the twenties and early thirties were an eclectic mix of art deco, arts and crafts, futurism, and other international modernist currents in architecture. Although movements like futurism were associated with a particular politics in Europe, within the Japanese context the admixture of styles expressed a playful spirit of experimentation and a vague cosmopolitan progressivism more than a particular ideological or political stance. This eclectic internationalism was harnessed to local culture to articulate a modernist regional style. As the record of the 1926 Sapporo Exhibition put it: "Exhibition architecture is by its nature temporary, and therefore you see a variety of new forms appearing. Though in the past Hokkaido architecture did not have a definitive character, now is the time to try and develop a unified style of architecture for the prefecture. Thus, in the design for the exhibition grounds, as much as possible we wanted to create something refined and elegant that symbolizes the development of Hokkaido."[41] Blueprints for the main gate, the central exhibition hall, the history pavilion, and the machine hall were all drawn up with the execution of a "refined and elegant" Hokkaido style in mind. In this way, exhibition planners saw architecture as the means of both formulating and presenting a local style that conveyed progress and development.

Through the combination of machine halls and entertainment pavilions, displays of artifacts and new inventions, and presentations of local specialty products from throughout the country, organizers sought to convey a totality of Japanese economic culture within the artificial confines of the fairgrounds. In what Todd Henry called an effect of "time-space compression," Japanese exhibitions allowed visitors within the space of several hours and a few city blocks to canvas the reaches of Japan and to travel from the ancient past into the future.[42] While the interwar fairs did project a sense of "Japan" as an economic and cultural totality, the stronger take-home message related to regionalism. In contrast to their Meiji predecessors, the expositions of the Taishō and the early Shōwa juxtaposed new and old in order to foreground a regional, rather than a national, brand.

Industrial fairs communicated this message by making regional products the centerpiece of exhibition display. Exposition sponsors invited participation from throughout the country and the colonial territories. Some, like the Kanazawa Exposition in 1932, boasted displays from all forty-three prefectures; the special municipalities of Tokyo, Osaka, and Kyoto; and Japan's colonies. Localities were represented by their specialty products, turning economic production into a local brand. Such commercial strategies complemented the marketing of regionalism through the emerging tourist industry. Just as travel guides compressed a city into a series of famous sights, expositions condensed local culture into its key products. In the process, a city like Sapporo became identified with beer, the Hokkaido region with the dairy industry. This reinforced companies' use of particular places for product trademarks. For example, packaging and advertisements for "Snow Brand" cheese, butter, and ice cream—produced in Sapporo at one of the country's largest commercial dairies—used the readily identifiable outline of Hokkaido to highlight the association with local climate and geography. Branding worked both ways, creating the association of beer with Sapporo and Sapporo with beer.[43]

The idea of local branding guided the organization of the Sapporo National Products Exposition of 1926. Of the forty-five buildings on the main fairgrounds, the majority were devoted to the exhibition and sale of regional products. Three buildings were set aside entirely for exhibits from communities in Hokkaido. In addition, the major regional cities of Sapporo, Otaru, Hakodate, and Asahikawa commanded separate exhibition halls and sales pavilions. While Tokyo businessmen sent enough display items to fill their own building, most participants from outside Hokkaido arranged their displays in the main exhibition hall. As the organizing committee explained its goals, the Sapporo National Products Fair specifically eschewed a common set of guidelines for layout, leaving it to the exhibitors to determine the arrangement of their own displays. The point was to "display the distinctive characteristics of regional production" and raise public awareness of the distribution of regional industry.[44]

Within this smorgasbord of the nation's industries, visitors got a taste of each prefecture. Hyōgo was the place "where the great trading port of Kobe is located." Merchant organizations highlighted its variety of the "most advanced manufactures"—everything from tires, to matches, to hair pomade. Gumma prefecture focused its display on its "famous dyes," and Saitama on its position as the "weaving center of the Kantō region." Chiba was renown for soy sauce and *mirin* (sweet rice wine), Ibaragi for its plum varieties, and Ishikawa for its artisan crafts.[45] After visitors passed through the sequence of prefectural displays in the main exhibition hall, the exposition route guided them into the more detailed exhibitions in the Hokkaido pavilions. Here the number and variety of items on display multiplied, presenting a textured, locally differentiated portrait of the regional economy. Fifteen localities from throughout Hokkaido contributed displays. While variations in layout conveyed the sense of local difference, the displays worked together to advertise Hokkaido's capacity for progress and development.

For this overwhelmingly agricultural region, it was striking how much of the display space was devoted to manufactures. For example, Ishikari, a rural district located near Sapporo, gave prime position to its manufacturing products. Fuji Paper's Ebetsu factory provided samples of the paper they produced; the accompanying text pointed out that the factory supplied local newspaper production. Agricultural displays stressed technical innovation, recasting Hokkaido's agriculture as a trope of futurism. Sorachi, an agricultural district in central Hokkaido, provided a display showing the advanced cultivation techniques used in its large-scale stock farming. The district also showcased its bright future as "Greater Sorachi": photographs and descriptions highlighted the extent of electrification and suggested how a new rail linkup positioned the region at the forefront of agricultural development. Shiribeshi, in Hokkaido's southwest, also made agriculture seem new and exotic. The Shiribeshi display introduced the specialty products asparagus and green peas by telling a story of innovation that highlighted the recent introduction of these crops to the Japanese archipelago. The display underscored their novelty: the entrance to the exhibit was adorned with photographs of asparagus and asparagus stalks blown up to a gigantic height.[46]

Other displays stressed the importance of the region to the national economy by calling attention to Hokkaido's exports and strategically important industries. The explanatory text next to the exhibit devised by Oshima (a district in southwest Hokkaido, next to the port city of Hakodate) focused on the long history of contact with the mainland. Surveying the large range of local products destined for export, the exhibit emphasized the importance of its production of fish and seaweed. As the text pointed out, fish were sent to markets in China and elsewhere and were a key export for both Hokkaido and Japan. Muroran, a port city on Hokkaido's southern coast, exhibited its heavy industrial products—ammunitions, weaponry, propellers, and machine tools produced by a local factory for Japan Steel.[47] The totality of exhibits in the Hokkaido pavilions left visitors with a fine-grain portrait of the region's economic geography, sending the message that Hokkaido's distinctive production culture positioned it at the forefront of economic progress.

As the locus of advanced manufacture and home to the broadest array of products, cities collectively held a special position within the mosaic of distinctive regional brands promoted through the industrial fairs. At the Sapporo Special Products Fair, Tokyo, Osaka, and Kyoto mounted their own exhibits. Tokyo's was especially extensive. Japan's three major cities projected a kind of superbrand, capturing certain emblematic elements of the national culture. While the promotional material described Tokyo as "the fashion capital," Kyoto was characterized as the "city of arts and crafts," and Osaka as the "city of commerce and industry."[48] To illustrate its iconic status as the center of fashion, the Tokyo exhibit featured the latest in "western-style umbrellas" (including something called a "radio umbrella"), the "first rank" of fashion in raincoats, bags, brushes, towels, and cosmetics, and even the very latest in building materials.[49] Nearby, the Osaka display featured an even larger range of consumer, industrial, and construction goods—from soap to sake, fabrics to rubber products, as well as machine tools of great variety. While the Tokyo display signaled Japan's sophisticated fashion, Osaka spoke to the nation's status as a fully industrialized and commercialized economy, a country whose range of manufactures satisfied a well-developed consumer market and whose industries had achieved the sophistication to produce precision and quality in machine tools. For its part, Kyoto was represented by fine artisanal crafts, the very products whose display in the world's fairs of the nineteenth century had set off an international fashion in Japonism: art pottery, fine weaving, and metal filigree work.

Though the three municipalities were presented as centers of a national economic culture, in this context they provided the backdrop to the city of Sapporo, which occupied the center stage. Just as the mosaic of prefectural displays in the main exhibition hall was set up to showcase the rich distinctiveness of Hokkaido's regional economy, the metropolitan superbrands provided a frame for Sapporo to promote its own unique urban brand. The Sapporo display was housed in a spacious hall of its own, with exhibits from the city's larger commercial and manufacturing establishments, from local merchant associations, and from producer cooperatives. The Imai Department Store occupied the commanding position at the entrance to the hall: its display cases featured manikins clothed in the latest urban fashion. Commercial and manufacturer's collectives sent samples of woodwork, toys, and Buddhist religious paraphernalia. The Sapporo Carpenters' Union provided a display of elegant western-style furniture. Imperial Linen, Greater Japan Beer, and Hokkaido Condensed Milk secured exhibit space, as did local manufacturers of skis and other sporting equipment. Such product displays highlighted Sapporo's identity as a "manufacturing city" that specialized in agricultural processing. Its manufactures were embedded within a local agricultural economy and the distinctive natural wonderland of Hokkaido that supplied milk for the dairy industry, hops for beer, lumber for furniture, hides for leather, and so forth. The exhibition text wove the identity of the city into the recent history of manufacturing and plotted out a promising trajectory for the local brand: "The top-class products seen on display here have developed out of the history of manufacturing in Hokkaido. Beginning with hemp spinning, and moving to beer, bricks, lumber, and leather manufacture, eventually all kinds of industries established a manufacturing base here. A national market for goods showed that Greater Sapporo has a bright future as a commercial and industrial city."[50]

Though several other Hokkaido cities also commanded their own exhibition halls, Sapporo's was noticeably larger and more centrally positioned. Even more important, the exhibition's "Hall of History" and "Hall of Knowledge" (sankō-kan) took Sapporo as their main subject, offering in-depth explorations of the city's past, present, and future. The Hall of History included several thousand documents, as well as archeological and historical artifacts, that presented visitors with an urban biography of the city "from prehistory until the present day."[51] Following a narrative being developed in the context of the local-history movement, the Hall of History grounded Sapporo's identity in its unique geographic heritage, the culture and land use of the Ainu that originally inhabited the area, and Sapporo's history as a frontier town and the gateway to Japanese colonization of the island. While the Hall of History provided viewers with the highlights of Sapporo's past, the Hall of Knowledge offered them a glimpse into its future. And just as the historical narrative condensed Sapporo's history into a time line of local development, the Hall of Knowledge spotlighted the sources of economic growth and the spirit of innovation that would propel the city into the future. From the spectacular to the mundane, an enormous array of new products under development packed the hall: ham, sausage, and cheese from Sapporo's experimental farms; the latest telephonic and wireless machines introduced into the Sapporo Communications Bureau; improvements to railway technology being implemented by the Sapporo Railway Bureau; and patents pending by Hokkaido University researchers for new kinds of soap, rice flour products, and so on.[52] A museum of Sapporo inventions and local inventiveness, the Hall of Knowledge showcased the city as the epicenter of regional knowledge production and innovation. The time line of local identity hitched Sapporo's heritage to a "bright future" of development and progress.

Since the late nineteenth century, industrial fairs had provided Japanese with a venue for thought experiments about their future. Building on strategies of display and the overarching theme of progress that had circulated internationally through the world's fairs of the late nineteenth century, the regional products fairs of the interwar years telegraphed the message that manufactures were the engines of local progress and development. The focus of the Japanese industrial fair shifted from "civilization and enlightenment" and national developmentalism in the nineteenth century to regional development and the local brand in the teens, twenties, and thirties. When the idea of progress took a regional turn, the single path of national improvement laid down by the concept of "civilization and enlightenment" branched off into the multiple tracks of local development. Through the regional exhibitions, the idea of progress became harnessed to the construction of regional identity and the local brand.

Several points can be made about the impact of the exhibitions. First, they defined local culture in economic terms, as a culture of production and in particular as a culture of modern manufacturing. Here, local developmentalism focused on the economy: identifying the place with its economic base and the community with its main product. Second, exhibitions portrayed cities as the centers of this local culture, as engines of regional development. Cities attracted pools of productive talent—business acumen, technological ingenuity, intellectual inventiveness—whose creative synergy generated a successful local product. Guided by this pool of talent, cities became the workshop for the regional economy. And third, in privileging cities, anointing them as epicenters of regional progress, exhibitions provided a new visibility for the urban brand. Harnessed to the project of local development, the urban brand carried a freight of expectations that it would bring the city and its people into a bright future. In all these ways, exhibitions helped construct a narrative of progress that was etched in local colors, a futurescape where regions were differentiated by their industries and cities by their brands.

And yet, this vision of a future marked by local difference competed with a more powerful narrative of convergence, which also found expression in the exhibition boom. Expositions privileged cities as the spectral sites for the world of tomorrow. They identified urban space with science and technology, with speed and novelty, with innovation and experimentation. They spotlighted cities as the source of vision and leadership, ushering in a future of progress and bounty. They portrayed them as experimental laboratories of social and mechanical engineering. All this both reinforced the temporal consciousness of the city—a sense that cities ran on a faster clock, that their developmental trajectory placed them ahead of the countryside. Like the vision of Ginza-ization, where all cities converged on a unitary future, the urban world of tomorrow on display in the exhibition boom distilled "the city" into symbols of a universal modernity. Whereas the Ginza represented the modern life of the entertainment district and consumer culture, the world of tomorrow at the exhibitions figured modernity as technotopia. Here the wonders of science engineered a brave new world of economic plenty and conspicuous consumption, a world where the social problems of the present were displaced by a future controlled by technology.

TECHNOTOPIA

Because the industrial revolution ushered in a continuous stream of inventions in the nineteenth century, observers associated the modern age with an ongoing technical revolution. Just as gaslight, the steam train, and factory machinery captured the imaginations of Japanese writers and artists in the late nineteenth century, the early twentieth century was the age of the airplane, electricity, and wireless communications. Along with the imports of novel gadgets and scientific inventions, a wave of translations of science fiction and adventure literature introduced the western preoccupation with the utopian and distopian possibilities of scientific advance. Beginning in the late nineteenth century, European and American writers like Edgar Allen Poe, Mary Shelly, Jules Verne, and H. G. Wells were translated into Japanese. They inspired the development of crossover forms combining elements of western adventure, detective stories, and science fiction that became a staple feature of boys' magazines and the like in the teens and twenties. Unno Jūza (1897–1949), Kigi Takatarō (1897–1969), Edogawa Rampo (1894–1965), and others wrote stories that explored the relationship between the modern city and the machine. But although stories like "Hell of Mirrors" (Edogawa Rampo) and "Incident of Death in the Electric Bath" (Unno Jūza) depicted the distopic possibilities of science, for the most part representations of technology conveyed an overwhelming aura of optimistic wonderment and utopian possibility.[53] Urban boosters embraced the potential of science to usher in an era of ever expanding production and ever improving lifestyle. This future cornucopia was part of the cult of the new.

As the explosive urban growth of the teens and twenties brought with it a transformation of the built environment, new technology and modern inventions became part of a novel sensory world that people encountered as they moved through urban space. City guides presented a technologically enhanced urban physiognomy as a central feature of modern urban life. Urban planners embraced the possibilities of technology to make their cities bigger and better and to enhance their particular natural endowments. In the dreamworlds of the future on display in town plans and industrial fairs, science provided a kind of magical solution to the problems of the present.

One of the main sites for the exhibition of technotopia was in the machine halls of the industrial fairs. Here urban residents encountered the latest in industrial design and a narrative of progress inscribed in products for the factory, the workplace, and the home. A splendid modernist building, the machine hall in the Hokkaido Special Products Fair of 1926 featured more than two hundred display items, including "all types of motorized, electrical machines." One commemorative book paid tribute to displays that "exhibited movement" of the machinery and provided attendants to demonstrate the workings of the machines. Through their central position within the exhibition route, through impressive architecture, and through extensive and eye-catching displays, the machine hall conveyed the message that the future was tied to the age of the machine. Moreover, in advertising the role of mechanization in local factories, as well as the variety of mechanized gadgets these factories produced, machine halls placed the machine at the heart of modern economic production and of modern everyday life.

Product exhibits organized by business groups and individual companies prominently placed company logos and promotional material within their displays. The effect was a mutually reinforcing message: while mechanization was key to the future of Japanese industry, Japanese businesses stood at the forefront of the technological revolution. The Hokkaido Special Products Fair included some leading names in the business world. Firms like Mitsui, Mitsubishi, and Tokyo Electric sent displays to Hokkaido that highlighted their leadership in developing new heavy industrial, chemical, and electrical products and in introducing to their factories the latest innovations in mechanized production. Packaged to showcase the local factory, such displays stressed the foresight of the city's leaders in bringing manufacturing to Sapporo, the efficacy of a partnership between the companies at the vanguard of Japan's industrial innovation, and the city's business acumen and production culture.

Machine hall displays included machines for both household and industrial use. Thus, the Hokkaido Machine Hall featured a family-size miso maker as well as a larger model for mass production. Displays of rice polishers, grain mills, and barley mills, of the Fukushima dehusker and the Honda rice huller, highlighted the ingenuity of Sapporo's factory engineers in designing products to process local goods and to sell to a domestic market. Numerous varieties of pumps appeared in the Machine Hall display: the Portugal pump, the gasoline pump, the hand pump, the well pump, and the hydraulic pump. Designed to transfer energy to a machine, pumps were fundamental to the process of factory mechanization: their display called attention to the shift to new mechanized forms of factory production. Even as machine hall exhibits marketed particular products for sale, they engaged to sell the power of the machine more generally, demonstrating its capacity to improve and expand local factory production. As local product fairs emphasized, not only had the machine age come to Japan, but machines were also now rooted in the local community.[54]

The magic of the new machine culture was reinforced in local guidebooks like *A Handbook to Niigata City* (*Niigata-shi yōran*), brought out in 1926. Pictures and advertisements in the book featured machinery developed and sold by local businesses, such as the Yamide-zeru engine distributed by Yamamoto Shōkai Tekkō Busei and an FK propeller used by Fujishima Seisakujo to build ships at the local docks. Photographs of new refrigerators (packed with beer) and a two-wheeled pram (under patent application) conveyed again the message that local machines changed production as well as consumption.[55] An extension of the machine hall, city guides like the *Niigata Handbook* provided a visual exhibition of the wonderful world of engines, propellers, and refrigerators that were transforming the household and the factory floor and promised more to come. Boosters of local development expressed an enchantment with gadgets, technology, and machines. These wonders of science raised efficiency and provided the key to economic progress; they brought economic plenty and wealth to the locality. They were presented as a spectacle and indeed appeared spectacular.

Another prominent site for new forms of display, department stores reinforced the message proffered by the machine halls, turning their spaces into a showcase of technological gadgets and scientific wonders. In the process, department stores promoted a vision of modernity as a utopia of mechanization and convenience. Equipped with the latest scientific gadgets and electrical machinery, department stores transported shoppers into a future of magical possibilities and ever improving lifestyles. In most cities, department stores offered citizens their first glimpse of an elevator. In Tokyo, a number of large banks and government offices had elevators, but the department stores were the only buildings to open their elevators to the public. In Okayama, the Tenmaya store was the first building in the city to install an elevator, and tourist guidebooks recommended that sightseers visit the department store to try it out. Escalators possessed the same magnetic appeal and drew crowds to the department store for the chance to ride up and down the moving stairs. Along with elevators and escalators, department stores introduced the public to a cornucopia of scientific and engineering marvels: air conditioning that heated and cooled the interior; indoor toilets; automated cash registers and vending machines; telescopes and movie projectors; and for the children, miniature cars, trains, and other rides in rooftop amusement centers. Deploying new technologies and making them freely available to the public, department stores positioned themselves at the center of the diffusion of technology that had revolutionized industrial production and was now revolutionizing consumption.[56]

Beyond the machine halls of the industrial fairs and the department stores, streetscapes of cities transformed by the construction boom of the teens and twenties offered an open-air venue for the display of revolutionary technology. Electrification of streets, homes, and factories; widening and paving of streets; railway and streetcar expansion; wharf, bridge, and tunnel construction; and the erection of more and bigger buildings turned cityscapes into objects of curiosity and wonderment. Magazine commentary and city guides trumpeted the eruption of an eclectic modernist architecture in their midst. Photograph collections and picture postcards captured the new multistory buildings from angles that emphasized their height and bulk and highlighted their exotic facades. Artists were fascinated by the geometry of the new rows of electrical lines, the rail grids, and straight paved streets.

For example, a 1926 guidebook to Niigata opened, like most guidebooks, with a series of photos of the city. These included the prefectural office building designed in a hybrid style that joined western and Japanese elements, and a neoclassically inspired police headquarters and city hall. All three buildings were shot from a distance, capturing their towering presence along a wide, straight road. These were typical shots of government buildings, conveying the authority of municipal government as the local inflection of state power.[57] Another guidebook included a photo of the multistory Niigata Chamber of Commerce building shot to emphasize the electrical poles flanking the building on either side. As the caption to a shot of the prefectural office building explained, "Three-story reinforced concrete conveys a strong, modern feel to passersby."[58] The guidebook captured the flavor of the modern cityscape that so fascinated observers of the time: concrete multistory buildings, electricity, and the new urban thoroughfares—the boulevard.

The photographs that adorned the pages of guidebooks emphasized the newness of these buildings by juxtaposing recent constructions with pictures of Edo-period structures. The same Niigata guidebook featured a photograph of the traditional wooden bridge that marked the entry to the city's landmark Hakusan Shrine, opposite a photo of the recently rebuilt Bandai Bridge, sleek and modern. One marked the entry to a sacred space that preserved the spirit of an earlier incarnation of the city; the latter marked the gateway into "Greater Niigata."[59] Other photos showed the gleaming new facilities of the recently expanded wharf, with several large ocean liners in dock. A guidebook favorite was the panoramic view of the city taken from the roof of a downtown building.[60] Such devices emphasized those elements of the city that were newly developed and where engineering science created a modernist facade for the built environment. The keen admiration for grand height and scale, like the fixation on the panoramic viewpoint, reflected a desire to grasp the city in a single gaze.

In contrast to the traditional famous sites that captured the cultural essence of older urban space, these so-called new famous sites (*shin meisho*) illustrated the marvels of science and engineering. And whereas the old *meisho* (*meisho kyūseki*) opened a window into previous lifeworlds and were wreathed in an aura of archaic survival, the new *meisho* emphasized change and novelty. In a typical example, the *San'yo shinpō* designated the prefecture's first "sunken highway" as a "new famous site." Opened with great fanfare in 1936, National Highway 2 ran from Okayama to the neighboring city of Kurashiki. At a point in the city where the road crossed the main rail tracks, instead of creating a level crossing the city engineered the road to run under the tracks. As the newspaper triumphantly announced, Okayama's sunken highway was the "first of its kind": "The magnificent scale of the construction reflects a desire to appeal to pedestrians. Made entirely of concrete, the sunken roadway is flanked on both sides by elevated walkways that are separated from the road by a blue painted iron railing. The whole project cost 56,414 yen."[61] Monumental architecture—bridges, tunnels, and multistory buildings—highlighted the ways that engineers were remaking the physical environment of the city. And the encomiums for such engineering wonders never failed to mention the large price tag, calling attention to the scale of public investments in monumental city space. The power of the engineer to control the built environment offered an appealing metaphor for an urban citizenry whose social environment seemed so volatile and unpredictable.

Like the gadgets and machines promoted through industrial fairs and department stores, and like the engineering wonders on the new city streets, the revolution in transportation technologies captured the imagination of urbanites in the early twentieth century. The automobile emerged as an icon of the modern cityscape, as did the streetcar. Airplanes and high-speed trains created new connections between cities; proliferating transportation links and higher travel speeds compressed the time and space that separated cities from one another. As the mechanization of home and factory signaled the transformation of everyday life of the future, transportation technologies provided an instrument for mastering space. The possibilities this opened up were regarded with wonder and anticipation.

Writing about the new developments in the city of Niigata, a 1936 handbook applauded the opening of a rapid train service connecting "the hinterland of the Northeast through the port of Niigata to the great economic center of Japan in the Kantō region. The Jōetsu Railroad crosses [the main island] of Honshū in only seven hours, bringing you to the capital city of Tokyo. A regular air route between Niigata and Tokyo covers the same distance in only two and a half hours."[62] New high-speed trains captured the spirit of the "age of the three *S*'s"—speed, sports, and screen. The *Niigata shinbun* commended the inauguration of Niigata's Echigo Express to Tokyo on December 9, 1930, for putting the locality on par with the famous Tsubame Express that ran between Tokyo and Kobe.[63] Such encomiums expressed the exhilarating sensation of speed even while they reinforced the trend toward urban-centrism. On the new mental maps created by transportation networks, the countryside represented dead time, space to be passed through rather than stayed in.

While the high-speed train presented a powerful metaphor for a society racing forward in time, the airplane represented the next frontier in transportation technology. The development of air travel in Japan began in the teens, after the Wright brothers' sensational flight of 1909 galvanized Japanese interest in the airplane. The same year, the government sent two junior officers to France to purchase a plane and receive training; they returned to carry out Japan's first successful air flight in 1910. The government followed with investments in airfields and an air fleet. A joint army-navy air force of nine planes was deployed in World War One, mostly for reconnaissance missions. The move to civil aviation accelerated in the 1920s with the establishment of a research center for air transport (1922), the promulgation of a law governing air travel (1925), the foundation of the first airline and inauguration of domestic air travel (1928), and the opening of the first international air route between Japan and Manchuria (1929).[64]

A growing audience of air enthusiasts followed these moves avidly. The market for actual air travel may have been limited to government officials and business executives, but the fan base of spectators for the proliferating number of air shows and demonstrations was expanding rapidly. For urban communities the opening of a local airport became a matter of pride and a sign of being up-to-date. Flying competitions, the use of airplane stunts for advertisements, and public investments in airfields, all spread what the *Niigata kōyū* called "an airplane fever."[65]

Okayama prefecture's first air flight took place in 1912, sponsored by the Chūgoku Railway and Nishidaiji Streetcar companies as a way to capture the aura of the airplane for their own brands of transportation. The *San'yō shinpō* advertised the air show in advance, headlining its story with: "The Phoenix Takes to the Air." As the newspaper reported the spectacle, some two thousand soldiers lined up to watch the plane take off from the parade grounds of the Seventeenth Division in Okayama city. Groups of students from local schools crowded a field already jammed with spectators while a military band entertained the eager crowd. The pilot walked out onto the field a few minutes short of 11:30 A.M., dressed smartly in a military uniform. Onlookers watched entranced as the plane took off and circled for eight minutes before coming back to land in the parade grounds once more.[66]

This was the first of many air shows in Okayama. After the city opened an airport in 1915, this "gateway to the skies" was used more frequently for air shows than for actual air travel. An air show commemorating the first anniversary of the airport featured a program of skydiving and aerial acrobatics, attracting a large crowd of air flight enthusiasts. Several months later, the local newspaper sponsored another big air show to honor an Okayama pilot who was killed in a plane crash in America. In a spectacular memorial service that celebrated a local hero and martyr to air flight, the crowds watched as the airplane flew to the birthplace of the dead pilot, circled overhead, then came back to land. The newspaper reported, "The airplane looked like a grain of sesame as it disappeared into the clouds . . . and then glided back out into the clear air. The excited crowd . . . watched in awe as the plane danced through the sky."[67]

In Okayama, the craze for air shows was stirred up by the intense rivalry between the two local newspapers, which competed to outdo one another in lavish air displays. In 1916, the *Chūgoku minpō* invited the internationally renowned aerialist Art Smith to come to the Okayama airfield and demonstrate the "loop the loop" before a "record-breaking crowd." Reporters triumphantly announced crowd estimates in the tens of thousands, which amounted to "at least three times [that of] the [rival] *San'yō shinpō* air show of the previous year." The *Chūgoku minpō* issued postcards to commemorate the event and followed up with related human-interest stories, like the article on a local youth who dreamed of a glamorous career as a pilot.[68]

Aerial acrobatics and other flying shows drove home to a largely urban audience the message that the airplane was an astonishing new technology capable of tricks and stunts in the hands of an intrepid pilot. At the same time, municipal investments in airfields and the opening of air service between Japanese cities brought the airplane into the realm of urban communication and made the airplane more than just an entertainment novelty.

The rapid growth of a domestic and colonial network of airfields brought these two features together and made the airplane a mode of advertisement with a unique market reach. Kanazawa city deployed an advertising campaign for its 1932 Exhibition on Industry and Tourism that ingeniously drew on the symbolic power of the airplane. The main advertising poster portrayed the fairgrounds with their eclectic mix of modernist architecture, the familiar outlines of a temple and the municipal building to one side, and the famous Hakusan Mountains in the background; overhead flew an airplane trailing an advertisement streamer that announced the Kanazawa Exhibition on Industry and Tourism. Organizers of the fair distributed this poster to train stations, government buildings, and chambers of commerce throughout the country; they issued it widely in the form of a news release. They sent the poster along with a diorama of Kanazawa's Kenrokuen Garden and a local product display for the city's exhibit at the Nagoya fair in the fall of 1931. They sent out a large number of New Year's cards with the airplane poster and applied it to matchbox covers and picture postcards.

Recognizing the utility of the plane, exhibition planners wrote, "In recent times airplanes have played an enormous role in advertising. On the 14th of May, 10,000 flyers were dropped from an airplane over different parts of the prefecture. This was an enormous success because people in regions of the prefecture without airstrips, and who had not seen or experienced an airplane, heard the tremendous noise and saw the flyers dropped from the sky. Thousands fought to grab them out of the air." The futurist exoticism of the airplane made it a particularly effective vehicle for advertising the Kanazawa exposition. Such tactics also drove home the association of the provincial city with modernity and progress.[69]

The advent of trains, planes, and automobiles helped to nurture a preoccupation with speed and the sense that the technologies transforming urban life were making city time run faster. By the same token, novel visual and aural technologies appeared one after another, creating new forms of perception. While machine culture enhanced the capacity of humans to manipulate their environment, inventions like cameras, telescopes, phonographs, and amplifiers expanded the realm of sensory experience. Cultural historians of the interwar era often stress the impact of the moving picture on urban popular culture, but the advent of radio was equally significant. From the first experiment in radio transmission in Japan in 1905, this novel, occult technology transfixed urban populations. Radio stations, manufacturers of equipment, and entertainment industries all promoted radio as a vehicle for news and entertainment. But more than this, radio transmission became a spectacle in itself, a powerful symbol of urban technotopia and its transformation of the world of the senses.

As local broadcasting spread to city after city in the late 1920s, radio stations emerged as so-called new famous sites (*shin meisho*). Housed in multistory concrete buildings, broadcast stations became a requisite stop on the tourist circuit to "show and tell" the latest in scientific advance. Between two and three hundred people lined up to visit the Osaka radio station every day.[70] A Niigata guidebook urged visitors to include a stop at JOQK, an imposing "reinforced concrete building" located at the summit of a hill in the scenic northwestern part of the city. A Sapporo guidebook likewise called attention to their station's modern architecture and locale. A trip to Sapporo's radio station rewarded visitors with a tour of the station's two recording studios, where they could take a close look at a radio control panel just imported from England, as well hear as the latest in microphone technology.[71]

An article in an Okayama business magazine in 1931 captured the sense of local pride in the radio station. Celebrating the inauguration of local broadcast several months earlier, the magazine printed the text of a speech by the studio's new celebrity announcer. Lured away from Osaka's BK station, the new announcer addressed the citizens of Okayama under the title "From the JOKK Studio." In his speech, which was accompanied by a large photograph of the sleek modern building that housed the new station, the announcer lavished praise on the "magnificent new studio" and the possibilities it offered to realize future ambitions for "the greatest city of the Chūgoku region." Confessing that he "felt a kind of homesickness" when first arriving in "unknown Okayama," this big-city transplant quickly came to embrace his new home and developed an admiration for the "outstanding performance" of "a leader, by far, of other broadcast stations." Radio broadcasting, the new tower buildings, and cultural celebrities all lined up in a train of associations that emphasized the new urban brand.

Such expressions of local pride and ambition (by a recent in-migrant) were explicitly linked to the technological cachet of the radio. The technological specifications of the station's microphone were elaborated in loving detail in the magazine article, which instructed readers that the microphone was called a *maiku* for short. "It is the only machine in the studio and is a deceptively simple device." Imported from England for the staggering sum of one thousand yen, this "tiny object with such awesome power . . . picks up a range of sound—soft, loud, strong, and weak—amazingly. Hidden behind a curtain you think you can safely yawn but the sound is caught and you are exposed! Is there anything as honest as a *maiku?*" Outfitted with this occult technology, the studio was transformed into a "palatial hall marking the boundary of a mysterious and sacred space."[72] For Japanese audiences, radio was surrounded by an aura of technological wonder.

Part of its magic was the anticipation of future developments. What might this technology look like in ten years time? An Okayama city exhibition captured the futuristic cachet of radio in a display captioned "At the Front Line of Culture" (*bunka no saizensen*). As a reporter covering the exhibit observed, the single greatest attraction was a television: "What is a television? The simplest explanation is a photographic image sent electronically. In America and Europe, research began fifty years ago on something called an electric telescope. . . . Though development is still in its infancy, the true dawn of this technology will come when we can see and hear a performance or a baseball game." This imagined future projected the idea of television as improved radio, allowing the next generation of live broadcast to be experienced as both a visual and an audio event. Along with the story, the local newspaper ran a photo of the experimental television on display, flanked by a radio engineer dispatched from Osaka for the demonstration and surrounded by an astonished crowd. As he ran through the "miraculous operations" of the experimental machine (one of three in the country), the radio engineer demonstrated with "passionate enthusiasm" the transmission of the visual image of a person speaking on the telephone to a nearby receiver. Like a successful magic show, this demonstration of the "strange and wonderful power" of the television sought to astonish and convince at the same time.[73] The power of science gave them radio today, television tomorrow, and it promised other wonders yet to come.

Events celebrating technology began to thin out after 1937, when the outbreak of war with China triggered state campaigns for spiritual mobilization that cast a shadow on urban technotopia. Slogans like "Luxury is the enemy!" and appeals to "tradition" discouraged the consumption of electrical novelties; laws outlawing neon lights in 1939 stripped entertainment districts of their futuristic illumination. Urban fashion seemed to revert to an earlier era. Nevertheless, throughout the teens and twenties and well into the thirties, bullish descriptions of a technological revolution in urban life helped put in place the idea of city as technotopia. To the interwar generation this was both the age of the city and the age of the machine. Bringing together man and his machines, the city created a space in which to engineer a more perfect world. Envisioning technology as the means for mastering nature rather than being mastered by it, urban technotopia contributed to the hubris of urban triumphalism. To be sure, there were critics of the modern city and plenty of ambient fear about where it was heading. Yet for the most part, queasiness about the future did not find a purchase in the ideas about technology in the twenties and thirties. Rather, it settled on a different set of images entirely, for the specter of the modern girl bore the freight of anxiety about the urban future.

GENDER DISQUIET

In the iconography of interwar Japan, women emerged as the quintessential symbol of modern life. In cartoons, advertisements, and magazine covers, in fiction and movies, women dominated the portraits of new urban space. Magazines like the monthly entertainment guide *Modan Kanazawa* paid worshipful tribute to the figure of the modern woman. The brainchild of a local café owner and self-proclaimed "modern boy," *Modern Kanazawa* celebrated the effervescent cultural life centered on the premier entertainment district of Kōrinbō. On nearly every page, alongside reviews of movies, cafés, and restaurants; announcements of events; or the local gossip, appeared pictures of women—studio stills of movie stars, art deco drawings of flappers, photographs of young matrons striding down the street, images of café waitresses, bus conductors, and dancing girls. Women appeared in western dress, in strikingly modern kimono patterns, in bathing costumes, and in the iconic white apron of the café waitress. Throughout the teens, twenties, and thirties, the Sapporo Beer Company carried out a lavish advertising campaign that relied on such images: an elegant young lady playing golf, a café waitress serving beer, a celebrity beauty against the backdrop of the dance hall—all looking directly at the viewer, wearing charming smiles and fashionably bobbed hair.[74] Like other companies in many similar ad campaigns, Sapporo beer promoted an association between consumption of its product, an up-to-date urban life, and the modern girl. In the process, they drew on and amplified the multifaceted symbolism of the modern woman. Whether in the bustling shopping district or the dance hall, the department store or beach resort, whether working in a café or the telephone exchange, women in these images conveyed freedom, sexual assertiveness, consumerism, philistinism, and material wealth. Such images associated women with the space of the *sakariba* and with the new service capitalism that was defining the future of the city.

As literature on the modern girl has pointed out, the *moga* was in many ways a phantasm—a spectral image stitched together from stereotypes of an array of new subject positions that women had begun to occupy at home, in the workplace, within the political sphere, and in the marketplace for mass culture.[75] Whether they were assembled out of new social fields of consumers, producers, or political activists, what these images shared was an association with the urban middle class. Much like the middle class more generally, the throngs of *moga* that populated representational space were wholly out of proportion with their real-life numbers. Also like the prominence of the middle class in the iconography of modernity, the ubiquity of the *moga* reflected the disproportionate social power wielded by middle-class women as urban consumers and producers. And yet when segregated from their male cohort, middle-class women seemed decidedly more disturbing. In contrast to admiring portraits of middle-class men and their families, the figure of the modern woman could be both alluring and alarming. As ambient anxieties about the upending of social hierarchies were projected onto depictions of women in urban culture space, competing images of the *moga* emerged, as upwardly mobile achiever on the one hand, and as meretricious strumpet on the other. Such tensions reflected the complicated ways that new gender and class norms inflected one other. While the middle class as a whole exercised hegemony by defining itself as normative and aspirational, women's class privilege was undercut by gender disadvantage. Much as workers lacked the media platform to counter negative stereotypes of slum life, women were unable to insulate themselves from the pathological narratives projected onto them by middle-class men. They were unable to prevent a gender panic.

Why did women become the face of a distopic urban future? Although the *moga* may have been a spectral figure, it was no accident that women were selected to represent modern life. Indeed, there were good reasons that women appeared as the symbols of social change, for over the course of the 1920s and 1930s women had moved out of the home and into public space in ways that affected ideas about public and private social life. They staked claims to public space through political and social activism, pushing for women's suffrage and other political rights, for changes in the civil code to expand women's property rights and autonomy within the family, and for better conditions for women workers. At the same time, the wave of industrialization during the teens and twenties, as well as the expansion of the local government and a municipal service sector, opened up avenues for women in the workplace. The rise of new forms of commerce and entertainment like department stores and amusement parks brought women into the center of an urban-based public culture of consumption. All this situated women at the vanguard of social change.

These developments were magnified by a boom in women's magazines and the formation of a mass culture of reading. *Fujin kōron (Ladies' Review), Fujin sekai (Ladies' World), Shufu no tomo (The Housewife's Friend)*, and other women's magazines boasted larger circulations than other mass magazines, arguably becoming the model for a new form of mass culture. As Barbara Sato explains in her book *The New Japanese Woman*, these magazines became a forum for women to express their reactions to the changes in the urban world around them. Women's magazines provided a feminine perspective on new work opportunities and shifting expectations for marriage. They expressed views on everything from mothers-in-law to love marriage, from women in sports to women in politics; they offered tips on employment, hobbies, child raising, and household budgets. In these ways the phenomenon of women's magazines brought into public view not only women as social actors but also something identified as a "woman's perspective." Neither had been conspicuously present within a national citizenry and public sphere that had both been gendered as male.[76]

Although Sato's book focuses on Tokyo, the phenomenon she describes holds true for provincial cities as well. The 1920s and 1930s saw the emergence of a new women's culture and a new interest on the part of local media in courting women readers. Radio stations, newspapers, and magazines all ran special columns, series, and programs that targeted a female audience, offering advice on the same set of issues that preoccupied the national women's magazines. They provided a forum to promote local campaigns for women's suffrage and against prostitution and drinking. The proliferation of women's organizations and the increasing attention they received in the local media helped create a laundry list of "women's issues" that inflected a distinctive political and social identity for the "modern woman."

Local newspapers were active agents in promoting a new sense of community among women. In Sapporo, the *Hokkai taimusu (Hokkaido Times)* began in 1924 to hold special events for female audiences. Over the next fourteen years the newspaper sponsored eighty-three different events, attracting more than sixteen thousand spectators. These included field trips to the Sapporo Beer factory and a local cheese maker, a visit to a livestock farm, and a trip to the nearby city of Otaru. The newspaper brought a lecturer from Denmark to speak on the women's movement and invited female readers to special art exhibitions and musical concerts at Hokkaido University. The paper organized tours of the university hospital and the medical college, of Sapporo's municipal government offices, of the city's state-of-the-art agricultural experimental station and industrial research laboratory, and of the famous Ishikari Fisheries.[77] Editors saw such events as a means of courting new readers among the city's female residents, as well as a means of staking out a progressive position on issues of concern to local women's organizations. In the process, newspapers created a public space for women to gather and define themselves as a community of interest.

Women embraced such opportunities enthusiastically. Shortly after announcing their first event, editors at the *Hokkai taimusu* were astonished at the "avalanche of requests" to participate. Letters to the paper from women who joined these groups of participants framed their reactions within narratives of enlightenment and emancipation. As one woman wrote, "For women who have only just been liberated from the shackles of a life of servitude, this is indeed a wonderful opportunity: we are grateful to the *Hokkai taimusu* for making it possible. Women are finally awakening to the prospect of a new life. This event comes at a great moment: it has ignited our quest for improvement and galvanized our search for meaning in this new life."[78] Such letters gave expression to a shared consciousness among "modern women." Here, collective identity was harnessed to a trajectory of liberation and progress that public political and social activities such as these made possible.

Women's magazines, too, were central to the creation of this imagined community. In Sapporo, social and political organizations established house journals and created a readership for local women's magazines such as the *Gekkan fujin taimusu* (Ladies' monthly) and *Shokugyō Fujin* (The professional woman). In their drive to expand circulation into local markets, the leading metropolitan magazines forged connections between local communities of women that helped to constitute "modern women" as a national interest group. *Fujin kōron, Fujin sekai, Shufu no tomo, Fujōkai, Fujin kurabu*, and *Josei* all bought ads on the front page of Sapporo's *Hokkai taimusu*. To foster a loyal readership they organized "reader's clubs" in Sapporo and other provincial cities. Like the newspapers, they sponsored events for women and created opportunities for public assembly. In 1923 *Fujōkai* brought the celebrated writer and critic Kikuchi Kan from Tokyo as keynote speaker at a reception at Sapporo's premier public girl's higher school, an event that drew three thousand of the magazine's readers. The same year, more than a thousand women attended a *Shufu no tomo* concert and lecture held at a local elementary school. Marketing efforts by the metropolitan-based magazines were critical to linking local publics to a national movement.[79]

As scholars like Barbara Sato, Sarah Frederick, and William Gardner point out, women's magazines explored new social and sexual practices and offered women a range of role models that challenged prevailing mores. In Sato's formulation, the three main incarnations of the "new Japanese woman" were the "bobbed haired, short-skirted modern girl, the self-motivated housewife, and the rational extroverted professional workingwoman."[80] All three defied stereotypes of Japanese femininity as docile, traditional, and hidden within the home. The significance of such shifts in gender roles invited much debate—in women's magazines and in virtually every form of media in the interwar period. And as Gardner observes, while there were many competing viewpoints in the controversy over gender roles, nearly everyone conceded that a restructuring of these roles and relationships was irreversible. More than any other single measure of social change, new gender roles defined the experience of "modern life."[81]

Much of the discussion of gender roles revolved around the significance of new employment opportunities for urban women. Female shop clerks, female typists, female bus conductors, and female telephone operators had become a conspicuous presence in Japanese cities. The *Japan Labor Almanac* estimated that, nationwide, close to a million women worked in professional jobs in 1926. Responding to the rising demand for such jobs after World War One, municipalities established employment offices for professional women (*shokugyō fujin*) as part of their expanding network of social services.[82] Even before this time, women had long worked in a variety of occupations—from the premodern period as agricultural laborers, domestic servants, and entertainers; and from the late nineteenth century as workers in Japan's new textile factories, where women constituted about 80 percent of the workforce.[83] Thus what drew commentary in the 1920s was not work per se but the kinds of work women were now involved in, specifically female employment in the new service economy in what were considered middle-class jobs. To many observers of the urban world, these workingwomen became the public face of the new urban economy. As such, they symbolized both opportunity and danger. In one sense, they captured hopes for social mobility and remaking everyday life, for self-cultivation and social progress. At the same time, in challenging expectations for wives, mothers, and daughters, workingwomen seemed to threaten the stability of the family—and by extension the broader fabric of society.

Most of the new jobs for women indicated by the category *shokugyō fujin* required an educational credential. From the beginnings of higher education for women in the late nineteenth century, the three so-called divine callings (*tenshoku*)—nursing, teaching, and midwifery—offered daughters of the Meiji elite a narrow path to a professional career. Many of the new "white collar" service jobs in the 1920s—like department store clerk—also required higher degrees. This meant that these employment changes were intimately linked with expansion in educational opportunities for women. Beginning in the late nineteenth century, national law required both girls and boys to attend four years of compulsory elementary school (expanded to six in 1907). After that an elective system of higher education divided into a series of tracks. Among girls, elementary school graduates could continue on to higher elementary school (*kōtō shogakkō*) and from there to teacher's college (*shihan gakkō*) or technical school (*jitsugyō gakkō*). Alternatively, they could aim for the more prestigious track by applying for entry into a girl's higher school (*kōtō jogakkō*). Despite ideological, social, and economic constraints on women's higher education, the numbers of these institutions expanded dramatically in the early decades of the twentieth century. In Niigata, for example, while a normal school was established in 1872, institutions expressly for girls came later. Two higher schools for girls opened in 1900—Niigata Prefecture Girl's Higher School and Niigata Girl's Private Technical College. In 1921 the municipal government opened a second girl's higher school.[84] Nationwide there were 193 girls' higher schools in 1910, 514 in 1920, and 975 in 1930.[85]

This translated into real opportunities for female students. By 1939, close to 5,000 students attended Kanazawa's girls' schools (both technical and higher schools), about a quarter of the city's higher-school student population. More than half (2,780) went to one of the city's five higher schools for girls.[86] Like their male counterparts, students at girl's schools expected to work when they graduated. For women and their families, education was an investment in their earning potential as well as in the social and cultural capital a higher degree conferred. As it did for male youth, education offered young women entry into the new middle class of professional workers set apart from other forms of work through payment of a monthly rather than a daily wage.

At a time when social and cultural divisions between the working and middle classes were beginning to cohere, these professional opportunities for women raised an interesting question. Where did women holding professional jobs fit in with concepts of a middle class increasingly defined by the example of the "salaryman"? Common opinion identified the professional workingman in terms of white-collar employment, a monthly wage structure, and "intellectual" rather than manual labor. In both popular imagery and social reality, middle-class professions for men offered access to the so-called cultured life in the new streetcar suburbs of the urbanizing world. A working wife or daughter was not part of the package; women figured rather as the rational and self-motivated housewife, who was cultured and independent and ran the household.

The category of professional workingwoman stood in uneasy tension with this normative portrait of the middle-class family with a salaryman husband and his stay-at-home wife. Sapporo's *Hokkai taimusu* ran a series in 1927 on conditions facing professional workingwomen that fleshed out what this term meant. The series focused on new occupations for women such as telephone switchboard operator, department store clerk, railway employee, typist, and bus conductor. As the paper pointed out, these jobs provided women with good wages, working conditions, and social status. Telephone operators, for example, were paid one yen per day, an excellent wage for women. The telephone exchange employed girls between thirteen and fifteen years of age and provided them with three months of training and a four-year apprenticeship before they were paid a regular wage. Nurses earned a monthly wage of forty yen (1926) and bus conductors fifteen yen (1934). Even jobs that required less training and education offered better pay and shorter working hours than factory work, where women worked fifteen-hour days for about half the wages. This included jobs such as hairdresser, department store model or "manikin girl," movie house usherette, and taxi driver.[87] While the women who held these jobs might not seem to fit with those who had professional occupations like nursing or teaching, they were grouped together under the rubric of *shokugyō fujin*. What set them apart as a coherent social group was their association with the new urban economy, their need for postelementary school education, and their remuneration in monthly rather than daily wages: they were the female counterparts to the salaryman.

Like the salaryman, the professional workingwoman was regarded as an upwardly mobile and self-improving individualist. The positions that workingwomen held were secured through a meritocratic educational system and a highly competitive employment market. It required hard study and hard work to get the job, a point driven home by the newspaper series—which also stressed the good wages and high status that were the rewards of this effort. These were the success stories of the self-made woman. Moreover, new forms of middle-class employment were regarded as a sign of social progress. The expansion of the urban middle class ushered in an era of increasing wealth, improving lifestyles, and an ever more literate and sophisticated citizenry. For women, especially, self-improvement of the individual was associated with the social progress of the group.

While all middle-class professionals were associated with narratives of rising in the world and self-improvement, the *shokugyō fujin* differed from salarymen in one key respect. They were social pioneers breaking stereotypes, upending gender hierarchies. The salaryman was anonymous, but the professional workingwoman always had a face; he was one of a multitude, but she possessed the singularity of a movie star, the rarified aura of being "the first."[88] Several articles in the *San'yo shinpō* showcased professional women as the face of a new social world, trail-blazing exemplars of the urban future. As a piece on the new occupation of "woman chauffer" pointed out, the two women working for a new Okayama city taxi company were the only women drivers in the prefecture. Not only was the idea of women driving entirely new, but also automobiles themselves were something of an exotic novelty.[89] Through her associations with department stores, telephones, automobiles, and the like, the professional workingwoman became a homology for the new technologies colonizing urban space; like them, she was regarded as an object of wonder.

Much like the car hire company, other Okayama businesses placed women in prominent public service positions, in part to advertise the progressive nature of the business, and in part to associate it with both the glitter of being "the first" and the sheen of "the new." The Okayama Tenmaya department store was a classic example. When it opened for business in 1925, Tenmaya took what was, for Okayama, the unprecedented step of hiring eight higher-school-educated women and assigned them to work the newly acquired cash registers. For this experiment, management took care to locate acknowledged beauties from prominent local families. As Tenmaya hoped they might, the women caused a sensation, winning commentary in the local newspapers and drawing customers in to witness the spectacle of women handling money and operating machinery. Tenmaya drew on the social capital of its first female employees to enhance the reputation and status of the store; later employees drew on Tenmaya's social capital to enhance their own reputations, as employment at Tenmaya became a guarantee of character and background for prospective marriage candidates.[90] Using educated female clerks as advertisements for the department store's belief in progressive business practices, Tenmaya helped shape a positive local image of the *shokugyō fujin*, or white-collar workingwoman.

Yet even while businesses like the Tenmaya Department Store associated the self-made, professional workingwomen with the well-bred daughters of the elite and looked on her appearance as a marketing opportunity, others raised questions about the impact of female ambition on the family. A series on professional workingwomen that ran in an Okayama business magazine revealed some of the anxieties triggered by the entry of women into the new white-collar workforce.

> The world is changing, and women's sense of independence is rising fast. Before they marry, women now want to have economic security. Every day, every month, more and more women enter the labor market, and the trickle has become a flood. . . . This desire to work among women today is the product of modern thought. Individualism has spread, and at the same time attitudes toward marriage have changed. This affects women's roles in the home. They are no longer satisfied with staying in the house as they did in the past. If something does not challenge their creativity, they refuse to do it. . . . In the past marriage was a way of life [seikatsu shudan] and practiced according to tradition, but now women compete with men in the job market and jockey for position economically.[91]

As the writer concluded, these changes meant that Japan's "modern woman" had cast off her subordination to men—not just in the workplace but also in the home.

Such sentiments were echoed in many quarters and revealed views on the shokugyō fujin that decidedly ran counter to the celebratory accounts of the "self-made woman." While women's magazines and department stores might applaud the desire for self-expression, creativity, and economic independence, elsewhere the spread of "individualism" and female desires to strive and succeed threatened men in what amounted to a zero-sum game: women's gain was men's loss. Not only did women become competitors in an increasingly difficult job market, but also aspirations for self-improvement raised new expectations about marriage. For critics of the modern woman, the qualities of independence and initiative that drove success in the workplace made women demanding at home, undermining domestic harmony. A willingness to take on new social roles in public translated into a disregard for traditional household duties and responsibilities. But whether they welcomed or decried the advent of women in the white-collar workforce, everyone agreed that employment outside the home transformed social relations inside it.

Critics of these developments frequently expressed their anxieties through satire. In fiction, film, and cartoons, male intellectuals lampooned the modern girl as immoral and vacuous, and the modern housewife as selfish and domineering. They denigrated professional women by stereotyping them as sexually promiscuous. The Okayama series on the professional working-woman made this point by focusing on the café waitress as representative of the new workingwomen.[92] "When you look at the front lines of the employment wars, what truly stands out are café and bar waitresses. This is a new type of employment for women and materially rewarding to boot. Indeed, the café waitress is the top prize in the job market." As the writer went on to say, the success of the café as a business enterprise rested on the sexual appeal of the café waitress. "What is it about a café that is beautiful? The source of the café's allure is the café waitress. . . . She represents the beauty of love, she creates an Eden of modern pleasure."[93]

Equating the professional workingwoman with the café waitress high-lighted the eroticism associated with some of the new jobs for women. Many businessmen hired female clerks as sex symbols in order to facilitate difficult business transactions and attract male clientele. Women in quite a few of the new "middle-class" jobs became known as "such-and-such girl": "shopgirl" (*shoppu gaaru*), "cinema girl" (*kinema gaaru*), "manikin girl" (*manekin gaaru*), and "gasoline girl" (*gasorin gaaru*). Whether they guided patrons to their seats in movie theaters, served as live clothing models in department stores, or beckoned taxi drivers into gas stations, such jobs eroticized women workers and invited the public to project sexual fantasies onto them. But while new kinds of public service employment may have made women into objects of sexual curiosity, the kind of eroticized service expected of café waitresses and bar girls was not a conspicuous element of most women's jobs.[94] And yet, conflating the *shokugyō fujin* with the café waitress derogated women's employment and minimize its social impact.

The slippage between the professional workingwoman and the café wait-ress reduced the assertive independence of the self-made woman to sexual aggressiveness. As one of the articles in the Okayama series on working-women declared, "The *jokyū* [café waitress] wears a ridiculously flashy kimono, a huge, wide *obi* [kimono belt], thick makeup, and a thin line of eyebrow." When the café waitress is decked out in this slatternly get up, sug-gested the writer, men become slaves to her bidding. "The temptress beckons them in, and the men follow one after the other. Café waitresses are aggres-sive and pressure customers relentlessly. But modern men like *jokyū!* This is what they define as entertainment."[95] Rather than competing with men on a level playing field and rising to the top on their own merits, such commentary implied, modern women deployed sexual lures to gain advantage over men. Depictions of the waitress as demanding and sexually aggressive undercut the progressive and wholesome image of the self-made woman and the narrative of social progress for women that she represented. Indeed, the Okayama writer extended the denunciation of café-waitress-type behavior to include the general fashion of the urban middle class. "Whether young ladies [ojōsantachi] mimic the appearance of café waitresses or waitresses ape the style of today's wives and daughters, when you are out on the street, there you see the Shōwa woman: standing boldly upright, waving the sleeves of her gaudy kimono, striding briskly along. The modern woman you see on the street displays the style and fashion of the café waitress."[96] In other words, claims on the public space of the street expressed in gestures of independence—an assertive posture, a determined gait, a fashionable kimono pattern—were characterized as mere sexual aggressiveness. The modern woman's quest for self-improvement and self-expression was reduced to the shallow and brazen blandishments of the bargirl.

More than anything else, the imaginary of the modern woman was the product of the culture industries and the mass media. Because of the sociology of the marketplace, consumption was gendered as well as classed; much like divisions between the middle and lower classes, social segmentation in the cultural marketplace was both cause and effect of gender formations. Complicating this further, many forms of mass culture, like movies, constructed "women" as both consumers and commodities. Thus, women were constituted as department store consumers, loyal magazine readers, and music hobbyists, but they were also commodified for male consumption in movie houses and cafés. Moreover, as artists and writers, women created products in the new cultural marketplace. What they tended *not* to be were managerial decision-makers in the mass media, entertainment industries, or municipal bureaucracy who exercised control over which products would circulate and which would not. This meant that middle-class women were much less in control of their own image than were middle-class men, who were able to generate and spread flattering self-images such as the farsighted and resourceful engineer or the talented and discerning man of culture. These appealing stereotypes of middle-class men offer a striking contrast with the dangerous, alluring *moga*, whose shallow and brazen persona overhung the wholesome image of the self-made woman.

If the mechanized futurescape of the Hall of Science conveyed confidence in the power of scientific and technological discoveries to engineer progress, meditations on the social future of the family portended a decidedly less optimistic set of possibilities. Although as symbols of the future in the present, women may have been as ubiquitous as the machines, they accumulated a more ambivalent freight of expectations. In satire, social criticism, and derogatory jokes, people fixed on the figure of the modern girl their ambient anxieties about the urban future. When the complex, multidimensional social changes affecting gender relations were crystallized into the image of the café waitress, they expressed excitement and fear, pleasure and disquiet. In this sense, women occupied a different territory of the imagination than other symbols of "the new." Within the system of representations that made up the city idea of the interwar years, the cult of the machine played out a fantasy of omnipotence. The new woman, on the other hand, referenced feelings of loss of control—the exhilaration and panic induced by a social world where the familiar ground has fallen away. Yet both were part of the dreamworlds of city life, where urban residents explored thought experiments in new social configurations and projected forward the possibilities opened up by changes in their material environment. Such ambivalence haunted the celebratory narratives of urban progress that spread through the cult of the new. They spoke to the misgivings about where things were headed that lurked just beneath the surface of urban triumphalism in interwar Japan.

Whether it was the fad for modernology or the exhibition boom, the cult of the machine or the disquiet about the modern girl, interwar cities became identified with the future. Cities were the place where one might behold the signs of things to come. Although the promotion of specialty products and urban brands suggested that this future could contain a variety of local colors, portraiture of radio towers and women in western dress augured a future where all moderns tended to look the same. While radio programming, as much as the provincial press, was a vehicle for regional culture movements, in the imagery of the modern city the local radio station tended to be viewed as a sign of uniformity, and the local newspaper as a sign of difference. Just as the idea of diffusion from the center outward masked flows in the reverse direction, this narrative of convergence concealed the varieties of modern urban form.

The city idea that took hold in the 1920s and 1930s recast urban space as a chronotope. If the late nineteenth century provided the moment when the nation crystallized the nexus of time-space, in interwar Japan the time-space of the modern coalesced around the social imaginary of the city. The turn from nation to city shifted the iconography of the modern. The modern monarch, the steam railway, and the young men of Meiji setting forth to enlighten themselves and their nation: these were the symbols of the new age and the new Japan in the late nineteenth century. By World War One, the modern girl emerged as the preeminent symbol of modern life, the automobile and the streetcar eclipsed the train as the emblems of the new age, and the city stood as the shining beacon into Japan's future.

This focus on the future and the intensification of temporal strategies for urban development and community-building must be understood within the broader context of the regional turn in the interwar period. The drive to create local identities emerged at multiple levels—within cities and prefectures, and more diffusely, along spatial units like the Kansai or Hokuriku regions. The agents of regionalism operated within the political-administrative structures created during the institution-building of the Meiji period that had established a strong local base by the interwar years. This included the educational system and local self-government, as well as the political parties, cultural organs, and business associations that grew up alongside public institutions and that mirrored them in spatial scope. The concentration of these institutions in provincial cities directly contributed to the development of strong urban identities. Compared to the diffuse sense of belonging to the Hokuriku region or even the consciousness of being a resident of Ishikawa prefecture, the more powerful sense of what it meant to be a Kanazawa citizen was a product of the relative density of place-based organizations in cities. Whether these were newspapers, poetry associations, chambers of commerce, or government institutions, because the greatest number operated at the municipal level, their collective voice dominated public discourse. They commanded more public space in their efforts to interpellate the subject.

The regionalist movements of Japan's interwar cities bequeathed to later generations libraries, museums, folklore associations, and a host of other institutions. They also helped produce a new concept of "the city"—one that imagined the city not simply as a point on a map but as a community that existed through time, bound by a shared set of cultural practices and a common history. Cities were defined by their economic bases and local brands; they were stamped by the personalities of their founding fathers. They were also projects, the locus of planning efforts and development schemes. This meant the modern city was forward-looking: it anticipated the future and created opportunities to grow and improve. This conceptualization of the city as a work-in-progress was systematized after World War Two in *machizukuri*—community building—policies that became a cornerstone of urban governance.

The technologies of *machizukuri* invented in the twenties and thirties mobilized time to create "the city." Linking the city idea to a (mostly) particularized past and a (mostly) universal future, this created a hallmark tension within the modern urban form. On the one hand, the cult of the new produced a sense of homogeneous time among urban residents, implicitly juxtaposed with an imagined particularity of the countryside. Modernology and Ginza-ization posited the city as a place where clocks run faster (than in the countryside); the city became a chronotope that situated urban people in a temporal space and subject position that was always already ahead of the countryside. But on the other hand, the regional history movements and the tourist industry generated urban biographies and mapped them onto the built environment of the city, knitting urban residents together into a particularized community that set them apart from other cities and regions.

The doubled nature of the modern urban form as both universal and particular closely resembled tensions within nationalism, from which urban-centrism borrowed many of its structural elements and ideological technologies. As Manu Goswami writes of "the discourse on nationhood": "It is both one of the most universally legitimate articulations of group identity and one of the most enduring and pervasive forms of modern particularism. It is precisely the doubled form of nationalism as simultaneously universal and particular."[97] Substitute *city* for *nation* and the same observation holds true for the modern urban form. Just as the nation proved the dominant political form in the global capitalist economy, and just as the interstate system helped forge an institutionalized tie between nationhood and statehood, the bureaucratic-administrative logics of nation-states and their internal governmentality insured the rise of the city as the dominant political-social form, a dominance sustained by the universalizing logic of capitalism. If we apply the insights of recent theorizations of nationalism to the operations of the modern urban form, it becomes clear that "the city" operated at multiple levels, representing at once a spatiotemporal, institutional, and ideological form.

The master narratives of modern Japan tell the story of the rise of militarism and ultranationalism in the 1930s in terms of the rejection of the progressive social movements of the preceding decade, and a "return" to native tradition. But viewed from the vantage point of the provincial city, this story line of a right-wing repudiation of modernism begins to break apart. Though discourses on the nation allied time and history to a mythic Japanese culture, urban social imaginaries figured past and future according to different systems of reference. While some of these, like the images of the modern girl and the idea of urban biography, abstracted universal meanings of the modern city, others were particular to a single city—Niigata as a country of geisha, snow, and oil refineries. Like the national imaginary, these urban systems of reference offered plenty of scope for right-wing appropriation.[98] Some regional war-support movements mobilized local myth; others invoked the cult of the machine. There was, in other words, much local variation in the culture of militarism and the forms of wartime social mobilization. What they shared was the hubris of modernist conceptions of time, a kind of imperialism of the present that envisioned the past as available for collecting and the future as available for engineering.

Epilogue

URBANISM AND TWENTIETH-CENTURY JAPAN

In visible and invisible ways, the urban expansion of the interwar period left its mark on the twentieth century. As urban projects created a network of urban-centered institutions that sustained the modern city, urbanism entwined itself with modern life and became the face of the future. The underlying foundations of the urban form and the city idea laid down in these years have proved remarkably tenacious in the face of the dramatic changes of the past century. Among them, the regional transportation system still hews to the contours of the light-rail grid laid down during the building boom of the interwar years; the regulatory and financing mechanisms established by the 1919 city planning law continue to provide instruments for urban development; the tourist circuits of *meisho* created in the golden age of the city feature as points of interest in guidebooks to contemporary cities.

Although a shift to the right began to challenge some of its progressive elements, urban modernism was not simply repressed by the rise of the militarist and the fascist movements of the 1930s. Rather, the modernist movements of the interwar period changed form through the political turn. Left-wing modernism morphed into right-wing modernism. Eclectic cosmopolitanism reoriented itself from Euro-American internationalism to a multiracial Asian empire. Wartime slogans such as "One hundred million hearts beating as one" and the cult of sacrifice repudiated consumerism and the individualist culture of the hobby in favor of a modernist vision of the masses as a well-oiled machine. Yet while urban modernism proved adaptable to appropriation for total war, equally striking were the ways that wartime mobilization turned against cities. As elsewhere during warfare, Japan's urban centers became ground zero for the physical destruction of battle. Even so, in the aftermath of war and defeat, cities emerged stronger than ever. In spite of the scope of physical destruction, the mental structures, the human capital, and the organizational vehicles of urban form were left intact: these provided the foundation upon which the postwar city rebuilt itself. The concluding reflections that follow speak to the contemporary legacy of interwar urbanism, sketching out in broad strokes its connections to what has been called Japan's "urban monolith." Just as second cities earlier helped usher in a new urban age, their postwar impact transcended the stage of the provincial city, shaping the broader forces of urban-centrism and urban growth.

WARTIME AND THE CITY

The construction of a national defense state began with the Manchurian Incident of 1931, and it accelerated dramatically with the invasion of China in 1937 and the onset of the Pacific War in 1941. Especially in the final years of the Asia-Pacific War, the intensification of total war mobilization turned the state against urban areas. During this brief yet critical period, Japanese cities came under siege. Until the late 1930s, urban industries soaked up military demand and the booming economy made these good years for cities of all sizes. But troubling signs began to appear, as an increasingly antiurban tone crept into nationalist discourse and the wartime state seemed to cast its lot with agrarian fundamentalism. Wartime appeals to the "national community" were often explicitly hostile to cities. At the height of the Pacific war, campaign slogans such as "Luxury is the enemy" demonized urban mass culture with its permanent waves, neon lights, and dance halls. As consumerism became unpatriotic, modern urban life was denigrated as western-style excess and a sign of the alien within. In the process, the modern city itself was targeted as the enemy of the imperial nation.

Wartime disadvantaged cities in other ways as well, as national concerns overrode local concerns. As the war continued and the scope of fighting expanded to multiple fronts, the centralization of authority and growth of wartime state apparatuses reasserted the preeminence of the nation over the region and the city. The needs of individual cities fell down the priority list. In a world of increasing scarcity and rationing, competition for resources was usually settled in favor of national priorities, scuttling carefully laid schemes for municipal development. The late-wartime period thus signaled the loss of power and autonomy for municipalities. Moreover, just as cities had borrowed the technologies of nationalism to forge regional identities, the national government mobilized regionalism in the service of total war. Regionalist organizations were tapped for wartime projects such as mass emigration to the empire and for home-front support movements. Wartime aesthetics reclaimed futurism for a fascist programmatic as the cult of the machine merged into a cult of the nation and grand schemes for building the Greater East Asian Co-prosperity Sphere eclipsed the bright tomorrow of urban technotopia. The total-war state likewise reclaimed growthism from city planners; pronatalist policies that encouraged the proliferation of national bodies, and five-year plans that targeted the growth of strategic industries, transferred the imperatives of expansion from the city to the nation.

The intensification of total war mobilization in the 1940s turned to cities as a last reserve of material and manpower, hollowing them out in a final bottom-scraping search for resources. An increasingly desperate hunt for labor in strategic industries and for military conscripts evacuated cities of their intelligentsia and their new middle-class professionals. Urban colonies of writers and artists, as well as the culture industries themselves, were turned over to the wartime propaganda machine. Wartime rationing largely shut down the domestic consumer industry and the service sector—the lifeblood of urban economies. By the end, total war had stripped away much of what had come to define "the city" during the interwar years. Although urban centers had benefited from nation-making and state-building efforts since the nineteenth century, the war, ironically, reversed the logic of Meiji developmentalism. While the Meiji state had ruthlessly sacrificed the countryside to develop the modern city, now the machinery of total war ground up urban resources and raided the coffers of cities to feed the war machine.

The wartime assault on the city reached its nadir with the bombing campaigns of the last months of the war. The prodigious extent of urban destruction resulted in part from new techniques of air power deployed in World War Two, especially the use of carpet-bombing against densely populated urban areas. Japan had been one of the first to bomb civilian targets in China, prompting outrage and condemnation from the United States. But as historian Michael Sherry notes, by the final phase of the war, scruples on all sides were brushed aside as air power became an instrument of "Armageddon."[1] It was more than a shift in Allied military tactics that made the last months of the war so calamitous for Japan's cities, however. Even when it was clear to all that Japan had lost the war, the nation's leaders made a deliberate decision to sacrifice their cities. In a feckless attempt to buy time for a final face-saving battle that might improve the terms of surrender, the leadership continually postponed the inevitable. As they waited for the propitious moment, the American air assault put city after city to the flame.

The U.S. bombing offensive began in November 1944, initially using so-called precision bombing to target strategic facilities such as aircraft arsenals, oil refineries, and munitions factories. In March of 1945, bombing tactics shifted abruptly to firebombing cities—assaulting civilian targets in order to destroy productive capacity and crush morale. By this time America had taken Saipan and, from this air base, could launch mass B-29 air raids on the Japanese home islands at will. The urban area assaults began with a devastating attack on Tokyo in the evening of March 9, 1945. In a single night, 1,667 tons of incendiary bombs were dropped on a fifteen-square-mile zone that covered Tokyo's most densely populated areas. In the conflagration that followed, 185,000 people were killed and wounded; everything within the target zone burned to the ground.[2]

Within the last months of a war that had lasted nearly fifteen years, Japan's cities—big and small—went to the torch. Not including Okinawa, which was the target of an extensive land assault, 215 cities suffered direct attack, most by aerial bombing and a few by shelling from American warships. Of these, 115 experienced destruction extensive enough to qualify for assistance under the occupation government's reconstruction program (*Sensai fukkō toshi keikaku*).[3] Strangely enough, Sapporo, Kanazawa, and Niigata were among the handful of Japanese cities that escaped air attack. Like Kyoto, alone among the "big six" to avoid bombing through the intercession of American Secretary of State Henry Stimson, Sapporo, Niigata, and Kanazawa were each spared by a stroke of fortune. Sapporo was passed over as the American command concentrated on nearby Hakodate, seen as the more strategic target given the importance of knocking out Hakodate's harbor and eliminating ferry traffic between Honshu and Hokkaido. Though Sapporo came out unscathed, other Hokkaido cities, including Hakodate and Muroran, suffered extensive physical damage.[4] Niigata was kept off the conventional bombing list for the same reason as Kokura, Hiroshima, and Nagasaki: all were reserved as targets for the atomic bomb. Because the American Command wanted a clean site to assess the effects of the atomic bomb, none of the four were subjected to prior attack. Kanazawa too was spared, like Sapporo, because more important targets were nearby, in this case the cities of Fukui (86 percent destroyed) and Toyama (99 percent destroyed). As a city of crafts, Kanazawa had little strategic industry; to the city's good fortune the war ended before bombers made their way down the priority list. Okayama's fate was more typical of Japan's provincial cities: repeated air raids destroyed 70 percent of the city.[5] The strange twist of fate that saved Sapporo, Niigata, and Kanazawa, much like Stimson's impulsive sparing of Kyoto, were the very rare exceptions to the shelling and bombing that defined the virtually universal experience of Japan's cities in the last months of the war.

Surveys of war damage estimate that the urban bombing campaigns ravaged 63,153 hectares of urban territory and destroyed 2,316,000 houses. The U.S. Strategic Bombing Survey calculated that 40 percent of the built area was destroyed in the sixty-six cities where major firebombing was conducted. The same report noted that 30 percent of the entire urban population lost homes and many of their possessions in the air attacks; industrial losses were on a similar scale. Incendiary bombs also damaged electric distribution systems and virtually eliminated all small- and medium-size structures within the bombed zones. Although the railway system was not subject to attack and still in good condition after surrender, local transportation within cities was heavily damaged. About 25 percent of the urban population—8.5 million people—fled or were evacuated during the air raids. Of those who remained, 331,000 were killed and 427,000 injured, mostly due to burns.[6]

Over the spring and summer of 1945, the accumulations of centuries of urban life went up in flame. Fires burned down daimyo estates and temple buildings; they destroyed countless old *meisho* that stood as symbols of local pride. Bombs also brought down monuments to the modern city—radio towers, department stores, central train stations. Fires consumed libraries, municipal records, and museum archives. The precious investments of capital and resources, the best that creative energy and intelligent minds could produce—all the hopes and dreams, the flash and bombast concentrated on Japanese cities in the interwar period—this, too, was laid waste in the final conflagrations of the Asia-Pacific War. In the end, military leaders discarded these emblems of a triumphant modernity as just so much scrap to cast into the war machine. Though Sapporo, Kanazawa, and Niigata were spared the firebombing, they suffered along with other urban centers the deprivations of the war and the wartime state's sacrifice of the city.

In all these ways, the final phase of World War Two and its immediate aftermath were years of calamity for cities, as these beacons of progress went dark. Vanished was the sense of boundless possibility, the self-confidence of a new middle class to engineer a better world, the pride in cultural traditions. The foundations for the imperialism of the present had fallen away. Evacuated of their population, their buildings, and their wealth, all that remained for Japan's cities was exhaustion, deprivation, and despair. In the immediate aftermath of defeat, cities were the gathering point for this toxic brew of misery.

Given the intensity of the assault and the scale of destruction, one might expect the postwar city to look quite different from its prewar predecessor. And yet, the wartime rupture appeared to leave little mark on the contemporary city. Reconstruction offered the opportunity to execute unfulfilled city plans and to widen main roads. Beyond this, however, not much radically changed. Cities of all sizes were largely rebuilt along earlier maps and communications grids. Cities such as Niigata and Sapporo that had been regional centers before the war reemerged as regional centers after the war. Tokyo-centrism only increased; and the geography of uneven development that privileged the Pacific coast and marginalized the Japan Sea side remained in force. The train renewed its position as the axis of economic development, helping to create a Tōkaidopolis centered on high-speed rail. Railroad politics reemerged with a vengeance, and Niigata, with its sterling political connections, rose as undisputed victor in the railway sweepstakes. The hegemony of the new middle class as agents of municipal governance and symbols of Japan's future reappeared in the rise of technocracy and the triumph of a "middle-class myth," where a purported 90 percent of Japanese considered themselves to be "middle class."[7] This was particularly true of second-tier cities, where the reliance on government administration to sustain urban economies grew stronger over time. The colonization of rural areas continued, as successive waves of annexations expanded the territorial scope and administrative power of cities such as Niigata and Sapporo. The tourist industry lovingly preserved the mystique of the "old hometown" (*kokyō*) and the attractions of consuming the countryside in Kanazawa's hot springs and Niigata's ski slopes. Regional industries such as Kanazawa's craft manufactures and Sapporo's dairy products reestablished themselves, and municipalities promoted their urban brands. The ideas about urban community building and the regional heritage movement also reemerged, as *machizukuri* (community building) and *toshizukuri* (city making) became the watchwords of urban planning.[8] The hundreds of local histories produced in the late 1980s and early 1990s to commemorate the centennial of cities and prefectures founded through the administrative revolution of the Meiji era provided testament to the vibrancy of regional identities. Such continuities speak to the power of the urban form and the city idea that took root in the decades before World War Two. Placed within the longer sight lines of the twentieth century, the wartime assault on the city registered as a tiny blip, quickly submerged within the larger forces of urban-centrism.

SECOND CITIES IN THE URBAN MONOLITH

As we are repeatedly told, Japan is among the most urbanized societies in the world today. Tokyo, with a population close to 35 million, is the largest city on the planet. At the opening of the twentieth century, 15 percent of the Japanese population lived in cities; by its close, nearly 80 percent did. Renewed waves of urban expansion after World War Two had so thoroughly colonized the country that scholars could claim that distinctions between urban and rural had become meaningless. As geographers Junjiro Takahashi and Noriyuki Sugiura note, "By about 1970, nearly three-quarters of the total population were defined as urbanites, and perhaps more importantly, even a small town in a remote area was functionally integrated into one nationwide urban and regional 'umbrella' system." Takahashi and Sugiura call this the "monolithic urban system."[9]

Most of the urban population is concentrated in the so-called Tōkaidopolis—the Pacific corridor stretching from Kobe in the west to Tokyo in the east. In large part the Tōkaidopolis is the product of successive waves of national developmentalism. This began in the late nineteenth century with the creation of a railroad grid and the emergence of the "big six" along its central axis, but picked up with renewed vigor after World War Two. Starting with the Economic Self-Sufficiency Plan (1955), the New Long-Term Economic Plan (1957), and the National Income-Doubling Plan (1960) that followed made the "Pacific belt concept" the focal point of industrial planning by concentrating nearly 80 percent of public investment along this stretch of the Pacific coast.[10] The result of such policies was the emergence of a vast network of cities and "urban infill" of sprawling settlement occupying the interstices between urban centers. The Tōkaidopolis represents an immense concentration of human, financial, and productive resources. Nine of the nation's ten largest cities are clustered within it; Sapporo is the sole exception. The cities of the Tōkaidopolis house the institutions of the central government, provide headquarters for most large industrial and financial institutions, are home to the nation's most prestigious universities, and bring together all of the major publishing and communications industries. If the

Pacific belt is extended to include Fukuoka, two-thirds of the Japanese population resides within the Tōkaidopolis; 85 percent of GDP is generated along this belt.[11]

The analysis of the contemporary city is largely the province of urban geography, which has developed the conceptual coordinates through which we understand postwar Japanese urbanism. While giving a nod to the cities of the Edo period, urban geographers usually trace Japan's astonishing urbanization back to the modernizing reforms that followed the Meiji Restoration of 1868. In a typical example, P. P. Karan divides the rise of Japanese urbanism into four phases. The first, from 1868–1930, saw the urban population rise from 10 percent to 24 percent and the proportion of people engaged in agricultural production shrink to 50 percent. During the second phase, from 1930–1950, the numbers of people residing in cities rose from 24 to 37 percent; by 1940 there were more than 45 cities with populations over one hundred thousand. By the end of the third phase in 1970, 70 percent of the population lived in cities. Between 1950 and 1970 9 million people moved to the cities of Nagoya, Osaka, and Tokyo alone. Together with other urban in-migration, 150 cities now topped the one hundred thousand mark, and 6 cities exceeded 1 million in population. During the final phase, from 1970 to the present, both economic growth and urban in-migration entered an initial period of sharp decline, as the oil crisis and the rise in the value of the yen cut into Japanese exports. But while Nagoya and Osaka lost some of their edge, other cities along the Tōkaidopolis continued to grow; by the turn of the twenty-first century, 10 cities topped the 1 million mark. As Japan became a creditor nation and global financial center (along with London and New York), and industrial planning shifted to the new frontier of high-technology and information systems, Tokyo reemerged as a key target for in-migration and principal focus for investment in the "information economy."[12] Such time lines frame our understanding of contemporary Japan, showing how 150 years of pursuit of economic development has made the country into one of the most urbanized societies on the planet.

What did this mean for second-tier cities? How did it shape the four prefectural capitals that are the focus of this book? All shared in the wave of urban expansion and economic development; all experienced the changes that defined postwar urbanism—*danchi* (blocks of public housing), cram schools, a succession of consumer fads. And yet, images of urban Japan based on the Tōkaidopolis and the concept of the urban monolith mask the enormous variety in contemporary urban form, much as the ideology of the metropolis did for interwar urbanism. Indeed, even the urban giants that make up the core of the Tōkaidopolis—Osaka, Tokyo, Yokohama, Kyoto, Kobe, and Nagoya—are strikingly different from one another. Making sense of their legendary rivalries and cultural stereotypes would require an entire history in itself. As in Japan's megacities, postwar national developmentalism and the sociospatial coordinates of the Pacific belt profoundly shaped the fates of Okayama, Sapporo, Niigata, and Kanazawa. But this was not the only social field within which cities operated, as the singularities of their stories demonstrate.

Okayama's case reveals some surprises for a city situated in the coveted zone of Pacific belt developmentalism, for this positioning did not prefigure its growth into an industrial megacity. During the 1960s era of "high growth," with national developmental funds flooding into the region, the governor of Okayama prefecture unveiled an ambitious scheme for a vast heavy-industrial zone that would cover the southern half of the prefecture. Part of the plan involved merging thirty-three cities, towns, and villages into a single administrative unit—the "million city" (*hyakuman toshi*)— and deploying technocratic planning and efficiencies of scale to engineer prosperity for the prefecture. Fierce opposition from community groups and public unions, as well as from the mayors of the two largest cities, Okayama and Kurashiki, forced the governor to scale back his plan. In the end, Okayama city was situated in close proximity to the Mizushima heavy industrial zone, but not directly within it. As the zone took off, Okayama city became sidelined, transformed into a supply center of construction goods and services for Mizushima. Although Okayama's signature light industries such as textiles and food processing continued to thrive, and city leaders advertised the city's capacities as a warehousing and transshipment center, the city's position as a multifunctional regional center had clearly diminished. Reversing the logic of the suburb, the heavy industrial belt became the force field through which the city of Okayama now pulsed; its power as a center of administration and culture was overwhelmed by the sheer economic might of Mizushima industry.[13] As Okayama's case suggests, the geography of the Tōkaidopolis was not destiny. Much as community groups mobilized to take charge of urban politics during the Taishō democracy movement, Okayama city's long tradition of social activism generated an oppositional politics to counter the boosters of high-growth developmentalism. In consequence of their efforts, Okayama did not become a megacity along the Pacific belt.

Positioned some distance north of the Tōkaidopolis, as administrative center of a large and wealthy region, Sapporo told a different story. Unlike Okayama, Sapporo became a megacity and moved into the first tier of "million plus." While Okayama's role as a regional hub was diluted by its position within a crowded field of large cities along the Pacific belt, Sapporo's importance over the past fifty years has only increased as command post for Hokkaido's agricultural processing industry, the banking and service sector, and regional commerce. Sapporo continued to house the headquarters of the region's largest newspaper company and provide a home to the prestigious Hokkaido University, both of which remain intellectual anchors of the city. Municipal leaders pursued urban development by building on Sapporo's multiple strengths, following strategies developed before the war. The city undertook a series of mergers that extended city limits to incorporate the seven suburbs and established an ambitious program of transportation and infrastructure development that encompassed subways, road building, waterworks, and the electric supply. Sapporo inaugurated several high-profile yearly events to help promote tourism (the enormously successful Sapporo Snow Festival), enhanced the local brand through investments in local museums (the Sapporo Beer Museum), and expanded the municipal civil service to staff a variety of community-building projects. One of the latter was the Municipal History Office (Sapporo-shi Kyōiku Iinkai), which publishes an enormous variety of local history, including the *New History of Sapporo City*, brought out to commemorate the centennial of the city's founding.[14] Matching these investments, the city built up a network of performance and gallery spaces to nurture a community of artists and musicians; it supported local media and facilitated collaborations with the information technology industry and related research at the University of Hokkaido.[15] In all these ways, the city pursued an aggressive growth agenda by building on established strengths, enhancing its role as a center of regional culture and a player in the information economy. Drawing on its power as an administrative core of an important regional economy, Sapporo grew into the sole megacity outside the Tōkaidopolis.

Kanazawa and Niigata likewise constitute an interesting exhibit in urban contrasts. Both cities remain on Japan's "back coast," which not only left them outside the flood zone of investments that washed over the Pacific coast, but also, until trade reopened with China in the 1970s, limited the potential value of an Asia-facing port. In spite of their shared location on the Japan Sea coast, a position all the more significant in the era of the

Tōkaidopolis, urban development followed radically divergent paths in these two "back coast" cities. While Niigata took full advantage of the American "special procurements" program during the Korean War to jumpstart its economic recovery, Kanazawa was unable to refit local factories to meet American orders, even though the city had survived the war in an excellent competitive position with its industrial infrastructure intact.[16]

In large part, Kanazawa continued its earlier strategy of turning remoteness into a virtue, promoting the city as a center of crafts and an old-world tourist site: a so-called little Kyoto. Brochures of Kanazawa invariably highlight *meisho* such as Kenrokuen Garden (one of the "three most beautiful gardens in Japan") as symbols of the city and monuments to the feudal era, when this "100 *koku* domain" was among the most powerful in the country. Much like Sapporo, Kanazawa built on prewar investments in regional culture, adding a variety of amenities that showcase its local heritage. But while Sapporo's regional culture has a contemporary inflection, for Kanazawa, "local culture" points to the past. For example, the city supported trade associations to promote traditional products such as lacquerware and its signature gold crafts: gold leaf, gold filigree, and gold-flake tea from the "gold [*kana*] marsh [*zawa*]" city. Kanazawa also advertised its literary and artistic heritage as a badge of local identity, investing in museums (the Tokuda Shūsei Museum, the Murō Saisei Museum, the Izumi Kyōka Museum, and the Kanazawa City Museum of Modern Literature) and awarding prizes (the Izumi Kyōka Literary Prize) that commemorate celebrated figures from the city's past. In striking contrast to most other cities, Kanazawa has been aggressive in the preservation of historic districts. Though this does not seem to apply to anything built after the Meiji Restoration, the Tokugawa-era geisha quarters, samurai districts, and merchant quarters are lovingly preserved as a tribute to the castle town. As a 1979 series in the *Hokkoku shinbun* exploring the image of "modern Kanazawa" explained, the city brand is built around a number of core elements: the city's attractions as a site for consumption, its position as a regional center, its importance as a "city of culture," and its heritage as a castle town. In all these ways, Kanazawa celebrated the old-world charm of a Japan Sea coast city, turning the slower pace of urban development into a point of local pride. As the *Hokkoku shinbun* put it, this "livable" community, with its plentiful green space and abundant amenities, represented a "model provincial city" (*tenkeiteki chihō toshi*).[17]

Niigata, also positioned on the back coast and separated by a mountainous divide from the high-speed-rail grid along the Pacific coast, saw its opportunities differently. Unlike Kanazawa, which celebrated the qualities bestowed by location on the Japan Sea coast, Niigata strove mightily to overcome its remoteness. The capital city of a heavily agricultural prefecture, Niigata's tale of rapid post-war industrialization illustrated the triumph of political economy over economic geography. Local-boy-made-good and onetime prime minister Tanaka Kakuei stands as the most prominent symbol of the political savvy and ruthless ambition that vaulted Niigata city into the coveted ranks of "designated city" (a kind of supercity with enhanced budgetary and administrative power) by 2007, in spite of the disadvantages of its location. With a base in Niigata's rural districts, Tanaka created a formidable support organization, which provided the vehicle for funneling local money into his campaign machine in exchange for central government funds that flowed into local infrastructure projects. The most spectacular of these was the Jōetsu Shinkansen, built in 1982 and offering high-speed train service between Niigata and Tokyo. But even before Tanaka made Niigata synonymous with pork-barrel politics and shady quid pro quos, city leaders charted a path for urban development that relied on forging effective political connections with power brokers in the center. During the height of the "high growth" era of the 1960s, the city effectively lobbied for designation as one of thirteen "industrial development targets" outside the Pacific belt. Central government funds helped create a heavy industrial zone attached to a new expanded port facility, making the city a center of heavy industrial production, including iron, oil refining, machinery, nonferrous metals, and shipbuilding. This strategy proved enormously successful for economic growth and justified the city in expanding its administrative control. Over the postwar decades, successive waves of annexations, most recently a series of mergers in 2005, multiplied the territory within Niigata's jurisdiction and increased its population to more than eight hundred thousand.[18]

Like all four cities, Niigata is a multifaceted symbol of the choices made in pursuit of urban development. Much like Tanaka himself, the city represents a brash rags-to-riches success story. Even though Niigata's image was tarnished by the political corruption scandals that brought Tanaka down, as well as by the dubious distinction of being home to one of the "big four" pollution diseases (caused by untreated mercury waste dumped into the Agano River), it remains for many an exemplary model for second-city development. Likewise, the Okayama story can be read alternatively as the heroic resistance of community groups to a power grab by corporate interests, or the tragic failure of a governor whose vision for economic development was ahead of its time. However one judges the merits of the choices made by

Kanazawa or Sapporo, the tales of second-city development in the age of the Tōkaidopolis point to the conclusion that these paths were consciously chosen and not simply fated. Moreover, their stories suggest that master narratives of convergence and homogenization can be misleading—that the urban monolith in fact subsumes enormous variation. Such differences between cities reflected, on the one hand, the unevenness of social and economic space, and on the other, the power of local particularity as a project of urban development.

While captivated by the manic energy of Japanese cities, scholars note that contemporary urbanism presents a number of urgent policy challenges to government planners. These include the overconcentration of people and resources in Tokyo, a seemingly intractable problem that continues to feed on itself in spite of serial attempts to promote the dispersal of economic activity throughout the archipelago. They also include ongoing tensions between environmental and quality-of-life concerns, on the one hand, and imperatives of economic development, on the other. Like many advanced industrial societies, Japan has an "inner-city problem," or what Niigata planners refer to as "the donut."[19] Here, this term signifies not the decay of the central city but rather the disappearance of a residential community from the old downtown areas. The flight to the suburbs is driven by precipitous increases in central city land values. As the downtown is reserved for high-priced office towers, government buildings, and upscale commerce, the search for affordable housing forces people to ever longer commutes from ever more distant dormitory communities. All told, contemporary analyses of the Japanese city present a cogent critique of the uneven benefits of postwar economic success, where government policy has tended to privilege corporations at the expense of the urban citizenry, an imbalance captured in the phrase "rich Japan; poor Japanese."

While insightful in certain respects, this master narrative of contemporary urbanism provides us with a stereotype of the city that obscures local difference. Images of an urban monolith and a taxonomy of cities based on whether they are located inside or outside the Tōkaidopolis does not fully explain the postwar development of Kanazawa, Sapporo, Okayama, or Niigata. Reducing urban change largely to economic determinants, it overlooks the multiple agents at work in the construction of urban form. Moreover, knitted into this critique of the contemporary condition is an uncritical embrace of the ideology of urban-centrism that is heir to the interwar city idea. Portraits of the modern Japanese city tend to endorse the mantra that (controlled) urban growth is a social good. Their narratives rest on the premise that industrial (and postindustrial) modernization and urban expansion are one and the same. Their argument builds on the claim that modernity invariably has an urban face. And they take it on faith that the urban monolith is inescapable.

However, as this book has argued, ideas such as urban growthism and the conviction that bigger is better or the equation of the city with modernity and the future are not simple descriptive and timeless Truths about cities. Rather, they represent surviving tenets of the city idea that took shape in the early decades of the twentieth century. Instead of signifying some natural law of urban development, these ideas compose strands of a belief system that privileges a particular way of looking at the city. The legacy of the interwar city idea in contemporary Japan has helped to naturalize the current social order and technocratic rule; it continues to legitimate uneven development, unequal distribution of resources, and unrelenting urban development in pursuit of private profit. Furthermore, there was nothing inevitable about the urban monolith. Tokyo-centrism, the Tōkaidopolis, and the persistence of economic and cultural geographies that structure space within the Japanese archipelago are all products of specific historical forces set in motion by institutions, ideas, and ultimately, individuals.

CITIES AND MODERN HISTORY

In Japan, as elsewhere, the particular configurations of the city took their characteristic modern form in the early decades of the twentieth century. This is not to claim that all of Japanese urbanism traces its roots to this single origin point, but rather that the explosive urban growth, the urban-focused social and cultural movements, and the extensive institution building that took place in these years left their mark on the formative structures of the modern city. In particular, I have focused on two critical developments that correspond to the main sections of the book. "Geo-Power and Urban-Centrism," examines the social production of regional and urban space as well as the ideology of urban-centrism. "Modern Times and the City Idea" explores the rise of "the city" as the locus of regional community and the identification of urbanism with the future. Each section shows how cities respond to what Steven Kern identified as a novel "culture of time and space"—in the first instance by taking on a particular sociospatial form and in the second by becoming a chronotope.[20] In both cases, the history of second cities in interwar Japan helped generate the master narratives of modern life. As "Geo-Power" suggests, a nested hierarchy of urban centers emerged alongside a diffusionist model of modernization. And as "Modern Times" shows, an imagined community of the city developed in concert with the belief that cities will converge on a single, homogeneous future. Not only do these master narratives of diffusion and convergence equate modernity with the city, but by identifying the metropolis as modernity's source and fullest development they also reinforce Tokyo-centrism. In short, they blind us to the ways that cities are mutually constituted and to the enormous variety in modern urban form.

"Geo-Power and Urban-Centrism" contends that the creation of a national and regional transportation grid and the establishment of elite educational and publishing institutions reorganized economic and cultural space into a system of centers and peripheries. Instruments of national developmentalism such as the communications infrastructure and the school system emitted economic and cultural force fields that privileged urban centers within the social space of the nation and led to an urban hierarchy with Tokyo at its apex. Geo-power fueled the mechanisms of urban-centrism, funneling wealth and talent into cities and channeling these resources up the urban hierarchy. Moreover, such institutions defined a characteristically modern relationship between town and country, one that elevated the claims of cities on rural areas as necessary to secure the future. Urban-centrism legitimated the relentless outward drive of suburbanization, colonizing the countryside to expand urban industry and to house and provide for its citizenry. In the process, the country became modernity's Other, a foil for the urban-centered subject.

"Modern Times and the City Idea" looks at the emergence of a novel urban form harnessed to the temporality of modern times. As cities rose in power and prominence within the national landscape, as they became the architects of economic development and the staging ground for social and political change, people began to view them in new and different ways. At the same time, as cities were destabilized by successive waves of annexations and in-migration, urban elites cast about for a means to bring together a society of strangers. Regionalist culture and development movements represented one response to the growth of urban power and spread of urban chaos. Regional developmentalism redefined "the city" as an organic unity and sovereign subject—and an imagined community to which urban residents belonged. Urbanites envisioned cities as self-enclosed lifeworlds and as forces unto themselves. They also associated cities with the future—with the prospects for their localities, the progress of the nation, and their own opportunities to prosper. The modern incarnation of the city idea reworked the relationship between the city, the region, and the nation established in the late nineteenth century, as cities became the focal points of regional identity. Although urbanism, regionalism, and nationalism often worked in concert and reinforced one another, they constituted distinct "projects" whose interests did not always align, as the wartime interregnum dramatically revealed.

Just as proliferating networks of railroads and schools generated competing impulses toward standardization and differentiation, the regionalist movements produced tensions between universalism and particularism within the urban form. In the tracks of regional identity, historians, collectors of crafts, folklorists, and other "hobbyists of the local" embarked on ventures of discovery that contributed to the idea of the city as a cultural community that persisted through time. In pursuit of urban development, business organizations cultivated a distinctive local brand associated with a regional culture of production. Alongside such agents of urban particularism, the spread of a service economy, the communications revolution, and other institutions of urban-expansionism shaped a shared experience of modern city life, where the seeming ubiquity of department stores, the rush hour, and other phenomenology of the modern portended a single time line to the future.

Much like nations, cities are composed of both institutions and ideas; they are grounded in material and ideological power. As I conceive it, "the city" encompassed the underlying material structures, institutional scaffolding, and built environment of the city, as well as the social and cultural networks that together gave it shape. It also included the social imaginaries, thought experiments, and ideological currents that ran through the city idea. On the one hand, Tokyo-centrism represented an ideology that naturalized the uneven distribution of resources and channeled wealth and talent to the center. The ideology of the metropolis concealed this flow toward the center beneath a narrative of diffusion and advance, masking the provincial origins of metropolitan culture and encouraging the self-marginalization of regional culture. But on the other hand, Tokyo-centrism signified the structures that produced and reproduced Tokyo's dominance—the system of higher education, publishing institutions, and the social formation of the literati. The same was true for urban expansionism and the railroad, which were at once a set of ideas—the imperative of growth, the mystique of the railway—and institutions—city planning regulations, the railroad grid. Cities became imagined communities and agents of the future through industrial exposi-tions and the images they disseminated, local-history texts and the urban biographies they invented, tourist guidebooks, and the ideologically satu-rated concept of the *meisho*. Like two sides of the same coin, thought and institutions, ideology and structure, the city idea and the urban form came together to constitute "the city."

The operations of this fusion of ideological and material power emerged with particular clarity in the social iconography of interwar Japan. Images of the salaryman, the modern girl, the *narikin*, and the Tokyo literati circulated widely within urban culture-space. They became archetypes for the new age, stand-ins for novel social formations and new ways of thinking about social relationships. Likewise "Ginza," the suburb, the hometown (*kokyō*), and the railroad worked as effective symbols of the modern because they crystallized key elements in the experience of modern life. Conjoining material social structures with the social ideology that infused them, these social symbols operated to shape and explain the new social order. Thus, the ubiquitous figure of the modern girl reflected the appearance of new educational and job opportunities for women as well as their rising social and consumer power, all of which generated much ambient social anxiety. At the same time, ideas about the *moga* encoded new gender relations, their "natural" hierarchies, and norms of social behavior. Just as the modern girl became a mechanism for producing an ideology of marriage and the family, images of the suburb and the *sakariba* combined material and mythic power to naturalize other changes in urban life.

These symbols of the modern city were striking for their sheer numbers and for how fluid they could be. Much like the social and ideological struc-tures they represented, social symbols were mediated in complicated ways. Produced and consumed by multiple agents, they could signify different things to different people. For some the "urban mass" was a frightening, potentially insurrectionary crowd. For others it was an untapped consumer market. The Ginza meant one thing to the Tokyo citizenry and another to Kanazawa residents. Class and gender inflected views of the modern girl, making her an object of both admiration and fear. In other words, social symbols were multivalent—they were open to contested meanings and mul-tiple interpretations. The fluid and multivocal quality of these social symbols suggested that their underlying structure and thought systems were also less than solid. What was made could be unmade; institutions designed for one purpose could be recaptured for other agendas. Although a central tenant of urban ideology was the inexorable rise of the city, urban triumphalism fell like a house of cards before the exigencies of the wartime state.

Conceived in these ways, the city offers a point of departure for rethinking Japan's twentieth century, as well as modernity more generally. Although our master narratives of modern history are dominated by the rise of the nation-state, capitalism, and globalization, the story of the city is also central to this history. As Michel de Certeau famously wrote: "The city is simultaneously the machinery and the hero of modernity."[21] Since the history of modernity is inseparable from the history of the category itself, the project of urban history involves critical examination of both the institutions and the idea of the city. While we tend to understand the modern city in universal terms, as evidence of a natural law of convergence where modernity necessarily brings with it the erasure of cultural particularity, this study suggests just the opposite. While they share many characteristics, the cities studied here are also quite different from one another. In this sense, even "global cities" are radically distinctive places.

Since every city is the product of a particular structural matrix and a specific confluence of circumstances, the project of urban history directs us to think about cities as sociospatial forms and as fields of dynamic interaction between multiple forces. The social space of the city intersected with other social spaces: region, nation, globe, each of which in turn was composed of ideas and institutions.[22] In the early twentieth century the social space of the globe was made up of the interstate system and the gold standard, stock exchanges and the League of Nations, all of which structured interactions within this space. National and local governments, educational systems and armies, constitutional assemblies and business organizations, operated at national, regional, and municipal levels and produced social space at different scales. Viewing the twentieth century from the vantage point of the provincial city allows us to analyze action along the intersections of these multiple spatial scales and theorize interactions between the global, the national, and the local. In this sense, a second-city frame of reference helps us rethink the diffusionist assumptions and the narratives of convergence that govern our understandings of terms such as *modernity*—and to locate agency in the wide world beyond the metropolis.

NOTES

INTRODUCTION

1. This insight comes from Carol Gluck, *Japan's Modern Myths: Ideology in the Late Meiji Period* (Princeton, NJ: Princeton University Press, 1985).

2. Minami Hiroshi and Shakai Shinri Kenkyūjo, *Taishō bunka, 1905–1927* (Tokyo: Keisō Shobō, 1987), 184.

3. Akimoto Ritsuo, *Nihon shakaigaku shi keisei katei to shisō kōzō* (Tokyo: Waseda Daigaku Shuppanbu, 1979), 158–68.

4. The classic examples are the canonical works on mass culture by Minami Hiroshi and Shakai Shinri Kenkyūjo: *Taishō bunka, 1905–1927* (Tokyo: Keisō Shobō, 1987) and *Shōwa bunka, 1925–1945* (Tokyo: Keisō Shobō, 1987). Though the essays in these twin volumes on Taishō and Shōwa culture claim to speak for a "Japanese mass culture," the data for analysis is drawn virtually exclusively from Tokyo. In English, Edward Seidensticker's authoritative account of the metropolis likewise collapses the history of Tokyo culture with Japanese intellectual and cultural history: *Tokyo Rising: The City since the Great Earthquake* (New York: Knopf, 1990), and Edward Seidensticker, *Low City, High City: Tokyo from Edo to the Earthquake: How the Shogun's Ancient Capital Became a Great Modern City, 1867–1923* (New York: Knopf, 1983).

5. There are a number of excellent English-language studies on cities outside Tokyo. My project builds on the pathbreaking work by Jeff Hanes, James McClain, Michael Lewis, Richard Torrance, Gary Allinson, and others: Jeffrey E. Hanes, *The City as Subject: Seki Hajime and the Reinvention of Modern Osaka* (Berkeley: University of California Press, 2002); James L. McClain and Wakita Osamu, eds., *Osaka, the Merchant's Capital of Early Modern Japan* (Ithaca, NY: Cornell University Press, 1999); James L. McClain, *Kanazawa: A Seventeenth-Century Castle Town* (New Haven, CT: Yale University Press, 1982); Michael Lewis, *Becoming Apart: National Power and Local Politics in Toyama* (Cambridge, MA: Harvard University Asia Center, 2000); Gary Allinson, *Japanese Urbanism: Industry and Politics in Kariya, 1872–1972* (Berkeley: University of California Press, 1975);

Richard Torrance, *The Fiction of Tokuda Shūsei and the Emergence of Japan's New Middle Class* (Seattle: University of Washington Press, 1994); Richard Torrance, "Literacy and Literature in Osaka, 1890–1940," *Journal of Japanese Studies* 31, no. 1 (Winter 2005): 27–60; and Richard Torrance, "Literacy and Modern Literature in the Izumo Region, 1880–1930," *Journal of Japanese Studies* 22, no. 2 (Summer 1996): 327–62. John Mock's anthropological study of Sapporo underscores the fact that Japan's second tier cities "are not smaller versions of metropolitan centers but rather display unique characteristics of their own which contribute to the heterogeneity that makes up much of the color and flavor of modern Japan." *Culture, Community, and Change in a Sapporo Neighborhood, 1925–1988: Hanayama* (Lewiston, NY: Edwin Mellon Press, 1999), 2. See also Hoyt Long's study of regional culture, *On Uneven Ground: Miyazawa Kenji and the Art of Making Place* (Stanford, CA: Stanford University Press, 2011).

6. Earlier on, in the first phase of industrialization, export-led growth privileged the Pacific corridor running from Osaka to Tokyo; hence Japan's "big six" metropolitan centers absorbed most of the initial resources of national development and assumed their commanding position at that time. To the west the tri-city Kansai complex of Osaka, Kyoto, and Kobe became the heart of the national textile industry. To the east Tokyo and Yokohama, the great cities of the Kantō plain, became the base of national government, the gateway to the west, and the center of nearly everything else. Nagoya sat strategically in between.

7. My usage of the term *second tier* follows from the Japanese government's population-based rankings and administrative distinction between the "big six" and the next tier of cities, mainly prefectural capitals.

8. Cornelius Castoriadis, *The Imaginary Institution of Society* (Boston: MIT Press, 1987). See also Charles Taylor, *Modern Social Imaginaries* (Durham, NC: Duke University Press, 2004). For an illuminating account of the city idea and Tokyo, see Henry D. Smith, "Tokyo as an Idea: An Exploration of Japanese Urban Thought until 1945," *Journal of Japanese Studies* 4, no. 1 (Winter 1978): 45–80.

9. Nicholas B. Dirks, Geoff Eley, and Sherry B. Ortner, eds., *Culture/Power/History: A Reader in Contemporary Social Theory* (Princeton, NJ: Princeton University Press, 1993), 13.

ONE. WORLD WAR ONE AND THE CITY IDEA

1. For an illuminating discussion of samurai dominance over the castle town, see James L. McClain, "Castle Towns and Daimyo Authority: Kanazawa in the Years 1583–1630," *Journal of Japanese Studies* 6, no. 2 (Summer 1980): 267–99.

2. See Henry Smith's discussion of Japanese urban thought in "Tokyo as an Idea: An Exploration of Japanese Urban Thought until 1945," *Journal of Japanese Studies* 4, no. 1 (Winter 1978): 45–80.

3. Okayama-shi, *Taishō 9-nen Okayama-shi tōkei nenpō* (Okayama: Okayama-shi, 1922), 87; Sapporo-shi Kyōiku Iinkai, *Shin Sapporo-shi shi.Dai 3-kan* (Sapporo: Sapporo-shi, 1994), 296.

4. Kanazawa-shi, *Taishō 9-nen Kanazawa-shi tōkeisho* (Kanazawa: Kanazawa-shi, 1920), 43.

5. Niigata Shōkō Kaigisho, *Niigata shōkō kaigisho 60-nen shi* (Niigata: Niigata Shōkō Kaigisho, 1958), 209–11.

6. Ibid.

7. Sapporo-shi Kyōiku Iinkai, *Shin Sapporo-shi shi. Dai 3-kan*, 296; Okayama-shi, *Okayama-shi 100-nen shi. Jō-kan* (Okayama: Okayama-shi, 1989), 565–66; Kanazawa-shi, *Taishō 9-nen Kanazawa-shi tōkeisho*, 88.

8. Niigata Shōkō Kaigisho, *Niigata shōkō kaigisho 60-nen shi*, 224–25.

9. *San'yō shinpō*, July 3, 1919, reprinted in San'yō Shinbunsha, *Shinbun kiji to shashin de miru sesō Okayama. Shōwa senzen, Meiji, Taishō-hen* (Okayama: San'yō Shinbunsha Shuppankyoku, 1990), 175.

10. Sapporo-shi Kyōiku Iinkai, *Shin Sapporo-shi shi. Dai 3-kan*, 248–49.

11. "Jitsuroku Ishikawa-ken shi" Henshū Iinkai, *Jitsuroku Ishikawa-ken shi 1868–1989: Gekidō no Meiji, Taishō, Shōwa zen kiroku* (Kanazawa: Noto Insatsu Shuppanbu, 1991), 236; Maki Hisao, ed., *Kanazawa shōkō kaigisho 100-nen shi* (Kanazawa: Kanazawa Shōkō Kaigisho, 1981), 118–21.

12. Niigata-ken, *Niigata-ken shi. Tsūshi-hen; 7* (Niigata: Niigata-ken, 1988), 553–56; 567–68.

13. Okayama-shi, *Okayama-shi 100-nen shi. Jō-kan*, 624–25; Hōgō Iwao, *Me de miru Okayama no Taishō* (Okayama: Nihon Bunkyō Shuppan, 1986), 44; San'yō Shinbunsha, *Shinbun kiji to shashin de miru sesō Okayama. Shōwa senzen, Meiji, Taishō-hen*, 165.

14. See the discussion of Kon Wajirō, Gonda Yasunosuke, and other students of modern culture in the 1920s in Miriam Silverberg, "Constructing the Japanese Ethnography of Modernity," *Journal of Asian Studies* 51, no. 1 (February 1992): 30–54.

15. Okayama-shi, *Okayama-shi 100-nen shi. Jō-kan*, 312–13.

16. San'yō Shinbunsha, *Shinbun kiji to shashin de miru sesō Okayama. Shōwa senzen, Meiji, Taishō-hen*, 146, 61, 71, and 77.

17. Translations in the text here and throughout are my own unless otherwise indicated. Ishikawa-ken, *Ishikawa-ken shi. Gendai-hen 2* (Kanazawa: Ishikawa-ken, 1962), 454–60.

18. For a discussion of early speculative fevers, see Steven J. Ericson, "Railroads in Crisis: The Financing and Management of Japanese Railway Companies during the Panic of 1890," in *Managing Industrial Enterprise: Cases from Japan's Prewar Experience*, ed. William Wray (Cambridge, MA: Council on East Asian Studies, Harvard University, 1989), 121–82.

19. Tsurumi Shunsuke, *Narikin tenka: 1912–1923* (Tokyo: Chikuma Shobō, 1962), 6. See also Michael Lawrence Lewis's discussion of *narikin* in *Rioters and Citizens: Mass Protest in Imperial Japan* (Berkeley: University of California Press, 1990), 1–2.

20. San'yō Shinbunsha, *Shinbun kiji to shashin de miru sesō Okayama. Shōwa senzen, Meiji, Taishō-hen*, 176; Hōgō Iwao, *Me de miru Okayama no Taishō*, 58–59.

21. Uchida Shin'ya, "Mitsui o tobidashite kara, *Seikatsu*, March 1918, cited in Tsurumi, *Narikin tenka: 1912–1923*, 4.

22. Matsunō Takasawa, "Kome sōdō to rōdōsha," *Nihon seikatsu fūzoku shi: Sangyō fūzoku 3* (1961), cited in Tsurumi, *Narikin tenka: 1912–1923*, 3.

23. Sapporo-shi Kyōiku Iinkai, *Shin Sapporo-shi shi. Dai 3-kan*, 655.

24. Of Japan's forty-seven prefectures, only Aomori, Iwate, and Akita in the Northeast and Okinawa in the South experienced no riots.

25. Lewis, *Rioters and Citizens: Mass Protest in Imperial Japan*, 84. Lewis's study divides riots into three types: city riots, rural riots, and coalfield riots. According to Lewis, rural riots tended to be driven by a sense of upset to the "moral economy" and a desire to restore traditional social norms. In urban centers, in contrast, protest was "transformed when carried out by the heterogeneous populations of growing Japanese cities. . . . [The] violent struggle for freer political expression and economic rationality waged by city dwellers and coal miners appeared to deny the very paternalistic authority that rioters elsewhere sought to restore" (xxiii).

26. In Edo period terminology, *ikki* stood for peasant uprisings, while *uchikowashi*, or "house smashing," referred to urban rioting. The etymology of the term *sōjō* goes back to classical times; but from the late nineteenth century, the term translated the European legal-political term *sedition*: Nihon Daijiten Kankōkai, *Nihon kokugo daijiten* (Tokyo: Shōgakukan, 1975–1976).

27. For a discussion of the development of crowd action and culture of disputes, see Andrew Gordon, *Labor and Imperial Democracy in Prewar Japan* (Berkeley: University of California Press, 1991), 26–62. Quote from p. 32.

28. Ōshima Mitsuko, Satō Shigerō, Furumaya Tadao, and Mizoguchi Toshimaro, *Niigata-ken no 100-nen* (Tokyo: Yamakawa Shuppansha, 1990), 183.

29. Hashimoto Tetsuya and Hayashi Yūichi, *Ishikawa-ken no 100-nen* (Tokyo: Yamakawa Shuppansha, 1987), 130–33.

30. The Sapporo anomaly had to do in part with farsighted action on the part of local officials, who diffused public anger by making subsidized cheap rice available in abundant supply early on, and in part to the fortunate circumstance of a recently opened industrial fair that had left the local economy flush and residents less vulnerable to rice price inflation: Sapporo-shi Kyōiku Iinkai, *Shin Sapporo-shi shi. Dai 3-kan*, 622.

31. Hashimoto, *Ishikawa-ken no 100-nen*, 130–35.

32. Niigata-ken, *Niigata-ken shi. Tsūshi-hen; 7*, 844–49.

33. Okayama-shi, *Okayama-shi 100-nen shi. Jō-kan*, 793–99.

34. Lewis, *Rioters and Citizens*.

35. Hashimoto Tetsuya, *Chihō dentōteki toshi no kasō minshū to minshū undō* (Tokyo: Kokusai Rengō Daigaku, 1980), 10–28.

36. The *burakumin* were descendants of feudal outcast groups who, despite the abolition of such status categories in the sweeping social reforms of the 1870s, remained subject to widespread social prejudice. They were victims of residential segregation, job discrimination, and other forms of social exclusion.

1. Until the late seventh century, Japanese rulers had not felt the need for a permanent capital, which was simply the ruler's palace, abandoned at the ruler's death to avoid the pollution associated with death. After that point, growth in the bureaucracy of state prompted the need for a fixed base of government, and the first permanent capital was established in Fujiwara. Over the next hundred years the capital shifted to Nara, then Nagaoka, then Heian (Kyoto), where it remained for the next thousand years. During the Tokugawa period (1600–1868), three cities emerged as major urban centers. Edo, seat of shogunal power, overshadowed the other two politically. With a population more than 1 million, it was Japan's largest city. Osaka rose to become the merchant capital and the heart of the expanding commercial economy. Kyoto, where the emperor's court was housed, remained the nominal capital. It was a center of courtly culture, temples, and shrines, and of a vigorous merchant and artisan community. For a general overview and some excellent maps, see Martin Collcutt, Marius Jansen, and Isao Kumakura, *Cultural Atlas of Japan* (New York: Facts on File, 1988).

2. Henry D. Smith, "The Edo-Tokyo Transition: In Search of Common Ground," in *Japan in Transition: From Tokogawa to Meiji*, ed. Marius B. Jansen and Gilbert Rozman (Princeton, NJ: Princeton University Press, 1986), 347–76. See also Henry D. Smith, "Tokyo as an Idea: An Exploration of Japanese Urban Thought until 1945," *Journal of Japanese Studies* 4, no. 1 (Winter 1978): 45–80; and Smith, "Tokyo and London: Comparative Conceptions of the City," in *Japan: A Comparative View*, ed. Albert Craig (Princeton, NJ: Princeton University Press, 1979), 49–104.

3. See Herbert Passin, *Society and Education in Japan* (New York: Columbia University, 1965).

4. Donald Roden, *Schooldays in Imperial Japan: A Study in the Culture of a Student Elite* (Berkeley: University of California Press, 1980), 3–7, 39–40.

5. Additional imperial universities were established in Fukuoka (Kyūshū University) in 1910 and Sapporo (Hokkaidō University) in 1918, as well as Seoul (Keijo University, 1924), Taipei (Taihoku University, 1928), Nagoya (1931), and Osaka (1939). On establishment of provincial higher schools, see ibid., 64–67.

6. Kumamoto was the location for Fifth Higher School.

7. Niigata-ken, *Niigata-ken shi. Tsūshi-hen;* 7 (Niigata: Niigata-ken, 1988), 615.

8. Kanazawa-shi, *Kanazawa-shi shi* (Kanazawa: Kanazawa-shi, 2006), 252. City leaders in Hiroshima and Okayama competed aggressively to become the site of Sixth Higher. Like Kanazawa, Okayama won the contest by contributing a large fraction of the costs of establishing the school. See Amano Ikuo, *Gakureki no shakai shi. Kyōiku to Nihon no kindai* (Tokyo: Shinchōsha, 1992), 23.

9. Niigata-ken, *Niigata-ken shi. Tsūshi-hen;* 7 (Niigata: Niigata-ken, 1988), 609–20; Ōshima Mitsuko, Satō Shigerō, Furumaya Tadao, and Mizoguchi Toshimaro, *Niigata-ken no 100-nen* (Tokyo: Yamakawa Shuppansha, 1990), 167–68.

10. Okayama-ken, *Okayama-ken shi. Dai 11-kan* (Okayama: Okayama-ken, 1987), 594–614.

11. Rachel DeNitto's wonderful study of Hyakken introduces this intriguing writer to an English-speaking audience: *Uchida Hyakken: A Critique of Modernity and Militarism in Prewar Japan* (Cambridge, MA: Harvard University Asia Center, 2008). Here and throughout, Japanese writers are referred to by their pen names (i.e., Hyakken) if they have adopted one; in all other cases I call them by their surnames.

12. Okayama-ken, *Okayama-ken shi. Dai 10-kan* (Okayama: Okayama-ken, 1986), 796–99.

13. Okayama-ken, *Okayama-ken shi. Dai 11-kan*, 642–43; Okayama-shi, *Okayama-shi 100-nen shi. Jō-kan* (Okayama: Okayama-shi, 1989), 954.

14. Okayama-ken, *Okayama-ken shi. Dai 10-kan*, 642; see respective biographical entries in Sanseidō Henshūjo, *Konsaisu jinmei jiten. Nihon-hen* (Tokyo: Sanseidō, 1976).

15. Special Council on Higher Education 1917, cited in Donald Roden, *Schooldays in Imperial Japan: A Study in the Culture of a Student Elite* (Berkeley: University of California Press, 1980), 198–99.

16. This culture is described in captivating detail in ibid.

17. Okayama-ken, *Okayama-ken shi. Dai 11-kan* (Okayama: Okayama-ken, 1986), 643.

18. Okayama-shi, *Okayama-shi 100-nen shi. Jō-kan*, 952–59. Kinoshita Rigen (1886–1924), the son of a high-ranking domainal official, became a notable poet. Like many young men of aristocratic background, Rigen studied at Gakushūin Peers School and continued on to Tokyo Imperial University. While at Gakushūin he made the acquaintance of Shiga Naoya, Mushanokōji Saneatsu, and other members of the Shirakaba group. Arimoto Hōsui (1886–1976) was born in the city of Himeiji and went to Okayama for middle school, continuing on to Waseda for university. After graduating he went to work for the publishing company Jitsugyo no Nihonsha and wrote the popular poetry collection *Nihon shōnen*, much loved for its romanticism and sweetness.

19. The Izumi Kyōka Prize was established in 1973, and the Tsubota Jōji Prize in 1985. In Kanazawa, the Ishikawa Kindai Bungakukan enshrined artists like Tokuda Shūsei, Izumi Kyōka, and Murō Saisei.

20. Murai Takeo, "Kanazawa to bunjin," *Kankō no Kanazawa*, no. 4 (April 1935): 42–46.

21. Hokkai Shuppansha, *Hokkaidō nenkan. Showa 4-nen* (Sapporo: Hokkai Shuppansha, 1929), 445.

22. Sapporo-shi Kyōiku Iinkai, *Sapporo jinmei jiten* (Sapporo: Sapporo-shi, 1993), 190; Hokkai Taimususha, *Hokkai taimusu nenkan. Shōwa 15-nendo ban* (Sapporo: Hokkai Taimususha, 1939), 541–42.

23. Edward Fowler, *The Rhetoric of Confession: Shishōsetsu in Early Twentieth-Century Japanese Fiction* (Berkeley: University of California Press, 1988), 129.

24. An illuminating discussion of canon can be found in James A. Fujii, *Complicit Fictions: The Subject in the Modern Japanese Prose Narrative* (Berkeley: University of California Press, 1993), 130–31.

25. Fowler, *The Rhetoric of Confession*, 129–31.

26. Donald Keene, *Dawn to the West: Japanese Literature of the Modern Era* (New York: H. Holt, 1987), 222–23.

27. Poet and critic Masaoka Shiki developed "sketching from life" (*shasei*) as a realistic technique for his "new poetry" movement. He advocated *shasei* as a way to make poetry express the experiences of modern, everyday life. See ibid., 50, 98–100.

28. Discussions of the *bundan* can be found in Fowler, *The Rhetoric of Confession*; Keene, *Dawn to the West*; Fujii, *Complicit Fictions*; Shūichi Kato, *A History of Japanese Literature* (Tokyo, New York: Kodansha International, 1979); and Tatsuo Arima, *The Failure of Freedom: A Portrait of Modern Japanese Intellectuals* (Cambridge, MA: Harvard University Press, 1969).

29. Arima, *The Failure of Freedom*; Keene, *Dawn to the West*; Kato Shūichi, *A History of Japanese Literature*.

30. Carol Gluck, *Japan's Modern Myths: Ideology in the Late Meiji Period* (Princeton, NJ: Princeton University Press, 1985), 182–83.

31. Kanazawa was also home to critic Miyake Setsurei, philosopher Nishida Kitarō, and religious thinker Suzuki Daisetsu. Studies of writers from Kanazawa include Richard Torrance, *The Fiction of Tokuda Shūsei and the Emergence of Japan's New Middle Class* (Seattle: University of Washington Press, 1994); and Miriam Silverberg, *Changing Song: The Marxist Manifestos of Nakano Shigeru* (Princeton, NJ: Princeton University Press, 1990).

32. Fujita Fukuo, *Kanazawa no bungaku* (Kanazawa: Hokkoku Shuppansha, 1971), 71–73.

33. Mori Ōgai's classic novel *Gan* (*Wild Geese*), 1911–13, is another example of this narrative, as is Kawabata Yasunari's celebrated work, *Yukiguni* (*Snow Country*), 1935–48. Kyōka's story itself was reworked many times for stage and screen, though the basic plot outline remained. The first version was published in *Yomiuri shinbun* in 1894, reworked as the *shimpa* play *The Water Magician (Taki no shiraito)* in 1896 and as a film by the same name in 1912. Many stage and film versions were subsequently produced, the most famous of them a 1933 Mizoguchi film, *Taki no shiraito*. See Keene, *Dawn to the West*, 206–10, 212; Donald Richie, *A Hundred Years of Japanese Film: A Concise History, with a Selective Guide to DVDs and Videos* (Tokyo: Kodansha international, 2005), 79; Keiko I. McDonald, *From Book to Screen: Modern Japanese Literature in Film* (Armonk, NY: M. E. Sharpe, 2000), 10–11.

34. This analysis was inspired by Johannes Fabian's provocative discussion of temporal strategies in anthropological practice, in *Time and the Other: How Anthropology Makes Its Object* (New York: Columbia University Press, 1983).

35. Fujita, *Kanazawa no bungaku*, 27–32; Fujimoto Noriaki, *Hokuriku no fūdo to bungaku: Kanazawa no bungaku o chūshin toshite* (Tokyo: Kasama Shoin, 1976), 90–92.

36. Fujita, *Kanazawa no bungaku*, 31.

37. Though with the exception of *Furusato no yuki* and *Machi no odoriba*, Shūsei's fiction was not literally set in Kanazawa. His work was shot through with concern about the relationship between center and periphery. For an illuminating discussion of the ways the town-and-country opposition operates as a metaphor to

structure his work, see Fujii, *Complicit Fictions*, 153–63. For a discussion of naturalist imagery, see Fujimoto, *Hokuriku no fūdo to bungaku*, 75.

38. Fujita, *Kanazawa no bungaku*, 47–52.

39. Ibid., 51.

40. This also characterized the work of Takehisa Yumeiji, who was born in Okayama but who moved to Kyoto and Tokyo to make his career as an artist. A celebrated magazine illustrator, Yumeiji produced an iconographic image of the Taishō woman as a languid, kimono-clad beauty. Although Yumeiji never moved back to Okayama, his illustrations, much like those of the White Birch Society writers, evoke a longing for a lost childhood in the countryside during a simpler time. For an example, see his print titled "Hometown of My Dreams" reproduced in Chiaki Ajioka and Jackie Menzies, *Modern Boy, Modern Girl : Modernity in Japanese Art, 1910–1935 = [Mobo, Moga]* (Sydney, NSW: Art Gallery of NSW, 1998), 48.

41. Fujita, *Kanazawa no bungaku*, 50; Keene, *Dawn to the West*, 277–78.

42. Keene, *Dawn to the West*, 279–80. I have used Keene's translation, except for *miyako no machi no tōku yori*, which I rendered as "far beyond the streets of the capital" instead of "from the distant city streets."

43. Minami Hiroshi and Shakai Shinri Kenkyūjo, *Taishō bunka, 1905–1927* (Tokyo: Keisō Shobō, 1988), 233–34.

44. Suzuki Shōzō, *Nihon no shuppankai o kizuita hitobito* (Tokyo: Kashiwa Shobō, 1985), 161–64.

45. Mori Eiichi, *Monogatari: Ishikawa no bungaku* (Kanazawa: Noto Insatsu Shuppanbu, 1985), 97–111.

46. Ibid., 105.

47. Ibid., 106.

48. Ibid., 110–11.

49. For a lucid and informative account of the establishment of the press in Meiji Japan, see D. Eleanor Westney, *Imitation and Innovation: The Transfer of Western Organizational Patterns to Meiji Japan* (Cambridge, MA: Harvard University Press, 1987).

50. Ibid., 154.

51. Ibid., 177–202.

52. Nihon Shinbun Kyōkai, ed., *Chihō betsu Nihon shinbun shi* (Tokyo: Nihon Shinbun Kyōkai, 1956), 191.

53. Ibid.

54. Kobayashi Teruya and Hokkoku Shinbunsha Henshūkyoku, *Hokuriku. Meisaku no butai* (Kanazawa: Hokkoku Shinbunsha, 1991), 2–4.

55. Nihon Shinbun Kyōkai, *Chihō betsu Nihon shinbun shi*, 194–95.

56. Teitsū was established as Japan's first press agency in the mid-1880s, and Dentsū in 1901 as a combination advertising, wireless, and news agency. Hajima Tomoyuki, *Gekidōki no shinbun* (Tokyo: Nihon Tosho Sentā, 1997), 38.

57. Nihon Shinbun Kyōkai, *Chihō betsu Nihon shinbun shi*, 194.

58. Yamamoto Taketoshi, *Kindai Nihon no shinbun dokushasō* (Tokyo: Hōsei Daigaku Shuppankyoku, 1981), 264–71; Westney, *Imitation and Innovation*.

59. Nihon Shinbun Kyōkai, *Chihō betsu Nihon shinbun shi*, 198–200.

60. *Nihon shinbun nenkan. Shōwa 14-nen ban* (Tokyo: Nihon Shinbun Kenkyūjo, 1938). Reprinted as *Nihon shinbun nenkan. Dai 17-kan* (Tokyo: Nihon Tosho Sentā, 1986).

61. Nihon Shinbun Kyōkai, *Chihō betsu Nihon shinbun shi*, 173.

62. *Nihon shinbun nenkan; Shōwa 14-nen ban* (Tokyo: Nihon Shinbun Kenkyūjo, 1938), Dai 2-hen, "Gensei," 75. Reprinted as *Nihon shinbun nenkan. Dai 17-kan* (Tokyo: Nihon Tosho Sentā, 1986).

63. Ibid., 80–81.

64. Ibid., 133.

65. Ibid., 99.

66. Okayama-ken, *Okayama-ken shi. Dai 11-kan* (Okayama: Okayama-ken, 1987), 657–58.

67. Westney, *Imitation and Innovation*, 187–90; Yamamoto, *Kindai Nihon no shinbun dokushasō*, 313–19.

68. *Nihon shinbun nenkan. Shōwa 14-nen ban*, 99.

69. Sapporo-shi Kyōiku Iinkai, *Shin Sapporo-shi shi. Dai 3-kan* (Sapporo: Sapporo-shi, 1994), 778–81.

70. Ibid., 776–78.

71. Nihon Shinbun Kyōkai, *Chihō betsu Nihon shinbun shi*, 175.

72. Niigata-ken, *Niigata-ken shi. Tsūshi-hen; 7*, 630.

73. Mori, *Monogatari: Ishikawa no bungaku*, 158–71.

74. Ibid., 100.

75. Ibid., 159.

76. Niigata-ken, *Taishō 13-nen Niigata-ken tōkeisho* (Niigata: Niigata-ken, 1924), 93–97.

77. Kihara Naohiko, *Hokkaidō bungaku shi: Taishō, Shōwa senzen-hen* (Sapporo: Hokkaido Shinbunsha, 1976), 125–31.

78. Niigata-shi, *Niigata-shi shi. Tsūshi-hen; 4* (Niigata: Niigata-shi, 1997), 174. *Niigata-shi shi. Tsūshi-hen; 3* (Niigata: Niigata-shi, 1996), 409–11. For a similar story in Sapporo, see list of local music stores in Ōtsuka Takatoshi, *Dai Sapporo an'nai* (Sapporo: Kinseisha, 1931), 149–53.

79. Sapporo-shi Kyōiku Iinkai, *Shin Sapporo-shi shi. Dai 3-kan* (Sapporo: Sapporo-shi, 1994), 764–65. Sapporo-shi Kyōiku Iinkai, *Sapporo jinmei jiten* (Sapporo: Sapporo-shi, 1993), 63.

80. Sapporo-shi Kyōiku Iinkai, *Shin Sapporo-shi shi. Dai 3-kan*, 769–70, Sapporo-shi Kyōiku Iinkai, *Sapporo jinmei jiten*, 7.

81. Keene, *Dawn to the West*, 106–18; Sapporo-shi Kyōiku Iinkai, *Sapporo jinmei jiten*, 7, 63, 84. On newspapers and the arts, see Sapporo-shi Kyōiku Iinkai, *Shin Sapporo-shi shi. Dai 3-kan*, 764–81.

82. Keene, *Dawn to the West*, 108–9.

83. Sapporo-shi Kyōiku Iinkai, *Shin Sapporo-shi shi. Dai 3-kan*, 770.

84. Ibid., 774. Headline in *Hokkai taimusu*, November 19, 1906.

85. Ibid., 774–78.

86. Mori, *Monogatari: Ishikawa no bungaku*, 131.

87. Okayama-ken, *Okayama-ken shi. Dai 11-kan*, 666–69.

88. The poem appeared in the poetry collection *Manifesto on Civilization* (*Bunmei no senpu*), published in 1926 by Daichisha. See Mori, *Monogatari: Ishikawa no bungaku*, 113–15.

THREE. COLONIZING THE COUNTRY

1. Raymond Williams made this point in an analysis of English literature since the sixteenth century, where he argues that mythologies of the town/country dualism justified social order. *The Country and the City* (London: Chatto and Windus, 1973).

2. Kären Wigen, *The Making of a Japanese Periphery, 1750–1920* (Berkeley: University of California Press, 1995).

3. Manu Goswami wrote in her book on the creation of a national economy in India: "During the last quarter of the nineteenth century, railways were chief instruments of national-economy making in the United States, Germany, France, Russia, and Japan. In these contexts, massive state investments in railroads, ports, canals, and educational systems and the proliferation of protective tariffs entailed the reorganization of economic space into distinct national blocs and a general movement toward autarkic, protectionist, and closed national economies.... Yet what distinguished the produced space of colonial India was the emergence of a distinct set of regional, urban, and local markets that were more tightly interwoven with imperial markets than with each other." Manu Goswami, *Producing India: From Colonial Economy to National Space* (Chicago: University of Chicago Press, 2004), 61–63. For an excellent study of the changes in social and economic geography of one region across the nineteenth century, see Kären Wigen, *The Making of a Japanese Periphery, 1750–1920* (Berkeley: University of California Press, 1995).

4. Sapporo-shi Kyōiku Iinkai, *Shin Sapporo-shi shi. Dai 2-kan* (Sapporo: Sapporo-shi, 1991), 477.

5. Ericson, *The Sound of the Whistle*, 114; F. C. Jones, *Hokkaido: Its Present State of Development and Future Prospects* (London: Oxford University Press, 1958), 18.

6. Ericson, *The Sound of the Whistle*, 83–84.

7. Shibata Hajime and Ōta Ken'ichi, *Okayama-ken no 100-nen* (Tokyo: Yamakawa Shuppansha, 1986), 137–41.

8. *Hokuriku shinpō*, 23 February 1893, reprinted in "Jitsuroku Ishikawa-ken shi" Henshū Iinkai, *Jitsuroku Ishikawa-ken shi 1868–1989: Gekidō no Meiji, Taishō, Shōwa, zen kiroku* (Kanazawa: Noto Insatsu Shuppanbu, 1991), 110.

9. Service to Fukui began in 1896 and extended to Komatsu in 1897, opening Ishikawa prefecture to rail traffic. The following year, the Hokuriku Railway completed track to Kanazawa and opened the city station for service. With the completion of the line to Takaoka in 1899, train service linked Kanazawa with Toyama prefecture. At the same time, work began on a feeder line that would drive north

into the Noto peninsula and Nanao, connecting Kanazawa to the main port in the region and granting improved access to markets on the Asian continent when the line opened in 1900. The Nanao line ran between Tsubata (the next station after Kanazawa on the Hokuriku line) and Yatashin (Nanao port). Hashimoto Tetsuya and Hayashi Yūichi, *Ishikawa-ken no 100-nen* (Tokyo: Yamakawa Shuppansha, 1987), 42–43, 123–25.

10. Today this term retains a stigmatizing nuance, and because of protest by regional politicians, the mass media refrain from using it. Furumaya Tadao, *Ura Nihon: Kindai Nihon o toinaosu* (Tokyo: Iwanami Shoten, 1997).

11. Ōshima Mitsuko, Satō Shigerō, Furumaya Tadao, and Mizoguchi Toshimaro, *Niigata-ken no 100-nen* (Tokyo: Yamakawa Shuppansha, 1990), 158–59; Niigata-shi, *Niigata-shi shi. Tsūshi-hen; 4* (Niigata: Niigata-shi, 1997), 47.

12. Carol Gluck, *Japan's Modern Myths: Ideology in the Late Meiji Period* (Princeton, NJ: Princeton University Press, 1985), 101.

13. *Tokyo nichinichi shinbun*, June 1888; cited in Ericson, *The Sound of the Whistle*, 64. On popular views of the railroad in the Meiji period, see Ericson, *The Sound of the Whistle*, 62–94, esp. 62–66.

14. Ericson, *The Sound of the Whistle*, 31–32; quote is on p. 32.

15. Okayama-shi, *Okayama-shi 100-nen shi. Jō-kan* (Okayama: Okayama-shi, 1989), 538–39; 568–70.

16. I am grateful to Andy Gordon for pointing this out and directing me to a dissertation that deals with railway politics: Nakano Yoichi, "Negotiating Modern Landscapes" (PhD diss., Harvard University, 2007).

17. Niigata-shi, *Niigata-shi shi. Tsūshi hen; 3* (Niigata: Niigata-shi, 1996), 347–49; Niigata Shōkō Kaigisho, *Niigata shōkō kaigisho 60-nen shi* (Niigata: Niigata Shōkō Kaigisho, 1958), 86–95.

18. Niigata-shi, *Niigata-shi shi. Tsūshi-hen; 3* (Niigata: Niigata-shi, 1996), 350–52.

19. Niigata-ken, *Niigata-ken shi. Tsūshi-hen; 8* (Niigata: Niigata-ken, 1988), 522–27; Niigata-shi, *Niigata-shi sangyō yōran* (Niigata: Niigata Sangyōka, 1937), 107. On reorientation of the economy toward Asia, see Louise Young, *Japan's Total Empire: Manchuria and the Culture of Wartime Imperialism* (Berkeley: University of California Press, 1998).

20. Hashimoto and Hayashi, *Ishikawa-ken no 100-nen*, 124.

21. The Onsen Denki (16.8 miles) connected Kanazawa, Komatsu, and Tsuruga to four hot springs resorts in the southern part of the prefecture. The Kanaiwa Dentetsu (4.5 miles) ran between Kanazawa and the coastal town of Ōno. The Nomi line (9.8 miles) connected Neagari and Yamakami; the Okoya Tetsudō (10.4 miles) ran between Komatsu and Nishio; and the Matsugane Sen (5.4 miles) linked Mattō and Nomachi. The Asanogawa Dentetsu (3.8 miles) ran between Kanazawa and Fukatsu; the Noto Tetsudō (15.8 miles), between Hakui and Togi; and the Kinmei Tetsudō (11.2 miles), between Tsurugi and Torigoe. Finally, the city tramway, Kanazawa Denki, operated a city route (6.3 miles) as well as lines from Mattō to Nomachi (5.4 miles), and from Shiragiku to Tsurugi (9 miles). Hashimoto and Hayashi, *Ishikawa-ken no 100-nen*, 123–24.

22. Sapporo-shi Kyōiku Iinkai, *Shin Sapporo-shi shi. Dai 4-kan* (Sapporo: Sapporo-shi, 1997), 355–57.

23. In 1911 Echigo Railway began work on a new line from Hakusan to Kashiwazaki, completing the track in 1913. The first stations were opened in Hakusan and Uchino in 1913, but by 1915 additional stations were completed at Sekiya, Terao, and Akatsuka. Niigata-shi, *Niigata-shi shi. Tsūshi-hen; 4* (Niigata: Niigata-shi, 1997), 46–47. On the electric streetcar, see Niigata-shi, *Niigata-shi sangyō yōran* (Niigata: Niigata Sangyōka, 1937), 107.

24. Niigata-shi, *Niigata-shi sangyō yōran* (Niigata: Niigata Sangyōka, 1929), 90; Niigata-shi, *Niigata-shi sangyō yōran* (Niigata: Niigata Sangyōka, 1937), 107–8.

25. Niigata-shi, *Niigata-shi shi. Tsūshi-hen; 3* (Niigata: Niigata-shi, 1996), 348–52.

26. Watanabe Shun'ichi, *Toshi keikaku no tanjō: Kokusai hikaku kara mita Nihon kindai toshi keikaku* (Tokyo: Kashiwa Shobō, 1993), 235–56; on the city planning process in Niigata, see Niigata-shi, *Niigata-shi shi. Tsūshi-hen; 4* (Niigata: Niigata-shi, 1997), 84–85.

27. Okayama-shi, *Okayama-shi 100-nen shi. Jō-kan* (Okayama: Okayama-shi, 1989), 622–23.

28. Kojima Jūzō, *Jidōsha no Okayama* (Okayama: Yoshida Shoten, 1933), 4–8; Hōgō Iwao, ed., *Me de miru Okayama no Taishō* (Okayama: Nihon Bunkyō Shuppan, 1986), 16.

29. In Hokkaido, 140 bus companies operated 403 vehicles over routes that covered 3,040 miles. Comparable statistics for Niigata prefecture were 104 companies, 519 vehicles, and 1,740 miles; for Ishikawa, 73 companies, 195 vehicles, and 958 miles. Tokyo Shisei Chōsakai, *Nihon toshi nenkan 2* (Tokyo: Tokyo Shisei Chōsakai, 1933), 480–81.

30. Fujisawa Susumu, *Okayama no kōtsū* (Okayama: Nihon Bunkyō Shuppan, 1972), 66–70.

31. Niigata-ken, *Niigata-ken shi. Tsūshi-hen; 8* (Niigata: Niigata-ken, 1988), 393.

32. Niigata-shi, *Niigata-shi shi. Tsūshi-hen; 3* (Niigata: Niigata-shi, 1996), 427–29.

33. Ibid., 361–64.

34. Niigata-shi, *Niigata-shi shi. Tsūshi-hen; 4* (Niigata: Niigata-shi, 1997), 98–100.

35. The precise number was 3,255,952 tsubo, equivalent to 1,085.32 cho or hectares.

36. Niigata-shi, *Niigata-shi shi. Tsūshi-hen; 4*, 12–16.

37. The city's territory then totaled twenty-eight square miles. Niigata-shi, *Niigata-shi shi. Tsūshi-hen; 4*, 378–81.

38. Okayama-shi, *Okayama-shi 100-nen shi. Jō-kan*, 163–78; Tokyo Shisei Chōsakai, *Nihon toshi nenkan 1* (Tokyo: Tokyo Shisei Chōsakai, 1931), 1–7, 24–26.

39. "Niigata-kō uta," in *Yakushin Niigata no zenbō*, by Junkan Niigatasha (Niigata: Junkan Niigatasha, 1936), unpaginated front material.

40. Ibid., 19.

41. Kanazawa-shi, *Kanazawa shimin dokuhon* (Kanazawa: Kanazawa-shi, 1928), 140–45.

42. Ōtsuka, *Dai Sapporo an'nai*, 181.

43. Population statistics must be taken as indicating general trends, since there are inconsistencies in population figures depending on the source. These are from Junkan Niigatasha, *Yakushin Niigata no zenbō*, 4.

44. Ibid., 22.

45. Kanazawa-shi, *Kanazawa shimin dokuhon*, 140–45.

46. Ibid.

47. Kobayashi Masao, "Nobiyuku Okayama," *Shōkō ōrai* 3, no. 4 (April 1932): 42–45.

48. "Okayama-shi ka," in "Nobiyuku Okayama," by Kobayashi Masao, *Shōkō ōrai* 3, no. 4 (April 1932): 42.

49. Ōtsuka, *Dai Sapporo an'nai*, 269, 270.

50. Ibid., 203.

51. Niigata-shi, *Niigata-shi shi. Tsūshi-hen;* 4, 378–79.

52. Okada Shō, "Okayama-shi no chiiki kakuchō," *Shōkō ōrai* 3, no. 2 (February 1932): 28–29.

53. Ibid., 29.

54. Ibid.

55. Ibid.

56. For example, see depictions of Tokyo suburbs in Tanizaki Jun'ichirō's novel *Chijin no ai* (1924) and Ozu Yasujiro's film *Umarete wa mita keredo* (1932).

57. My analysis of the taxonomy of suburban development is indebted to the painstaking detective work and wealth of detail furnished in the discussion of Sapporo's satellite villages in the *New History of Sapporo City:* Sapporo-shi Kyōiku Iinkai, *Shin Sapporo-shi shi. Dai 3-kan* (Sapporo: Sapporo-shi, 1994), and Sapporo-shi Kyōiku Iinkai, *Shin Sapporo-shi shi. Dai 4-kan* (Sapporo: Sapporo-shi, 1997).

58. F. C. Jones, *Hokkaido: Its Present State of Development and Future Prospects* (London: Oxford University Press, 1958), 14.

59. Kobayashi Takiji's *Fuzai jinushi* was published in 1929 in the journal *Chūō kōron*. See the English translation: *The Factory Ship and the Absentee Landlord*, trans. Frank Motofuji (Seattle: University of Washington Press, 1973).

60. Sapporo-shi Kyōiku Iinkai, *Shin Sapporo-shi shi. Dai 3-kan*, 190–96.

61. Ibid., 155–59; Sapporo-shi Kyōiku Iinkai, *Shin Sapporo-shi shi. Dai 4-kan*, 158; Sapporo-shi Kyōiku Iinkai Bunka Shiryōshitsu, *Sapporo rekishi chizu. Shōwa-hen* (Sapporo: Sapporo-shi, 1981), 17.

62. Sapporo-shi Kyōiku Iinkai, *Shin Sapporo-shi shi. Dai 4-kan*, 158, 166, 168; Sapporo-shi Kyōiku Iinkai, *Shin Sapporo-shi shi. Dai 3-kan*, 183.

63. Sapporo-shi Kyōiku Iinkai, *Shin Sapporo-shi shi, Dai 3-kan*, 161–62.

64. The value of economic production rose from 1,719,453 yen to 3,362,368 yen. Population figures of 4,169 in 1910 rose only modestly, to 4,414 in 1921 and 4,729 in 1930; but Teine caught up with Kotoni in 1939, with a population of 9,879. Ibid., 159–60, 167–69; Sapporo-shi Kyōiku Iinkai Bunka Shiryōshitsu, *Sapporo rekishi chizu. Taishō hen* (Sapporo: Sapporo-shi, 1980), 51; Sapporo-shi Kyōiku Iinkai, *Shin Sapporo-shi shi. Dai 3-kan*, 183.

65. The population of Shiroishi-chō rose from 489 in 1920 to 4,874 in 1925: Sapporo-shi Kyōiku Iinkai Bunka Shiryōshitsu, *Sapporo rekishi chizu. Taishō hen*,

42–43, 52; Sapporo-shi Kyōiku Iinkai, *Shin Sapporo-shi shi. Dai 4-kan*, 162–63, 285.

66. Production in Shiroishi rose from 1,567,470 in 1925 to 2,693,969 yen in 1939. Sapporo-shi Kyōiku Iinkai, *Shin Sapporo-shi shi. Dai 4-kan*, 166–69; Sapporo-shi Kyōiku Iinkai, *Shin Sapporo-shi shi. Dai 3-kan*, 178–82.

67. A rich and illuminating analysis of the garden city and its relationship to discourses on domesticity can be found in Jordan Sand, *House and Home in Modern Japan: Architecture, Domestic Space and Bourgeois Culture, 1880–1930* (Cambridge, MA: Harvard University Asia Center, 2005).

68. Sapporo-shi Kyōiku Iinkai, *Shin Sapporo-shi shi. Dai 4-kan*, 355–56, 362.

69. Sapporo-shi Kyōiku Iinkai, *Sapporo seikatsu bunka shi Taishō, Shōwa senzen-hen* (Sapporo: Sapporo-shi, 1986), 42.

70. Sapporo-shi Kyōiku Iinkai, *Shin Sapporo-shi shi. Dai 4-kan*, 151–53.

71. Sapporo-shi Kyōiku Iinkai, *Shin Sapporo-shi shi. Dai 3-kan*, 169, 183; Sapporo-shi Kyōiku Iinkai, *Shin Sapporo-shi shi. Dai 4-kan*, 166.

72. Sapporo-shi Kyōiku Iinkai, *Shin Sapporo-shi shi. Dai 4-kan*, 161; Sapporo-shi Kyōiku Iinkai, *Shin Sapporo-shi shi. Dai 3-kan*, 171, 552–54. As in Shiroishi, sections of the old village annexed to the city in 1910 created a seamless transition into the new village. The river made a natural boundary that defined the former limit between the city and village.

73. Sapporo-shi Kyōiku Iinkai, *Shin Sapporo-shi shi. Dai 4-kan*, 161; Sapporo-shi Kyōiku Iinkai Bunka Shiryōshitsu, *Sapporo rekishi chizu. Taishō-hen*, 47.

74. Sapporo-shi Kyōiku Iinkai, *Shin Sapporo-shi shi. Dai 3-kan*, 175.

75. Ōtsuka, *Dai Sapporo an'nai*, 15–16. Sapporo-shi Kyōiku Iinkai, *Shin Sapporo-shi shi. Dai 3-kan*, 176–77.

76. Sapporo-shi Kyōiku Iinkai, *Shin Sapporo-shi shi. Dai 4-kan*, 168–69.

77. Ibid.

78. Ibid., 168–69, 183.

79. Sapporo-shi Kyōiku Iinkai Bunka Shiryōshitsu, *Sapporo rekishi chizu. Shōwa-hen*, 12.

80. Sapporo-shi Kyōiku Iinkai, *Shin Sapporo-shi shi. Dai 4-kan*, 148–49; Sapporo-shi Kyōiku Iinkai Bunka Shiryōshitsu, *Sapporo rekishi chizu. Taishō-hen*, 52.

81. Sapporo-shi Kyōiku Iinkai, *Shin Sapporo-shi shi. Dai 4-kan*, 155–58; Sapporo-shi Kyōiku Iinkai, *Shin Sapporo-shi shi. Dai 3-kan*, 149–54.

82. Sapporo-shi Kyōiku Iinkai, *Shin Sapporo-shi shi. Dai 4-kan*, 375–77, 155–58; Sapporo-shi Kyōiku Iinkai, *Shin Sapporo-shi shi. Dai 3-kan*, 149–54.

83. Sapporo-shi Kyōiku Iinkai, *Shin Sapporo-shi shi. Dai 3-kan*, 153, 183; Sapporo-shi Kyōiku Iinkai, *Shin Sapporo-shi shi. Dai 4-kan*, 170–71, 166–69; Andō Yoshio, ed., *Kindai Nihon keizai shi yōran* (Tokyo: Tokyo Daigaku Shuppan, 1975), 14.

FOUR. THE PAST IN THE PRESENT

1. As Takeo Yazaki notes in his encyclopedic urban history, "The castle towns, which constituted the majority of pre-Meiji cities, suffered most under the Meiji

transformation. Feudal lords left their castle centers for Tokyo under government orders, and most of the castles were destroyed when the domain system was abolished and the prefectures were established in 1871. The warrior groups, consistently more than half of castle town populations, were left without stipends or status. Bankrupted by such sudden and drastic measures, some managed to enter bureaucratic service, though many turned to operating shops of their own and many more returned to the farms. Losing their best customers, the merchants faced severe depression, and the castle towns dwindled in size, structure, and prestige as their former integrative place and function came to an end." Takeo Yazaki, *Social Change and the City: From Earliest Times through the Industrial Revolution*, trans. David L. Swain (Tokyo: Japan Publications, 1968), 314.

2. My argument about localism as an invented tradition builds on a number of excellent studies, including Theodore C. Bester, *Neighborhood Tokyo* (Stanford, CA: Stanford University Press, 1989); Jennifer Robertson, *Native and Newcomer: Making and Remaking a Japanese City* (Berkeley: University of California Press, 1994); and Michael Lewis, *Becoming Apart: National Power and Local Politics in Toyama, 1868–1945* (Cambridge, MA: Harvard University Asia Center, 2000).

3. Taguchi Shōichirō, *Akita-ken no 100-nen* (Tokyo: Yamakawa Shuppansha, 1983), 225.

4. Nagayama Usaburō, *Okayama-ken. Tsūshi. Jō-hen* (Okayama: Okayama-ken, 1930); Nagayama Usaburō, *Okayama-ken. Tsūshi. Ka-hen* (Okayama: Okayama-ken, 1930); San'yō Shinpōsha, *Shōwa 12-nen San'yō nenkan bessatsu. Okayama-ken 70-nen shi* (Okayama: San'yō Shinpōsha, 1936); Takakura Shin'ichirō, *Hokkaidō no rekishi* (Sapporo: Nihon Hōsō Kyōkai Hokkaidō Shibu, 1933).

5. Okayama also published a city history in this period, though it was a comparatively modest single volume: Okayama-ken, *Okayama-ken shi. Dai 11-kan* (Okayama: Okayama-ken, 1987), 649. Kanazawa-shi, *Kōhon Kanazawa-shi shi* (Kanazawa: Kanazawa-shi, 1916–1937); Sapporo-ku, *Sapporo-ku shi* (Sapporo: Sapporo-ku, 1911).

6. Both works were published by producer organizations. Haraguchi Kiyoshi and Un'no Fukuju, *Shizuoka-ken no 100-nen* (Tokyo: Yamakawa Shuppansha, 1982), bibliography, p. 22; Dai Nihon Bīru Kabushiki Kaisha Sapporo Shiten, *Sapporo bīru enkaku shi* (Tokyo: Dai Nihon Bīru Kabushiki Kaisha, 1936).

7. For example: Sapporo Tanuki Kōji Shōtengai Shōgyō Kumiai, *Sapporo tanuki kōji hatten shi* (Sapporo: Sapporo Tanuki Kōji Shōtengai Shōgyō Kumiai, 1938); Hokkaidō Sapporo Shihan Gakkō, *Hokkaidō Sapporo shihan gakkō 50-nen shi* (Sapporo: Hokkaidō Sapporo Shihan Gakkō, 1936).

8. Suzuki Zensaku, *Chihō hattatsu shi to sono jinbutsu—Shikoku no maki* (Takamatsu: Kyōdo Kenkyūsha, 1942).

9. *Ishikawa-ken shi. Gendai-hen 3* (Kanazawa: Ishikawa-ken, 1964), 296.

10. Revised and expanded from a 1913 edition: Hosokawake Hensanjo, *Higohan kokuji shiryō. Kaitei ban* (Kumamoto: Kōshaku Hosokawake Hensanjo, 1932).

11. Morita Seiichi, Hanatachi Saburō, and Ikai Takaaki, *Kumamoto-ken no 100-nen* (Tokyo: Yamakawa Shuppansha, 1987), 244; Yamazaki Masatada, *Yokoi Shōnan ikō* (Tokyo: Nissin Shoin, 1942).

12. Ishikawa-ken, *Ishikawa-ken shi. Gendai-hen 3*, 296; Kanazawa-shi, *Kōhon Kanazawa-shi shi*.

13. Niigata-shi, *Niigata-shi shi. Jō-kan, Ge-kan* (Niigata: Niigata-shi, 1934).

14. Okayama-ken, *Okayama-ken shi. Dai 11-kan*, 649.

15. Ishikawa-ken, *Ishikawa-ken shi. Gendai-hen 3*, 291–93.

16. Louise Young, *Japan's Total Empire: Manchuria and the Culture of Wartime Imperialism* (Berkeley: University of California Press, 1998), 379.

17. Miyoshi Shōichirō, Matsumoto Hiroshi, and Satō Masashi, *Tokushima-ken no 100-nen* (Tokyo: Yamakawa Shuppan, 1992), 166.

18. Okayama Culture Study Group (Okayama bunka benkyōkai); Central Japan Folklore Studies Association (Chūgoku Minzoku Gakkai): Okayama-ken, *Okayama-ken shi. Dai 11-kan*, 648.

19. Ishikawa-ken, *Ishikawa-ken shi. Gendai-hen 3*, 293.

20. Taguchi, *Akita-ken no 100-nen*, 225; Miyoshi, Matsumoto, and Satō, *Tokushima-ken no 100-nen*, 174.

21. Ishikawa-ken, *Ishikawa-ken shi. Gendai-hen 2* (Kanazawa: Ishikawa-ken, 1963), 874–75.

22. Kanazawa Culture Association (Kanazawa Bunka Kyōkai); Ishikawa Prefecture Geography Society (Ishikawa-ken Chiri Gakkai); Kanazawa Folklore Association (Kanazawa Minzoku Danwakai); Ishikawa-ken, *Ishikawa-ken shi. Gendai-hen 3*, 299–301; Ishikawa-ken, *Ishikawa-ken shi. Gendai-hen 2*, 874–75.

23. See W. G. Beasley and Edwin G. Pulleyblank, *Historians of China and Japan* (London: Oxford University Press, 1962); John Whitney Hall, "Materials for Study of Local History," in *Studies in the Institutional History of Early Modern Japan*, ed. John Whitney Hall and Marius B. Jansen (Princeton, NJ: Princeton University Press, 1968), 143–46.

24. Margaret Mehl, "Scholarship and Ideology in Conflict: The Kume Affair, 1892," *Monumenta Nipponica* 48, no. 3 (Autumn 1993): 337–57; Margaret Mehl, "The Mid-Meiji 'History Boom': Professionalization of Historical Scholarship and Growing Pains of an Emerging Academic Discipline," *Japan Forum* 10, no. 1 (1998): 67–83; Peter Duus, "Whig History, Japanese Style: The Min'yūsha Historians and the Meiji Restoration," *Journal of Asian Studies* 33, no. 3 (May 1974): 415–36.

25. Niigata-shi, *Niigata-shi shi. Jō-kan*, 1.

26. Susan L. Burns, *Before the Nation: Kokugaku and the Imagining of Community in Early Modern Japan* (Durham, NC: Duke University Press, 2003); Stefan Tanaka, *Japan's Orient: Rendering Pasts into History* (Berkeley: University of California Press, 1993); John S. Brownlee, *Japanese Historians and the National Myths, 1600–1945* (Vancouver: University of British Columbia, 1997), 89–91.

27. Niigata-shi, *Niigata-shi shi. Jō-kan*, preface pp. 1–3, main text pp. 1–11.

28. Ibid., preface p. 2, main text pp. 12–26; quote on preface p. 2.

29. Ibid., preface p. 3, main text pp. 79–198.

30. Ibid., preface p. 3, main text pp. 91–198.

31. Kanazawa-shi, *Kōhon Kanazawa-shi shi. Shigai-hen, Dai 1* (Kanazawa: Kanazawa-shi, 1916), 233–51.

32. Kanazawa-shi, *Kanazawa shimin dokuhon* (Kanazawa: Kanazawa-shi Kyōikukai, 1928), 1.

33. Ibid., 1–3.

34. Ibid., 4.

35. Ibid., 2–5.

36. Ibid., 10–12.

37. Hokkaidō-chō, *Shinsen Hokkaidō shi. Dai 1-kan; Gaisetsu* (Sapporo: Hokkaidō-chō, 1936–37).

38. Sapporo-shi Shōgakkō Kyōiku Kenkyūkai Chirika Kenkyūbu, *Sapporo-shi chiri dokuhon* (Sapporo: Sapporo-shi Kyōikukai, 1927), 3.

39. Ibid., 1–5.

40. Text of song in unpaginated front matter of Junkan Niigatasha, *Yakushin Niigata no zenbō* (Niigata: Junkan Niigatasha, 1936), n.p.

41. Kanazawa-shi, *Kanazawa shimin dokuhon* (Kanazawa: Kanazawa-shi Kyōikukai, 1928), 139.

42. Ibid., 139–41.

43. "Okayama-shi ka" in Kobayashi Masao, "Nobiyuku Okayama," *Shōkō ōrai* 3, no. 4 (April 1932): 42.

44. Broadly speaking, the second wave occurred in the sixties and seventies and the third in the 1980s and 1990s to commemorate the centennial of the 1889 founding of prefectures, towns, and villages.

45. Kanazawa-shi, *Kōhon Kanazawa-shi shi. Kōgei-hen, Dai 1* (Kanazawa: Kanazawa-shi, 1925).

46. My use of Koselleck's concept here is not an attempt to condense his densely theoretical and deeply historical argument. *Futures Past: On the Semantics of Historical Time*, trans. Keith Tribe (New York: Columbia University Press, 2004).

47. See the excellent discussion of the tensions and overlaps between the social movements led by Yanagi and Yanagita, in Kim Brandt, *Kingdom of Beauty: Mingei and the Politics of Folk Art in Imperial Japan* (Durham, NC: Duke University Press, 2007), 72–82. On Yanagita, see Gerald Figal, *Civilization and Monsters: Spirits of Modernity in Meiji Japan* (Durham, NC: Duke University Press, 1999), 105–52; and Marilyn Ivy, *Discourses of the Vanishing: Modernity, Phantasm, Japan* (Chicago: Chicago University Press, 1995), 66–97.

48. "Hongo shippitsusha no gairyaku," *Koshiji* 1 (January 1935): 42. As Kim Brandt points out, the decades of the twenties and thirties constituted a critical moment marking a shift from an older culture of aristocratic aesthetics to a broader hobbyist culture of dilettantism (*Kingdom of Beauty*, 38–82).

49. "Koshijikai o shōkai su," *Koshiji* 1 (January 1935): 41.

50. Ibid.

51. Ivy, *Discourses of the Vanishing*, 1–28.

52. Andō Bumpei, "Niigata kyōdo dokuhon," *Koshiji* 1 (January 1935): 9.

53. Nakano Shiromizu, "Echigo Sado tokuyū no densetsu," *Koshiji* 4 (April 1935): 15.

54. Hirazawa Kō, "Hōgen," *Koshiji* 5 (May 1935): 1.

55. Katsura Matasaburō, "Hashigaki," in *Okayama densetsu shū* (Okayama: Bunken Shobō, 1931), n.p. Katsura Matasaburō also headed the folklore studies group Bunken Kenkyūkai, which published the *Okayama bunka shiryō* from 1928 to 1931 (3 vols.). A larger group, the Chūgoku Minzoku Gakkai, began publication of *Chūgoku minzoku kenkyū* in 1932.

56. Okayama-shi, *Bizen Okayama* (Okayama: Okayama-shi, 1929), 26–27.

57. Oka Chōhei, *Okayama konjaku ki* (Okayama: Okayama Minpōsha, 1935), 79–80.

58. Ibid.

59. Okayama-shi, *Bizen Okayama*, 26–27.

60. Harry Harootunian, *Overcome by Modernity: History, Culture, and Community in Interwar Japan* (Princeton, NJ: Princeton University Press, 2001), 306–28. See also Ivy, *Discourses of the Vanishing*, 66–97, Gerald Figal, *Civilization and Monsters;* and Michael Foster, *Pandemonium and Parade: Japanese Monsters and the Culture of Yokai* (Berkeley: University of California Press, 2008).

61. Niigata-shi, *Niigata-shi shi. Ge-kan* (Niigata: Niigata-shi, 1934), 543–93; *kawa hiraki:* 572–53; *o-bon bon odori (o-bon* festival dancing)*:* 561–62; *kakoi bune:* 574–76.

62. Ibid., 547–48; Louis Frédéric, *Japan Encyclopedia*, trans. Käthe Roth (Cambridge, MA: Belknap Press of Harvard University Press, 2002), s.v. "dōsojin."

63. Ibid., 543.

64. The section in the *Niigata City History* on customs includes entries on meat eating, short hair, housing, and so on, which likewise track the changes in cultural practice effected by Edo-period sumptuary legislation and Meiji regulations concerning dress and hairstyles. Entries pointed out that customs were influenced by other local factors, such as political regime, climate, and agricultural practices. Again, the discussion makes the point that local customs, while they define a particularized local subject, were historically rooted and changed over time.

65. Niigata-shi, *Niigata-shi shi. Ge-kan* (Niigata: Niigata-shi, 1934), 543–93, *dōsojin:* 547–48; *kadomatsu:* 544–45; Frédéric, *Japan Encyclopedia*, s.v. "dōsojin."

66. The central agency for organized tourism in prewar Japan, the Japan tsūristo būro (JTB) was founded in 1912, initially to promote foreign tourism in Japan and its colonies. Recognizing the possibilities of using tourism as a tool for cultural policy and economic development, the government expanded the JTB to focus on Japanese travelers in 1924. The JTB maintained an expanding network of service centers in cities throughout Japan and the empire; it produced travel literature and the magazine *Tabi* (Travel). The JTB worked with the Bureau of Railways to promote passenger travel on the national rail network and with the Home and Education Ministries to develop group summer travel programs for schoolchildren designed to encourage hiking, skiing, and mountain climbing. These and other sports connected tourism to the countryside as a form of public health. Tourism became a major element of fascist cultural policy in the 1930s. See Takaoka Hiroyuki, "Kankō, kōsei, ryokō: Fashizumuki no tsūrizumu," in *Bunka to fashizumu: Senjiki Nihon ni okeru bunka no kōbō*, ed. Akasaka Shirō and Kitagawa Kenzō (Tokyo: Nihon Hyōronsha, 1993), 9–52.

67. See, for example, Okayama-shi, *Okayama* (Okayama: Okayama-shi, 1927).

68. Okada Izumi, *Kankō Okayama* (Okayama: Hanayanagi Shinbunsha, 1936).

69. Ibid.; Okayama-shi, *Okayama*.

70. Okayama-shi, preface to *Bizen Okayama* (Okayama: Okayama-shi, 1929), n.p.

71. The initial impetus behind these laws was the Iwakura Mission of 1871–73. During this trip to Europe and America, Japanese government leaders were impressed with the use of museums and historic preservation as tools of nation-building and means of protecting cultural relics with "national" associations. In Japan in 1871, the Law for Preservation of Ancient Artifacts was passed and the first national museum opened. In 1897, partly in reaction to the wave of destruction of temples and a flood of exports of Japanese artworks, the government passed the Law to Preserve Ancient Shrines and Temples. In 1919, the idea of preservation expanded to encompass *meisho* with the Historic Sites, Places of Scenic Beauty, and Natural Monuments Preservation Law. Ellen P. Conant, "Introduction: A Historiographical Overview," in *Challenging Past and Present: The Metamorphosis of Nineteenth-Century Japanese Art*, ed. Ellen P. Conant (Honolulu: University of Hawai'i Press, 2006), 16–19.

72. Alice Y. Tseng, *The Imperial Museums of Meiji Japan: Architecture and the Art of the Nation* (Seattle: University of Washington Press, 2008), 18–38.

73. Laura Nenzi, *Excursions in Identity: Travel and the Intersection of Place, Gender, and Status in Edo Japan* (Honolulu: University of Hawai'i Press, 2008), 38–39, 94–101.

74. Constantine N. Vaporis, *Breaking Barriers: Travel and the State in Early Modern Japan* (Cambridge, MA: Council on East Asian Studies, Harvard University, 1994); Marcia Yonemoto, "The 'Spatial Vernacular' in Tokugawa Maps," *Journal of Asian Studies* 59, no. 3 (August 2000): 647–66; Marcia Yonemoto, *Mapping Early Modern Japan: Space, Place, and Culture in the Tokugawa Period, 1603–1868* (Berkeley: University of California Press, 2003); Nenzi, *Excursions in Identity*. Yonemoto cities the authoritative early modern bibliography *Kokusho sōmokuroku*, which includes several thousand titles under the category of travel literature: Yonemoto, *Mapping Early Modern Japan*, 46.

75. Vaporis, *Breaking Barriers;* Sarah Thal, *Rearranging the Landscapes of the Gods: The Politics of a Pilgrimage Site in Japan, 1573–1912* (Chicago: University of Chicago Press, 2005).

76. Manu Goswami's analysis of nationalism helped inspire this formulation of urban community and the city idea. As she writes, "The historically constituted 'family resemblances' between modern nationalisms include the pervasively institutionalized tie between nationhood and statehood; the understanding of culture, history, and territory as the 'frontier signs' of the modern nation; the emphasis on a territorial correspondence between people, culture, economy, and state; the claim to a collective archaic past and a linear, developmental conception of the future; the concept of 'direct membership' according to which individuals are understood as integral parts of a national collective and as formally equivalent." "Rethinking the Modular Nation Form: Toward a Sociohistorical Conception of

Nationalism," *Comparative Studies in Society and History* 44, no. 4 (October 2002): p. 776. See also Goswami, *Producing India: From Colonial Economy to National Space* (Chicago: University of Chicago Press, 2004), 31–72, esp. p. 67.

77. Niigata Shisei Kisha Kurabu, "Niigata-shi no konjaku," in *Niigata-shi an'nai* (Niigata: Niigata Shisei Kisha Kurabu, 1918), 1–3.

78. Oka Chōhei, *Okayama konjaku ki*, unpaginated front matter.

79. Niigata Shisei Kisha Kurabu, *Niigata-shi an'nai* (Niigata: Niigata Shisei Kisha Kurabu, 1918), 72.

80. Okayama-shi Kangyōka, *Okayama* (Okayama: Okayama-shi Kangyōka, 1927), 80–81.

81. Ibid., 77–82; Okayama-shi, *Bizen Okayama* (Okayama: Okayama-shi, 1929), 46.

82. Utani Takeji, preface to *Okayama no yūran* (Okayama: Saikinsha, 1929), n.p.

83. Utani Takeji, *Okayama no yūran* (Okayama: Saikinsha, 1929), 38–39.

84. Ibid., 43–44.

85. Ibid., 51–53.

86. Ibid., 54–55, 57.

FIVE. THE CULT OF THE NEW

1. For a discussion of fashion and the department store, see Hatsuda Tōru, *Hyakkaten no tanjō: Meiji Taishō Shōwa no toshi bunka o enshutsu shita hyakkaten to kankōba no kindai shi* (Tokyo: Sanseidō, 1993), 74; and Jinno Yuki, *Shumi no tanjō: Hyakkaten ga tsukutta teisuto* (Tokyo: Keisō Shobō, 1994), 124–29.

2. Hiromi Mizuno, *Science for the Empire: Scientific Nationalism in Modern Japan* (Stanford, CA: Stanford University Press, 2009). The phrase comes from the title of the last chapter of the book.

3. For a wonderful treatment of the rise of scientific management in Japan, see William M. Tsutsui, *Manufacturing Ideology: Scientific Management in Twentieth-Century Japan* (Princeton, NJ: Princeton University Press, 2001).

4. Kimura Sōhachi writes that what was called *iki* in the mid-nineteenth century became "high-collar" and "modern" in mid-Meiji. Kimura, *Gendai fūzoku chō* (Tokyo: Tōhō Shobō, 1952). See entry in Kabashima Tadao, Hida Yoshifumi, and Yonekawa Akihiko, eds., *Meiji, Taishō shingo zokugo jiten* (Tokyo: Tōkyōdō Shuppan, 1996), 305.

5. I am adapting the concept of the chronotope from Soviet literary critic M. M. Bakhtin, who used the term to identify the intrinsic interconnectedness of time and space in fictional space. Mikhail Bakhtin, "Forms of Time and of the Chronotope in the Novel: Notes Toward a Historical Poetics," in *The Dialogic Imagination: Four Essays*, trans. Caryl Emerson and Michael Holquist (Austin: University of Texas Press, 1981).

6. San'yō Shinbunsha, *Shinbun kiji to shashin de miru sesō Okayama. Shōwa senzen, Meiji, Taishō-hen* (Okayama: San'yō Shinbunsha Shuppankyoku, 1990), 202; Ōtsuka Takatoshi, *Dai Sapporo an'nai* (Sapporo: Kinseisha, 1931), 103.

7. Much of modern argot derives from terms like *moga* and *mobo*, the abbreviations of, respectively, *modan gāru* and *modan bōi*. *Ginbura* is an abbreviation of the phrase "Ginza o burabura suru." For reference to *Furabura*, see Satō Ensaku, *Funae no hana* (Niigata: Tōhoku Jihō, 1936), 7–8.

8. Hattori Keijirō, "Ginza, soshite Ginzanaizēshon," *Toshi mondai* 67, no. 5 (May 1976): 63–80, cited in Yoshimi Shun'ya, *Toshi no doramaturugī: Tōkyō sakariba no shakai shi* (Tokyo: Kōbundō, 1987), 244. See also the special issue of *Modan Kanazawa* on Ginza: *Modan Kanazawa: Ginza kaikan-go* 3, no. 19 (June 1933). On Ginza in mass magazines, see Yoshimi's discussion of such articles as "Ginza Economics," "Ginza Alps," "Ginza Rising," "Scenes from the Ginza Intelligentsia," which were published in *Chūō kōron* and *Kaizō*, in Yoshimi, *Toshi no doramaturugī*, 222–23.

9. Tanizaki's parody of the domestic life of the new middle class, *Naomi*, took readers on a voyeuristic journey through cafés, dance halls, and movie theaters in Tokyo's entertainment zones; likewise Kafū's elegiac short stories about down-market red-light districts and Kawabata's montage of Asakusa condensed the character of Tokyo into its *sakariba*. In *Topographies of Japanese Modernism* (New York: Columbia University Press, 2002), Seiji Lippit makes a similar point, arguing that the novel of the twenties and thirties demonstrated a peculiar affinity for urban space, and that this constituted the grounds for Japanese modernism.

10. Komota Nobuo, Shimada Yoshifumi, Yazawa Kan, and Yokazawa Chiaki, *Nihon ryūkōka shi. Jō* (Tokyo: Shakai Shisōsha, 1994), 260–61.

11. For brief accounts of the earthquake, see Andrew Gordon, *A Modern History of Japan from Tokugawa Times to the Present* (New York: Oxford University Press, 2003); and Edward Seidensticker, *Tokyo Rising: The City Since the Great Earthquake* (New York: Knopf, 1990).

12. Yoshimi, *Toshi no doramaturugī*, 219–44, esp. 242–44.

13. Seidensticker, *Tokyo Rising*, 21–87.

14. David Harvey, *The Condition of Postmodernity : An Enquiry into the Origins of Cultural Change* (Oxford: Blackwell, 1989).

15. "Tōkyō o omou," trans. Donald Keene, *Dawn to the West: Japanese Literature of the Modern Era* (New York: H. Holt, 1987), 750.

16. Kamoi Yū, *Kanazawa shin fūkei* (Kanazawa: Hokkoku Shinbunsha Shuppanbu, 1933), 7.

17. Yoshimi, *Toshi no doramaturugī*, 59–74.

18. *Modan Kanazawa* 3, no. 19 (June 1933), 26–27.

19. Kamoi, *Kanazawa shin fūkei*, 7.

20. Ibid., 24.

21. Ibid., 8.

22. Ibid., 24.

23. *Modan Kanazawa*, special issue, *Ginza kaikan-go* 3, no. 19 (June 1933): 1.

24. Kamoi, *Kanazawa shin fūkei*, 12.

25. In the Japanese measurement system, 1 ken equals 2 yards. Ibid., 20–21.

26. The largest fire in modern Kanazawan history, the devastating Hikizō Fire of 1927, resulted in seven hundred houses burned and three thousand people injured. A

major hospital and Kanazawa Prefectural Commercial College were both destroyed. Kanazawa-shi, *Kanazawa-shi shi. Tsūshi-hen; 3* (Kanazawa: Kanazawa-shi, 2006), 442–44.

27. Kamoi, *Kanazawa shin fūkei*, 20–21.

28. Ibid., 20.

29. Ibid.

30. Ibid., 24–25.

31. Maki Hisao, ed., *Kanazawa shōkō kaigisho 70-nen shi* (Kanazawa: Kanazawa Shōkō Kaigisho, 1960), 188; Kokusai Shinkō Hakurankai Hensanbu, *Kokusan shinkō hakurankai shi* (Sapporo: Hokkai Taimususha, 1927), 1.

32. Nagayama Sadatomi, *Naigai hakurankai sōsetsu narabini wagakuni ni okeru bankoku hakurankai no mondai* (Tokyo: Suimei Shoin, 1933), 84–91.

33. Ibid., 1.

34. Maki, *Kanazawa shōkō kaigisho 70-nen shi*, 188–89.

35. Nagayama, *Naigai hakurankai sōsetsu narabini wagakuni ni okeru bankoku hakurankai no mondai*, 82, 400–401.

36. Sapporo-shi Kyōiku Iinkai, *Shin Sapporo-shi shi. Dai 3-kan* (Sapporo: Sapporo-shi, 1994), 661–71.

37. Maki, *Kanazawa shōkō kaigisho 70-nen shi*, 188–90; Kanazawa-shi, *Kanazawa* (Kanazawa: Kanazawa-shi, 1932); Sangyō to Kankō no Dai Hakurankai Kyōsankai, *Kanazawa-shi shusai sangyō to kankō no dai hakurankai kyōsankai shi* (Kanazawa: Sangyō to Kankō no Dai Hakurankai Kyōsankai, 1933), 195.

38. P. F. Kornicki, "Public Display and Changing Values: Early Meiji Exhibitions and Their Precursors," *Monumenta Nipponica* 49, no. 2 (Summer 1994), 167–96.

39. *Shūkan Asahi hyakka. Nihon no rekishi. 106: Hakurankai kindaika to gijutsu iten* (Tokyo: Asahi Shinbunsha, 1988), 194–95.

40. Sangyō to Kankō no Dai Hakurankai Kyōsankai, *Kanazawa-shi shusai sangyō to kankō no dai hakurankai kyōsankai shi* (Kanazawa: Sangyō to Kankō no Dai Hakurankai Kyōsankai, 1933), 386–89.

41. Kokusan Shinkō Hakurankai Hensanbu, *Kokusan shinkō hakurankai shi*, 54.

42. Todd Henry, "The 1940 Exposition in Late Colonial Korea" (public lecture, University of Wisconsin-Madison Center for East Asian Studies, fall 2008).

43. Sapporo-shi Kyōiku Iinkai, *Sapporo seikatsu bunka shi. Taishō, Shōwa, senzen-hen* (Sapporo: Sapporo-shi, 1986), 56–57.

44. Kokusan Shinkō Hakurankai Hensanbu, *Kokusan shinkō hakurankai shi*, 131–32.

45. Ibid., 179–81.

46. Ibid., 135–36.

47. Ibid., 136, 139.

48. Ibid., 170.

49. Ibid.

50. Ibid., 283–84.

51. Ibid., 131.

52. Ibid., 185.

53. Unno Hiroshi, ed., *Kikai no metoroporisu* (Tokyo: Heibonsha, 1990), 471–77.

54. Kokusan Shinkō Hakurankai Hensanbu, *Kokusan shinkō hakurankai shi*, 207–16.

55. *Niigata-shi yōran* (Niigata: Jitsugyō no An'naisha, 1926).

56. Maruyama Atsushi, "Toshi bunka no kyoten toshite no hyakkaten: Chihō toshi Kanazawa no hyakkaten," in *Mentarite Kanazawa: "Asobi" kara mieru mono*, ed. Maruyama Atsushi (Kanazawa: n.p., 1995), 221–52; Tenmaya Shashi Hensan Iinkai, *Tenmaya 150-nen shi* (Okayama: Tenmaya, 1979), 56; Hyakkaten Jigyō Kenkyūkai, *Hyakkaten no jissō* (Tokyo: Hyakkaten Jigyō Kenkyūkai, 1935), 52–53.

57. *Niigata-shi yōran*.

58. Shunkan Niigatasha, *Yakushin Niigata no zenbō* (Niigata: Shunkan Niigatasha, 1936).

59. *Niigata-shi yōran*.

60. See, for example, Satō Ensaku, *Funae no hana* (Niigata: Tōhoku Jihō, 1936).

61. *San'yo shinpō*, May 1, 1936, reprinted in San'yō Shinbunsha, *Shinbun kiji to shashin de miru sesō Okayama. Shōwa senzen, Meiji, Taishō-hen*, 300.

62. Shunkan Niigatasha, *Yakushin Niigata no zenbō*, 13.

63. Ninomiya Jun'ichi, Nagai Kō, Niigata Nippōsha, *Niigata-ken no Shōwa shi* (Niigata: Niigata Nippō Jigyōsha, 1989), 66.

64. "Hikōki," in *Kadokawa Nihon shi jiten*, 2nd ed. (Tokyo: Kadokawa Shoten, 1983).

65. "Hikōki netsu o hakki suru," *Niigata kōyū*, January 1, 1915.

66. *San'yō shinpō*, December 21, 1912, reprinted in San'yō Shinbunsha, *Shinbun kiji to shashin de miru sesō Okayama. Shōwa senzen, Meiji, Taishō-hen, 147*.

67. *San'yō shinbun*, April 16, 1989, reprinted in San'yō Shinbunsha, *Shinbun kiji to shashin de miru sesō Okayama. Shōwa senzen, Meiji, Taishō-hen*, 160.

68. *Chūgoku minpō*, May 28, 1916, reprinted in San'yō Shinbunsha, *Shinbun kiji to shashin de miru sesō Okayama. Shōwa senzen, Meiji, Taishō-hen*, 147, 60.

69. Kanazawa-shi, *Kanazawa*; Sangyō to Kankō no Dai Hakurankai Kyōsankai, *Kanazawa-shi shusai sangyō to kankō no dai hakurankai shi* (Kanazawa: Sangyō to Kankō no Dai Hakurankai Kyōsankai, 1933), 360, 367–68.

70. "JOKK stajio kara," *Shōkō ōrai* 2, no. 2 (January 1931): 44.

71. Niigata Shōkō Kaigisho, *Niigata jijō* (Niigata: Niigata Shōkō Kaigisho, 1934), 60, 63; Sapporo-shi, *Sapporo-shi shi. Bunka shakai-hen* (Sapporo: Sapporo-shi, 1958), 416; Satō Seijirō, *Sapporo an'nai* (Sapporo: Sōryū Shuppan, 1931), 10.

72. "JOKK stajio kara," 44–45

73. "Yobimono wa terebijon," *San'yō shinpō*, October 2, 1931, reprinted in San'yō Shinbunsha, *Shinbun kiji to shashin de miru sesō Okayama. Shōwa senzen, Meiji, Taishō-hen*, 245.

74. Posters are on display in a permanent exhibition at the Sapporo Beer Museum in Sapporo.

75. See, for example, Barbara Hamill Sato, *The New Japanese Woman: Modernity, Media, and Women in Interwar Japan* (Durham, NC: Duke University Press, 2003), 48.

76. Ibid., 1–7. See also Sarah Frederick, *Turning Pages: Reading and Writing Women's Magazines in Interwar Japan* (Honolulu: University of Hawai'i Press, 2006); and Maeda Ai, "The Development of Popular Fiction in the Late Taishō Era: Increasing Readership of Women's Magazines," in *Text and the City: Essays on Japanese Modernity*, ed. James Fujii (Durham, NC: Duke University Press, 2004), 163–222.

77. For this account, I am indebted to the pioneering research on professional working women in *The New History of Sapporo: Sapporo-shi Kyōiku Iinkai, Shin Sapporo-shi shi. Dai 4-kan* (Sapporo: Sapporo-shi, 1997), 682–83.

78. January 1, 1927, cited in ibid., 682.

79. Ibid., 684.

80. Sato, *The New Japanese Woman*, 7.

81. William O. Gardner, *Advertising Tower: Japanese Modernism and Modernity in the 1920s* (Cambridge, MA: Harvard University Asia Center, 2006), 151.

82. Sato, *The New Japanese Woman*, 115; Sapporo-shi Kyōiku Iinkai, *Shin Sapporo-shi shi. Dai 4-kan*, 684.

83. Sarah Frederick, introduction to *Turning Pages: Reading and Writing Women's Magazines in Interwar Japan* (Honolulu: University of Hawai'i Press, 2006).

84. Niigata Shōkō Kaigisho, *Niigata jijō*, 10–11.

85. Sato, *The New Japanese Woman*, 25.

86. Niigata Shōkō Kaigisho, *Niigata jijō*, 10–11. Kanazawa-shi, *Shōwa 14-nen Kanazawa shisei ippan* (Kanazawa: Kanazawa-shi, 1941), 28–29.

87. Sapporo-shi Kyōiku Iinkai, *Shin Sapporo-shi shi. Dai 4-kan*, 684–89.

88. Cindy I-Fen Cheng, "The Culture of the First: Asian Americans and the Discourse on Model Minority in Early-Cold-War America" (public presentation, University of Wisconsin-Madison, February 14, 2005).

89. *San'yō shinpō*, May 18, 1921, and January 15, 1927, both reprinted in San'yō Shinbunsha, *Shinbun kiji to shashin de miru sesō Okayama. Shōwa senzen, Meiji, Taishō-hen*, 182, 225.

90. Tenmaya Shashi Hensan Iinkai, *Tenmaya 150-nen shi*, 55.

91. Okada Itsusaburō, "Shokugyō sensen no fujin tenbō (6)," *Shōkō ōrai 2*, no. 9 (October 1931): 42.

92. The occupation of café waitress involved erotic (though not sexual) service, serving drinks, food, and companionship.

93. Okada Itsusaburō, "Shokugyō sensen no fujin tenbō (2)," *Shōkō ōrai 2*, no. 4 (April 1931),: 43–44.

94. Sato, *The New Japanese Woman*, 118–27.

95. Okada Itsusaburō, "Shokugyō sensen no fujin tenbō (2)," *Shōkō ōrai 2*, no. 4 (April 1931): 44.

96. Ibid., 42–43.

97. Manu Goswami, "Rethinking the Modular Nation Form: Toward a Socio-historical Conception of Nationalism," *Comparative Studies in Society and History* 44, no. 4 (October 2002): 770–99, quote on p. 775.

98. On right-wing modernism in national culture, see Hiromi Mizuno, *Science for the Empire: Scientific Nationalism in Modern Japan* (Stanford, CA: Stanford University Press, 2009); Alan Tansman, ed., *The Culture of Japanese Fascism* (Durham, NC: Duke University Press, 2009); Janis Mimura, *Planning for Empire: Reform Bureaucrats and the Japanese Wartime State* (Ithaca, NY: Cornell University Press, 2011).

EPILOGUE

1. Michael S. Sherry, *The Rise of American Air Power: The Creation of Armageddon* (New Haven, CT: Yale University Press, 1987).

2. *U.S. Strategic Bombing Survey: Summary Report (Pacific War)* (Washington, DC.: Government Printing Office, 1946), 16–17.

3. Ishida Yorifusa, "Japanese Cities and Planning in the Reconstruction Period: 1945–55," in *Rebuilding Urban Japan after 1945*, ed. Carola Hein, Jeffrey M. Diefendorf, and Ishida Yorifusa (New York: Palgrave Macmillan, 2003), 17–18.

4. Nagai Hideo and Ōba Yukio, *Hokkaido no 100-nen* (Tokyo: Yamakawa Shuppansha, 1999), 252.

5. *U.S. Strategic Bombing Survey*, 16–21; Kanazawa-shi, *Kanazawa-shi shi. Tsūshi-hen; 3.* (Kanazawa: Kanazawa-shi, 2006), 573–74; Shibata Hajime and Ōta Ken'ichi, *Okayama no 100-nen* (Tokyo: Yamakawa Shuppansha, 1986), 287–90.

6. *U.S. Strategic Bombing Survey*, 16–21; Ishida, "Japanese Cities and Planning in the Reconstruction Period," 17–18.

7. Kenji Hashimoto, *Class Structure in Contemporary Japan* (Melbourne, Australia: Trans Pacific Press, 2003), ix–x, 27–33.

8. A wonderful example of this is the twenty-volume series "The Urban Future," brought out in the early 1980s. Two volumes are entirely devoted to "city-making": *Atarashii toshizukuri* (vol. 2) and *Toshizukuri: sono aidia, hassō* (vol. 20); and the other books in the series are peppered with discussions of the concept. This series brought together an astonishing diversity of urban experts and professionals, including civil servants, leaders in community movements, architects, historians, urban planners, and prominent figures from the media and educational world. This army of people, largely drawn from provincial cities, was called upon to rethink the urban future. As the preface to the series announced, the mission of the project was to create a vision for the coming "age of the region." The political backdrop for this ambitious publishing venture was the succession of plans to decentralize economic production, beginning with Tanaka Kakuei's aborted "Plan to Redevelop the Japanese Archipelago." Other titles in the series included: *Town and Country* (vol. 3), *The City and the Citizen* (vol. 9), *The Urban Community* (vol. 10), *The City and Culture* (vol. 11), *The City and Education* (vol. 12), *The City and Public Servants* (vol. 13), *The City and the Regional Economy* (vol. 18), and *The Problem of*

the Metropolis (vol. 19). Isomura Eiichi et al., *Ashita no toshi*, 20 vols. (Tokyo: Chūō Hōki Shuppan, 1981).

9. Junjiro Takahashi and Noriyuki Sugiura, "The Japanese Urban System and the Growing Centrality of Tokyo in the Global Economy," in *Emerging Cities in Pacific Asia*, ed. Fu-chen Lo and Yue-man Teung (Tokyo: United Nations University Press, 1996), 103.

10. Jeremy D. Alden, Moriaki Hirohara, and Hirofumi Abe, "The Impact of Recent Urbanisation on Inner City Development in Japan," in *Planning for Cities and Regions in Japan*, ed. Philip Shapira, Ian Masser, and David W. Edgington (Liverpool, U.K.: Liverpool University Press, 1994), 34.

11. Andre Sorenson, *The Making of Urban Japan: Cities and Planning from Edo to the Twenty-first Century* (London: Routledge, 2002), 1; Cotton Mather and P. P. Karan, "Urban Landscapes of Japan," in *Urban Growth and Development in Asia. Volume I: Making the Cities*, ed. Graham P. Chapman, Ashok K. Dutt, and Robert W. Bradnock (Aldershot, U.K.: Ashgate, 1999), 402–5, esp. 402–3.

12. P. P. Karan, "The City in Japan," in *The Japanese City*, ed. P. P. Karan and Kristin Stapleton (Lexington: University of Kentucky Press, 1997), 22–23; Jeremy D. Alden and Hirofumi Abe, "Some Strengths and Weaknesses of Japanese Urban Planning," in *Planning for Cities and Regions in Japan*, ed. Philip Shapira, Ian Masser, and David W. Edgington (Liverpool, U.K.: Liverpool University Press, 1994), 13; Takahashi and Sugiura, "The Japanese Urban System and the Growing Centrality of Tokyo in the Global Economy," 101–43.

13. Okayama-shi, *Okayama-shi 100-nen shi. Ge-kan* (Okayama: Okayama-shi, 1991), 20–23, 473–86, 545–49; Shibata Hajime and Ōta Ken'ichi, *Okayama-ken no 100-nen* (Tokyo: Yamakawa Shuppansha, 1986), 318–25.

14. These publications have been invaluable resources for this book, as were the archives generously opened to me at the Municipal History Office. The ten-volume *Shin Sapporo-shi shi* (Sapporo: Sapporo-shi Kyōiku Iinkai, 1986–2002), represents an ambitious project of collaborative research and writing carried out by the staff of the Municipal History Office. Prior to the *New History of Sapporo City*, the office brought out the one-hundred-volume *Sapporo bunko* (Sapporo Library) series, with books ranging from studies of local music, the history of the entertainment district, Sapporo arts, and the history of local publishing. The same office maintains an extensive archive and publishes an in-house journal, *Sapporo rekishi*.

15. Nagai Hideo and Ōba Yukio, *Hokkaidō no 100-nen* (Tokyo: Yamakawa Shuppansha, 1999), 349–53; Sapporo-shi Kyōiku Iinkai, *Shin Sapporo-shi shi. Dai 5-kan. Tsūshi 5. Jō* (Sapporo: Sapporo-shi, 2002), 193–250, 423–40, 843–936.

16. Kanazawa-shi, *Kanazawa-shi shi. Tsūshi-hen; 3* (Kanazawa: Kanazawa-shi, 2006), 597–99; Ōshima Mitsuko, Satō Shigerō, Furumaya Tadao, and Mizoguchi Toshimaro, *Niigata-ken no 100-nen* (Tokyo: Yamakawa Shuppansha, 1990), 302–7.

17. "Shin Kanazawa kō," *Hokkoku shinbun*, January 5, 1979–May 11, 1979: cited in Motoyasu Hiroshi, "Chihō toshi Kanazawa: Sono rinkaku to shiteki bunseki no shikaku," in *Kindai Nihon no chihō toshi: Kanazawa/jōkamachi kara kindai toshi e*, ed. Hashimoto Tetsuya (Tokyo: Nihon Keizai Hyōronsha, 2006), 2–4.

This is a pathbreaking study on Kanazawa, an example of new work on the history of regional modernity. See also the latest Kanazawa City history: Kanazawa-shi, *Kanazawa-shi shi. Tsūshi-hen; 3* (Kanazawa: Kanazawa-shi, 2006), the first of twenty-two planned volumes in the series.

18. Ōshima Mitsuko, Satō Shigerō, Furumaya Tadao, and Mizoguchi Toshimaro, *Niigata-ken no 100-nen* (Tokyo: Yamakawa Shuppansha, 1990), 310–17; Niigata-shi, *Niigata-shi shi. Tsūshi-hen; 5* (Niigata: Niigata-shi, 1997), 205–8, 213–17, 303–6, 326–37.

19. Niigata-shi, *Niigata-shi shi. Tsūshi-hen; 5* (Niigata: Niigata-shi, 1997), 329.

20. Steven Kern, *The Culture of Time and Space, 1880–1918* (Cambridge, MA: Harvard University Press, 2003).

21. Michel de Certeau, *The Practice of Everyday Life*, vol. 1, trans. Steven Rendall (Berkeley: University of California Press, 1984), 95.

22. I have been inspired to think about urban space in this way through Henri Lefebvre's provocative theorization of the social production of space, *The Production of Space*, trans. Donald Nicholson-Smith (Oxford: Blackwell, 1991). I am also indebted to David Harvey and Manu Goswami for their development of Lefebvre's ideas, in Manu Goswami, *Producing India: From Colonial Economy to National Space* (Chicago: University of Chicago, 2004); and David Harvey, *The Condition of Postmodernity: An Enquiry into the Origins of Cultural Change* (Oxford, U.K.: Blackwell, 1989).

BIBLIOGRAPHY

Ajioka, Chiaki, and Jackie Menzies. *Modern Boy, Modern Girl: Modernity in Japanese Art, 1910–1935 = [Mobo, Moga]*. Sydney, NSW: Art Gallery of NSW, 1998.

Akimoto Ritsuo. *Nihon shakaigaku shi keisei katei to shisō kōzō*. Tokyo: Waseda Daigaku Shuppanbu, 1979.

Alden, Jeremy D., and Hirofumi Abe. "Some Strengths and Weaknesses of Japanese Urban Planning." In *Planning for Cities and Regions in Japan*, edited by Philip Shapira, Ian Masser, and David W. Edgington, 12–22. Liverpool, U.K.: Liverpool University Press, 1994.

Alden, Jeremy D., Moriaki Hirohara, and Hirofumi Abe. "The Impact of Recent Urbanisation on Inner City Development in Japan." In *Planning for Cities and Regions in Japan*, edited by Philip Shapira, Ian Masser, and David W. Edgington, 33–59. Liverpool, U.K.: Liverpool University Press, 1994.

Allinson, Gary. *Japanese Urbanism: Industry and Politics in Kariya, 1872–1972*. Berkeley: University of California Press, 1975.

Amano Ikuo. *Gakureki no shakai shi. Kyōiku to Nihon no kindai*. Tokyo: Shinchōsha, 1992.

Andō Yoshio, ed. *Kindai Nihon keizai shi yōran*. Tokyo: Tōkyō Daigaku Shuppankai, 1975.

Arima, Tatsuo. *The Failure of Freedom: A Portrait of Modern Japanese Intellectuals*. Cambridge, MA: Harvard University Press, 1969.

Bakhtin, Mikhail. *The Dialogic Imagination: Four Essays*. Translated by Caryl Emerson and Michael Holquist. Austin: University of Texas Press, 1981.

Beasley, W. G., and Edwin G. Pulleyblank. *Historians of China and Japan*. London: Oxford University Press, 1962.

Bester, Theodore C. *Neighborhood Tokyo*. Stanford, CA: Stanford University Press, 1989.

Brandt, Kim. *Kingdom of Beauty: Mingei and the Politics of Folk Art in Imperial Japan*. Durham, NC: Duke University Press, 2007.

Brownlee, John S. *Japanese Historians and the National Myths, 1600–1945*. Vancouver: University of British Columbia, 1997.

Burns, Susan L. *Before the Nation: Kokugaku and the Imagining of Community in Early Modern Japan*. Durham, NC: Duke University Press, 2003.

Castoriadis, Cornelius. *The Imaginary Institution of Society*. Boston: MIT Press, 1987.

Collcutt, Martin, Marius Jansen, and Isao Kumakura. *Cultural Atlas of Japan*. New York: Facts on File, 1988.

Conant, Ellen P., ed. *Challenging Past and Present: The Metamorphosis of Nineteenth-Century Japanese Art*. Honolulu: University of Hawai'i Press, 2006.

Dai Nihon Bīru Kabushiki Gaisha Sapporo Shiten, ed. *Sapporo bīru enkaku shi*. Tokyo: Dai Nihon Bīru Kabushiki Gaisha, 1936.

de Certeau, Michel. *The Practice of Everyday Life*. Vol. 1. Translated by Steven Rendall. Berkeley: University of California Press, 1984.

DeNitto, Rachel. *Uchida Hyakken: A Critique of Modernity and Militarism in Prewar Japan*. Cambridge, MA: Harvard University Asia Center, 2008.

Dirks, Nicholas B., Geoff Eley, and Sherry B. Ortner, eds. *Culture/Power/History: A Reader in Contemporary Social Theory*. Princeton, NJ: Princeton University Press, 1993.

Duus, Peter. "Whig History, Japanese Style: The Min'yūsha Historians and the Meiji Restoration." *Journal of Asian Studies* 33, no. 3 (May 1974): 415–36.

Ericson, Steven J. "Railroads in Crisis: The Financing and Management of Japanese Railway Companies during the Panic of 1890." In *Managing Industrial Enterprise: Cases from Japan's Prewar Experience*, edited by William Wray, 121–82. Cambridge, MA: Council on East Asian Studies, Harvard University, 1989.

———. *The Sound of the Whistle: Railroads and the State in Meiji Japan*. Cambridge, MA: Council on East Asian Studies, Harvard University, 1996.

Fabian, Johannes. *Time and the Other: How Anthropology Makes Its Object*. New York: Columbia University Press, 1983.

Figal, Gerald. *Civilization and Monsters: Spirits of Modernity in Meiji Japan*. Durham, NC: Duke University Press, 1999.

Foster, Michael Dylan. *Pandemonium and Parade: Japanese Monsters and the Culture of Yokai*. Berkeley: University of California Press, 2008.

Fowler, Edward. *The Rhetoric of Confession: Shishōsetsu in Early Twentieth-Century Japanese Fiction*. Berkeley: University of California Press, 1988.

Frédéric, Louis. *Japan Encyclopedia*. Translated by Käthe Roth. Cambridge, MA: Belknap Press of Harvard University Press, 2002.

Frederick, Sarah. *Turning Pages: Reading and Writing Women's Magazines in Interwar Japan*. Honolulu: University of Hawai'i Press, 2006.

Fujii, James A. *Complicit Fictions: The Subject in the Modern Japanese Prose Narrative*. Berkeley: University of California Press, 1993.

Fujimoto Noriaki. *Hokuriku no fūdo to bungaku: Kanazawa no bungaku o chūshin toshite*. Tokyo: Kasama Shoin, 1976.

Fujisawa Susumu. *Okayama no kōtsū*. Okayama: Nihon Bunkyō Shuppan, 1972.

Fujita Fukuo. *Kanazawa no bungaku*. Kanazawa: Hokkoku Shuppansha, 1971.

Furumaya Tadao. *Ura Nihon: Kindai Nihon o toinaosu*. Tokyo: Iwanami Shoten, 1997.

Gardner, William O. *Advertising Tower: Japanese Modernism and Modernity in the 1920s.* Cambridge, MA: Harvard University Asia Center, 2006.

Gluck, Carol. *Japan's Modern Myths: Ideology in the Late Meiji Period.* Princeton, NJ: Princeton University Press, 1985.

Gordon, Andrew. *Labor and Imperial Democracy in Prewar Japan.* Berkeley: University of California Press, 1991.

———. *A Modern History of Japan from Tokugawa Times to the Present.* New York: Oxford University Press, 2003.

Goswami, Manu. *Producing India: From Colonial Economy to National Space.* Chicago: University of Chicago Press, 2004.

———. "Rethinking the Modular Nation Form: Toward a Sociohistorical Conception of Nationalism." *Comparative Studies in Society and History* 44, no. 4 (October 2002): 770–99.

Hajima Tomoyuki. *Gekidōki no shinbun.* Tokyo: Nihon Tosho Sentā, 1997.

Hall, John Whitney. "Materials for Study of Local History." In *Studies in the Institutional History of Early Modern Japan*, edited by John Whitney Hall and Marius B. Jansen, 143–68. Princeton, NJ: Princeton University Press, 1968.

Hanes, Jeffrey E. *The City as Subject: Seki Hajime and the Reinvention of Modern Osaka.* Berkeley: University of California Press, 2002.

Haraguchi Kiyoshi and Un'no Fukuju. *Shizuoka-ken no 100-nen.* Tokyo: Yamakawa Shuppansha, 1982.

Harootunian, Harry. *Overcome by Modernity: History, Culture, and Community in Interwar Japan.* Princeton, NJ: Princeton University Press, 2001.

Harvey, David. *The Condition of Postmodernity: An Enquiry into the Origins of Cultural Change.* Oxford: Blackwell, 1989.

Hashimoto Kenji. *Class Structure in Contemporary Japan.* Melbourne, Australia: Trans Pacific Press, 2003.

Hashimoto Tetsuya. *Chihō dentōteki toshi no kasō minshū to minshū undō.* Tokyo: Kokusai Rengō Daigaku, 1980.

———, ed. *Kindai Nihon no chihō toshi: Kanazawa/jōkamachi kara kindai toshi e.* Tokyo: Nihon Keizai Hyōronsha, 2006.

Hashimoto Tetsuya and Hayashi Yūichi. *Ishikawa-ken no 100-nen.* Tokyo: Yamakawa Shuppansha, 1987.

Hatsuda Tōru. *Hyakkaten no tanjō: Meiji Taishō Shōwa no toshi bunka o enshutsu shita hyakkaten to kankōba no kindai shi.* Tokyo: Sanseidō, 1993.

Hattori Keijirō, "Ginza, soshite Ginzanaizēshon," *Toshi mondai* 67, no. 5 (May 1976): 63–80.

Hōgō Iwao, ed. *Me de miru Okayama no Taishō.* Okayama: Nihon Bunkyō Shuppan, 1986.

Hokkaidō-chō. *Shinsen Hokkaidō shi.* Dai 1-kan; Gaisetsu. Hokkaidō: Hokkaidō-chō, 1937.

Hokkaidō Sapporo Shihan Gakkō. *Hokkaidō Sapporo shihan gakkō 50-nen shi.* Sapporo: Hokkaidō Sapporo Shihan Gakkō, 1936.

Hokkai Shuppansha. *Hokkaidō nenkan, Shōwa 4-nen.* Sapporo: Hokkai Shuppansha, 1929.

Hokkai Taimususha. *Hokkai taimusu nenkan: Shōwa 15-nendo ban.* Sapporo: Hokkai Taimususha, 1939.

Hyakkaten Jigyō Kenkyūkai. *Hyakkaten no jissō.* Tokyo: Hyakkaten Jigyō Kenkyūkai, 1935.

Ikimi Kenkichi, ed. *Higohan kokuji shiryō.* Kumamoto: Kōshaku Hosokawake Hensanjo, 1932.

Ishida Yorifusa. "Japanese Cities and Planning in the Reconstruction Period: 1945–55." In *Rebuilding Urban Japan after 1945,* edited by Carola Hein, Jeffrey M. Diefendorf, and Ishida Yorifusa, 17–49. New York: Palgrave Macmillan, 2003.

Ishikawa-ken. *Ishikawa-ken shi. Gendai-hen 2.* Kanazawa: Ishikawa-ken, 1963.

———. *Ishikawa-ken shi. Gendai-hen 3.* Kanazawa: Ishikawa-ken, 1964.

Isomura Eiichi et al. *Ashita no toshi.* 20 vols. Tokyo: Chūō Hōki Shuppan, 1981.

Ivy, Marilyn. *Discourses of the Vanishing: Modernity, Phantasm, Japan.* Chicago: Chicago University Press, 1995.

Jinno Yuki. *Shumi no tanjō: Hyakkaten ga tsukutta teisuto.* Tokyo: Keisō Shobō, 1994.

"Jitsuroku Ishikawa-ken shi" Henshū Iinkai. *Jitsuroku Ishikawa-ken shi 1868–1989: Gekidō no Meiji, Taishō, Shōwa zen kiroku.* Kanazawa: Noto Insatsu Shuppanbu, 1991.

Jones, F. C. *Hokkaido: Its Present State of Development and Future Prospects.* London: Oxford University Press, 1958.

Junjiro Takahashi and Noriyuki Sugiura. "The Japanese Urban System and the Growing Centrality of Tokyo in the Global Economy." In *Emerging Cities in Pacific Asia,* edited by Fu-chen Lo and Yue-man Teung, 101–43. Tokyo: United Nations University Press, 1996.

Junkan Niigatasha. *Yakushin Niigata no zenbō.* Niigata: Junkan Niigatasha, 1936.

Kabashima Tadao, Hida Yoshifumi, and Yonekawa Akihiko, eds. *Meiji, Taishō shingo zokugo jiten.* Tokyo: Tōkyōdō Shuppan, 1996.

Kadokawa Nihon shi jiten. 2nd ed. Tokyo: Kadokawa Shoten, 1983.

Kamoi Yū. *Kanazawa shin fūkei.* Kanazawa: Hokkoku Shinbunsha Shuppanbu, 1933.

Kanazawa-shi. *Kanazawa.* Kanazawa: Kanazawa-shi, 1932.

———. *Kanazawa-shi shi. Tsūshi-hen; 3.* Kanazawa: Kanazawa-shi, 2006.

———. *Kanazawa shimin dokuhon.* Kanazawa: Kanazawa-shi, 1928.

———. *Kōhon Kanazawa-shi shi.* 14 vols. Kanazawa: Kanazawa-shi, 1916–1937.

———. *Shōwa 14-nen Kanazawa shisei ippan.* Kanazawa: Kanazawa-shi, 1941.

———. *Taishō 9-nen Kanazawa-shi tōkeisho.* Kanazawa: Kanazawa-shi, 1920.

Karan, P. P. "The City in Japan." In *The Japanese City,* edited by P. P. Karan and Kristin Stapleton, 12–39. Lexington: University of Kentucky Press, 1997.

Kato, Shūichi. *A History of Japanese Literature.* Tokyo: Kodansha International, 1979.

Katsura Matasaburō. *Okayama densetsu shū.* Okayama: Bunken Shobō, 1931.

Keene, Donald. *Dawn to the West: Japanese Literature of the Modern Era.* New York: Holt, Rinehart, and Winston, 1987.

Kern, Steven. *The Culture of Time and Space, 1880–1918.* Cambridge, MA: Harvard University Press, 2003.

Kihara Naohiko. *Hokkaidō bungaku shi: Taishō, Shōwa senzen-hen.* Sapporo: Hokkaidō Shinbunsha, 1976.

Kimura Sōhachi. *Gendai fūzoku chō.* Tokyo: Tōhō Shobō, 1952.

Kobayashi Takiji. *The Factory Ship and the Absentee Landlord.* Translated by Frank Motofuji. Seattle: University of Washington Press, 1973.

Kobayashi Teruya and Hokkoku Shinbunsha Henshūkyoku. *Hokuriku. Meisaku no butai.* Kanazawa: Hokkoku shinbunsha, 1991.

Kojima Jūzō. *Jidōsha no Okayama.* Okayama: Yoshida Shoten, 1993.

Kokusan Shinkō Hakurankai Hensanbu. *Kokusan shinkō hakurankai shi.* Sapporo: Hokkai Taimususha, 1927.

Komata Nobuo, Shimada Yoshifumi, Yazawa Kan, and Yokazawa Chiaki. *Nihon ryūkōka shi. Jō.* Tokyo: Shakai Shisōsha, 1994.

Kornicki, P. F. "Public Display and Changing Values: Early Meiji Exhibitions and Their Precursors." *Monumenta Nipponica* 49, no. 2 (Summer 1994): 167–96.

Koselleck, Reinhart. *Futures Past: On the Semantics of Historical Time.* Translated by Keith Tribe. New York: Columbia University Press, 2004.

Lefebvre, Henri. *The Production of Space.* Translated by Donald Nicholson-Smith. Oxford: Blackwell, 1991.

Lewis, Michael Lawrence. *Becoming Apart: National Power and Local Politics in Toyama.* Cambridge, MA: Harvard University Asia Center, 2000.

———. *Rioters and Citizens: Mass Protest in Imperial Japan.* Berkeley: University of California Press, 1990.

Lippit, Seiji. *Topographies of Japanese Modernism.* New York: Columbia University Press, 2002.

Long, Hoyt. *On Uneven Ground: Miyazawa Kenji and the Art of Making Place.* Stanford, CA: Stanford University Press, 2011.

Maeda Ai. *Text and the City: Essays on Japanese Modernity.* Edited by James Fujii. Durham, NC: Duke University Press, 2004.

Maki Hisao, ed. *Kanazawa shōkō kaigisho 70-nen shi.* Kanazawa: Kanazawa Shōkō Kaigisho, 1960.

———, ed. *Kanazawa shōkō kaigisho 100-nen shi.* Kanazawa: Kanazawa Shōkō Kaigisho, 1981.

Maruyama Atsushi, ed. *Mentarite Kanazawa: "Asobi" kara mieru mono.* Kanazawa: n.p., 1995.

———. "Toshi bunka no kyoten toshite no hyakkaten: Chihō toshi Kanazawa no hyakkaten." In *Mentarite Kanazawa: "Asobi" kara mieru mono.* Edited by Maruyama Atsushi, 221–52. Kanazawa, 1995.

Mather, Cotton, and P. P. Karan. "Urban Landscapes of Japan." In *Urban Growth and Development in Asia.* Vol. 1, *Making the Cities,* edited by Graham P. Chapman, Ashok K. Dutt, and Robert W. Bradnock, 402–15. Aldershot, U.K.: Ashgate, 1999.

McClain, James L. "Castle Towns and Daimyo Authority: Kanazawa in the Years 1583–1630." *Journal of Japanese Studies* 6, no. 2 (Summer 1980): 267–99.

McClain, James L., and Wakita Osamu, eds. *Osaka, the Merchant's Capital of Early Modern Japan*. Ithaca, NY: Cornell University Press, 1999.

Mehl, Margaret. "The Mid-Meiji 'History Boom': Professionalization of Historical Scholarship and Growing Pains of an Emerging Academic Discipline." *Japan Forum* 10, no. 1 (1998): 67–83.

———. "Scholarship and Ideology in Conflict: The Kume Affair, 1892." *Monumenta Nipponica* 48, no. 3 (Autumn 1993): 337–57.

Mimura, Janis. *Planning for Empire: Reform Bureaucrats and the Japanese Wartime State*. Ithaca, NY: Cornell University Press, 2011.

Minami Hiroshi and Shakai Shinri Kenkyūjo. *Shōwa bunka, 1925–1945*. Tokyo: Keisō Shobō, 1987.

———. *Taishō bunka, 1905–1927*. Tokyo: Keisō Shobō, 1987.

Miyoshi Shōichirō, Matsumoto Hiroshi, and Satō Masashi. *Tokushima-ken no 100-nen*. Tokyo: Yamakawa Shuppansha, 1992.

Mizuno, Hiromi. *Science for the Empire: Scientific Nationalism in Modern Japan*. Stanford, CA: Stanford University Press, 2009.

Mock, John. *Culture, Community, and Change in a Sapporo Neighborhood, 1925–1988: Hanayama*. Lewiston, NY: Edwin Mellon Press, 1999.

Mori, Eiichi. *Monogatari: Ishikawa no bungaku*. Kanazawa: Noto Insatsu Shuppanbu, 1985.

Morita Seiichi, Hanatachi Saburō, and Ikai Takaaki. *Kumamoto-ken no 100-nen*. Tokyo: Yamakawa Shuppansha, 1987.

Motoyasu Hiroshi. "Chihō toshi Kanazawa: Sono rinkaku to shiteki bunseki no shikaku." In *Kindai Nihon no chihō toshi: Kanazawa/jōkamachi kara kindai toshi e*, edited by Hashimoto Tetsuya, 1–108. Tokyo: Nihon Keizai Hyōronsha, 2006.

Nagai Hideo and Ōba Yukio. *Hokkaidō no 100-nen*. Tokyo: Yamakawa Shuppansha, 1999.

Nagayama Sadatomi. *Naigai hakurankai sōsetsu narabini wagakuni ni okeru bankoku hakurankai no mondai*. Tokyo: Suimei Shoin, 1933.

Nagayama Usaburō. *Okayama-ken. Tsūshi. Jō-hen*. Okayama: Okayama-ken, 1930.

——— *Okayama-ken. Tsūshi. Ka-hen*. Okayama: Okayama-ken, 1930.

Nakano Yoichi. "Negotiating Modern Landscapes." PhD diss., Harvard University, 2007.

Nenzi, Laura. *Excursions in Identity: Travel and the Intersection of Place, Gender, and Status in Edo Japan*. Honolulu: University of Hawai'i Press, 2008.

Nihon Daijiten Kankōkai. *Nihon kokugo daijiten*. Tokyo: Shōgakukan, 1975–1976.

Nihon Shinbun Kyōkai. *Chihō betsu Nihon shinbun shi*. Tokyo: Nihon Shinbun Kyōkai, 1956.

Nihon shinbun nenkan. Dai 17-kan. Tokyo: Nihon Tosho Sentā, 1986.

Niigata-ken. *Niigata-ken shi. Tsūshi-hen; 3*. Niigata: Niigata-ken, 1987.

———. *Niigata-ken shi. Tsūshi-hen; 7*. Niigata: Niigata-ken, 1988.

———. *Niigata-ken shi. Tsūshi-hen; 8*. Niigata: Niigata-ken, 1988.

———. *Taishō 13-nen Niigata-ken tōkeisho*. Niigata: Niigata-ken, 1924.

Niigata-shi. *Niigata-shi sangyō yōran.* Niigata: Niigata Sangyōka, 1929.

———. *Niigata-shi sangyō yōran.* Niigata: Niigata Sangyōka, 1937.

———. *Niigata-shi shi. Ge-kan.* Niigata: Niigata-shi, 1934.

———. *Niigata-shi shi. Jō-kan.* Niigata: Niigata-shi, 1934.

———. *Niigata-shi shi. Tsūshi-hen; 3.* Niigata: Niigata-shi, 1996.

———. *Niigata-shi shi. Tsūshi-hen; 4.* Niigata: Niigata-shi, 1997.

———. *Niigata-shi shi. Tsūshi-hen; 5.* Niigata: Niigata-shi, 1997.

Niigata Shisei Kisha Kurabu. *Niigata-shi an'nai.* Niigata: Niigata Shisei Kisha Kurabu, 1918.

Niigata-shi yōran. Niigata: Jitsugyō no An'naisha, 1926.

Niigata Shōkō Kaigisho. *Niigata jijō.* Niigata: Niigata Shōkō Kaigisho, 1934.

———. *Niigata shōkō kaigisho 60-nen shi.* Niigata: Niigata Shōkō Kaigisho, 1958.

Ninomiya Jun'ichi, Nagai Kō, and Niigata Nippōsha. *Niigata-ken no Shōwa shi.* Niigata: Niigata Nippō Jigyōsha, 1989.

Oka Chōhei. *Okayama konjaku ki.* Okayama: Okayama Minpōsha, 1935.

Okada Izumi. *Kankō Okayama.* Okayama: Hanayanagi Shinbunsha, 1936.

Okayama-ken. *Okayama-ken shi. Dai 10-kan.* Okayama: Okayama-ken, 1986.

———. *Okayama-ken shi. Dai 11-kan.* Okayama: Okayama-ken, 1987.

Okayama-shi. *Bizen Okayama.* Okayama: Okayama-shi, 1929.

———. *Okayama.* Okayama: Okayama-shi, 1927.

———. *Okayama-shi 100-nen shi. Ge-kan.* Okayama: Okayama-shi, 1991.

———. *Okayama-shi 100-nen shi. Jō-kan.* Okayama: Okayama-shi, 1989.

———. *Taishō 9-nen Okayama-shi tōkei nenpō.* Okayama: Okayama-shi, 1922.

Okayama-shi Kangyōka, *Okayama.* Okayama: Okayama-shi Kangyōka, 1927.

Ōshima Mitsuko, Satō Shigerō, Furumaya Tadao, and Mizoguchi Toshimaro. *Niigata-ken no 100-nen.* Tokyo: Yamakawa Shuppansha, 1990.

Ōtsuka Takatoshi. *Dai Sapporo an'nai.* Sapporo: Kinseisha, 1931.

Passin, Herbert. *Society and Education in Japan.* New York: Columbia University, 1965.

Richie, Donald. *A Hundred Years of Japanese Film: A Concise History, with a Selective Guide to DVDs and Videos.* Tokyo: Kodansha International, 2005.

Robertson, Jennifer. *Native and Newcomer: Making and Remaking a Japanese City.* Berkeley: University of California Press, 1994.

Roden, Donald. *Schooldays in Imperial Japan: A Study in the Culture of a Student Elite.* Berkeley: University of California Press, 1980.

Sand, Jordan. *House and Home in Modern Japan: Architecture, Domestic Space, and Bourgeois Culture, 1880–1930.* Cambridge, MA: Harvard University Asia Center, 2005.

Sangyō to Kankō no Dai Hakurankai Kyōsankai. *Kanazawa-shi shusai sangyō to kankō no dai hakurankai kyōsankai shi.* Kanazawa: Sangyō to Kankō no Dai Hakurankai Kyōsankai, 1933.

Sanseidō Henshūjo. *Konsaisu jinmei jiten. Nihonhen.* Tokyo: Sanseidō, 1976.

San'yō Shimpōsha. *Shōwa 12-nen Sanyō nenkan bessatsu. Okayama-ken 70-nen shi.* Okayama: San'yō Shimpōsha, 1936.

San'yō Shinbunsha. *Shinbun kiji to shashin de miru sesō Okayama. Shōwa senzen, Meiji, Taishō-hen.* Okayama: San'yō Shinbunsha Shuppankyoku, 1990.

Sapporo Tanuki Kōji Shōtengai Shōgyō Kumiai. *Sapporo tanuki kōji hatten shi.* Sapporo: Sapporo Tanuki Kōji Shōtengai Shōgyō Kumiai, 1938.

Sapporo-ku. *Sapporo-ku shi.* Sapporo: Sapporo-ku, 1911.

Sapporo-shi. *Sapporo-shi shi. Bunka shakai hen.* Sapporo: Sapporo-shi, 1958.

Sapporo-shi Kyōiku Iinkai. *Sapporo jinmei jiten.* Sapporo: Sapporo-shi, 1993.

———. *Sapporo seikatsu bunka shi. Taishō, Shōwa, senzen-hen.* Sapporo: Sapporo-shi, 1986.

———. *Shin Sapporo-shi shi. Dai 2-kan.* Sapporo: Sapporo-shi, 1991.

———. *Shin Sapporo-shi shi. Dai 3-kan.* Sapporo: Sapporo-shi, 1994.

———. *Shin Sapporo-shi shi. Dai 4-kan.* Sapporo: Sapporo-shi, 1997.

———. *Shin Sapporo-shi shi. Dai 5-kan. Tsūshi 5. Jō.* Sapporo: Sapporo-shi, 2002.

———. *Shin Sapporo-shi shi.* 10 vols. Sapporo: Sapporo-shi, 1986–2002.

Sapporo-shi Kyōiku Iinkai Bunka Shiryōshitsu. *Moiwa, Maruyama.* Sapporo: Sapporo-shi, 1980.

———. *Sapporo rekishi chizu. Shōwa-hen.* Sapporo: Sapporo-shi, 1981.

———. *Sapporo rekishi chizu. Taishō-hen.* Sapporo: Sapporo-shi, 1980.

Sapporo-shi Shōgakkō Kyōiku Kenkyūkai Chirika Kenkyūbu. *Sapporo-shi chiri dokuhon.* Sapporo: Sapporo-shi Kyōikukai, 1927.

Sato, Barbara Hamill. *The New Japanese Woman: Modernity, Media, and Women in Interwar Japan.* Durham, NC: Duke University Press, 2003.

Satō Ensaku. *Funae no hana.* Niigata: Tōhoku Jihō, 1936.

Satō Seijirō, *Sapporo an'nai.* Sapporo: Sōryū Shuppan, 1931.

Seidensticker, Edward. *Low City, High City: Tokyo from Edo to the Earthquake.* New York: Knopf, 1983.

———. *Tokyo Rising: The City since the Great Earthquake.* New York: Knopf, 1990.

Sherry, Michael S. *The Rise of American Air Power: The Creation of Armageddon.* New Haven, CT: Yale University Press, 1987.

Shibata Hajime and Ōta Ken'ichi. *Okayama-ken no 100-nen.* Tokyo: Yamakawa Shuppansha, 1986.

Shūkan Asahi hyakka. Nihon no rekishi. 106: Hakurankai kindaika to gijutsu iten. Tokyo: Asahi Shinbunsha, 1988.

Shunkan Niigatasha. *Yakushin Niigata no zenbō.* Niigata: Shunkan Niigatasha, 1936.

Silverberg, Miriam. *Changing Song: The Marxist Manifestos of Nakano Shigeru.* Princeton, NJ: Princeton University Press, 1990.

———. "Constructing the Japanese Ethnography of Modernity." *Journal of Asian Studies* 51, no. 1 (February 1992): 30–54.

Smith, Henry D. "The Edo-Tokyo Transition: In Search of Common Ground." In *Japan in Transition: From Tokugawa to Meiji*, edited by Marius B. Jansen and Gilbert Rozman, 347–76. Princeton, NJ: Princeton University Press, 1986.

———. "Tokyo and London: Comparative Conceptions of the City." In *Japan: A Comparative View*, edited by Albert Craig. Princeton, NJ: Princeton University Press, 1979, 49–104.

———. "Tokyo as an Idea: An Exploration of Japanese Urban Thought until 1945." *Journal of Japanese Studies* 4, no. 1 (Winter 1978): 45–80.

Sorenson, Andre. *The Making of Urban Japan: Cities and Planning from Edo to the Twenty-first Century.* London: Routledge, 2002.

Suzuki Shōzō. *Nihon no shuppankai o kizuita hitobito.* Tokyo: Kashiwa Shobō, 1985.

Suzuki Zensaku. *Chihō hattatsu shi to sono jinbutsu: Shikoku no maki.* Takamatsu: Kyōdo Kenkyūsha, 1942.

Taguchi Shōichirō. *Akita-ken no 100-nen.* Tokyo: Yamakawa Shuppansha, 1983.

Takahashi, Junjiro, and Noriyuki Sugiura. "The Japanese Urban System and the Growing Centrality of Tokyo in the Global Economy." In *Emerging Cities in Pacific Asia,* edited by Fu-chen Lo and Yue-man Teung, 101–43. Tokyo: United Nations University Press, 1996.

Takakura Shinichirō. *Hokkaidō no rekishi.* Sapporo: Nihon Hōsō Kyōkai Hokkaidō Shibu, 1933.

Takaoka Hiroyuki. "Kankō, kōsei, ryokō: Fashizumuki no tsūrizumu." In *Bunka to fashizumu: Senjiki Nihon ni okeru bunka no kōbō,* edited by Akasaka Shirō and Kitagawa Kenzō, 9–52. Tokyo: Nihon Keizai Hyōronsha, 1993.

Tanaka, Stefan. *Japan's Orient: Rendering Pasts into History.* Berkeley: University of California Press, 1993.

Tansman, Alan, ed. *The Culture of Japanese Fascism.* Durham, NC: Duke University Press, 2009.

Taylor, Charles. *Modern Social Imaginaries.* Durham, NC: Duke University Press, 2004.

Tenmaya Shashi Hensan Iinkai. *Tenmaya 150-nen shi.* Okayama: Tenmaya, 1979.

Thal, Sarah. *Rearranging the Landscapes of the Gods: The Politics of a Pilgrimage Site in Japan, 1573–1912.* Chicago: University of Chicago Press, 2005.

Tokyo Shisei Chōsakai. *Nihon toshi nenkan. 1.* Tokyo: Tōkyō Shisei Chōsakai, 1931.

———. *Nihon toshi nenkan. 2.* Tokyo: Tōkyō Shisei Chōsakai, 1933.

Torrance, Richard. *The Fiction of Tokuda Shūsei, and the Emergence of Japan's New Middle Class.* Seattle: University of Washington Press, 1994.

———. "Literacy and Literature in Osaka, 1890–1940." *Journal of Japanese Studies* 31, no. 1 (Winter 2005): 27–60.

———. "Literacy and Modern Literature in the Izumo Region, 1880–1930." *Journal of Japanese Studies* 22, no. 2 (Summer 1996): 327–62.

Tseng, Alice Y. *The Imperial Museums of Meiji Japan: Architecture and the Art of the Nation.* Seattle: University of Washington Press, 2008.

Tsurumi Shunsuke. *Narikin tenka: 1912–1923.* Tokyo: Chikuma Shobō, 1962.

Tsutsui, William M. *Manufacturing Ideology: Scientific Management in Twentieth-Century Japan.* Princeton, NJ: Princeton University Press, 2001.

Unno Hiroshi, ed. *Kikai no Metoroporisu.* Tokyo: Heibonsha, 1990.

U.S. Strategic Bombing Survey: Summary Report (Pacific War). Washington, DC: Government Printing Office, 1946.

Utani Takeji. *Okayama no yūran.* Okayama: Saikinsha, 1929.

Vaporis, Constantine N. *Breaking Barriers: Travel and the State in Early Modern Japan*. Cambridge, MA: Council on East Asian Studies, Harvard University, 1994.

Watanabe Shun'ichi. *Toshi keikaku no tanjō: Kokusai hikaku kara mita Nihon kindai toshi keikaku*. Tokyo: Kashiwa Shobō, 1993.

Westney, D. Eleanor. *Imitation and Innovation: The Transfer of Western Organizational Patterns to Meiji Japan*. Cambridge, MA: Harvard University Press, 1987.

Wigen, Kären. *The Making of a Japanese Periphery, 1750–1920*. Berkeley: University of California Press, 1995.

Williams, Raymond. *The Country and the City*. London: Chatto and Windus, 1973.

Yamamoto Taketoshi. *Kindai Nihon no shinbun dokushasō*. Tokyo: Hōsei Daigaku Shuppankyoku, 1981.

Yamazaki Masatada. *Yokoi Shōnan ikō*. Tokyo: Nissin Shoin, 1942.

Yazaki, Takeo. *Social Change and the City: From Earliest Times through the Industrial Revolution*. Translated by David L. Swain. Tokyo: Japan Publications, 1968.

Yonemoto, Marcia. *Mapping Early Modern Japan: Space, Place, and Culture in the Tokugawa Period, 1603–1868*. Berkeley: University of California Press, 2003.

———. "The 'Spatial Vernacular' in Tokugawa Maps." *Journal of Asian Studies* 59, no. 3 (August 2000): 647–66.

Yoshimi Shun'ya. *Toshi no doramaturugī: Tōkyō sakariba no shakai shi*. Tokyo: Kōbundō, 1987.

Young, Louise. *Japan's Total Empire: Manchuria and the Culture of Wartime Imperialism*. Berkeley: University of California Press, 1998.

INDEX

city-country binary, railway development affecting, 584–88

city idea, 11–12, 15, 23, 115, 139, 147, 157, 186–87, 191, 236–38, 253–55, 256, 283n8; the city as a machine, 21, 215, 257; ideology of the metropolis, 37, 238, 252–53, 255, 257; interwar period and, 3, 6, 12, 13–14, 105, 142, 179, 236–37, 238, 252, 253–54; universalism and particularism encompassed in, 191, 204, 238; urban futurism, 190–91, 204, 254–55. *See also* urban biographies; urban-centrism; urban expansionism; urbanization

city parks, 101, 162, 207, 227

city planning, 23, 42, 105, 110–11, 125–26, 203, 240, 255–56; City Planning Law (*toshi keikaku hō*) of 1923, 101; city planning movement, 83, 101, 108–9, 115, 134, 142, 196, 203–4

Colonization Bureau, 162

communications infrastructure, 4, 110, 136; radio, 222–24, 236; television, 224

community: connecting to the past through local history institutions, 150, 153, 157, 165, 172, 173, 176, 185; as a culture formation, 164–65, 186–87; recreating a sense of, 141–42, 143, 168, 171; uniqueness of local culture (*see also* folk festivals), 170, 173, 185, 186

community building (*machizukuri*), 144, 190, 237, 238, 245, 249, 283n8

consciousness of the modern, 92, 109–10, 152; and railways, 91, 92

construction industry, 162, 194, 201, 211, 248; construction boom, 20, 21–23, 90, 123, 205, 217–18. *See also* industrial development and production

cosmopolitanism, 240

country. *See* rural areas

Cuckoo (*Hototogisu*), 76–77

cultural geography, 39–42, 45, 53–54, 61, 81–82; centers and peripheries, 13, 33, 41, 42, 81–82, 84, 186, 254

culture industry, 189

danchi (public housing), 247

demographic movements, 22, 41–42, 271n63. *See also* urbanization

DeNitto, Rachel, 264n11

department stores, 199–200, 212; Tenmaya department store, 232–33

Dōshisha University, 25

dystopia, and gender (*see also* gender roles), 224–29, 236–37

Earth, The, Shimada Seijirō, 58–60

Echigo Railway, 100, 270n23

economic decline: Japan's Great Depression, 196; nationwide bank failures of 1927, 196; postwar depression, 26–27, 136

economic development: interwar boom, 17, 18, 23–26, 192, 204; and the Pacific coast, 8, 83–84, 86–87, 90, 91, 245–46, 249–51; rags-to-riches stories, 24–25; railway-led development (*see also* railways), 84, 115, 137; service economy growth, 189, 229, 255; trade (*see also* exports; ports), 17, 161, 162–63; World War One and, 16–20, 23, 24, 32. *See also* communications infrastructure; industrial development and production; transportation

Edo, 20, 38, 177–78; Edo castle, 193

Edo period, 160–61, 162

Edogawa Rampo, "Hell of Mirrors," 215

Edo period, 163, 170, 182, 206, 218, 247, 262n26, 276n64. *See also* Meiji government

educational system, 39–43, 187, 254; girls' education, 230; Meiji government policies, 37, 39–40; secondary schools, 40, 42, 43–44, 158; university track, 40. *See also* higher education; intellectuals

electrification, 20, 218

Emi Suiin, 48

emperor(s), 4; Emperor Jimmu, 180, 182

Enlightenment News, 63–64. See also *Hokkoku shinbun*

Euro-American internationalism, 240

Euro-centric universalism, 153

Exhibition on Industry and Tourism, Kanazawa, 222

exhibitions and fairs, 205, 206–8; demonstrating local identity, 208–14;

industrial fairs, 188, 190, 204–5, 209,
211–13, 215; Meiji era, 206–7
exhibitions and fairs—by locality:
Hokkaido, 208–9, 211, 216; Kanazawa,
205, 206, 208, 222; Okayama, 205, 221;
Osaka, 205; Sapporo, 205–6, 208–9
exports, 18, 26, 91, 132, 189, 204, 211, 247,
260n6, 277n71
expositions and industrial fairs, 204–14

factory employment and the working class,
8, 9, 15, 19, 26, 28, 31, 40, 106–7, 120,
137, 148; dekasegi labor system, 82, 84
factory production, 5, 18, 19, 120;
transforming the rural landscape, 134–35
factory towns, 120–30, 134
family, social future of, 236
famous places. See meisho (famous sites
and places)
fashion, 193, 224; western dress, 225
female employment, 229–31, 232, 282n92;
discriminating stereotypes, 234–35;
professional workingwoman, 231, 233,
234. See also gender roles; women
festivals: festival of Gongen, 169; Obon
"festival of the dead," 30, 171; "opening
of the river" (kawa hiraki) festival, 171,
172; Sapporo Snow Festival, 249;
Shinto god of the road festival (dōsojin
matsuri), 172–73
"Fifty-Three Views of the Tokaidō," 202
financial decline. See economic decline
financial industry, 37
folklore groups and narratives, 166–71,
179, 180–81; folklore enthusiasts,
168–71. See also festivals
Fowler, Edward, 51
Frederick, Sara, 229
Fuji, Mount, 176
Fuji Goro the hermit legend, 158–59
Fujin kōron (Ladies' Review), 227
future orientation, 187, 188–90, 203;
chronotopes of future and past, 13, 165,
189, 195; cult of the new, 188, 189, 190,
192–93; dystopia and gender, 226–27,
236–37; "Ginza-ization," 193, 197,
200, 203, 214, 238; Ginza symbolic of,
193–97; "new meisho," 190, 219;

"posthistory" analysis, 197; urban
futurism, 190–91, 204. See also
technical revolution and technotopia

Gakushūin school, 51
garden cities (den'en toshi), 114, 174, 272n65
Gardner, William, 229
geisha, 25, 193–94, 208, 239, 250; narratives
about, 54–55, 193
gender roles: dystopia and gender, 224–29,
236–37; the "modern woman/girl"
(moga), 8, 201, 226, 228–29, 235–36, 237,
239, 256; shifts in, 229–36. See also
women
Geography Reader (Sapporo chiri dokuhon),
161, 162
Ginza, 16, 194–95, 238, 256; café culture, 195;
Ginbura (to "hang out in the Ginza"),
193; "Ginza-ization," 193, 197, 200, 203,
214, 238; symbolic of modernity, 193–98
Glacier journal, 78
global economy, 4, 83
globalism, 257
Gluck, Carol, 91
Gōdō shinbun newspaper, 68
Great Exhibition on Asian Development
and National Defense, 205
Great History of Japan, 151
Great Kantō Earthquake, 194, 195, 196, 198
Great War. See World War One
Guide to Greater Sapporo, A, 110, 112, 193

haiku movement, 45, 73, 75–77. See also
poets and poetry
Hakodate Honsen Railroad, 118, 119
Hakusan Park, Niigata, 181
Hall of Science, 235
Handbook to Niigata City, 216–17
Hara Takashi, 59
Hattori Keijirō, 193
Heian period, 178; agricultural estate
(shōen), 158
Higashi Sapporo station, 123
higher education, 5, 13, 45, 61, 70, 71, 81, 84,
255; expansion during World War One,
43; higher education for women, 230;
institutions creating a cultural
geography, 39–42, 45, 53–54, 61, 81–82;

higher education, *(continued)*
  ranking of institutions, 40–41, 46;
  Tokyo as center of, 37–38, 44, 48–49,
  53, 56–58, 60–61, 195. *See also*
  educational system
Hiragishi hamlet, Sapporo, 128–29
historical factors, 141, 253–54, 257
historical materialism, 202
Historiographic Institute, 153
Hiwa Mountain, Niigata, 181
Hokkaido, 8, 49, 117; industrial
  development and exhibitions, 208–9,
  211, 216; literary and cultural
  movements, 49–50, 66–67, 75–76, 77;
  Sorachi, 210–11; urban biographies,
  159–63. *See also* Sapporo
Hokkaido University, 76, 132, 213, 228,
  249; as Hokkaido Imperial University
  (imperial era), 8, 41, 213, 228, 249. *See*
  also Sapporo Agricultural College;
  universities
Hokkaido Special Products Fair, 215–16
Hokkaido Yearbook, 50
Hokkai taimusu newspaper, 66–67, 227–28
Hokkoku nippō newspaper, 78
Hokkoku shinbun newspaper, 60, 63–64,
  65, 231
Hokuetsu Railway, 95, 96
Hokuriku Federation of Poetry groups,
  78–79
Hokuriku mainichi newspaper, 65
Hokuriku Railway, 90, 110, 268n9
Hokusai, *Thirty-Six Views of Mount Fuji*,
  177
hometown *(kokyō)*, metaphor and imagery,
  53, 80–81, 191, 245, 256
hometown education *(kyodo kyoiku)*, 143,
  148–49, 154, 159, 164, 187
homogenization, 252

ideology of the metropolis. *See* city idea
Ikuta Chōkō, 59
Imperial Palace, 194
independence, Japanese, 4
industrial capitalism, 3–4, 6, 22, 83–84,
  263n1; rural colonization and, 83
industrial development and production,
  17–19, 21, 102, 105, 130, 153, 253;

construction industry, 20–23, 90, 123,
  162, 194, 201, 205, 211, 217–18, 218, 248;
  exports, 18, 26, 91, 132, 189, 204, 211,
  247, 260n6, 277n71; industrial
  revolution, 4–6, 16–17, 236; policies, 4;
  rubber production, 122, 123, 211;
  shokusan kōgyo (industrial promotion),
  4; steel production, 211. *See also*
  construction; economic development;
  factory production; technical
  revolution and technotopia; *and by city*
industrial fairs, 188, 190, 204–5, 207, 209,
  211–13, 215–16
industrial satellites and factory suburbs,
  118–24, 129, 134, 271n72
inflation. *See* price inflation (bōtō)
Ikku Jippensha, *Shank's Mare*, 177
Inoue Michiyasu, 47–48
intellectuals, 73, 81, 193, 195; intellectual
  circuits uniting Tokyo and provinces,
  44–50; rise of, 5, 255; Tokyo as center
  of, 37–38, 44, 48–49, 53, 56–58, 60–61,
  195. *See also* higher education; literary
  and cultural movements; print media
interwar period: the city idea and, 3, 6, 12,
  13–14, 105, 142, 179, 236–37, 238, 252,
  253–54; development of regionalism
  during, 133, 144, 148, 185, 237; dualistic
  constructions of city and country
  during, 135; economic boom during, 17,
  18, 23–26, 192, 204; modernist
  movements during (*see also* modernity),
  240; population growth, 136; urban
  expansion during, 115, 240, 253
Irisawa Ryōgetsu, 79
Ishikawa prefecture, cultural
  institutions, 66
Ishikawa prefecture, 15–16
Ishikawa shinbun. See also *Hokkoku*
  shinbun
Ishikawa shinbun newspaper, 63–64
Izumi Kyōka, 39, 54; *Noble Blood, Heroic*
  Blood, 54–55
Iwakura Mission, 277n70

Japan, 87*map*, 159–61; government policies,
  4, 47; modern industrial economy in,
  15, 16–23, 193, 263n1; national history

literary magazines, 51–52, 76–77, 78
local branding, 209–10, 255
local culture, 164, 172, 173; honoring ancient regimes, 175–77, 179–80; interwar period movements, 144; temporal narratives of community, 164, 165–66; variation in, 62. *See also* folklore groups and narratives; regionalism
local history movement, 10, 13, 15, 19, 57, 145–48, 150–51, 152–53, 166, 175, 187, 284n14; commercialized aspects, 185; community institutions and, 150, 153, 157; regionalization and, 188. *See also* urban biographies
local identity: demonstrated by exhibitions and fairs, 208–14; multiple temporalities and, 147, 154, 160–61, 185, 185–86, 190–91, 204, 207; national identity and, 175–76, 204
localism, 78, 79, 207, 273n2; local-development movement, 203. *See also* city idea; regionalism
local specialty products (*meibutsu*), 169–70
locomotives. *See* railways; roads; traffic issues; vehicles

machine displays and cults, 209, 211–13, 215–17, 222, 236, 239, 240, 242
Manchukuo, Manchuria, 109
Manu Goswami, 238, 268n3, 277–78n76
Manyōshū, 20, 151
Masaoka Shiki, 75, 76–77, 265n27
Matsumae domain, 160–61
Matsuo Bashō, *The Road to the Far North*, 177
media: mass media, 37; radio, 145, 211, 222–23; regional press, 61–69; Tokyo publishing industry, 52, 61, 62, 64, 65, 66, 67. *See also* print media
meibutsu (local specialty products) 169–70
Meiji era: exhibitions and fairs, 206–7; news services, 64
Meiji government, 6, 16, 84, 162; education policies, 37, 39–40; growth agenda, 37,

50, 153–54, 204; news services (Teitsū, Dentsū). *See also* Edo period; Tokugawa period
Meiji railway system, 86–87
meisho (famous sites and places), 175–85, 256; the "new *meisho*," 190, 219
metropolis. *See* city idea; second-tier cities; urban-centrism; urban expansionism; urbanization
middle class, 5, 8, 119, 279n9; as agents of the new, 189–90; hegemony of, 189, 226, 245
military, *fukoku kyōhei* (rich country; strong military), 4; militarism and ultranationalism, 238–39
"mindless boosterism," 114
Mitani Takamasa, 44, 45–46
Mitsuda Shinzō, 46
Mizuno, Hiromi, 21, 188
modern woman/girl (*moga*), 8, 201, 226, 228–29, 235–36, 237, 239, 256. *See also* female employment
modernism/modernity (*modanizumu*), 10, 21–22, 257; architecture of modernism, 199–202, 207, 208–9, 216, 218–19, 222; consciousness of the modern, 92, 109–10, 152; convergence narrative, 13, 135, 191, 203–4, 214, 236, 252, 254, 257; Ginza symbolic of modernity, 193–97; modernist movements (*see also* Japanese modernism), 240; modernist movements/modernology (*kōgengaku*), 3–7, 11, 21, 83, 93, 99, 192–93, 194, 197–200, 236, 238; railways and, 91, 92; tenacity of, 240–41; the modern cityscape, 199–203. *See also* city idea; future orientation; industrial capitalism; technical revolution and technotopia
Modern Kanazawa magazine, 198, 225
Moiwa, Sapporo, 124–29
"monolithic urban system," 246–48, 252; historical factors, 253–55
Mori ōgai, *Gan* (Wild Geese), 22, 265n33
multiple temporalities, and local identity, 147, 154, 160–61, 185, 185–86, 190–91, 204, 207

pilgrimage, 178
poets and poetry, 44, 57, 73, 76, 264nn18–
19, 265n27; haiku movement, 45, 73,
75–77; poetry magazines, 70, 75–76,
79; regional poetry movement, 76–79.
See also literary and cultural
movements
popular protest, 9, 27–28, 31–32, 148,
262n25
population. *See* demographic movements
ports, 9, 20, 86, 162–63. *See also* trade
postwar period, 49, 241, 245–46, 251
poverty: educational access lacking, 40;
rural poor, 41; working poor, 31, 127
power and utilities, electric power, 20
prefectural capitals, 7
preindustrial culture: narratives of, 160,
165–66, 167; preservation of, 277n70.
See also folklore groups and narratives
price inflation (bōtō), 9, 19–20, 79, 96, 128,
219, 262n30; land inflation, 96, 252; rice
prices, 9, 27, 29–31
print media, 5, 6, 13, 61–62, 69–70, 178,
195; authors (*see also* by name), 52, 58,
73; publishing culture, 63; travel
literature, 177; university publications,
51–52. *See also* newspapers and
magazines; publishing industry
print media, regional and local presses,
61–69, 62–69; Kanazawa, 63–65;
Niigata, 66; Okayama, 67–68, 221;
Osaka, 62, 67, 68; Sapporo, 66–67;
Sapporo, 66–67
professionalism, rise of, 5
professional workingwoman, 231, 233, 234
Progressive Party, 63, 64
property inflation, 96, 252
Prospects for Niigata's Advance, 109, 110
protests, popular protests, 9, 27–28, 31–32,
148, 262nn25–26
provincial aristocracy, 53
publishing industry, 5, 6, 58, 61, 81, 195,
283n8; newspaper industry, 6, 62, 64,
65–66, 68, 266n56. *See also* print media

radio, 145, 211, 222–23
rail communications, 88
"railroad age," 99

railways, 4, 86, 87, 103, 245, 268–69n9,
269n21; and consciousness of the
modern, 91, 92; during the interwar
period, 134; high-speed trains, 219–20,
250–51; networks of, 91, 255; producing
social and economic space, 84–89; the
railroad revolution, 85–91; railway-led
development, 84, 115, 137; the railways
grid, 91–98, 94*map*; regional effects and
development, 91, 94*map*, 98–103, 129
recreational space: city parks, 101, 162, 207,
227; rural areas as, 137
red-light districts, 122–23
regionalism: development during interwar
period, 76, 133, 144, 148, 185, 237, 253;
regionalist movements, 143, 186–87,
237, 255. *See also* localism
regional presses, 61–69, 62–69
rice: cultivation of, 133, 137, 216; economic
benefits, 38, 163; rising prices, 9, 19,
27–31; rice riots, 9, 11, 15, 27, 29–31; rice
products, 120, 170, 210, 213; shortages,
9, 27; subsidies, 262n30; taxes on, 93;
urban expansion reducing rice paddies,
106, 108, 137
risshin shusse (rising in the world), 40
roads and highways, 86–87, 89, 109, 156,
219; highway network, 177; metaphor
of, 156, 202; Tōkaidō highway, 89*map*,
176, 177, 202
Roden, Donald, 46–47
rubber production, 122, 123, 211. *See also*
industrial development
rural areas: colonizing of, 83, 85, 254; as
recreational space, 137; social
conditions, 78–79; transformed by
factories, 134–35; villages and villagers
as "the other", 84, 203
rural industrialization, 83
Russian Revolution, 78
Russo-Japanese War, 64

Sakai Toshihiko, 59
sakariba (urban entertainment and
commercial centers), 37, 198–99
salaryman, 232, 256
samurai caste, 15–16, 38, 40, 41, 93, 109–10,
163, 178, 184, 206, 250

San'yō Railway Company, 90
San'yō shinpō newspaper, 19, 25, 31, 67–68, 219–21
Sapporo, 7, 30, *119*, 126, 174, 245, 246, 262n30; economic boom in, 17; exhibitions and fairs, 205–6, 208–9; expansion and suburbs, 108, 109, 116–17, 119*map*, 135; expositions, 204, 209–10, 211–13; history, 8; industrial development, 116–17, 118, 120, 130–31; industrial satellites (factory towns), 120–30; literary and cultural movements, 10, 39, 50, 76–77, 78; located outside the Tōkaidopolis, 246, 249; modernization, 21; Nakajima Park, 205–6; print media, 66–67; railway development and, 88, 90, 91; a university town, 77, 124; urban biographies, 8, 161–62, 213. *See also* Hokkaido; Sapporo agricultural suburbs; Sapporo factory/industrial suburbs; Sapporo residential suburbs
Sapporo Agricultural College, 25, 41, 76, 128. *See also* Hokkaido University
Sapporo agricultural suburbs, 132–33, 134; Sapporo village, *119*, 130, 131–32, 133; Shinoro, 133
Sapporo Beer, 227, 249
"Sapporo-centrism," 112
Sapporo factory/industrial suburbs, 118–22, 124; Kotoni, 118, 119*map*, 120, 122, 123–24, 134; Shiroishi, 122, 124, 129, 134; Teine, 118, 119*map*, 120, 121, 122, 123–24, 134, 271n62
Sapporo residential suburbs, *119*, 126–30; Kotoni, 120, 122; Moiwa residential development, 124–29. *See also* Toyohira (Sapporo suburb)
Sapporo Snow Festival, 249
Sapporo village, *119*, 130, 131–32, 133
Sasaki Kuni, 47
Sato, Barbara, *The New Japanese Woman*, 227, 229
Satō Giryū, 58
Sea of Japan coast, 8, 31, 86, 87*map*, 109, 167, 181, 250
Sea of Japan Regional Culture Exhibit, 149, 150

second-tier cities, 7, 88, 241, 252, 260n7; and the "monolithic urban system," 246–48, 252. *See also* localism; regionalism; *and by city*
Seidensticker, Edward, 195
service economy, 189, 229, 255; gender and, 225–26
sex trades, 122–23
shichōson (city-town-village), 6, 44
Shida Sōkin, 44, 45
Shimada Seijirō, 58, 60–61; *The Earth*, 58–60
Shima Yoshitake, 162
Shinano River, 20, 109
Shinchōsha publishing house, 58
Shinoro, Sapporo, 133
Shinto god of the road festival, 172–73
shipping magnates, 24, 26
Shirakaba (White Birch), 52, 53
Shiroishi, Sapporo, 122, 124, 129, 134
shogunate, 38
silk exports, 204
Sino-Japanese War, 64
social diversity, 127
social production, of urban space, 285n22
social production of space, 82, 116, 135, 253, 285n22
space, social production of, 82, 116, 135, 253, 285n22
stock market, Japan, 24, 57
suburbs, 134, 135, 254, 271n55; agricultural suburb(s), 132–33, 134; factory suburbs, 120–24; proliferation of, 108, 116–34; Sapporo expansionism and, 108, 109, 119*map*, 135; urban sprawl, 118. *See also* industrial satellites and factory suburbs; Sapporo agricultural suburbs; Sapporo residential suburbs; urban expansionism
Suzuki Daisetsu, Buddhologist, 39
Suzuki Kyūgorō, Buddhologist, 24

Taishō democracy movement, 5, 9, 59, 184, 248
Taishō exhibition, 207
Takahashi Satomi, 46
Takahashi, Junjiro and Noriyuki Sugiura, 246

urban-centrism, 5, 13, 35, 83, 111, 136, 186, 189; agrarianist movement and, 115; defined, 5; geo-power concept and, 35, 253–54; geo-power conception and, 254; Meiji elite embracing, 84; railroads and, 136, 220–21, 254, 255–56; rise of, 12–13, 116. *See also* city idea; Tokyo-centrism

urban crowd, 27–33; popular protests, 9, 27–28, 31–32, 148, 262n25

urban entertainment and commercial centers (*sakariba*), 37, 198–99. *See also* Kamoi Yū

urban expansionism, 95, 99, 105–8, 111–12, 189, 253, 255; annexations, 85, 105, 108, 114–15, 130, 131, 161, 245, 251, 254; the "big city" (*dai toshi*) movement, 12, 104, 105, 108, 111, 115, 135, 136; ideology of, 85, 111, 113, 115; opposition to, 113–14. *See also* suburbs

urban futurism, 190–91, 204, 254–55. *See also* future orientation

urban ideology, 37, 238, 252–53, 255, 257

urban investment, 17

urbanism, 240; industrial capitalism and, 4–5

urbanization, 6–7, 8, 135; industrial satellites and factory suburbs, 118–24, 129, 134, 271n72; runaway factor in, 23; *sakariba* (urban epicenters), 198–99; the "urban march" (Kamoi), 198; "wondrous development," 183. *See also* demographic movements

urban-rural relationship. *See* centers and peripheries; city-country binary

urban space, 21, 279n9, 285n22; chronotopes of, 54, 186, 192, 193, 198, 236, 238, 253. *See also* social production of space

Ushijima Tōroku, 76

Utani Takeji, 182–83, 184

Vaporis, Constantine, 178

vehicles, 22–23, 104t.; bus and streetcar service, 6, 20, 22, 23, 102–3, 104, 196, 205, 206, 270n29; bicycles, 23, 103; cars, 22–23, 90, 102–3, 196, 217, 219;

Okayama Prefecture report, 104t.; taxis, 22, 99, 101, 102, 206; traffic issues, 22, 23, 111, 127. *See also* railways; transportation

village politicians and entrepreneurs, 125

wartime: damage to cities, 241–45; occupation reconstruction program, 243; U.S. bombing offensive, 243. *See also* World War One; World War Two

Waseda University, 51

Western encounters and influences, 152, 192, 215, 225

Westney, Eleanor, 62

white collar employment, 5, 8, 106, 231

Williams, Raymond, 83, 268n1

Wilsonian internationalism, 78

women: girls' education, 230; "modern woman/girl" (*moga*), 8, 201, 226, 228–29, 235–36, 237, 239, 256; sense of community, 228; women's magazines, 227, 228; women's movement, 191–92, 227–29. *See also* female employment; geisha; gender roles

working class, 8, 9, 15, 19, 26, 28, 31, 40, 106–7, 120, 137, 148

world economy. *See* global economy

World War One, 4, 15, 204; economic development and, 9–10, 16–20, 23, 24, 32; prewar protests, 9. *See also* interwar period

World War Two, 164. *See also* postwar period

Yamamoto Isaburō, 24–25, 26

Yanagi Sōetsu, 166

yearly events (*nenjū gyōji*), 171–72; O-bon "festival of the dead," 30, 171; Shinto god of the road, 172–73. *See also* folk festivals

Yokohama, 62

Yomiuri shinbun newspaper, 64

Yoneda Shōtarō, 5

Yoshimi Shun'ya, 195

Yoshino Sakuzō, 5

Yumeji Takehisa, 266n40

STUDIES OF THE WEATHERHEAD EAST ASIAN
INSTITUTE, COLUMBIA UNIVERSITY

*The Studies of the Weatherhead East Asian Institute of Columbia
University were inaugurated in 1962 to bring to a wider public
the results of significant new research on modern and
contemporary East Asia.*

SELECTED TITLES

(Complete list at: http://www.columbia.edu/cu/weai/weatherhead-studies.html)

*The Nature of the Beasts: Empire and Exhibition at the Tokyo
Imperial Zoo*, by Ian J. Miller. University of California
Press, 2012.

Asia for the Asians: China in the Lives of Five Meiji Japanese, by
Paula Harrell. MerwinAsia, 2012.

Redacted: The Archives of Censorship in Postwar Japan, by
Jonathan E. Abel. University of California Press, 2012.

*Occupying Power: Sex Workers and Servicemen in Postwar
Japan*, by Sarah Kovner. Stanford University Press, 2012.

*Empire of Dogs: Canines, Japan, and the Making of the Modern
Imperial World*, by Aaron Herald Skabelund. Cornell
University Press, 2011.

Russo-Japanese Relations, 1905–17: From Enemies to Allies, by
Peter Berton. Routledge, 2011.

Realms of Literacy: Early Japan and the History of Writing, by
David Lurie. Harvard University Asia Series, 2011.

Planning for Empire: Reform Bureaucrats and the Japanese Wartime State, by Janis Mimura. Cornell University Press, 2011.

Passage to Manhood: Youth Migration, Heroin, and AIDS in Southwest China, by Shao-hua Liu. Stanford University Press, 2010.

Imperial Japan at its Zenith: The Wartime Celebration of the Empire's 2,600th Anniversary, by Kenneth J. Ruoff. Cornell University Press, 2010.

Behind the Gate: Inventing Students in Beijing, by Fabio Lanza. Columbia University Press, 2010.

Postwar History Education in Japan and the Germanys: Guilty Lessons, by Julian Dierkes. Routledge, 2010.

The Aesthetics of Japanese Fascism, by Alan Tansman. University of California Press, 2009.

The Growth Idea: Purpose and Prosperity in Postwar Japan, by Scott O'Bryan. University of Hawai'i Press, 2009.

National History and the World of Nations: Capital, State, and the Rhetoric of History in Japan, France, and the United States, by Christopher Hill. Duke University Press, 2008.

Leprosy in China: A History, by Angela Ki Che Leung. Columbia University Press, 2008.

Kingdom of Beauty: Mingei and the Politics of Folk Art in Imperial Japan, by Kim Brandt. Duke University Press, 2007.

Mediasphere Shanghai: The Aesthetics of Cultural Production, by Alexander Des Forges. University of Hawai'i Press, 2007.

Modern Passings: Death Rites, Politics, and Social Change in Imperial Japan, by Andrew Bernstein. University of Hawai'i Press, 2006.

The Making of the "Rape of Nanjing": The History and Memory of the Nanjing Massacre in Japan, China, and the United States, by Takashi Yoshida. Oxford University Press, 2006.